WRITING SCIENCE

EDITORS Timothy Lenoir and Hans Ulrich Gumbrecht

BOOTSTRAPPING

Douglas Engelbart,
Coevolution, and the Origins
of Personal Computing

THIERRY BARDINI

STANFORD UNIVERSITY PRESS

STANFORD, CALIFORNIA

Stanford University Press
Stanford, California

© 2000 by the Board of Trustees of the
Leland Stanford Junior University

Library of Congress Cataloging-in-Publication Data

Bardini, Thierry.
  Bootstrapping : Douglas Engelbart, coevolution, and the origins of personal
computing / Thierry Bardini.
    p.   cm — (Writing science)
  Includes bibliographical references and index.
    ISBN 0-8047-3723-1 (alk. paper) — ISBN 0-8047-3871-8 (paper : alk. paper)
    1. Microcomputers—History.   2. Human-computer interaction.   3. User
interfaces (Computer systems).   I. Title.   II. Series.
QA 76.17. B37   2000
004.16'09—dc21   00-056360

⊗ This book is printed on acid-free, recycled paper.

Original printing 2000
Last figure below indicates year of this printing:
09   08   07   06   05   04   03   02   01   00

Printed in the United States of America

CONTENTS

8 pages of photos follow page 142

Instead of starting from the individuality of the technical object, or even from its specificity, which is very unstable, to try to define the laws of its genesis in the framework of this individuality or specificity, it is better to invert the problem: it is from the criterion of the genesis that we can define the individuality and the specificity of the technical object: the technical object is not this or that thing, given hic et nunc, but that which is generated.

—GILBERT SIMONDON, *Du mode d'existence des objets techniques*

How did the creators of personal computer technology envision those who would use it? How did they perceive the future of computers within the larger society? What technical options were included, or excluded, from the hardware, systems software, and applications on the basis of these representations? How have technical designs based upon the values and visions of early technical innovators shaped the way users integrate present-day computers into their work?

To understand the answers to these questions, and with them, the origins of personal computing, it is necessary to begin by understanding the contributions of Douglas Engelbart and the concerns that motivated them. Famous and revered among his peers, Engelbart is one of the most misunderstood and perhaps least-known computer pioneers. This book proposes to remedy this, and not only for the sake of a case study or to claim a spot for Douglas Engelbart in the pantheon of the computer revolution, but also because such an enterprise teaches us many lessons in the development, diffusion, and effect of the defining technology of the twentieth century: the computer.

This book is intended for various audiences and answers different expectations accordingly. A first type of reader will find in the book ample historical results about the genesis of personal computing and a definitive account of Engelbart's research program at his lab, the Augmentation Research Center at the Stanford Research Institute. For this historically inclined reader, the interest of the book will stem from a well-documented thesis about the achievement and significance of the ARC laboratory that will go further than the published versions, which are generally characterized by a lack of theoretical focus. It shows how and why a significant part of what defines life as we now live it came into being.

A second type of reader will consider the book as my contribution to ongoing debates in sociology of science and technology or communication. For this scholarly reader, the strength and value of the book also will reside in the way the case study is carried out in order to cast a new light, based on an informed multidisciplinary perspective, on the sociology of science and technology. For the communications scholar, this book is informed by the current debates on the future of communication technologies and audiences and proposes an innovative argument to answer the fundamental question of the relationship between technology and user.

The research reported in this book started, oddly enough, with a report for the United Nations Food and Agricultural Organization (Rogers, Bardini, and Singhal 1992). I helped Dr. Everett M. Rogers advise this institution about the potential uses of microcomputers in the South. It resulted in more questions and frustrations than answers, and especially in one crucial question: what is a microcomputer?

Terry Winograd (1990, 443) once said that "we may sometimes forget how new it all is. . . . Not so long ago, there were just a few odd psychologists concerned with 'human factors,' who happened to study how people used computers." How new indeed: most current personal computer users do not realize that they have more computer power at their fingertips than NASA had to send a man on the moon. But if the computing technology is new, Winograd is right to say that the interest for its human users is even newer.

The call for a better understanding of the "human side of the computing technology," however, has been made repeatedly since the mid-1980's. Jonathan Grudin, for instance, noted that the effectiveness of computers "as agents in the world will increase in step with their greater understanding of us. For that reason, work to develop an understanding of people will remain at the very heart of the computer's development. It is the engine of change" (1990, 267). My work intends to develop such "an understanding of people" in connection to computers: not an understanding of the cognitive and physical processes of the individual user, but rather an understanding of users as collective entities emerging through time. It focuses on the history of the forms of agency in the human-computer interaction from a sociological perspective. It is a genealogy of the human-computer interface.

The earliest notion of an interface comes from the Greek *prosōpon,* a "face facing another face" (Heim 1993, 78). The interpersonal and unmediated *prosōpon* remains the ultimate model of the computer interface, the dream of a transparent, unintrusive medium. In computer-mediated communication, the interface has progressively emerged as a fundamental notion. Michael Dertouzos once noted that "when computers first appeared, input-output commands were minor afterthoughts to cohesive, often well-crafted and occasionally pretentious programming languages. Today, these commands occupy over 70 percent of programming systems' instructions" (1990, 1). Jonathan Grudin realized that the term "user interface" is "technologically-centered" and that in the engineering perspective that gave birth to this notion, "the equation of the 'user interface' to software and I/O devices means, ironically, that *'user interface' denotes the computer interface to the user ... not the user's interface to the computer*" (1993, 112, 115, emphasis in the original).

In this book, I look at the emergence of the personal computer interface in both senses, not just as the emergence of a technology independent of those who develop it and those who are thought of as using it. The slow and sometimes painful process of imagining the personal computer was not just a process of technological innovation, independent of uses and users, as tends to be the norm in the historical accounts of the development of the computer. In its inception, as the career of Douglas Engelbart shows, the development of the personal computer interface was a technology by and about people.

In more traditional accounts, the computer is first a batch-processing machine, an information-processing device that processes data, usually coded in punch cards, in huge batches. In a second phase, computing time is shared among users who can run specific tasks on the same computer simultaneously. In a third phase, each user has access to a devoted stand-alone machine that sits on his or her desktop. And finally, the stand-alone workstations of the previous phase are connected into a network.

Such a way to describe the evolution of computing focuses on the specific characteristics of the computer at a given time and usually puts the emphasis on a technological innovation that allowed the passage from one phase to the next: the time-sharing operating system, for example, the desktop metaphor of the human-computer interface, or packet switching network technologies.[1] While these innovations obviously contributed greatly to shaping the history of computing, the dynamic of personalization that characterizes the evolution of computing since the late 1940's played an equally important role. I describe the progressive construction of the user as a person, or, what sometimes amounted to the same thing, how the computer eventually got a personality. The creators of personal computer technology linked their innovations to ideologies or representations that explained and justified their designs. Those visions have become invisible, latent assumptions to the latter-day users of the personal computer, even as they shape these users' activities and attitudes. It is my task here to make them visible once again.

Like Steve Shapin, and "unlike some postmodernist and reflexivist friends, I write in the confident conviction that I am less interesting than the subjects I write 'about,' and accordingly, [that] much of this book can be read in the mode of old-fashioned historical realism" (1995, xv). Everything presented as a citation in this book is "real": somebody, whoever that is, told it to me in one way or another. I happen to have met most of the people I quote in this book, except the dead ones and the very famous others.

The story I tell begins not long before I was born, and I finish it around the time I was twenty years old, long before I had any interest in what I am writing about now. Many coincidences made my writing possible, most of which were encounters with people. As a sociologist, my pleasure is to meet people, hear them, and then write about them. This book is a testimony to my respect for them. I wish for you to hear their voices.

I am not an ironic, self-reflexive narrator, and my purpose is not to reveal the "ideology of representation." These are very valuable means and purposes that deserve serious consideration, but these are not my means and purposes.[2] Susan Leigh Star is right: "power is about *whose* metaphor brings worlds together, and holds them here" (1991, 52, emphasis in the original). This book is about power and marginality: my own power and marginality, as well as the respective power and marginality of the actors I represent in this book. When "you" read my account, my power is much stronger than the power of these represented actors. I decide who speaks and when. My respect for the people and things I represent is paralleled by the most abject and nevertheless constitutive lack of respect: I can silence them, transform their meaning by misquoting them, and so on. I assume this responsibility, and "trying my best" only means that I commit myself not to enact such horrors intentionally. Remaining errors and other unintentional betrayals are my responsibility.

In the remainder of the book, I will not write about power directly, which means that I will always write about power*s*. Indeed, this whole book is "about powers": powers of the user, of the designer, of the analyst. In the framework I present here, power is dispersed into multiple sites, and all these dispersed powers are tied together in the same dynamic, mutually constitutive: the attempt to control the central uncertainty of innovative practices. In this process, the actors and the author are playing symmetrical parts, all collaborating in the same process of cultural production and diffusion.[3]

My account is no more and no less definitive than the actors'. It is just *different*. I do not necessarily use the same resources, I do not necessarily intend my description to reach the same audience. I do not need to compare my narrative to the actors' narratives and refer to an allusive metaposition. There is no metaposition, there are only discourses—and maybe authors behind them—who want us to believe that they have more depth, that they know better. I know for a fact that I do not know better. I am a priori not more or less "shy," "agnostic" or else "informed" than the actors I represent. You will be the judge.

This book is witness to the respect I owe to a few individuals: Gabriel Degert, of ENSA Montpellier, who gave me a taste of interdisciplinary scholarly work in the social sciences and nurtured my passion for sociology in an hostile environment; Rigas Arvanitis, of ORSTOM Caracas, who opened new directions of research for me and introduced me to the relativist sociology of science and technology; Everett M. Rogers, of the University of New Mexico, who gave me the opportunity to do my job in the United States, was always ready to discuss and listen, and opened to me the doors of Silicon Valley; James R. Taylor, who gave me the opportunity to teach and do research in the best conditions possible and, therefore, to tackle such a crazy project as writing this book; and, last but not least, Douglas Engelbart, of the Bootstrap Institute, who agreed to answer my questions and cheerfully helped me in writing this book.

This book would not have existed without the patience and understanding of the people who told me their stories: Don Andrews, Bob Belleville, Peter Deutsch, Bill English, Charles Irby, Alan Kay, Butler Lampson, Harvey Lehtman, Ted Nelson, George Pake, Jeff Rulifson, Dave Smith, Robert Taylor, Keith Uncapher, Jacques Vallée, "Smokey" Wallace, and Jim Warren. Thank you all, and I sincerely hope that you will occasionally find your voice in these pages.

My deepest thank-yous go to my development editor, Bud Bynack, who made a book out of my manuscript, and to my editor, Nathan MacBrien, who always knew how to keep his cool when I did not keep mine. Thank you both for believing in this book and making it live up to your belief. I also want to acknowledge the contribution of the following colleagues who greatly helped in the making of this book: Frank Biocca and the participants in the 1993 International Communication Association panel that he organized, Harry Collins and the participants in the 1995 Fourth Bath Quinquennial Workshop, Tim Lenoir and the participants in the 1995 Stanford Technology and Economics Workshop, Henry Lowood, Michael Century, Peter Salus, Michael Friedewald, John Staudenmaier, Line Grenier, Aude Dufresne, Jean-Claude Guédon, Serge Proulx, Patrice Flichy, August Horvath, Toru Nakayama, and Tom Valente. I also thank my graduate students for their (much needed) patience and support while I was writing this book and all the undergraduate students at the Department of Communication at the University of Montréal, on whom I shamelessly tried some of the ideas of this book.

On an even more personal note, I would like to thank Lucy Ring, Riton V. and Maurice Dantec, my partners in crime, and Éric Le Ménédeu, *mon peintre préféré,* for their always wise advice, and Adriana Di Polo, for her support in the early stages of the project. Finally, thank you to Fabienne Lucet for standing by me when the book became one, through the tough times of revision and the glorious days, too, *pour ton oreille patiente et ton sourire lumineux.*

Some of the chapters or sections of this book appeared previously elsewhere in a shortened version. The Introduction and Chapter 1 were presented at the Fourth Bath Quinquennial Science Studies Workshop, Bath, England, July 27–31, 1995. Chapters 2 and 3 appeared in French in *Réseaux* 87, January–February 1998. Chapter 4 appeared in the *Journal of Computer Mediated Communication* 3, no. 2 (September 1997), in French in *Réseaux* 76 (summer 1996). Parts of Chapter 6 appeared in the *Journal of Communication* 45, no. 3 (summer 1995). I thank all the editors of these journals for granting me the permission to reprint and update parts of these publications.

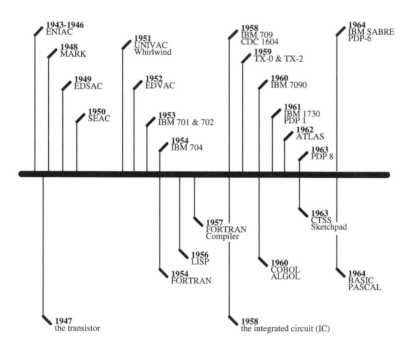

Developments in Computer Technology, 1943–1964

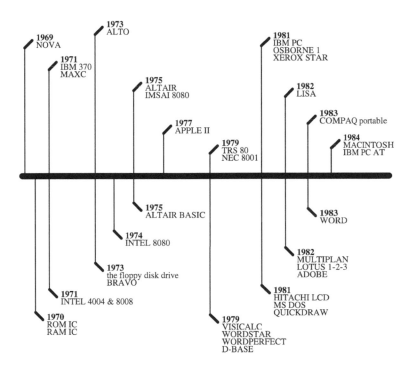

Developments in Computer Technology, 1969–1984
(Computers are shown above the line; software and components, below)

Douglas Engelbart's Crusade for the Augmentation of Human Intellect

Journal entry 37. Thoughts of the Brain are experienced by us as arrangements and rearrangements—change—in a physical universe; but in fact it is really information and information processing that we substantialize. We do not merely see its thoughts as objects, but rather as movement, or, more precisely, the placement of objects: how they become linked to one another. But we cannot read the patterns of arrangement; we cannot extract the information in it—i.e., it as information, which is what it is. The linking and relinking of objects by the Brain is actually a language, but not a language like ours (since it is addressing itself and not someone or something outside itself).

— PHILIP K. DICK, *Valis*

Very few people outside the computer industry know Douglas Engelbart, the leading figure of the Augmentation of Human Intellect project, and among those people, many still credit him only with technological innovations like the mouse, the outline processor, the electronic-mail system, or, sometimes, the windowed user interface. These indeed are major innovations, and today they have become pervasive in the environments in which people work and play. But Douglas Engelbart never really gets credit for the larger contribution that he worked to create: an integrative and comprehensive framework that ties together the technological and social aspects of personal computing technology.

Engelbart articulated a vision of the world in which these pervasive innovations are supposed to find their proper place. He and the other innovators of this new technology defined its future on the basis of their own aspirations and ideologies. Those aspirations included nothing less than the development, via the interface between computers and their users, of a new kind of person, one better equipped to deal with the increasing complexities of the modern world. In pursuing this vision, they created the conditions, both symbolic and material, that prescribe the possibilities and limits of the technology for the users of personal computer technology today.

Engelbart and his associates conceived of the personal interface as a hybrid entity derived from both the human and nonhuman participants. That is, it was understood to operate by means of representations, symbolic and material, derived from both, some appearing electronically via integrated circuits and display screens, some deriving from the physical and mental abilities of the people that the designers of the technology imagined using and benefiting from them.[1] The story of the personal interface thus is twofold. It is the story of a technological innovation. At the same time, it is the story of how Douglas Engelbart and the other designers of that technology conceived of the people who would use it. That part of the story involves how they understood humans to live and work, to think and act. It also involves more than that: how they believed humans could do better at living and working, thinking and acting. Both aspects of the story meet in what Douglas Engelbart always called his "crusade."

In the 1950's, computing technology was still in its early stages, characterized by massive machines devoted to number crunching. Input-and-output technology was rudimentary, only one user could access the computing power at a time, and a very few users indeed did so. The number of computers in use started to grow rapidly in the second half of the 1950's, from a few hundred worldwide in 1955 to approximately five thousand in 1959 (Norberg and O'Neill 1996, 75). Two intertwined trends at that time slowly started to shape the future of computing. First, the increased use of computers by large governmental and business organizations (and with it, the inception of their cultural presence and prestige), was driven in part by the development of programs and languages that made it possible to take the computer out of the research laboratory and put it to use. Second, with the development of these programs and languages, a caste of professionals, the computer "coders" or "programmers," started to appear. It was the time of the mainframe computer priesthood, who employed the power of the machine to serve the very large corporation or the military.

In the first trend, programmers began to acquire increased control over their machines via new layers of code imposed over the fundamental machine code, which is made of strings of binary digits or bits (0 or 1). Even if programming had improved dramatically with the use of stored electronic programs, rather than the hardware plugboards of the 1940's, the programs themselves still consisted of bits in machine code, and programming was exceedingly difficult, involving putting together long, unintuitive chains of 1s and 0s. By 1955, though, a relatively old idea, the use of metaprograms called assemblers and compilers, which worked as translators between some sort of more natural human language and machine code, finally became an idea whose time had come.

The computer pioneers had thought of just such a possibility. Alan Turing, for instance, had developed a "symbolic language" close to an assembly language and had even written that "actually one could communicate with these machines in any language provided it was an exact language, i.e. in principle one should be able to communicate in any symbolic logic, provided that the machines were given instruction tables which would enable it to interpret that logical system" (quoted in Hodges 1992 [1983], 358). Indeed, the need for higher-level programs and languages was recognized from the mid-1940's. BINAC and UNIVAC, two of the first digital computers, used "short code," a system similar to Turing's "instruction tables" in "symbolic language," and Atick Glennie, a programmer for the Manchester Mark I computer, wrote in 1952 that "to make it easy one must make coding comprehensible. Present notations have many disadvantages; all are incomprehensible to the novice, they are all different (one for each machine) and they are never easy to read. It is quite difficult to decipher coded programs even with notes and even if you yourself made the program several months ago" (quoted in Lubar 1993, 359).

The first compilers appeared with the first digital computers of the 1950's: the A-O compiler of the UNIVAC, and the compiler designed by J. Halcombe Laning and Niel Zierler for the Whirlwind computer in 1953 (Lubar 1993, 360).[2] But a major step in making the computer useful in the real world occurred between 1954 and 1957 with the development of the first widely diffused high-level programming language: IBM FORmula TRANslator, FORTRAN for short.[3] FORTRAN was designed for scientific users and soon became the standard programming language for scientific applications. It was soon followed by another language specifically designed to become the standard for business applications: COmmon Business Oriented Language, or COBOL. Even if these two languages were much closer to natural human languages, they still had two significant drawbacks by 1960: they were linear languages, much more like a spoken language than a language for thought, and their community of users was still relatively small. What is more, it was giving some signs that it wanted to stay small. The computer priesthood proved unwilling to give up its privileged position between the computer and the supplicants who wanted to make use of its power.[4]

Programming languages remained separate languages, still unnatural and arcane to average people. In the second trend, the programmers thus became a dedicated group of professionals, at ease with the difficulties of computer programming and the seemingly arcane nature of computer languages, a necessary intermediary between the computer's power and its end users. In 1957, there were fifteen thousand of them in the United States alone. By then, most of them had a science or math background, often a Ph.D. in mathematics (Lubar, 361).

At first, computers had been used by individual programmers who ran their programs one at a time in scheduled sessions. Because of the difficulties of the management of the computer peripherals (tape drives, card readers, card punches, printers), the computer processing unit was active only a small part of the time of the scheduled session (see Norberg and O'Neill 1996, 770). Along with the rise of computer languages and the community of computer programmers, the mid-1950's saw two crucial innovations that changed dramatically this situation and the nature of computing: the development of operating systems and the use of batch processing. The first innovation took care of the intricacies of managing input-output devices, while the second was a more economical way to manage computer time. Both consolidated the central position of computer specialists in the way computers were put to practical use.

The development of operating systems meant that "a machine is run by an operating system, not by an [individual] operator (Fred Brooks, quoted in Lubar 1993, 367). And in batch processing, programs were run in "batches" not, as previously, one at a time. So the individual user was displaced by computer operations departments that oversaw the running of the machine by the system software, with the computer and its attending priesthood usually isolated in a "computer center" far from the end users of the computer, whether they were able to program or not.

Such was the state of computing at the beginning of the 1960's, the era that brought revolutions—or attempts at revolutions—in many areas of life. Computing was to be one area where change was most dramatic. From an arcane exercise carried out by a close-knit community of specialists, computing became available to increasingly large segments of the population, an easily used means to a plethora of ends. How—and why—that revolution came about can best be seen by examining the career of one of its most important agents, Douglas Engelbart. Both because of Engelbart's efforts and, in some ways, despite them, the personal computer is what it is today.

FROM TECHNICIAN TO CRUSADER

The Genesis of the Augmentation of Human Intellect

Douglas C. Engelbart was born in Portland, Oregon, in 1925, the second of three children, to a couple of Scandinavian and German descent. His father was an electrical engineer and owned a radio shop there. He died when Douglas Engelbart was nine years old. This early loss shaped the young Engelbart's personality in two different ways: the electrical engineering background of his father provided an early influence, even if the advent of the Depression did not exactly allow a strong relationship at this level, and, perhaps more importantly, the loss itself had repercussions for his sometimes vexed relationships with later sources of authority:[5]

> I didn't have any clarity on what I'd like to do, because my father, during the Depression, had to work very hard, and what I remember is his coming home and eating dinner and going back to finish repairing radios. . . . I was nine, when he died—that's too young to die. . . . I realized some years later, when I got to college, that I must have been looking for that [some sort of role model after his father's death]. I'd become quite disappointed midway through the first semester, in one professor or another, and finally started realizing I would like them to be the father I didn't have, instead of being a professor. (Engelbart 1996)

Douglas Engelbart was a bright child who sailed through most of his school years with no apparent difficulties. He graduated from high school and spent two years at Oregon State University in Corvallis, where, with higher education on a wartime footing, he was trained as a radar technician before he was drafted into the U.S. Navy. (He was still in high school during Pearl Harbor.) The radar training he received in college and the navy proved to be central for the rest of his career and first triggered an absolute fascination in his young mind:

> I'd hear these rumors among the kids about this thing called radar, and that the navy had this program where they would train you by having you study, and you'd go behind closed fences and they'd take the books out of vaults and teach you and then search you when you left, and put the books back in the vaults. It all sounded so dramatic. Whatever the secret stuff, radar, was, it intrigued me. So I started saying, "Well, I think I'll sort of prepare, so that when I go into the service, maybe that's what I can do." And that's what I ended up doing. . . . It was pretty challenging to me to learn. . . . Without knowing the math and the physics underneath it, you could get a model for how it's operating so then you could understand how to service it, and troubleshoot, and repair. I would usually be groping for a deeper understanding. . . . We were technicians. We weren't aimed for being officers, we were a bunch of enlisted men being technicians. But it was challenging to learn that much, and put it together. (Engelbart 1996)

Douglas Engelbart was in the navy from 1944 to 1946 and was stationed for a year at the Philippines Sea Frontier, in Manila Bay. (His ship had embarked on VJ day, August 13, 1945.) He did not have to fight, and learned his trade instead. After the war, he went back to Oregon State to finish his degree in electrical engineering. He received his Bachelor of Science diploma in 1948 and then took a job at the Ames Navy Research Center in Mountain View, California, where he stayed for three years, from 1948 to 1950. He was recruited as an electrical engineer in the electrical section, a service-and-support group that helped develop specifications. It was a mixture of maintenance and building, basically a line job in electrical engineering. He was not dealing with computers at all. As Engelbart puts it: "I'll tell you what a computer was in those days. It was an underpaid woman sitting with a hand calculator, and they'd have rooms full of them, and that's how they'd get their computing done. So you'd say 'What's your job?' 'I'm a computer'" (Engelbart 1996).

Even at that time, however, computing was no longer being limited to human computing. During the three years Engelbart spent at the Ames Research Laboratory, IBM assembled their SSEC electromechanical computer, which first ran a stored program in January 1948. Manchester University's Mark I prototype ran the first fully electronic stored program on June 21 of the same year. Researches were under way on the EDSAC (at Cambridge University), UNIVAC and BINAC (first at the Moore School, and then at John P. Eckert's and John W. Maulchy's Electronic Control Company), ILLIAC (at the University of Illinois), JOHNNIAC (at the RAND Corporation in Santa Monica, California), MANIAC (at Los Alamos Laboratories, New Mexico), and most importantly, WHIRLWIND (at MIT).[6]

In the United States, these computing projects were all connected to military research and development activities in one way or another. By 1948, the Office of Naval Research was funding 40 percent of *all* basic research, and most advances in computing research were classified.[7] In August 1949, the Soviet Union exploded an atomic bomb, and the Cold War climate settled in, without any prospect for a thaw. Internally, the Committees on Un-American Activities of the House and Senate soon turned this climate into a general atmosphere of suspicion. All these conditions did not help diffuse a general awareness of computing's state of the art.[8]

Furthermore, Engelbart's awareness of computing research was also limited by the fact that on the West Coast, this research was mostly concentrated at RAND. A part of the military-industrial complex, RAND (an acronym for Research and Development) was founded in 1946 as a joint venture between the U.S. Air Force and Douglas Aircraft. In 1948, it separated from Douglas and became an independent, nonprofit think tank devoted to studying techniques of air warfare. During the 1950's, the air force funded RAND for approximately ten million dollars a year, and at its peak, in 1957, the institution had 2,605 employees (Edwards 1996, 165). It was definitely not in the business of disseminating research on computing.

"Flash"

In the narrative that Engelbart provides to describe how he decided to get involved in computing research, the actual vision of what he wanted to accomplish and even the understanding of how he wanted to accomplish it came in an instantaneous insight, yet at the same time was a complex development that encompassed most aspects of his personal and professional life at the time. Its result was his lifelong "crusade." The narrative itself is a remarkable tale of an intuition produced almost as an act of will as the result of hard work. It is a tale with deep resonances in the American tradition of self-made technological innovators, from Edison, Bell, and the Wright Brothers onward, and beyond that, in the tradition of self-reliance and self-invention, from Ralph Waldo Emerson to Fitzgerald's Jay Gatsby.

As Engelbart describes this period, "I was never the kind that would push everybody into talking about what I wanted to talk about. I guess I was looking around watching people and soaking it up" (Engelbart 1996). He was opening himself to various professional and moral discourses, trying to figure out a set of personal goals for his life. There was a reason for this serious reflection. After three years of working at a steady job, Engelbart had become engaged, in December 1950, at the age of twenty-five:

> I can just remember one half-hour driving to work, one day after I got engaged; that was a turning point. . . . I had all this excitement, "Oh, I'm engaged!" And I was riding to work, and I said to myself, "Well, let's see, I'd better get my mind on work. What am I gonna do today? Oh, well, gee, that's not terribly exciting. Is there anything this week that I can look forward to that's in any way a little bit exciting?" And suddenly I just realized that on ahead of me there were very nice people, it was a good place to work . . . but there was no excitement. I could have noticed that two years earlier, but being a bachelor, and busy trying to fill the rest of my life, I guess, it didn't really dawn on me. But it just dawned on me then. . . . By the time I got to work, I had this realization that I didn't have any more goals, and that getting married and living happily ever after was the last of my goals, which isn't very surprising. The Depression kids were likely to grow up getting a steady job, and getting married and having a family, that's about all. I was literally embarrassed to realize that. I was twenty-five. It was December 10th or 11th, 1950. For some reason, I just picked that as an explicit, conscious thing to do; I had to figure out a good set of professional goals. (Engelbart 1996)

In many ways, Engelbart indeed can be seen as a representative of the generation of "Depression kids," a generation born in adverse conditions and coming of age during and just after World War II. Not just for Engelbart, but for many Americans of his generation, "getting a steady job, and getting married and having a family," were important, but it was equally important to them that they never agree "that's about all" there is to life.

The historical conditions of postwar America created a specific cultural background that framed issues of material well-being, money, power, and morals in general. These issues revolved around what to do with their lives—

what ends to serve, and on what terms, at what cost. Both the New Deal and World War II had altered the American institutional landscape. As Richard Hofstadter noted, "the Second World War, like the first, increased the need for experts, not only the sort the New Deal employed but also men from previously untapped fields of scholarship—even classicists and archeologists were suddenly thought important because of their knowledge of the Mediterranean area" (1962, 421). But experts who were taken up into the matrices of large institutions and organizations thereby sacrificed the self-reliant autonomy that American culture so strongly valorized and that was epitomized by the "free intellectuals" of the Emersonian tradition. As Ross Evans Paulson has noted:

> The separation of the "academics" from the "free intellectuals" in the late 1930s and 1940s was accelerated by government assistance to higher education. . . . The balance of power in intellectual matters gradually shifted. The free intellectual became the "outsider"; academia swallowed the poet, the writer, the playwright, the philosopher. . . . A pervasive anti-intellectualism made the very notion of the free, unattached and critical individual seem somehow subversive. The free intellectual survived, if at all, as an exile, a supplicant for foundation grants and fellowships or as a foundation executive or expert.

The children of the Depression and World War II, prematurely turned adults, returned to a civilian life fundamentally altered in its institutional spaces and social roles. "Outsiders" of all sorts, intellectual, artistic, and even technical, had to decide what ends to serve, and how much, or how little, to compromise their autonomy and self-identity in serving them. For many, the problem of what to do with their lives in this new situation was exacerbated by a sense that they faced a paradoxical situation in which, with the dawn of the nuclear age and the arms race, science and technology had been the key to winning what was starting to look to many like a Pyrrhic victory. However, the idealistic opening of a new era also was full of hopes, fears, and a sense of moral obligation to prevent the events of the immediate past from ever happening again, an obligation to make fundamental efforts to solve the world's problems. It is against this cultural background that one should read Engelbart's recollection of the way he sorted out his goals in life:

> I tried to be a little general for a while, to say "What could be the guidelines, and what are my requirements?" Well, I could earn a lot of money, but I hadn't yet had any perception of what money was worth. I think I was earning three thousand dollars a year then, or something like that. Wage scales were different. But it was a steady job. I finally said, "Well, let's just put as a requirement I'll get enough out to live reasonably well." Then I said, "Well, why don't I try maximizing how much good I can do for mankind, as the primary goal, and with the proviso that

I pick something in there that will make enough livable income." So that was very clear, very simple. (Engelbart 1996)

Engelbart found here a specific way to situate himself with respect to the ambivalent feelings and goals of his generation—a way to commit his personal energies to something worthy of that commitment.

For him, the "primary goal," "maximizing how much good I can do for mankind," seemed best expressed in the military-religious metaphor of the "crusade," with its connotations of zeal and enthusiasm in the undertaking of a task of epic proportions. For a generation of engineers and scientists like Douglas Engelbart, who had known the military as the means of achieving moral goals, as well as the context in which they came of age and, later, as a potential source of funding, the military aspect of the metaphor was natural enough. In light of what eventually was to come of this crusade, however, it is the quasi-religious aspect of it that is worth emphasizing. The postwar era was as much an age of seekers and self-appointed seers as it was an age of complacency and suburban idylls, as much the age of Jack Kerouac and Norman Mailer as the age of Ozzie and Harriet, an age of rebels in search of a cause.[9] It is in this perspective that one should read Engelbart's recollections of the way he organized his thoughts on his professional future:

> So then I started poking around, looking at the different kinds of crusades you could get on. I soon realized that if I wanted to contribute in some maximum way, I'd need to provide some real driving force . . . because to just go be a soldier in somebody else's crusade is one way you can contribute, but not a way to be satisfied that you're doing the maximum you can. So I tried thinking, "Well, you need to know enough to help organize and drive your goals, so you need special education. So my God, would I have to go back and get retreaded?" If you think about understanding the social and economic picture, and trying to do something on either the sociological side or the economic side, you'd have to be retreaded. So I said, "Boy, here I am, at the ancient age of almost twenty-six, and I'd be in there competing with kids who had picked that kind of a line when they were eighteen, or something, and so I'd be getting behind. Then if I did get the education in one of those fields, what would make me feel that I could make some unusual commitment? So I'd better first pick a field that's really something, and if I find a set of goals that there's some way I can use the engineering training, then that would be very valuable." (Engelbart 1996)

The problem, as it was for so many in postwar America, was to find a concrete cause worthy of commitment:

> But I somehow had the feeling that that wasn't what the world's dominant needs were, more engineering, right then. They didn't have the Peace Corps, but there

were people who had been trying to fight malaria in the tropics, or trying to boost food productivity in some areas, or something like that. I remembered reading about the people that would go in and lick malaria in an area, and then the population would grow so fast and the people didn't take care of the ecology, and so pretty soon they were starving again, because they not only couldn't feed themselves, but the productivity of the land was going to go down. So it's a case that the side effects didn't produce what you thought the direct benefits would. I began to realize that it's a very complex world. If you can pick a target that if you succeed will indeed produce the benefits you wanted, or it might also have negative side effects that are going to counteract the benefit. You'd have to be very smart to be sure. Well, you can't be sure, so you say, this is the probability that if you succeed the benefits will be high. All right, then what's the probability of success? Then you start thinking about all the special difficulties of a crusade. (Engelbart 1996)

The "special difficulties" of a crusade also included finding a cause that could inspire others and that could be effectively organized and carried out:

There was also the problem of communicating to enough people to get them to share the goals enough to do the unusual things that a crusade generally demands of the people who work on it. And then there are the problems of raising the money to finance it. You're not selling a product. You have the problem of recruiting good people, finding a way to organize it, and managing it all so it's an effective campaign. It's much easier to organize a corporation, and get a guy who's going to be in charge of production, and who's got a long history of that, than it is to recruit people for a new crusade. (Engelbart 1996)

Crusades therefore "have many strikes against them at the outset" (Engelbart 1988, 188). But the problem posed by the complexity of the world's problems and the felt urgency to resolve them to do good "for mankind" together pointed to a more general and more lofty goal. Find a way to deal with *that* situation, and all the other solutions should follow. The solution came as a "flash":

I began to realize the probability of your achieving your goal isn't terribly high, and the probability if you do achieve it that it's a success is low. So, you'd better start learning about that. Someplace along there, I just had this flash that, hey, what that really says is that the complexity of a lot of the problems and the means for solving them are just getting to be too much. The time available for solving a lot of the problems is getting shorter and shorter. So the urgency goes up. So then I put it together that these two factors, complexity and urgency, are the measure for human organizations and institutions. The complexity/urgency factor had transcended what humans can cope with. I suddenly flashed that if you could do something to improve human capability to cope with that, then you'd really contribute something basic. (Engelbart 1996)

Cybernetics

The expression that Engelbart used to describe his crusade to improve human capability to cope with "the complexity/urgency factor" was the "augmentation of the human intellect," a term that, like "the complexity/urgency factor" itself, located his project firmly in the emerging field of cybernetics. It is striking to read Engelbart's formulation of that crusade alongside these few lines from Ross Ashby's "Design for an Intelligence Amplifier"(1956):

> There is certainly no lack of difficult problems awaiting solutions. Mathematics provides plenty, and so does almost every branch of science. It is perhaps in the social and economic world that such problems occur most noticeably, both in regard to their complexity and to the great issues that depend on them. Success in solving these problems is a matter of some urgency. We have built a civilization beyond our understanding and we are finding that it is getting out of hand. Faced with such problems, what are we to do? (1956, 215)

Engelbart was certainly aware of Ashby's writings on cybernetics during the 1950's. Cybernetics, the science of communication and control, was one of the most original and synthetic schools of thought to emerge in the cultural context of America at midcentury. (Heims 1991, 1–13). In the eight years between 1946, the year of the first in the series of conferences supported by the Josiah Macy Jr. Foundation, multidisciplinary meetings of the group of psychologists, mathematicians, engineers, and social scientists who created cybernetics, and 1954, when the second edition of Norbert Wiener's *The Human Use of Human Beings: Cybernetics and Society* was published, cybernetic concepts, methods, and metaphors gained a huge popularity.[10] As we will see in greater depth later, the writings of Ashby, Wiener, and others on cybernetics deeply influenced Engelbart, then in his maturing years, just as they influenced many computer scientists in the 1950's and 1960's.[11] To understand Engelbart's connection with cybernetics also helps us make sense of the solution to the problem of complexity and urgency that Engelbart proposed, and, more importantly, helps to situate that solution in the environment of post–World War II American culture.

Like Ashby, Engelbart proposed a fundamentally technical solution to the development of human intellect. As Ashby put it, "if intellectual power is to be developed, we must somehow construct amplifiers for intelligence—devices that, supplied with a little intelligence, will emit a lot" (Ashby 1956, 216). In his original report on the project in 1962, Engelbart admitted that, when he tried to formulate the idea of augmenting the human intellect, "at first this term was rejected on the grounds that in our own views one's only hope was to make a better match between existing human intelligence and the problem to be tackled, rather than by making man more intelligent. But . . . indeed this term does seem applicable to our objective" (Engelbart 1962, 19).

Here is how Engelbart later described the aftermath of his epiphany, his initial "flash" that it was by doing something to improve "human capability" to deal with the problem of the complexity and urgency factor that he could "contribute something basic":

> That just resonated. Then it unfolded rapidly. I think it was just within an hour that I had the image of sitting at a big CRT screen with all kinds of symbols, new and different symbols, not restricted to our old ones. The computer could be manipulating, and you could be operating all kinds of things to drive the computer. The engineering was easy to do; you could harness any kind of a lever or knob, or buttons, or switches, you wanted to, and the computer could sense them, and do something with it. . . .
>
> I knew about screens, and you could use the electronics to shape symbols from any kind of information you had. If there was information that could otherwise go to a card punch or a computer printer, that they had in those days, you could convert that to any kind of symbology you wanted on the screen. That just all came from the radar training, and the engineering I'd had, too, knowing about transistors. It's so easy for the computer to pick up signals, because in the radar stuff, you'd have knobs to turn that would crank tracers around and all. So the radar training was very critical, about being able to unfold that picture rapidly. . . .
>
> And I literally at that time didn't know how the computer worked. But I just knew that much, that if it could do the calculations and things, it could do what I wanted. . . . Just to complete the vision. I also really got a clear picture that one's colleagues could be sitting in other rooms with similar work stations, tied to the same computer complex, and could be sharing and working and collaborating very closely. And also the assumption that there'd be a lot of new skills, new ways of thinking that would evolve. Within a matter of hours, that image came, and I just said, "AHA!" I very rarely make my decisions in such a definite way. That one just unfolded and went "Bam!" and I just said, "Boy, that's it. That just fills all kinds of different needs." (Engelbart 1996)

On the basis of this epiphany and the vision it brought, Engelbart decided to go back to graduate school. He applied to both Stanford and Berkeley and finally went to Berkeley on money from the GI Bill of Rights. At an engineering society meeting at which a Berkeley professor, Paul Morton, was giving a talk, he eventually found that Berkeley had a computer program: "I went up there and sat, and afterward went up, as shy as you could be, just asking if there was any space for more people, that I was interested in it. It was an easy choice, because they already had something going, building a computer, and Stanford had never even heard of it" (Engelbart 1996). The program Engelbart learned about was the CALDIC project (for California Digital Computer), headed by Paul Morton, sponsored by the Navy, and running since 1947 or 1948. Once enrolled in the program, Engelbart learned how a computer worked and he started applying this knowledge in the field of symbolic logic:

> I was interested all the time in how, instead of just doing numeric computations, how it [the computer] could manipulate symbols. I was even conjecturing how I could connect it up to make a teaching machine. So I found people in the psychology department who said, "Oh that sounds very interesting." But the computer people just weren't interested—I don't know whether they were insulted to think of using it for such a mundane thing, or what. Then I looked into symbolic logic. That began to intrigue me a lot, to realize that the computer could manipulate the symbolic logic, and really help you in the kind of reasoning that is formal enough to employ that kind of symbolism. (Engelbart 1996)

It became clear to Engelbart very soon in the course of completing his Ph.D. at Berkeley, however, that he could not do what he wanted to do. He was interested in working with computers on symbolic logic, and not necessarily on computation, which is what concerned both his mentor at Berkeley and most of his colleagues in the then-emerging field of computer science. Part of his motivation for such an undertaking stemmed from a personal assessment of his own capacity and tastes: "I never really go very strongly in for any numeric manipulation at all. I'm practically helpless in that domain." In the end, however, he managed to shift the required curriculum to avoid studying advanced differential equations. Instead, he took courses in logic in the philosophy department. He was "the only engineer in there." "We didn't particularly travel in circles of all engineering graduate students," Engelbart recalls, and he enjoyed socializing with "the English Lit. majors," although nobody in the humanities had any sympathy for what he was undertaking, either. "It was part of my personality," Engelbart says he realized later, "you might almost say it was a defect. . . . I was always sort of different. Other people knew what they were doing, and had good guidance, and had enough money to do it. I was getting by, and trying. I never expected, ever, to be the same as anyone else" (Engelbart 1996). Always something of an outsider, at Berkeley, Engelbart had become the outsider as free intellectual, fitting uneasily into the regimen of incentives and rewards proffered by the America of the mid-1950's.

Douglas Engelbart eventually got his Ph.D. in electrical engineering in 1956 (John Woodyard was his adviser). For his Ph.D. work, he had developed a shift register based on a bistable gaseous phenomenon: "It was a very common thing, people trying to find all sorts of weird things that you could get something into one or two states it would stay, and then there were ways you could trigger it back and forth" (Engelbart 1996). Altogether, his Ph.D. at Berkeley had not diminished his commitment to his crusade, but it had not provided him, at least directly, with the means to research and implement his ideas, either.

A Place for an Outsider

As a newly minted Ph.D., Engelbart was a valuable candidate for doing research, either in or out of academia. But still entirely committed to his crusade, he refused several offers for part-time or full-time positions at Berkeley, the University of Washington, General Electric Research Labs, and RAND.

> The university didn't offer a very attractive place at all at the time. . . . I realized that if you came in as junior faculty, your job was to prove yourself by research and publishing, if you wanted to progress to get to be an independent full professor with tenure. So that what you had to do was do that which would be viewed as good research. Talking with different older people around the university, it became clear that, whatever the department was, it's suicide if you think you're going off in some independent direction that isn't popular or acceptable. (Engelbart 1996)

Large corporations were scarcely more inclined to let a young engineer work independently. Instead, Engelbart decided to form his own corporation, Digital Techniques, to capitalize on his Ph.D. work on gas-discharge devices. But the corporation did not last long. Digital Techniques closed down in 1957 after an assessment report from a team of experts concluded that the advent of solid-state semiconductors soon would doom the project. Indeed, since 1945, solid-state physics research and development had slowly permitted progress that replaced the existing gas-tube technology with the transistor and soon with the integrated circuit (Augarten 1984). So in the summer of 1957, Engelbart joined Stanford Research Institute (SRI):

> I said to myself, "Universities are out, where else?" I realized it would be very hard. One of the difficulties was selling somebody on supporting my ideas. How would you know what company you could go to, and hope that that management would be able to sell it? I realized if you go to a place like SRI, you have a chance to approach almost anybody in the world to put up money, to do it there. . . . It [SRI] had established itself quite well. It had been operating for about ten years. (Engelbart 1996)

Stanford Research Institute was funded the same year as RAND, in the autumn of 1946, and its first board meeting was held on January 8, 1947. It was founded to provide a center for sponsored industrial research in the West. It was an independent research institution, but founded with the possibility of there being a close "working connection" with Stanford University. According to Weldon B. Gibson, a former SRI vice president, "both SRI and Stanford might have been better served if more attention had been given at the time

[1946] to operating connections between the two organizations. In many respects, the question was left to the future" (1980, 62). The essence of SRI lay in the notion of "public service," to:

> *Promote* the educational purposes of Stanford University through research in the physical, life, and social sciences, engineering and the mechanic arts.
> *Extend* scientific knowledge in the several pursuits and professions of life and assist Stanford University in extending learning and knowledge.
> *Apply* science in developing commerce, trade and industry and in improving the general standard of living and peace and prosperity of mankind.
> *Publish* research results deemed to be of general public interest. (Ibid., vi)

Unlike RAND, which was conceived of as a paramilitary think tank, SRI was designed to connect mainly with the industrial and business communities of the West Coast. SRI soon developed successful economics, management, and social-science programs, and by 1956 "had become one of the largest research groups of its kind in the world" (ibid, ix). The early development of SRI occurred according to the basic plan outlined by Dr. Henry T. Heald, then president of the Illinois Institute of Technology:

> The Pacific Coast area will be best served by a research organization which is equipped to provide a direct service to industry in the solution of specific scientific and engineering problems appropriate to the region. . . . Such an organization should provide patent protection to the sponsors of projects, should accept only one project in a specific field, and should have sponsored research as its primary responsibility. . . . An effective research foundation or institute can expect to undertake projects sponsored by:
> (a) Individual companies for the solution of specific company problems.
> (b) Groups of companies acting through associations which are interested in problems of common interests.
> (c) Federal governmental agencies such as the Army and Navy. A substantial amount of continuing research will be done in this field.
> (d) State or local governmental agencies interested in work of public interest of a regional character. (quoted in Gibson 1980, 57)

SRI provided Engelbart with an environment that he saw was perhaps suited to the implementation of his crusade and that at the same time was connected to the industrial and business world, relatively free of academic commitments and burdens, but still in something resembling an academic setting. For an outsider on a crusade, it was about the best he could do.

Scouting the Frontier

Most of the individuals who directly influenced Engelbart, as we will see, also were outsiders, other "free intellectuals" such as Norbert Wiener,[12] Alfred

Korzybski, and Benjamin Lee Whorf, and all of whom directly suffered from the pervasive anti-intellectualism of American culture before and after World War II. Engelbart, however, was a radar technician turned computer engineer, and therefore certainly was well positioned to be absorbed into some large organization as a "technical expert." But as an engineer, his interest in the social and the human aspects of contemporary problems definitely set him at odds with the purely technical roles he would be asked to play in such organizations. The subversive belief, for an engineer, that "more engineering was not the dominant need of the world at the time" was in his mind to stay, and in a letter dated March 21, 1961, to Dr. Morris Rubinoff of the National Joint Computer Committee, he again insisted on the need to consider the "human side" of the technology:

> I feel that the impact upon society which can reasonably be predicted from the present state of the computer art, the present state of our society, the trends of both, and the history of both, is not being given enough attention. . . . The blossoming and the impact of computer technology are going to be more spectacular and socially significant than any of us can actually comprehend. I feel that comprehension can only be attained by considering the entire socio-economic structure, a task which the people in the know about computer technology aren't equipped for, and a job about which the people who might be equipped properly are not yet stimulated or alerted.

One has to turn to unpublished manuscripts from this era to get a better grasp of both the importance of these ideas for Engelbart and how the way that he was able to articulate them helped put him in a position to realize their potential:

> I think that there is enough understanding within our society to develop a good preview, but it is a scattered understanding that is dispersed among a number of different disciplines of professional thought. . . . It may well be that the true picture of what computer technology is going to do to our social structure represents too drastic a change to expect our inelastic little minds to face up to. On the other hand, it is clear that almost everything in our society is experiencing an accelerated evolution. This is the result of a number of social forces, the list of which will not be topped by socially evident human thoughtfulness. We are playing for high stakes (you bet your life, or your kids'), and we are going to have to learn how to scout our horizons and to control our progress more effectively. In an instance where something looms on the horizon as imposingly as does computer technology, we should be organizing scouting parties composed of nimble representatives from different tribes—e.g. sociology, anthropology, psychology, history, economics, philosophy, engineering—and we shall have to adapt to continual change.

This idea of "organized scouting parties" is very close to the classical cybernetic ideal of collaboration among specialists, "each possessing a thoroughly sound and trained acquaintance with the fields of his neighbors," in order to explore the "no-man's-land between the various established fields . . . the boundary regions of science" (Wiener 1961, 3, 2). The "scouting" metaphor also locates those who feel themselves to be outsiders at a privileged place, the frontier, where distance from the norms of what currently is taken for granted becomes a mark of distinction, making the outsider into a pathfinder for those who meekly must follow later, a "roughly clad eccentric who leaves the safety of the settlement and reappears unpredictably, bringing a mixture of firsthand reports, rumors, and warnings about the wilderness ahead" (Toulmin 1980, 38).[13] And the description of the various disciplines of academic expertise as "tribes" reappropriates their knowledge from the inside to the outside, from the organized metropolis to the wild frontier, while at the same time employing the cybernetic vocabulary of "differentiation in the style and function" (Heims 1991, 53) discovered in human groups by Margaret Mead and Gregory Bateson, the leading social scientists of the cybernetics circle. Scouting the frontier to try to find out "what computer technology is going to do to our social structure" would give those who were developing that technology a progressive social role:

> I think that part of our adaptation will have to be in the form of giving more definite attention to the path ahead. For example, I feel that our resources for research could be much better invested if we spent more of it on "organized scouting," to give us a chance to have the research results fit the world that *is* when it is done, not the world that *was* when it was planned. Our society is a big entity, with huge and ever-increasing momentum, and what steering we can do should have the benefit of as much knowledge as possible of conditions up ahead. I guess my plea is for more recognition that in the long-range thinking there is payoff for any segment of society that has to adapt and perhaps compete in a rapidly changing society.
>
> Computer technology is going to blossom so spectacularly, and hit our society so hard, that I am both thrilled and frightened. I am interested in where computer development is going to go; after all, I am a computer engineer. But I'm also a human, with an extremely sensitive interest in where the development of human culture is going to go. I happen to think that none among our "big thinkers" can stretch his mind to the dimensions needed for anticipating the extent of the computer's future role in our society. This covers both breadth and depth—How many kind of ways are computers going to be applied, and how significantly?

Engelbart here was not just deploying the rhetoric of the American frontier, but also following Norbert Wiener, who "had redefined the function of a scientist or engineer from mere expertise to competence and sophistication in the difficult, exacting task of anticipating the social effects of his work" (Heims 1980, 337). In a paper entitled "Some Moral and Technical Consequences of Automation" that appeared in *Science* a few months before Engelbart's writing, Wiener had claimed that "for the individual scientist, even the partial appraisal of the liaison between the man and the [historical] process requires an imaginative forward glance at history which is difficult, exacting and only limitedly achievable" (quoted in Heims 1980, 337). Like Wiener, Engelbart demonstrated a special concern for a technological responsibility that can be attained only through human compassion and the intellectual power of "this imaginative forward glance." The joining of historical knowledge and analogical reasoning was for Engelbart one way to develop this "forward glance":

> Consider the parallel to the individually manned automotive vehicles. . . . No one would particularly be ruffled by hearing that "automotive power technology is going to remake our lives, our cities, our schools" . . . because, of course, they had their mental picture of railroads and steamships making ever greater impact upon our lives. And then came the cars, trucks, fork lifts, bulldozers, motor scooters, jeeps . . . and our unruffled listener realized that he had been listening only with his ears.
>
> The first uses of our automatic-information-handling (computer) equipment was in the large installation, formal-schedule class too, with tremendous impact upon society. And we all agree, without being at all ruffled, that our lives will be re-made by this technology. But are we really *listening* as we nod? I suggest that the parallel of the individually manned auto-motive vehicles will develop in the computer field, contributing changes to our social structure that we can't comprehend easily. The man-machine interface that most people talk about is the equivalent of the locomotive-cab controls (giving a man better means to contribute to the big system's mission), but I want to see more thought on the equivalent of the bulldozer's cab (giving the man maximum facility for directing all that power to his individual task).

This is the first reference to personal computing in Engelbart's thinking: the difference between locomotives and automobiles or bulldozers points to a difference between technological servitude and technological liberation, between individuals being subsumed into a task defined by some massive technological innovation and that innovation being put at the service of autonomous individuals—in fact, being a condition of their autonomy. In social terms, however, no autonomy is unconditional. One way in which Engelbart tried to imagine the human-computer relationship was almost Hegelian, cast in terms of a human master and a mechanized "slave":

> Imagine what it might be like to have information-handling "horsepower" available for your personal use, with means for interaction and control so that you

could get useful help in your daily activities and with procedures and environment developed to facilitate its use and take advantage of its capabilities. I am betting on an emergence of this type of development. . . .

Think ahead to the day when computer technology might provide for your very own use the full-time services of a completely attentive, very patient, very fast symbol-manipulating slave who has an IQ adequate for 95% of your today's mental tasks. This is a plausible possibility. But dream on,—assume that you and that machine know how to work together so that you can still pursue your professional tasks as a free-wheeling operator, but with your slave doing most of the work involved in that pursuit that is within its capability. This means, of course, that the ball bounces back and forth very often between you and your slave, because your high-order activity is greatly dispersed among the low-order tasks.

This unself-conscious enthusiasm for the computer as "slave" ignores the way that all master-slave relationships tend to be problematic—for the master, as well as, of course, for the slave. But the kind of relationship between computer user and computer that Engelbart was trying to imagine using these highly charged terms was in fact an exact image of the way he hoped the computer would be conceptualized and developed: as something subjugated to and serving the desire and will of the user.

OTHER VISIONS

J. C. R. Licklider and Artificial Intelligence

The effort to construct a relationship in which the computer is subordinated to the individual, although not completely isolated or even original, however, was a marginal endeavor in the computer-science community of the 1960's in the United States. Two main projects had stemmed from the rise of cybernetics: intelligence amplification, including Engelbart's Augmentation of the Human Intellect project, on the one hand, and the effort to produce artificial Intelligence (AI), on the other.[14] It was the latter that received most of the attention—and the bulk of the funding. The person who best articulated the effort to produce artificial intelligence after World War II and who differentiated it from projects like Engelbart's was a young psychologist at MIT in the Department of Electrical Engineering and in the Lincoln Laboratory, J. C. R. Licklider, part of the group around Norbert Wiener and a member of the cybernetics circle at MIT.

In 1960, his paper "Man-Computer Symbiosis" laid the groundwork for a program of action for interactive computing, computing that involved real-time, two-way exchanges across the interface between user and machine (Licklider 1960). Mainframe computers were used during the 1950's for the batch processing of numbers. Such "number crunching" was not interactive. A user would hand over a data set plus the instructions for analyzing these data, and then typically wait for some hours before getting the results, which often led to a further request, and so on. With his idea of "man-computer symbiosis," Licklider proposed a new representation of the human-computer interaction in a programmatic call inspired by cybernetics. The fact that to portray the human-computer interaction Licklider chose the biological concept of symbiosis, which he defined as the "cooperative living together in intimate association or even close union, of two dissimilar organisms," clearly inscribed his project in the perspective of cybernetics, which describes animals and machines with the same vocabulary. " 'Man-computer symbiosis' is a subclass of 'man-machine systems.' There are many man-machine systems. At present however, there are no man-computer symbioses." The vision of man-computer symbiosis was "that the resulting partnership will think as no human brain has ever thought and process data in a way not approached by the information-handling machines we know today." In calling for a machine that would think "as no human brain has ever thought," this vision parted company with the notion of augmenting human intelligence.

As a concept, man-computer symbiosis is different in an important way from what North [15] has called "mechanically extended man." In the man-machine systems of the past, the human operator supplied the initiative, the direction, the integration, and the criterion. The mechanical parts of the systems were mere extensions, first of the human arm, then of the human eye.

These systems certainly did not consist of "dissimilar organisms living together. . . . " There was only one kind of organism—man—and the rest was there only to help him.

In one sense of course, any man-made system is intended to help man, to help a man or men outside the system. If we focus upon the human operator(s) within the system, however, we see that, in some areas of technology, a fantastic change has taken place during the last few years. "Mechanical extension" has given way to replacement of men, to automation, and the men who remain are there more to help than to be helped. In some instances, particularly in large computer-centered information and control systems, the human operators are responsible mainly for functions that it proved infeasible to automate. Such systems ("humanly extended machines" North might call them) are not symbiotic systems. They are "semi-automatic" systems, systems that started out to be fully automatic but fell short of that goal.

Man-computer symbiosis is probably not the ultimate paradigm for complex technological systems. It seems entirely possible that, in due course, electronic or chemical "machines" will outdo the human brain in most of the functions we now consider exclusively within its province. . . . In short, it seems worthwhile to avoid arguments with (other) enthusiasts for artificial intelligence by conceding dominance in the distant future of cerebration to machines alone. There will nevertheless be a fairly long interim during which the main intellectual advances will be made by men and computers working in intimate association.

Starting from a sense he shared with Engelbart that in technological change, "mechanical extension" had led to the "replacement of men, to automation," a situation in which "the men who remain are there more to help than to be helped," Licklider looked instead for a path of development that led not to autonomous individuals using personal computers as tools, or even as "slaves," but to a future in which "cerebration" was dominated by machines alone, a future toward which "man-computer symbiosis" was simply an evolutionary stage. Artificial intelligence and the augmentation of human intelligence might in the near term be compatible, but their ends were utterly divergent.

And Licklider had the resources to pursue this vision of artificial intelligence. He was an insider, not an outsider, and in October 1962 became the first director of the Information Processing Techniques Office (IPTO) at ARPA, the U.S. Defense Department's Advanced Research Projects Agency, which was to underwrite the development of the ancestor of the Internet. Licklider and his successors as directors of the IPTO in the 1960's had the opportunity to direct and influence the overall shape of computer science during their tenure at the head of the most important source of funding for this activity. Altogether, they allocated more than one hundred and fifty million dollars over a period of ten years to a dozen institutions that are still today at the leading edge of computing research.

Soon after President John F. Kennedy took office in 1960, global tensions with the Soviet Union led the federal government to stress technological competition with Russia. ARPA was established, Congress provided it with a large budget for research and development, and ARPA's Information Processing Techniques Office was created to fund R&D efforts in computing. ARPA-IPTO soon became the major source of funding for academic research in computer science.

At the beginning of his tenure at the IPTO, Licklider formed an advisory committee composed of the representatives of the main funding institutions involved in computing at that time. One member was another young psychologist, Robert Taylor, who was then heading a research program on computing at NASA.[16] In 1964, Licklider resigned from ARPA in order to return to MIT and was replaced as director of the IPTO by Ivan Sutherland, at that time a 26-year-old army lieutenant at Fort Meade, Maryland. Taylor served as Sutherland's associate director until 1965, when Sutherland accepted a faculty position at Harvard. Thus, Taylor became the third director of the IPTO.

Over the next five years, the IPTO funded twenty or so large research projects, mostly at U.S. universities.[17] Particularly heavy funding went to the computer science departments at MIT, Carnegie-Mellon University, and Stanford University, three departments still top-rated in computer science today. The IPTO served in a coordinating role, facilitating the formation of an invisible college among ARPA's R&D contractors in the computer field.[18]

Through the IPTO, Licklider and those who succeeded him established a network of computer scientists on the basis of a philosophy of conflict and cooperation. This organizational style and the management of the IPTO were to be central to the shaping of early personal computing. The key feature of the management style developed by Licklider at the IPTO was the absence of the peer review system, which was replaced by a more informal networking system. It created yet another group of insiders.

Licklider believed this networking system could spot "the best people doing the best projects related to its mission." [19] He described this networking mode in the following words: "I had been going to computer meetings for quite a while. I'd heard many of these people talk. . . . There is a kind of networking. You learn to trust certain people, and they expand your acquaintance. I did a lot of traveling, and in a job like that, when people know you have some money it's awful easy to meet people; you get to hear what they are doing" (Licklider 1988).[20] This informal networking system is best epitomized by the annual IPTO contractors' meetings, where the various principal investigators would give short presentations of their work and engage in quite lengthy arguments and debates. In this management style, according to Alan Kay, decisions were in the hands of the director of the office, himself a member of the community, and were usually based on controversy, rather than consensus.[21]

As some of the major figures in the community of IPTO contractors now see it, "To some extent, much of what we have in personal workstations is a result of the quality of research that Lick[lider] funded" (John Brackett); "One of the things that characterized ARPA's history was a selection of foci" (Allen Newell); "I think that ARPA, through Lick, realized that if you get *n* good people together to do research on computing, you're going to illuminate some reasonable fraction of the ways of proceeding because the computer is such a general instrument" (Alan Perlis).[22]

That may have been the outcome of the research, but everyone in this group agreed that there was not a commonly defined project to build a personal workstation. That is because the organization of the IPTO-contractor relationships reflected the belief that the computer is "a general instrument." As a result, present-day microcomputers and personal workstations are technological systems that reflect the legacy of the collective output of a network of creative individuals bound together in shaping them.

Engelbart and Licklider

In 1960, when J. C. R. Licklider was proposing his ideas on "man-computer symbiosis," Douglas Engelbart was beginning to implement his "crusade" to make humans better able to cope with the twin challenges of complexity and urgency at SRI. The full title of his research program was The Framework for the Augmentation of Human Intellect. Like Licklider's vision of a "man-computer symbiosis," Engelbart's project was based on the premise that computers should be able to perform as a powerful auxiliary to human communication. He, too drew on the biological notion of "symbiotic" association proposed earlier by Licklider. Engelbart proposed to extend the symbiotic model with his notion of "synergism" to represent the "actual source of intelligence":

> If we then ask ourselves where that intelligence is embodied, we are forced to concede that it is elusively distributed throughout a hierarchy of functional processes—a hierarchy whose foundation extends down into natural processes below the depth of our comprehension. If there is any one thing upon which this "intelligence" depends, it would seem to be *organization*. The biologists and psychologists use a term "synergism" to designate (from *Webster's Unabridged Dictionary*, second edition) the "cooperative action of discrete agencies such that the total effect is greater than the sum of the two effects taken independently." . . . This term seems directly applicable here, where we could say that synergism is our most likely candidate for representing the actual source of intelligence (Engelbart 1962, 18).

Engelbart was not heavily funded by ARPA-IPTO until 1967. His funding for the Augmentation of Human Intellect research, however, dates back to 1959, with a first small grant from the Air Force Office of Scientific Research, under the supervision of Rowena Swanson and Harold Wooster. His grants increased with continuous ARPA support beginning in February 1963, at varying levels—during 1965 about eighty thousand dollars. But this early, the IPTO's funding was relatively marginal:

> Lick was willing to put some more support into the direct goal (more or less as originally proposed), but the support level he could offer wasn't enough to pay for both a small research staff and some interactive computer support. . . . What saved my program from extinction was the arrival of an out-of-the-blue support offer from Bob Taylor, who at that time was a psychologist working at NASA headquarters.[23]

Thanks to Robert Taylor, NASA support started from midyear 1964 to midyear 1965 at a level of about eighty-five thousand dollars. Taylor's support became even more important when he became Ivan Sutherland's second in command at the IPTO in July 1964, and then when he took the direction of the IPTO, in June 1966.

Engelbart's approach differed from Licklider's both essentially and pragmatically, despite the apparent agreement on the need do some kind of human-computer symbiosis. Engelbart took what he called "a *bootstrapping* approach," considered as an iterative and coadaptive learning experience. The word "bootstrap" acquired several meanings during the twentieth century. As a noun in 1913, it meant "unaided effort" and "a loop strap sewed at the side or the rear top of a boot to help in pulling it on." As an adjective in 1926, it came to refer to being "designed to function independently of outside direction: capable of using one internal function or process to control another." Finally, in 1951, "bootstrap" became a transitive verb meaning "to promote or develop by initiative and effort with little or no assistance." Most readers are more familiar with the verb form of the word, "to boot": "To load and initialize the operating system on a machine." [24]

Although he did not use the word "bootstrap" in his original 1962 report, Engelbart indicated in his "research recommendations" that "tremendous value to the research objectives" was to be found in "the feeding back of positive research results to improve the means by which the researchers themselves can pursue their work" (Engelbart 1962, 118). In his 1968 presentation to the American Federation of Information Processing Societies Fall Joint Computer Conference, these researchers are dubbed "the bootstrap group [which] has the interesting recursive assignment of developing tools and techniques to make it more effective at carrying out its assignment" (Engelbart and English 1968, 396).

The basis of this approach is the cybernetic notion of positive feedback in the research process:

> This approach is designed to treat the redesign of a capability hierarchy by reworking from the bottom up, and yet to make the research on augmentation means progress as fast as possible by deriving practically usable augmentation systems for real-world problem solvers at a maximum rate. This goal is fostered by the recommendation of incorporating positive feedback into the research development—i.e., concentrating a good share of the basic research attention upon augmenting those capabilities in a human that are needed in the augmentation-research workers. (Engelbart 1962, 129)

Norbert Wiener gave many definitions and instances of feedback in his work. His most general definition is in *Cybernetics and Society*:

> *Feedback* [is] the property of being able to adjust future conduct by past performance. Feedback may be as simple as that of the common reflex, or it may be

a higher order feedback, in which past experience is used to regulate not only specific movements but also whole policies of behavior. Such a policy-feedback may, and often does, appear to be what we know under one aspect as a conditioned reflex, and under another as learning. (Wiener 1967, 47–48)

Wiener's statement summarizes an already long process that had slowly enlarged the sphere of application of the notion of feedback from engineering to biology and finally to the social sciences. Wiener noted very early that "it is manifest that the importance of information and communication as mechanisms of organization proceeds beyond the individual into the community" (1961, 18).

Engelbart's approach is an instance of this broad conception of feedback applied to "whole policies of behavior." It is the reflexive application of the notion of feedback to research management as an instance of learning. In Engelbart's framework, the tool system and the human system are equally important, and the technological development of computing is associated with the human capacity to change in order to take advantage of computing as a tool.

The first occurrence of the notion of feedback in a cybernetic sense appeared in an influential paper in *Philosophy of Science* entitled "Behavior, Purpose and Teleology" by Arturo Rosenblueth, Norbert Wiener, and Julian Bigelow (1943). In this often-discussed paper, the three authors, a cardiologist, a mathematician, and an engineer, respectively, generalized and redefined the classic notion of regulatory feedback mechanism exemplified by James Watt's 1784 "governor" and formalized mathematically by James Clerk Maxwell in 1868. They distinguished two kinds of feedback mechanisms: positive, when the mechanism amplifies the input signal (and therefore is of the same sign, $+/+$ or $-/-$), and negative, when the mechanism corrects the input signal (and therefore is of opposite sign, $+/-$ or $-/+$). This very crucial distinction led them to focus on negative feedback only, because they argued that all teleological behavior, that is, all behavior oriented toward a goal or purpose, can be considered to require negative feedback. Feedback correcting the input signal is what goes on when humans learn.

These fundamental ideas were presented by Rosenblueth and Wiener in person before an audience composed mostly of social scientists on the afternoon of March 9, 1946, the first day of the Feedback Mechanisms and Circular Causal Systems in Biology and the Social Sciences Meeting, effectively the second Macy meeting before they were named as such (Heims 1991, 21). It was during this second meeting that the sphere of application of the notion of feedback was effectively enlarged to the social sciences. Steve J. Heims insists, however, that it was a quite specific kind of social science that was represented at the Macy meetings:

> Controversial social theory, especially if it entailed socialist ideas, did not appear in the conferences any more than it did in academia generally. No historian or political scientist was ever invited, even as a guest, and the sole sociologist participating was safely interested only in statistical methods. With the exception of the first meeting, explicit philosophical discussion was muted. The ideal of purely scientific discourse dominated all the meetings after the first.

Indeed these social scientists were mostly psychologists, with the notable exception of the anthropologists Gregory Bateson and Margaret Mead and the sociologist Paul Lazarsfeld. Norbert Wiener, of course, as we have seen already, was well aware of the political and ethical dimensions of cybernetics as a new science that "embraces technical developments with great possibilities for good and for evil." Even if he felt at the time that he and his colleagues "stand in a moral position which is, to say the least, not very comfortable," he was nevertheless not very troubled by the lack of presence of such "controversial social science" (Wiener 1961, 28). He soon made clear his position in respect to the potential applications of cybernetics to the social sciences in his book *Cybernetics*:

> I mention this matter because of the considerable, and I think false, hopes which some of my friends have built for the social efficacy of whatever new ways of thinking this book may contain. They are certain that our control over our material environment has far outgrown our control over our social environment and our understanding thereof. Therefore, they consider that the main task of the immediate future is to extend to the fields of anthropology, of sociology, of economics, the methods of the natural sciences, in the hope of achieving a like measure of success in the social fields. From believing it necessary, they come to believe it possible. In this, I maintain, they show an excessive optimism, and a misunderstanding of the nature of all scientific achievement. (Wiener 1961, 162)

For Wiener, the roots of this crucial "misunderstanding of the nature of all scientific achievement" on the part of those social scientists, including Bateson and Mead, stemmed from their lack of respect for the "scientific" necessity to maintain "a high degree of isolation of the [observed] phenomenon from the observer." To the objection that the Heisenberg Uncertainty Principle had shown that such a degree of isolation between observer and phenomenon was illusional, even in physics, Wiener responded that "we do not live on the scale of the particles concerned, either in space or in time." Finally, the false hopes and misunderstandings of his social-scientist friends appeared to Wiener to be caused by the fact that "it is in the social sciences that the coupling between the observed phenomenon and the observer is the hardest to minimize" (Wiener 1961, 162, 163).

It seems therefore that both in his application of the notion of "positive feedback" at the level of the research approach ("bootstrapping") as well as in the notions of amplification and synergism, Engelbart would have appeared guilty of the same crime in Wiener's eyes, whatever the closeness of their moral position in respect to their responsibility as scientists. Engelbart, of course, never would have accepted such an abrupt condemnation of the kind of optimism that was at the root of his project: a reflexive application of the cybernetics principles as embodied in the notion of bootstrapping to help people learn how to become better at realizing their abilities to deal with the challenges that confronted them.

J. C. R. Licklider, by contrast, was very representative of the kind of specialist in the "human sciences" first attracted by the cybernetics project. After earning his Ph.D. at the University of Rochester in 1942, Licklider started his career as an experimental psychologist at Harvard Psycho-Acoustic Laboratory. He lectured at Harvard until 1951, when he left to start the MIT program in speech and hearing. He was invited to the seventh Macy meeting (March 23–24, 1950), where he gave a presentation on his work in psychoacoustics, describing "how the sound made by a person speaking, as well as distortion of that speech and noise, can be analyzed mathematically." Licklider's work on "intelligibility" was therefore very close to the work of Claude Shannon, who was also invited to the seventh meeting, but unlike Shannon's work, it included a formalization of the "human hearing mechanisms" (Heims 1991, 75).

Licklider, like many of his psychologist colleagues, believed that the human aspect of the question of communication and control should be understood in terms of "human mechanisms"—with the emphasis on "mechanisms." As John Stroud, another member of the cybernetics group, summarized the question: "so we have the human operator surrounded on both sides by very precisely known mechanisms and the question comes up 'what kind of machine have we put in the middle?'" (quoted in Heims 1991, 207). This "mechanist bias" was profoundly inscribed in the cybernetics project, and Licklider's decision to look at the computer as an organism in a symbiotic association must be placed in this context. It meant that the human participant could and should be seen as a machine.[25] The contrast with Engelbart's assumption about how and why human-computer interaction was possible could not have been greater.

Time Sharing

In Licklider's proposal, one of the main novel ideas was that human-computer interaction should be seen as a communicative act. But there were at least two major communication models underlying the various representations of what interactive computing should be: the computer could appear either as a means in a mostly human communication process, the way Engelbart understood it, or as a mechanical "partner in interaction." This opposition became inscribed in the structure of the ARPA-IPTO community itself. With his concept of man-machine symbiosis, J. C. R. Licklider launched an initial program of action for the then-emerging field of human-computer interaction (HCI): "to think in interaction with a computer in the same way you think with a colleague whose competence supplements your own will require much tighter coupling between man and machine than is suggested by the example and than is possible today" (Licklider 1960). For this first representation, then, HCI was conceptualized as a communicative act between the user and the computer modeled on a conversation between more or less equal "colleagues."

Licklider's model of a conversation between colleagues applied to human-computer interaction was a fundamental innovation because it cast a new light on what computing might be about. It introduced the computer as a new kind of medium: an extension of the brain. That conversation, however, could be conceptualized in the two very different ways that characterized the difference between Engelbart's and Licklider's approach. On the one hand, the computer could be seen as an autonomous entity unto itself, an "artificial" colleague. On the other, the user-machine conversation could be seen as a sort of internal dialogue, as if the computer were a prosthesis of the brain, an extension of the thinking processes of the user. Licklider made it clear that he believed that only the first was bound to happen, while the second was already passé.

The first program of action was developed into what is known as the program of Artificial Intelligence (AI). The idea was to enable the computer to behave as a colleague by mimicking the mechanisms of the highest human attribute, intelligence.[26] The second was taken over by Engelbart and his Augmentation Research Center (ARC) at Stanford Research Institute (SRI), working from a very distinct perspective:

> When interactive computing in the early 1970s was starting to get popular, and they [researchers from the AI community] start writing proposals to NSF and to DARPA, they said well, what we assume is that the computer ought to adapt to the human [. . .] and not require the human to change or learn anything. And that was just so antithetical to me. It's sort of like making everything to look like a clay tablet so you don't have to learn to use paper. (Engelbart 1992)

This trend was established before the early 1970's, and what Engelbart narrates here can be seen as the result of the way the contractors' community was structured as funded mainly by the IPTO. Between 1962 and 1967, three main research areas emerged in the IPTO's funding in computer science: time sharing, graphics, and artificial intelligence. But AI research was an emergent program, and ARPA budgets did not include it as separate item line until 1968. Bob Taylor gave the rationale for such a situation from his standpoint as the IPTO director:

> The AI people, who were getting support from ARPA when I was there, may have thought that the reason why I was supporting AI was because I believed in AI, qua AI. If they thought that, they were mistaken. I was supporting it because of its influence on the rest of the field, not because I believed that they would indeed be able to make a ping-pong-playing machine in the next three years, but because it was an important stimulus to the rest of the field. There was no reason for me to tell them that, of course. (Taylor 1989)

Engelbart's position thus was relatively marginalized in the institutional network that progressively emerged at that time, and his interest in the augmentation of the intellect of the user, and not in the intelligence of the computer, as in AI, finally never got much recognition inside the contractors' commmunity.[27]

Time sharing was without contest Licklider's first objective in the early 1960's.[28] To him, time sharing was a necessary step toward interactive computing; "we needed to have time-sharing systems before we could do man-computer interaction research" (Licklider 1988). The vision embodied in the "Man-Computer Symbiosis" article is "interactive computing" ("to think in interaction with a computer"), and interactive computing became an article of faith for Licklider:

> Every time I had the chance to talk, I said the mission is interactive computing. . . . I was just a true believer. I thought, this is going to revolutionize how people think, how things are done. . . . I was one of the very few people, at that time, who had been sitting at a computer console four or five hours a day—or maybe even more. It was very compelling. I was terribly frustrated at the limitations of the equipment we had, but I also saw how fast it's getting better. (Licklider 1988)

One of the first decisions Licklider made when he arrived at the IPTO was to revise the contract with System Development Corporation (SDC) in Santa Monica, which was the only contract he inherited. SDC, which had been the computing arm of the Department of Defense (DOD) since its work on the Sage System for the U.S. Air Force, was in possession of one of the four Sage DOD-owned IBM AFSQ32s, the largest computer of that time. Much to the dismay of some at SDC, Licklider reworked their work statement in order to design and build a time-sharing system for this machine.

At the same time, Licklider initiated another contract with the University of California at Berkeley, where David Evans and Harry Husky were the principal investigators. The work statement of this second contract was to put a

Model 33 teletype in the Berkeley lab and connect it up on-line to the time-sharing system at SDC. According to Robert Taylor, this second contract was made to help Licklider "evaluate, motivate and stimulate SDC's progress." [29]

Since his Ph.D. at Berkeley under Paul Morton's supervision in the early 1950's, Douglas Engelbart had kept some contacts with his alma mater. For instance, some Berkeley computer science students came to ARC for summer jobs. Engelbart, in connection with Evans's contract with the IPTO, also got to work on the SDC AFSQ32 on-line. The connection between ARC and Berkeley was reinforced when a second early time-sharing system grew out of Licklider's original contract. Some graduate students at Berkeley started their own time-sharing system with an SDS 930 computer purchased from Scientific Data Systems, a company based in El Segundo, near Los Angeles. This second project, entitled Project Genie, had a tremendous influence on the further progress of both Douglas Engelbart's "crusade" and the development of personal computing. Charles Thacker, Butler Lampson, and Jim Mitchell (and later Peter Deutsch) were the main architects of this SDS 940 time-sharing system. Robert Taylor later hired them to work at Xerox PARC, where they became the main architects of the Alto computer. However, at the time, Engelbart's position in the contractors' community amounted to one modestly funded project in the West Coast subnetwork centered on SDC-RAND.

Apart from this West Coast pole of the ARPA-IPTO contractors' network, Licklider established an East Coast pole centered in Boston and Cambridge, including institutions and projects like MIT Project MAC (for Machine-Aided Cognition and Multiple-Access Computer) and Lincoln Laboratories, Bolt, Beranek, and Newman (BBN), and a number of smaller projects and companies. In this second subnetwork, the IPTO's three main research areas were investigated by prestigious scientists such as John McCarthy, Marvin Minsky, Wesley Clark, Edward Fredkin, and younger members such as Ivan Sutherland. MIT also had operated an early time-sharing system since December 1958,[30] and Ivan Sutherland developed Sketchpad, the first graphics software, on the TX-2 computer. The research on artificial intelligence certainly gave strength to the East Coast subnetwork. Apart from the MIT-centered Boston community, it also included the Carnegie-Mellon University group led by Herbert Simon and Allen Newell (joined by Alan Perlis) after they had left RAND in the early 1960's.[31]

Almost everybody in this community agreed on the necessity of time sharing as a preliminary step toward interactive computing. John McCarthy was the first to champion the idea of time sharing, according to many accounts (Wildes and Lindgren 1985). Some, however, questioned this necessity. Wesley Clark, for instance, gave the rationale for such a critique of time sharing:

I still think that it's a bad idea. . . . Actually I think that's probably a transitional sense in which the term was used. It was first used in somewhat more of a constrained sense, simply to mean the moment-by-moment carving up of the time of a resource—among two or more cooperative users of a resource . . . to describe the mode in which parts of the resource were dedicated instant-by-instant to one thing and then to another. But the overall program or resource at the time was serving the function of only one principal task. And this was the matter of resource allocation to best meet that task without using too much equipment. That is a very limited sense.

There was, however, another sense:

The Time-Sharing—capital T, capital S notions which sort of grew up following observations of the behavior of . . . ideas that are on the SAGE system, and perhaps the TX-2 and TX-o as well. But most likely from the campus part of MIT, the Cambridge people . . . who could not fail to realize that access to the machinery, hands-on access, was a very happy thing to have. In that sense, it was quite a different one. It meant the competitive use of the same resource for different purposes. And unfortunately, the idea of time sharing became a bit confused, I believe. The access part was a good idea. Everybody should have good access to good computers; nobody can deny that. . . . But the trouble is, people generally wanted to use machinery that wasn't around. So they had to share in one way or another. And there were so many people that it was thought that the way to provide the access was to carve time up into little pieces and then alternate from one competitor to another, and to do that so fast in fact that no one realized that . . . or no one would have the perception that there were any other competitors around. And in fact, all of those competitors had to be kept in good order with respect to one another without their knowledge by the coordinating program, and the operating system, the time-sharing operating system for the resource. And that was going to take away a great deal from the efficiency of the machinery. So it's a very big price to pay. And in the time-sharing paradigm the more users you have the better. So the time slices get very small. And the number of coordination steps goes up, so the overhead costs become very, very large to run a time-sharing system like that. And what is perhaps worst of all, the idea was based on taking the largest machine that you could pay for, and then spread the costs around among all these users. But unfortunately, that meant that regardless of the need that the user might have, he had to pay for the entire machine during the fraction of the time that he was using it, whether he needs it or not. (Clark 1990)

This is very close to Engelbart's criticism of the way people become subservient to a big technological system like a steamship or locomotive, instead of being given their autonomy by a technological innovation such as the automobile. The paradox of time sharing, according to this rationale, is that it provided less "personal access," access to meet a personal task, because it was supposed to provide more access to individual users. Time sharing, therefore, as it developed inside the IPTO community, or rather, the "capital T, capital S notions" of how it should be implemented, proved to be alien to Engelbart's entire approach to personal computing. Once again, he was on the outside, going in a different direction entirely.

Engelbart's personality and communicative skills as a lifelong outsider didn't endear him to the IPTO contractors' community, either. John Backus, one of the leading developers of the programming language FORTRAN, recalls that although "programming in the America of 1950's had a vital frontier enthusiasm virtually untainted by either the scholarship or the stuffiness of academia," even on the frontier, you still had to fit in, and "recognition in the small programming fraternity was more likely to be accorded for a colorful personality, an extraordinary feat of coding, or the ability to hold a lot of liquor well than for intellectual insight" (1980, 126–27).[32] Engelbart's inability to compromise on his "crusade" did not help to attract much interest from a community whose interests lay elsewhere, and very often, on the contrary, helped to categorize him further as a "loner" doing "weird stuff." His project for the augmentation of human intellect was never discussed inside the IPTO contractors' community as a potential alternative to a research program in artificial intelligence.[33]

CHAPTER ONE

Language and the Body

If we "think" verbally, we act as biased observers and project onto the silent levels the structure of language we use, and so remain in our rut of old orientations, making keen, unbiased observations and creative work well-nigh impossible. In contrast, when we "think" without words, or in pictures (which involve structure and therefore relations), we may discover new aspects and relations on silent levels, and so may produce important theoretical results in the general search of similarity of structure between the two levels, silent and verbal. Practically all important advances are made that way.

— A L F R E D   K O R Z Y B S K I , *Manhood of Humanity*

Engelbart's "weird stuff" was in fact not weird at all. Instead, it was thoroughly grounded in what at that point was some of the most advanced thinking about how people think, act, and live in the world. It reflected what many influential thinkers—many of them also "outsider" free intellectuals— had been saying about language, thought, and reality, to use the terms that Benjamin Lee Whorf used to frame a book that helped blaze the path that Engelbart followed.

It is difficult to remember the time when computers could not deal with what is called "natural language," the ordinary, everyday language in which people speak and write. As strange as it can appear now, however, the notion of a natural-language interface between the computer and its user is a relatively new idea. The evolution of human-computer interfaces from specialized, artificial computer languages such as FORTRAN and COBOL to a natural-language interface was the result of a slow process of teaching both the user and the computer how to talk to each other, to find a common language. How that process worked out had significant consequences for the way the personal computer developed. The most significant consequence was Douglas Engelbart's

33

inclusion of the body of the user in the interaction between computers and
their users.

LANGUAGE

The history of how the computer and its relationship to its human users was
imagined is a dance of metaphors.[1] For Engelbart, as we have seen, the computer was to be less like a locomotive and more like a bulldozer or automobile, or more like a "slave" and less like an autonomous thinking machine. For
Licklider, it was to be an artificial "colleague" with whom the user could "interact" in a "conversation." Engelbart, in his effort to develop computers as a
kind of prosthesis, and those trying to develop them as a form of artificial intelligence, both agreed, however, that in one sense, the usual way of representing human-machine interaction was misleading. The user of a computer
should not be thought of as "operating" it, the way a construction worker operates a bulldozer. Instead, the user and the computer should be thought of as
"communicating" with each other.

> Prior styles of interaction between people and machines—such as driver and
> automobile, secretary and typewriter, or operator and control room—are all ex-
> tremely lean: there is a limited range of tasks to be accomplished and a narrow
> range of means (wheels, levers and knobs) for accomplishing them. The notion of
> the *operator* of a machine arose out of this context. But the user is not an opera-
> tor. He does not operate the computer, he communicates with it to accomplish a
> task. Thus we are creating a new arena of human action: communication *with*
> machines rather than operation *of* machines. (Card, Moran, and Newell 1983, 7,
> emphasis in the original)

In both the AI community and in Engelbart's lab at SRI, much effort was devoted to figuring out what this metaphor could mean in actuality and to making it work with real people and computer hardware.

As Engelbart saw it in 1962, the interaction between users and computers
is a process of information exchange that is not necessarily unique to humans
using computers. All such exchanges take place within a larger framework.
He called the larger framework as it operates with respect to computers the
"H-LAM/T System" for "Human using Language, Artifact, Methodology, in
which he is Trained." In this scheme, arrows represent flows of energy between
the "outside world" and both the user and the machine, the "artifact." A cap-
tion in the original representation refers to the shaded areas, the defining element of the "Man-Artifact Interface" shared by both humans and machines,
as "matching processes." Whereas these processes for computers heretofore
had been the domain of a few programmers and depended on artificial lan-

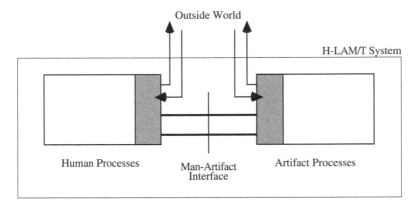

Figure 1-1. Engelbart's Portrayal of the H-LAM/T System. Source: Adapted from Engelbart (1962), p. 20.

guages to provide the computer with input, instruct it what to do with it, and obtain usable output, for Engelbart, they were ubiquitous, part of the givens with which humans interact with their environment:

> Where a complex machine represents the principal artifact with which a human being cooperates, the term "man-machine interface" has been used for some years to represent the boundary across which energy is exchanged between the two domains. However, the "man-artifact interface" has existed for centuries, ever since humans began using artifacts and executing composite processes, exchange across this "interface" occurs when an explicit-human process is coupled to an explicit-artifact process. Quite often these coupled processes are designed for just this exchange purpose, to provide a functional match between other explicit-human and explicit-artifact processes buried within their respective domains that do the more significant things. (Engelbart 1962, 20–21)

For Engelbart, what seemed promising about computers was that for these "artifacts," the processes that match human and machine to the outside world and to each other could be found in natural language, understood in both its physiological and its social dimensions, a language available to all. Of all the tools humans use to construct and modify the machines they use to transform themselves and their environment, language clearly seemed the meta-tool, the one that made all the others possible.

"I remember the revelation to me when I was saying, 'Let's look at all the other things that probably are out there in the form of tools,' and pretty soon focusing on language; realizing how much there was already that is added to our basic capability. . . . It amounts to an immense system that you essentially can say augments the basic human being" (Engelbart 1996). Because of the use of natural language in the matching processes connecting not just the user, but the computer with the outside world and with each other, the computer could appear both as an extension of the brain, in its physiological dimension, and as a medium, in its social dimension.

What Engelbart meant by "language" was "the way in which the individual parcels out the picture of his world into the concepts that his mind uses to model the world, and the symbols that he attaches to those concepts and uses in consciously manipulating the concepts" (Engelbart 1962, 9).

> A natural language provides its user with a ready-made structure of concepts that establishes a basic mental structure, and that allows relatively flexible, general-purpose concept structuring. Our concept of "language" as one of the basic means for augmenting the human intellect embraces all of the concept structuring which the human may make use of. . . . The other important part of our "language" is the way in which concepts are represented—the symbols and *symbol structures*. (Engelbart 1962, 35)

Language thus was conceived as operating at two levels: it structures concepts, but it also structures symbols in order to model and at the same time to represent "a picture of the world." The evolution of this definition of language during twenty years of Engelbart's publications shows that the meaning of the term remained constant in Engelbart's work, as one of its most constant assumptions. In *Vistas in Information Handling* (Engelbart 1963), the phrase "the way in which the individual parcels out the picture of his world" be-came "the way in which the individual classifies the picture of his world," but the rest remained unchanged. In "Toward High-Performance Knowledge Workers" (Engelbart 1982), the definition of "language" simply became "how we conceptualize, attach labels and symbols, externalize, portray, model, communicate."

As Engelbart himself pointed out, this understanding of what language is and does derives from the work of Benjamin Lee Whorf, and it both mirrors and extends the famous Sapir-Whorf Hypothesis:

> The Whorfian hypothesis states that "the world view of a culture is limited by the structure of the language which this culture uses." But there seems to be another factor to consider in the evolution of language and human reasoning ability. We offer the following hypothesis, which is related to the Whorfian hypothesis: Both the language used by a culture, and the capability for effective intellectual activity, are directly affected during the evolution by the means by which individuals control the external manipulation of symbols. (Engelbart 1962, 24)

In his extension of the Whorf Hypothesis, Engelbart postulates a dialectical relationship between the two sublevels of natural language, a relationship

in which the symbolic representation of concepts can affect the way these concepts structure the world. It is not simply the case that language structures our
world in a given way, without our having any influence on the matter. The
computerized display of new symbols should therefore allow us to affect the
way we conceptualize our world. The computer thus could become an open
medium that could be used to "make sense of the world," to map the structure
of the world as information flows in order to manage their increasing complexity. The computer medium would change intellectual activity radically. It
would not just improve its efficiency, make it faster, more economical, and so
on, although it would do these things, too. The basic means to augment human intellect would lie in the simultaneous development of computer and user
in a way that would exploit the potential of natural language to reconfigure
our concepts and change our world.

The key to this reconfiguration lay not in any single concept itself, but in
their being already configured—already given in nonlinear relationships that
could be identified, mapped, and changed. As Whorf himself put it in one of
his last statements on the issue, "Every language is a vast pattern-system, different from others, in which are culturally ordained the forms and categories
by which the personality not only communicates, but also analyzes nature, no-
tices or neglects types of relationships and phenomena, channels his reasoning,
and builds the house of his consciousness" (Whorf 1956 [1942], 252). Engelbart thus decided to focus on the configurations themselves, the "pattern-
system" or "network" ordering the concepts that make up our world, rather
than on the linear expression of those concepts, the way in which they usually
are communicated:

> With the view that the symbols one works with are supposed to represent a map-
> ping of one's associated concepts, and further that one's concepts exist in a "net-
> work" of relationships as opposed to the essentially linear form of actual printed
> records, it was decided that the concept-manipulation aids derivable from real-
> time computer support could be appreciably enhanced by structuring conventions
> that would make explicit (for both the user and the computer) the various types
> of network relationships among concepts. (Engelbart and English 1968, 398)

Engelbart proposed to use this pattern system as a way by which computers could become devices that would allow humans to expand the house of
their consciousness. When one stretches the notion of technology to include
the way humans use language—as Engelbart realized very early, according to
his own account—it becomes clearer how it was the influence of Whorf—and
beyond that, of a nexus of independent thinkers like him—that was central to
the development of the personal computer. The origin of the basic notions underlying hypertext offer one example.

Hypertext

As the personal computer has evolved, the one important way of employing "the various types of network relationships among concepts" has been the development of hypertext, "a style of building systems for information representation and management around a network of nodes connected together by typed links" (Halasz 1988, 836). Because of how he conceived of the way that natural language could function in the human-computer interface, Douglas Engelbart, along with Ted Nelson, often is credited for pioneering work in the field of hypertext or hypermedia. Many, however, trace the genealogy of hypertext not to Engelbart and his extension of the Sapir-Whorf Hypothesis, but to the work of Vannevar Bush.

In a famous article called "As We May Think," Vannevar Bush, who had done some pioneer work in analog computing in the 1920's and 1930's while he was a professor at MIT,[2] proposed a new kind of electro-optical device, the Memex, "an enlarged intimate supplement of an individual's memory." The result of "utopian fiction and speculative engineering," the Memex was an imaginary machine that existed entirely on paper and that never was constructed (Nyce and Kahn 1991b, 45). Bush was very close to the cybernetics project, and accordingly conceived his Memex on the basis of analogies between brain and machine, between electricity and information. Most authors dealing with hypertext or hypermedia systems usually refer to the following quotation, representative of this analogical thinking, as the conceptual origin of hypertext:

> The human mind . . . operates by association. With one item in its grasp, it snaps instantly to the next that is suggested by the association of thoughts, in accordance with some intricate web of trails carried by the cells of the brain. . . . Man cannot hope fully to duplicate this mental process artificially, but he certainly ought to be able to learn from it. . . . The first idea, however, to be drawn from the analogy concerns selection. Selection by association, rather than by indexing, may yet be mechanized. (Bush 1991 [1945], 101–2)

Some critics realized very early, however, that relying on such an individual process could create problems. For instance, in a private letter to Vannevar Bush sent on August 27, 1945, immediately after "As We May Think" appeared, John H. Weakland offered two main objections: "(1) Wouldn't the fact that association patterns are thoroly [sic] individual make a general use of the Memex difficult? (2) How would the tremendous bulk of information already recorded be made usable, especially for a searcher who wants to branch into lines of thought and knowledge that are quite new and unfamiliar to him?" (quoted in Nyce and Kahn 1991b, 60).[3]

James M. Nyce and Paul Kahn argue convincingly that "Weakland here anticipated two fundamental issues that were to appear again in hypertext system design," and they insist that since Bush's work, "whether access and use of the records should be based on abstract general principles or on personal, i.e., individual associations . . . has been the major issue separating information retrieval systems from hypertext" (ibid.). Hypertext systems in this formulation thus rely on the individual process of "association" as envisioned by Bush, rather than on "abstract general principles," and "for Bush, and later for Nelson and others engaged in hypertext research, Memex represented a very personal tool" (ibid., 60–61). The term "hypertext" wasn't coined until 1962 by Nelson, however, according to most accounts, including his own (Nelson 1993), and Bush himself never used the terms to describe his work. The regnant term at the time for what Bush was proposing was indeed "information retrieval," and Engelbart himself has testified to the power that a preconceived notion of information retrieval held for creating misunderstanding of his work on hypertext networks:

> I started trying to reach out to make connections in domains of interest and concerns out there that fit along the vector I was interested in. I went to the information retrieval people. I remember one instance when I went to the Ford Foundation's Center for Advanced Study in Social Sciences to see somebody who was there for a year, who was into information retrieval. We sat around. In fact, at coffee break, there were about five people sitting there. I was trying to explain what I wanted to do and one guy just kept telling me, "You are just giving fancy names to information retrieval. Why do that? Why don't you just admit that it's information retrieval and get on with the rest of it and make it all work?" He was getting kind of nasty. The other guy was trying to get him to back off. (Engelbart 1996)

It seems difficult to dispute, therefore, that the Memex was not conceived as a medium, only as a personal "tool" for information retrieval. Personal access to information was emphasized over communication. The later research of Ted Nelson on hypertext is very representative of that emphasis.[4]

It is problematic, however, to grant Bush the status of the "unique forefather" of computerized hypertext systems. The situation is more complicated than that.[5] For the development of hypertext, the important distinction is not between personal access to information and communication, but between different conceptions of what communication could mean, and there were in fact two different approaches to communication at the origin of current hypertext and hypermedia systems. The first is represented by Ted Nelson and his Xanadu Project, which was aiming at facilitating individual literary creativity. The second is represented by Douglas Engelbart and his NLS, as his oN-Line System was called, which was conceived as a way to support group collaboration. The difference in objectives signals the difference in means that characterized the two approaches. The first revolved around the "association" of ideas on the model of how the individual mind is supposed to work. The second revolved around the intersubjective "connection" of words in the systems of natural languages.

What actually differentiates hypertext systems from information-retrieval systems is not the process of "association," the term Bush proposed as analogous to the way the individual mind works. Instead, what constitutes a hypertext system is clear in the definition of hypertext already cited: "a style of building systems for information representation and management around a *network of nodes connected together by typed links*." A hypertext system is constituted by the presence of "links." And a process of association analogous to the way the individual mind works is not the only way of establishing links. The most important ones already are established in natural language.

Bush himself stated that "a provision whereby any item may be caused at will to select immediately and automatically another . . . is the essential feature of the memex. The process of tying two items together is the important thing" (Bush 1991 [1945], 103). For Bush, the individual can create links by association, jumping from one document ("node" in the current vocabulary) to another, thus creating a "trail" (a "path" or "tour" in the current vocabulary) (Oren 1991). Randy Trigg (1991, 353) also considers that such "trailblazing" is "the single most important process-related idea in Bush's Memex" and insists that "there is widespread agreement that the field of hypertext has its roots in just this notion of trailblazing." So what actually defines hypertext is the existence of links organizing the information in "trails" or paths, regardless of the process by which these links were created.

To put it another way, "association" is only one kind of "connection," and is in fact the least desirable kind, where communication is the goal, precisely because it *is* the way an *individual* mind works. The distinction was pointed out by Benjamin Lee Whorf:

> The "connection" of ideas, as I call it in the absence of any other term, is quite another thing from the "association" of ideas. In making experiments on the connecting of ideas, it is necessary to eliminate the "associations," which have an accidental character not possessed by the "connections." . . . "Connection" is important from a linguistic standpoint because it is bound up with the communication of ideas. One of the necessary criteria of a connection is that it be intelligible to others, and therefore the individuality of the subject cannot enter to the extent that it does in free association, while a corresponding greater part is played by the stock of conceptions common to people. The very existence of such a common stock of conceptions, possibly possessing a yet unstudied arrangement of its own, does not yet seem to be greatly appreciated; yet to me it seems to be a nec-

essary concomitant of the communicability of ideas by language; it holds the principle of this communicability, and is in sense the universal language, to which the various specific languages give entrance. (Whorf 1956 [1927], 36)

Associations can be individual and open-ended. "A common stock of conceptions," by contrast, tends to be limited, and "possibly possessing a yet unstudied arrangement of its own," often is structured, even hierarchical, and susceptible to rearrangement. Ted Nelson, who like Engelbart (1992) told me that he was very familiar with Whorf's writings, stressed that the main difference between his views and Engelbart's view indeed concerned the role of structure and hierarchy:

> To me hierarchy is a special case. I don't say that hierarchies are always invalid, it's just that because they're so convenient they've been used too much. And they represent many things very badly. . . . So hierarchy is fine where it correctly and appropriately matches up. And forcing it where it doesn't is wrong. So the whole point is create the structures that map correctly whatever you do. And if you're mapping thought or trying to present ideas, the likelihood that they are non-hierarchical is greater. (Nelson 1993)

For Engelbart, with his concern for communication, the opposite was the case:

> No human being can hold very many concepts in his head at one time. If he is dealing with more than a few, he must have some way to store and order these in some external medium, preferably a medium that can provide him with spatial patterns to associate with the ordering, e.g., an ordered list of possible courses of action. Beyond a certain number and complexity of interrelationships, he cannot depend upon spatial-pattern help alone and seeks other more abstract associations and linkages. (Engelbart 1961, 122)

Although most of the authors writing about hypertext mention Engelbart's work, most of them also usually fail to understand how crucial and direct Whorf's influence was. And of course, in a letter he wrote to Bush in 1962, Engelbart himself acknowledged the influence that Bush's famous article had on him:

> I might add that this article of yours has probably influenced me quite basically. I remember finding it and avidly reading it in a Red Cross library on the edge of the jungle on Leyte, one of the Philippine Islands, in the Fall of 1945. . . . I rediscovered your article about three years ago, and was rather startled to realize how much I had aligned my sights along the vector you had described. I wouldn't be surprised at all if the reading of this article sixteen and a half years ago hadn't had a real influence upon the course of my thoughts and actions. (Reprinted in Nyce and Kahn 1991a, 235–36)

Vannevar Bush was the founding father of the community of experts within the large-scale military and civilian organizations that grew out of World

War II and thrived during the Cold War, while Whorf, like Engelbart, was a "free intellectual" whose work had a significance that transcended disciplinary boundaries. Bush accumulated distinctions and honors at MIT,[6] where he was vice president and dean of engineering beginning in 1932. Whorf did not develop his passion for linguistics until the last fifteen years of life, between 1929 and 1944, "without even having undergone the usual preliminaries of formal academic study signalized by an advanced degree" (Carroll 1956, 1). It sometimes takes outsiders to see things differently. But the history of outsiders is not always the history that gets written. When it comes to understanding the ideas that made possible the development of the personal computer, however, understanding the role of outsiders, not just the role of officially sanctioned and funded efforts like the Artificial Intelligence program, is central. Without their inspiration, Engelbart would not have had the means to envision the body as part of the human-computer interface.

THE BODY

The use of natural language as a way to connect computers and their users was a central concern of the Artificial Intelligence research program, not just of Douglas Engelbart's project for the Augmentation of Human Intellect. Its attempt to use natural language as a human-machine interface was perhaps AI's utmost achievement and at the same time its worst failure, because the Artificial Intelligence research program failed to take into account the role that the body of the user could play in the human-computer interaction.

The point of contact between human and computer intelligence, the boundary that separates and joins them, usually has been located only via metaphor. There are two levels of justification for this claim. First, the very use of the word "boundary" in this context is itself metaphorical:[7] it suggests that there is a "space" where the processes of the mind and the processes of the machine are in contact, a line where one cannot be distinguished from the other except by convention—the sort of line usually drawn after a war, if one follows the lessons of human history.[8]

Second, to talk about the point of contact between human and computer intelligence at this specific time, the end of the twentieth century, has to be metaphorical because direct perception by sight, sound, or touch is still enough to know absolutely that humans and machines are different things with no apparent point of contact. Since the early days of computer science, however, the most common test to decide whether a computer can be considered an analog to a human being is the Turing Test, Alan Turing's variation on the imitation game whose experimental setting makes sure that there cannot be a direct perception (Turing 1950). In it, an interrogator sitting at a terminal who cannot see the recipients of his questions, one a human and one a machine, is asked to decide within a given span of time which one is a machine by means of their respective responses. In an elegant article called "A Simple Comment Regarding the Turing Test," Benny Shanon has demonstrated that "the test undermines the question it is purported to settle."

> But, of course, there are ways to tell the difference between computer and man. Everybody knows them. Confronted with candidates for identification, look at them, touch them, tickle them, perhaps see whether you fall in love with them. Stupid, you will certainly say: the whole point is to make the decision without seeing the candidates, without touching them, only by communicating with them via a teletype. Yes, but this, we have seen, is tantamount to begging the question under consideration. (1989, 253)

The question that the Turing Test dodges by physically isolating the interrogator from the human and the machine that is being tested is the materiality of the two respondents. And efforts to address this question simply continue the dance of metaphors. To say that "the mind is a meat machine," or, more accurately, that "the mind is a computer," is to make another metaphor: the statement relies on an analogy that "invites the listener to find within the metaphor those aspects that apply, leaving the rest as the false residual, necessary to the essence of the metaphor" (Newell 1991, 160). With the mind-as-a-computer metaphor, the greatest source of this false residual lies in the human's direct perception of the computer. Physically, materially, minds and machines or computers are fundamentally different things, however much there may be resemblances that permit metaphorical comparisons.

When one considers the mind-as-a-computer metaphor as a means to make sense of the "boundary" metaphor (a metaphor interpreting a metaphor), the obvious conclusion is that the topographical aspects are definitely not what determines the meaning: if the compared materiality of human beings and computers is the false residual of the mind-as-computer metaphor, one should conclude that there is no "natural" way to locate the boundary that distinguishes and joins them. There is no ontological connection, that is, between our materiality—our bodies—and the material manifestation of the computer. But the ultimate goal of the project to create artificial intelligence was to achieve the material realization of the metaphor of the computer as a "colleague," and therefore as a mind, a machine that can pass the Turing Test.

The greatest philosophical achievement of the AI research program might very well be that it provides an invaluable source of insight into the effect of the formal, conventional nature of language on efforts to think about the nature of the boundary between humans and machines. There is yet another metaphor to describe the traditional research program in Artificial Intelligence: the bureaucracy-of-the-mind-metaphor. For Terry Winograd, AI is the ultimate avatar of the Western philosophical program that, since Descartes, Hobbes, and Leibniz, has sought to "achieve rational reason through a precise method of symbolic calculation." This "mechanization of reason" relies heavily on the techniques of "formulation of rule-governed operations on symbol systems," which are to the mind what bureaucracy is to human social interaction (1991, 200). If this metaphor is used to interpret the metaphor of the human-machine boundary, the implication is that the boundary as a border is marked by the existence of a bureaucratic apparatus in charge of enforcing it, some sort of customs bureau and the immigration office. Here again, however, there is no "natural formation" at the border: no river nor mountain, no interface where carbon-based organization merges with silicon-based organization, but an arbitrary definition that states "here you are in machine territory, there, in human territory."

Winograd, however, argues that the computer ought to be seen as a "language machine," rather than as a "thinking machine": "The computer is the physical embodiment of the symbolic calculations envisaged by Hobbes and Leibniz. As such, it is really not a thinking machine but a *language machine*. The very notion of 'symbol system' is inherently linguistic, and what we duplicate in our programs with their rules and propositions is really a form of verbal agreement, not the workings of mind" (Winograd 1991, 216). When the AI project is understood in this way, the computer-as-mind metaphor points to the level of information processing and symbolic manipulation, not to the more general concept of "thinking."

The metaphor of the computer as a language machine makes sense of the boundary metaphor by locating the boundary more accurately, within the realm of "verbal agreement." One can still ask whether this claim does not also beg the question of material diffferences in the manner of the Turing Test, however. Even if "the very notion of 'symbol system' is inherently linguistic," there is more to natural language than the processing of symbols, more than conventional "rules and propositions" that lead to "verbal agreement." If the notion of "symbol system" is indeed inherently linguistic, everyday natural human language, on the other hand, cannot simply be reduced to the conventional manipulation of symbols.

Hubert L. Dreyfus has stated this objection regularly since 1972: there are things that computers (still) can't do because they function in a binary logic at odds with human reasoning, and binary translations into machine logic of symbols are far from enough to mimic human thinking.[9] Jean-François Lyotard has summarized the position taken by phenomenologists, from Husserl to Merleau-Ponty, on this issue, to conclude that:

A field of thought exists in the same way that there's a field of vision (or hearing): the mind orients itself in it just as the eye does in the field of the visible. . . . [This] analogy isn't extrinsic, but intrinsic. In its procedures it doesn't only describe a thought analogous to an experience of perception. It also describes a thought that proceeds analogically and only analogically—not logically. A thought in which therefore procedures of the type "just as . . . so likewise . . . " or "as if . . . then" or again "as *p* is to *q*, so *r* is to *s*" are privileged compared to digital procedures of the type "if . . . then . . . " and "*p* is not non-*p*." Now, these are the paradoxical operations that constitute the experience of a body, of an "actual" or phenomenological body in its space-time continuum of sensibility and perception. Which is why it's appropriate to take the body as model in the manufacture and programming of artificial intelligence if it's intended that artificial intelligence not be limited to the ability to reason logically.

It's obvious from this objection that what makes thought and the body inseparable isn't just that the latter is the indispensable hardware of the former, a material prerequisite of its existence. It's that each of them is analogous to the other in its relationship with its respective (sensible, symbolic) environment: the relationship being analogical in both cases. (1994, 293–94)

AI has been at the same time overly ambitious in its claim to model human intelligence and insufficiently ambitious in trying to understand the linguistic phenomenon and the path it opens to the body. Engelbart, following Whorf and a number of other independent thinkers, however, was able to see the ways in which the analogous character of natural language, thought, and the human body meant that as a "language machine," the computer could serve as a genuine boundary-spanning object.[10] In this perspective, the materiality of humans and computers takes on a different meaning than that of a "false residual" in a metaphor: both language and technology are inherently tied to the body on the human side of the border and to the circuits on the mechanical side. To understand this insight better, we need to delve further into the ideas that allowed Engelbart to arrive at it.

Cybernetic Time, Cybernetic Space

In an essay originally written in 1939 called "The Relation of Habitual Thought and Behavior to Language" and reprinted in the first edition of *Language, Thought, and Reality* in 1956, Benjamin Lee Whorf introduces his inquiry as follows: "That portion of the whole investigation here to be reported may be summed up in two questions: (1) Are our own concepts of time, space, and matter given in substantially the same form by experience to all men, or are they in part conditioned by the structure of particular languages? (2) Are there traceable affinities between (a) cultural and behavioral norms and (b) large-scale linguistic patterns?" (Whorf 1956 [1941]). As Emily Schultz's analysis of

Whorf's writing shows, the answers Whorf actually gave to these questions are considerably more nuanced than the bald formulations such as "language is culture" that sometimes are attributed to him (1990, 8–9).[11] In an illuminating parenthesis that a footnote makes even clearer, for example, Whorf adds: "I should be the last to pretend that there is anything so definite as a 'correlation' between culture and language. . . . We have plenty of evidence that this is not the case. . . . The idea of 'correlation' between culture and language is certainly a mistaken one" (1956 [1941], 139).[12] And a remark near the end of the article certainly reinforces this: "There are connections but not correlations or diagnostic correspondences between cultural norms and linguistic patterns" (ibid., 159).

For Whorf, the true nature of the relationship between language and culture was more subtle, as can be seen from an essay called "Linguistics as an Exact Science" published in 1940 in *Technology Review*:

> The phenomena of language are background phenomena, of which the talkers are unaware or, at the most, very dimly aware. . . . These automatic, involuntary patterns of language are not the same for all men but are specific for each language and constitute the formalized side of language, or its "grammar". . . . From this fact proceeds what I have called the "linguistic relativity principle," which means, in informal terms, that users of markedly different grammars are pointed by their grammars toward different types of observations and different evaluations of externally similar acts of observation, and hence are not equivalent as observers but must arrive at somewhat different views of the world. (Whorf 1956 [1940], 221)

Thus, Whorf's answer to the question of whether our concepts of time, space, and matter are universal and unconditioned or "in part conditioned by the structure of particular languages" was that both propositions are true: "Probably the apprehension of space is given in substantially the same form by experience irrespective of language . . . but the *concept of space* will vary somewhat with language, because, as an intellectual tool, it is so closely linked with the concomitant employment of other intellectual tools, of the order of time and matter, which are linguistically conditioned" (Whorf 1956 [1941], 159, emphasis in the original). Space may indeed be perceived in a similar fashion by every individual, and therefore be common to all human beings as a result of the basic conditions of human physiology, while at the same time the concept of space also is a linguistic construction and therefore varies with the different human groups singularized by their language. At group level, the level of language, said Whorf, belong "Newtonian" and "Euclidean" concepts of space (Whorf 1956 [1941], 158). Thus, for Whorf, the connections between language, cultural norms, and behavior are to be found at the level of observation and representation, not the level of perception.

This point turns on a distinction that is well explained by Jonathan Crary in terms of a fundamental shift in the understanding of how we see the world. In the classical model of the Enlightenment, all people were thought simply to receive the same impressions from the world as passive spectators. In the twentieth century, people began to become aware of the effect of the observer on observations:

> Unlike *spectare*, the Latin root for "spectator," the root for "observe" does not literally mean "to look at." Spectator also carries specific connotations . . . namely, of one who is a passive onlooker at a spectacle, as at an art gallery or theater. [But] *observare* means "to conform one's action, to comply with," as in observing rules, codes, regulations and practices. Though obviously one who sees, an observer is more importantly one who sees within a prescribed set of possibilities, one who is embedded in a system of conventions and limitations. And by "conventions" I mean to suggest far more than representational practices. If it can be said there is an observer specific to the nineteenth century, or to any period, it is only as an *effect* of an irreducibly heterogeneous system of discursive, social, technological, and institutional relations. There is no observer prior to this continually shifting field. (1990, 5–6, emphasis in the original)

For Whorf, the principle of linguistic relativity applies at the level of a "prescribed set of possibilities." However unconscious the part that language plays in this process may be, Whorf postulated that language always plays a central role in constituting "this continually shifting field," and his idea of a linguistic "connection" linking a given "common stock of conceptions" helped to convey this point: the construction of the "real world" stems from the process of sharing meaning through language.

To understand this point fully, one has to go back to Whorf's answer to his first question about the way particular languages may "condition" our concepts of time, space, and matter. Introducing language and its networks of connections into the question of how we know what we know, the question of epistemology, was part of the overthrow of the Kantian Enlightenment's notion of a universal time and space given in the fundamental conditions of human perception: "Concepts of time and matter are not given in substantially the same form by experience to all men but depend upon the nature of language or languages through the use of which they have been developed" (Whorf 1956 [1941], 159).

The relativity of time and space, of course, was not a notion limited to Whorf's work on comparative linguistics. It was fundamental to the scientific discoveries of the early twentieth century. Norbert Wiener likewise insisted on alternative conceptions of time, although not exactly in the perspective presented here by Whorf. In the first chapter of *Cybernetics*, entitled "Newtonian and Bergsonian Time," Wiener followed Henri-Louis Bergson's opposition "between the reversible time of physics, in which nothing new happens, and the irreversible time of evolution and biology, in which there is always something new" (ibid., 38). Wiener found the origin of all cybernetics thinking in the realization of the machine-organism analogy on the basis of this shifting notion of time: "the modern automaton exists in the same sort of Bergsonian time as the living organism; and hence there is no reason in Bergson's consideration why the essential mode of functioning of the living organism could not be the same as that of the automaton of this type" (1961 [1948], 30–44).

Geoffrey Bowker has said that cybernetics created a "new economy of sciences [that] challenged the traditional hierarchy, which reduced all knowledge epistemologically to physics" (1993, 118). According to Bowker, by means of the creation of new "universalist" language (which he also considers as a form of "imperialist rhetoric"), with its roots in industrial and technological thinking, "biological ideas could be imported into physics" (ibid., 119). Wiener's application of a "universal" vocabulary of communication and control to a broader set of situations formerly studied only within disciplinary limits, however, was as much a consequence as a cause of the challenge to the traditional scientific hierarchy proposed by the first cyberneticians. It was not in fact a new "vocabulary" that cybernetics introduced, or even a new "language." It was a fundamental change in our concepts of space and time, based on the widespread realization that something was wrong with traditional Newtonian mechanics and its worldview based on the notion of a reversible time:

> About the year 1900, it became apparent that there was something seriously wrong with thermodynamics, particularly where it concerned radiation. The ether showed much less power to absorb radiations of high frequency—as shown by the law of Planck—than any existing mechanization of radiation theory had allowed. [Max] Planck gave a quasi-atomic theory of radiation—the quantum theory—which accounted satisfactorily enough for these phenomena, but which was at odds with the whole remainder of physics; and Niels Bohr followed this up with a similarly *ad hoc* theory of the atom. Thus Newton and Planck-Bohr formed, respectively, the thesis and antithesis of a Hegelian antinomy. The synthesis is the statistical theory discovered by [Werner] Heisenberg in 1925, in which the statistical Newtonian dynamics of [Josiah Willard] Gibbs [the inventor of thermodynamics] is replaced by a statistical theory very similar to that of Newton and Gibbs for large-scale phenomena, but in which the complete collection of data for the present and the past is not sufficient to predict the future more than statistically. It is thus not too much to say that not only the Newtonian astronomy but even the Newtonian physics has become a picture of the average result of a statistical situation, and hence an account of an evolutionary process. (Wiener 1961 [1948], 37)

A former disciple of Einstein's, David Bohm, has summarized the effect that changes induced by the theory of relativity in physics had on the fundamental conditions of communication:

> Relativity introduces new notions concerning the order and measure of time. These are no longer *absolute*, as was the case in Newtonian theory. Rather, they are now *relative* to the speed of a coordinate frame. This relativity of time is one of the radically new features of Einstein's theory.
>
> A very significant change of language is involved in the expression of the new order and measure of time plied by relativistic theory. The speed of light is taken not as a possible speed of an *object*, but rather as the maximum speed of propagation of a *signal*. Heretofore, the notion of signal has played no role in the underlying general descriptive order of physics, but now it is playing a key role in this context.
>
> The word "signal" contains the word "sign," which means "to point to something" as well as "to have significance." A signal is indeed a kind of *communication*. So in a certain way, significance, meaning, and communication became relevant in the description of the general order of physics (as did also information, which is, however, only a *part* of the content or meaning of a communication). The full implications of this have perhaps not yet been realized, i.e., of how certain very subtle notions of order going far beyond those of classical mechanics have tacitly been brought into the general descriptive framework of physics. (1980, 123, emphasis in the original)

These points are crucial to cybernetics because they eventually allowed cyberneticians to justify the functional analogy between living organisms and machines, and hence between brains and computers. Wiener's assertion that "the modern automaton exists in the same sort of Bergsonian time as the living organism" appears then as the conclusion of a logical reasoning based on these premises: [13]

> It is clear of course, that the relation input-output is a consecutive one in time and involves a definite past-future order. What is perhaps not so clear is that the theory of the sensitive automata is a statistical one. We are scarcely ever interested in the performance of a communication-engineering machine for a single input. To function adequately, it must give a satisfactory performance for a whole class of inputs, and this means a statistically satisfactory performance for the class of inputs which it is statistically expected to receive. (Wiener 1961 [1948], 43–44)

We find here the key to the cybernetics reconstruction of "the meaning of life" in an ecological perspective and based on shifting the conception of time from the reversible and therefore completely determining Newtonian time to statistical time, fundamentally undetermined, where absolute time becomes the "statistical" time of "time series." Hence the relevance of a "new science of communication and control" that defined a message as "a discrete or continuous sequence of measurable events distributed in time—precisely what is called a time series by the statisticians" (ibid., 8–9). Wiener reinforces this idea when he states that "the great contribution of Heisenberg to physics was the replacement of this still quasi-Newtonian world of Gibbs by one in which time series can in no way be reduced to an assembly of determinate threads of development in time" (ibid., 92).

Reversible time is static. In it, events must be seen as rigidly determined. If, instead, time is in principle undetermined, however, it should be possible to make fundamental changes in how things occur. It should be possible, for example, to manage increasing complexity in an era of increasing urgency.

The revolution in how time and space were viewed helped make possible insights such as Whorf's, most notably via The General Semantics program epitomized by Alfred Korzybski's writings. Korzybski established a connection between the changing worldview in physics and an overall framework for social sciences that granted a new epistemological status to meaning and language. In fact, Whorf's "Relation of Habitual Thought and Behavior to Language" actually appeared in *ETC.: A Review of General Semantics*, the General Semantics International Society's journal.

For Korzybski (1926), "mankind" is not bound by time, but instead a *"time-binding"* class of life that "had survived in evolution by its ability to learn from past experiences and to pass this knowledge on from generation to generation through language" (Paulson 1983, 82). Trained as an engineer, but with as strong a background in philosophy, as well as in mathematics and physics, Korzybski wanted to realize the nineteenth century's positivist dream of a "mathematically sound, logically consistent *theory* of language and the hope for a psychologically valid, linguistically coherent *therapy* of language united in human action or *praxis* both to reveal and reorder the world" (ibid., 84).

For Korzybski and his followers, it was necessary to change the linguistic conception of the relationship between the "word" and the "thing-in-the-world." Korzybski (1933) best expressed this new perspective in his famous analogy between maps and language: "a map is *not* the territory" to which it corresponds, "words are not the things they represent" (quoted in Paulson 1983, 40–41). This central premise led him to question the fundamental basis of the Newtonian worldview, the Aristotelian logic system:

> I. The postulates and main characteristics of Newtonian physics are a necessary consequence of the postulates and main features of Aristotelian logic.
> II. The acceptance of a non-Newtonian physics calls for the acceptance of a non-Aristotelian logic. (Reiser 1989 [1940], 82)

Korzybski proposed to extend Aristotelian logic—hence his system is better described as non-Aristotelian rather than anti-Aristotelian—by revising three Aristotelian "laws of thought." [14] Korzybski's argument can be summed up as follows:

> (1) If the traditional Aristotelian metaphysics says that something (a word) is something else (a thing), then I say that something (a word) is "nothing" (that is, not a thing); (2) if Aristotelian grammar says that a word has a definite meaning (that is, means what it means as a defined term), then I say that a word has an indefinite range of meanings (that is, means what it means as an undefined term in a particular context or structure); and (3) if Aristotelian logic asserts that something cannot both *be* and *not be* at the same time (that is, must be *either* one thing *or* not be that one thing), then I say that according to modern quantum physics and relativity theory, something (light) can both *be* one thing (matter) and *not be* that one thing (that is, it can a be quantum of energy) at the same time. (Cited in Paulson 1983, 47, emphasis in the original)

The reference to the theory of relativity in these lines is far from accidental, and one can consider, as Oliver L. Reiser does, that Korzybski's general semantics lead to a "relativist" reformulation of the law of identity: "*identity is a relative matter*: relative to the history of the things considered, relative to the environment the thing is in, relative to our own practical purposes, relative to the frame of reference from which it is viewed, etc., and it is in fact and in principle impossible to reproduce *all* the conditions and circumstances which the statement, 'A is identical with B' would presuppose for verification" (1989, 85–86).

As in the shifting worldview in physics, the extension of the Aristotelian logic and its application to language in the General Semantics program relied heavily on a quasi-statistical approach, or more accurately, on a theory of classes, since words were not considered any more as "identical" with what they represented, but rather as a class of things that they *could* represent. [15] In other words, Korzybski sought a general reformulation of the basic epistemological foundations of scientific thought in mathematics (from Euclidean to non-Euclidean), physics (from Newtonian to non-Newtonian), and most crucially, in logic (from Aristotelian to non-Aristotelian), a reformulation that brought all these and more under the rubric of a "human science" that would include philosophy, linguistics, and psychology, a science that he dubbed "human engineering."

The social scientists of the cybernetics group were of course aware of this line of thought. As Margaret Mead wrote in 1928, "it is unthinkable that a final recognition of the great numbers of ways in which man, during the course of history and at the present time, is solving problems of life, should not bring with it in turn the downfall of our belief in a single standard." [16] But by the early 1940's, "relativity had become a popular catch-word implying a confluence of Einstein's physics and social anthropology and resting on a misunderstanding of both" (Heims 1991, 269). Indeed, Mead often had to defend herself from a politically or ethically trivial critique of cultural relativity that translated it as "all moral practices are limited in time and place and therefore lack any ultimate validity." She stated rather that "cultural relativity demands that every item of cultural behavior be seen as relative to the culture of which it is a part" (1942, 57–58).[17]

The connection between Korzybski's ideas and the social-science side of cybernetics appears in the synthesis provided by Gregory Bateson's writings. Bateson's work in diverse fields such as anthropology and psychiatry and his solid background in biology led him to propose a synthesis, an "open epistemology" [18] that he conceived as "a monistic and normative branch of natural history." The core of this synthesis revisited Korzybski's notion of the connection between "map" and "territory," and applied it at a basic level:

> The bridge between map and territory is *difference*. It is only *news of difference* that can get from the territory to the map, and this fact is the basic epistemological statement about the relationship between all reality out there and all perception in here: that the bridge must always be in the form of difference. Difference, out there, precipitates coded or corresponding difference in the aggregate of differentiation which we call the organism's mind. (Bateson 1977, 240)

In a famous illustration of this point, Bateson contended that:

> Language always says, "The lemon is yellow," and obscures the relationship between the yellow and the lemon, or it says that you have "five fingers." The correct answer to "How many fingers do you have?" is not "Five." The correct answer is that what I have is four relationships between fingers. . . . If you begin to look at your hand, or indeed any organic object, in terms of its relations and not in terms of its things, you will suddenly find that that object is about four times as beautiful as you thought it was.
>
>   Take your hand home and take a good look at it sometime. (Bateson 1991 [1980], 302–3)

Bateson knew that this epistemology "grew out of ethnographic work and cybernetic theory" (Bateson 1977, 236), but his work also redefined the basic cybernetic notion of "information." "Information" thus appears as "any difference that makes a difference" (Bateson 1979, 228).

Defined in these terms, for Whorf, what matters is not simply that language determines our concepts and that the relational network of our concepts determines our view of the world. What matters is the difference between perception on the physiological level and mental concepts on the level of language, a difference that itself has different implications, depending on which side of it is emphasized. For Korzybski, what matters is the difference between the map and the territory—not the map, by itself, or the territory. Difference is thus by definition the site of an interface. In the cybernetic formulations of Whorf, Korzybski, and Bateson, the interface, the difference that makes a difference, lies between the physical and the conceptual at a place where both can be seen to meet in the notion of "information." For Engelbart, that interface provided the possibility for the augmentation of human intellect via the computer as prosthesis.

Prosthesis and Coevolution

In *The Pencil: A History of Design and Circumstances*, Henry Petroski concludes that "the very commonness of the pencil, the characteristic of it that renders it all but invisible and seemingly valueless, is really the first feature of successful engineering. Good engineering blends into the environment, becomes a part of society and culture so naturally that a special effort is required to notice it" (Petroski 1992, 334).[19] This "becoming familiar," or "becoming a part of society and culture" was for Engelbart, too, the result of a process— the augmentation process:

> Individuals who operate effectively in our culture have already been considerably "augmented". . . . Increasing the effectiveness of the individual's use of his basic capabilities is a problem in redesigning the changeable parts of a system. The system is actively engaged in the continuous processes (among others) of developing comprehension within the individual and of solving problems; both processes are subject to human motivation, purpose and will. . . . To redesign a structure, we must learn as much as we can of what is known about the basic materials and components as they are utilized within the structure. (Engelbart 1962, 15–16)

For humans, perhaps the most distinguishing basic component used for solving problems other than natural language is the hand. The personal computer interface started with the hand, not with the brain (or the eyes, for that matter). The computer became "personal" the moment when it came into the hand's reach, via a prosthesis that the user could forget as soon as it was there.

A prosthesis that has this ability to disappear is a prosthesis that appears "natural," the evidence of a "good design" as Petroski would say.[20] As I. J. Good put it in a 1958 paper with the double-entendre title "How Much Science Can You Have at Your Fingertips?"—a paper that Engelbart annotated and underlined: "Even books and stone slabs must have been regarded as artificial or supernatural when they were first introduced. *Progress depends on artificial aids becoming so familiar that they are regarded as natural*" (Good 1958, 283, Douglas Engelbart's emphasis).[21] And what is more natural, for humans, and indeed, more universal, than perception? As Whorf has said, our concepts of space and time are conditioned by the connections supplied in our languages, but perception itself—sensation, the physiological response of the body to its environment—is not. For Whorf, among the attributes of this prelinguistic level are kinesthesia, the "sensing of muscular movement" and synesthesia, the "suggestion by certain sense receptions of characters belonging to others" [22] (Whorf 1956 [1941], 155). These form part of a general somesthetic manifold, the collection of bodily sensations.[23]

Whorf also postulated the existence of a feedback loop between the somesthetic and the linguistic, between prelinguistic sensations and linguistic images, concepts, and symbols. Kinesthesia, "though arising before language, should be made more highly conscious by linguistic use of imaginary space and metaphorical images of motion," while synesthesia "should be made more conscious by a linguistic metaphorical system that refers to nonspatial experiences by terms for spatial ones." In the West, art, especially in sculpture and music, employs this feedback loop to link the preconscious and somatic with the conscious level of linguistic concepts (ibid., 155–56). In other words, art functions by exploiting this difference that makes a difference, this interface between the physical and the conceptual.

So, in Engelbart's view, do the most elemental forms of learning, such as learning to use a pencil, for example, or learning to type, as well as the more advanced forms—in effect, learning how to learn. Engelbart's whole project dealt with information processing. This processing can be symbolic, as in the acquisition and development of skilled inscribing (and describing) practices. But this may not define all kinds of learning: Engelbart intuited that there could be another kind of practice, not necessarily linked to symbolic coding, as in writing and other inscribing practices, but rather to the kind of neuromuscular coding that emerges through the interaction of nerves, muscles, and limb groups during the acquisition and repetition of skills and practices (MacKenzie 1991). At a basic level, his project started with the intuition that such learning practices could have their place in the personal interface. That is the point of the "/T" in Engelbart's H-LAM/T system of information exchange: "Human using Language, Artifact, Methodology in which he is *Trained*."

Learning is not necessarily easy, especially at the somatic level. It is important not to confuse the way Engelbart conceived the prosthesis of the user-machine interface with later concepts such as "user friendliness." Quite the contrary. As Engelbart later put it, "Concern with the 'easy-to-learn' aspect of user-oriented applications systems has often been wrongly emphasized. For control of functions that are done very frequently, payoff in higher efficiency warrants the extra-training costs associated with using a sophisticated command vocabulary, including highly abbreviated (therefore non-mnemonic) command terms, and requiring mastery of challenging operating skills" (Engelbart 1973, 223).

Engelbart wasn't interested in just building the personal computer. He was interested in building the person who could use the computer to manage increasing complexity efficiently. For Engelbart, there were four stages in the evolution of the human intellect. In the first, "humans rose above the lower forms of life by evolving biological capability for developing abstractions and concepts." In the second, they "made another great step forward when they learned to represent particular concepts in their minds with specific symbols." In the third, they took "another significant step" when they developed "the means for externalizing some of the symbol manipulation activity, particularly in graphical representation" (1962, 21–23). In these first three stages, Engelbart was not concerned "with the value derived from human cooperation" made possible by these "manipulations," but "considered only the direct value for the individual." The development of abstractions and concepts, the linking of them to symbols, and then the externalization of those symbols so that individuals could manipulate them via representations pointed to the fourth stage, which was yet to come in human evolution: the prosthetic manipulation of symbols by a technology that would further augment the evolving human intellect.

> One way of viewing the H-LAM/T system changes that we contemplate—specifically, integrating the capabilities of a digital computer into the intellectual activity of individual humans—is that we are introducing new and extremely advanced means for externally manipulating symbols. We want to determine the useful modifications in the language and in the way of thinking that could result. This suggests a fourth stage to the evolution of our individual-human intellectual capability: (4) *automated external symbol manipulation*. In this stage, symbols with which the human represents the concepts he is manipulating can be arranged before his eyes, moved, stored, recalled, operated upon according to extremely complex rules—all in very rapid response to a minimum amount of information supplied by the human, by means of special cooperative technological devices. (Engelbart 1962, 25)

Whorf, too, had proposed that not only is language "a vast pattern-system," but that changes in the evolving pattern systems of language could be connected to the evolutionary processes of the physical world:

> The types of patterned relationships found in language may be but the wavering and distorted, pale, substanceless reflection of a CAUSAL WORLD. Just as language consists of discrete lexation-segmentation . . . and ordered patternment, of which the latter has the more background character, less obvious but more infrangible and universal, so the physical world may be an aggregate of discrete

entities (atoms, crystals, living organisms, planets, stars, etc.) not fully under-standable as such, but rather emergent from a field of causes that is itself a mani-fold of pattern and order. It is upon the bars of the fence, beyond which it would meet these CHARACTERS OF THE FIELD, that science is now poised. (Whorf, 1956 [1942], 269)

Among the early cyberneticians, it was Gregory Bateson who best followed the trail blazed by Whorf, Korzybski, and Wiener, and eventually synthesized their notion of an evolutionary process connecting the physical and the con-ceptual worlds. In the conceptual world, both the transmission and the trans-formation of what Whorf called "culturally ordained forms and categories" is the process by which people learn. The crucial point in Bateson's synthesis lay in the characterization of all such processes as "stochastic":

> Both genetic change and the process called *learning* (including the somatic changes induced by the environment) are stochastic processes. In each case there is, I believe, a stream of events that is random in certain aspects and in each case there is a nonrandom selective process which causes certain of the random com-ponents to "survive" longer than others. Without the random, there can be no new thing.
> . . . We face, then, two great stochastic systems that are partly in interaction and partly isolated from each other. One system is within the individual and is called *learning*; the other is immanent in heredity and in populations and is called *evolution*. One is a matter of the single lifetime; the other is a matter of multiple generations of many individuals.
> . . . these two stochastic systems, working at different levels of logical typing, fit together into a single ongoing biosphere that could not endure if either somatic or genetic change were fundamentally different from what it is. (Bateson 1979, 147–49)

"Coevolution" was for Bateson a way to describe the interacting evolution-ary processes connecting the physical and the conceptual worlds, including the learning processes, in which "every [physical] regularity must meet with complementary regularities; perhaps skills," and "the genesis of the skills . . . is the obverse, the other side of the process of evolution. It is *co-evolution*" (ibid., 51).[24]

It is to such ideas that Engelbart was referring when he retrospectively ex-plained the purpose and the working of his Framework for the Augmentation of Human Intellect as coevolution based on the "bootstrapping" approach, a coadaptive learning experience.

> It takes a long time (generations) to discover and implement all of the fruitful changes in the human system made possible by a given, radical improvement in technology. . . . The technology side, the *tool system*, has been inappropriately

driving the whole. What has to be established is a balanced coevolution between both parts. How do we establish an environment that yields this coevolution? Well, that's where the bootstrapping in a laboratory comes in. (Engelbart 1988, 217)

This bootstrapping philosophy was not originally conceived as a design principle, but as a basic methodology to attain the augmentation of the human intellect. The focus thus was not on a specific product or an artifact, but on a process that involved the coevolution of the user along with the computer. Here is how Douglas Engelbart was formulating the bootstrap strategy in 1968:

> I have been talking about what you would say is an evolutionary approach. You build a system; you evaluate it. You make some improvements. You evaluate those, and you constantly take what you can learn and achieve to make the next improvement. That's evolution in the standard sense of the word. But add an ingredient to this evolutionary characteristic: we are evolving techniques to help problem-solvers. Well, we're problem solvers, so if the actual sample cases we build, use and evaluate are those we ourselves can use to do the analysis, design, instrumentation and operation of our systems, then we learn about how to make people work effectively, the more effectively we can work in harnessing these improvements. It's an added ingredient of our research strategy that we call "bootstrapping." (Engelbart 1968, 23)

For Engelbart, the Framework for the Augmentation of Human Intellect was a systematic way to think and organize the coevolution between humans and their tools. The project was his effort to discover a coevolutionary path on which a radical technological improvement, a new kind of tool appropriately called in the nineteenth century "the Difference Engine," could lead to a radical improvement in "how to make people work effectively"—not just to an improvement in the way people are able to labor, but a fundamental improvement in the way people, as people, "work."

■■■■■■■■■

CHAPTER TWO

The Chord Keyset and the QWERTY Keyboard

Man must, in order to operate his instruments skillfully, internalize aspects of them in the form of kinesthetic and perceptual habits. In that sense at least, his instruments become parts of him and modify him, and thus alter the basis of his affective relationship to himself.

— JOSEPH WEIZENBAUM, *Computer Power and Human Reason: From Judgment to Calculation*

From 1957 to 1959, Douglas Engelbart earned his room and board at SRI by working on single-aperture devices, a kind of magnetic-core memory. His participation in these projects, however, was mostly motivated by his belief that he "had learned enough by then that his augmentation ideas did not grab anybody else as they grabbed him" (Engelbart 1996). But from 1959 on, thanks to a small grant from Harold Wooster and Rowena Swanson at the Air Force Office of Scientific Research, Engelbart, on a very small scale, and without a computer, started to implement his ideas about the augmentation of human intellect. Between 1959 and 1962, before he got more funding with the help of Robert Taylor and J. C. R. Licklider, Engelbart focused his efforts on teaching machines and psychomotor skills. Since his Ph.D. at Berkeley, he had kept his interest in teaching machines and symbolic logic, and he inscribed this interest into the core of his Framework for the Augmentation of Human Intellect. After all, augmentation was mostly based on systematic and organized learning, and teaching was its flip side.

THE CHORD KEYSET AND KINESTHETIC COMMUNICATION

Engelbart's project relied on a systematic appraisal of all the likely "candidates for change" in the H-LAM/T system, "the Human using Language, Artifact, and Methodology in which he is Trained." Perhaps because an early lack of funding prevented the dedicated use of a computer powerful enough, Engelbart first focused on some basic experiments involving the human components of the system, the teaching of psychomotor skills. In an SRI internal document dated September 23, 1960, entitled "A possible research activity toward a technique for teaching coordinate physical skills," Engelbart gave the general rationale for such an undertaking:

> We *have* to have a quick and direct way to lead the student's concept-handling device (his higher mental processes) through a sequence of already developed concepts from which we are composing a new, compound concept, so that the new association and relationships which are involved can impinge smoothly on the "lower processes" that somehow will fuse this into a single conceptual entity. My view is that it is essential, for an effective teaching technique, to have a neat encoding system which allows us to trigger within the student a desired sequence of elemental concepts in a form which is smooth enough to allow ready association and integration. . . .
>
> The basic new thing, I think, is the principle of using physical-stimulus cues that are more effective for prompting desired physical responses than are audio or visual cues, which generally have to be given more higher-center processing in our brains before they result in the desired physical response than the direct physical-stimulus cues. (1–4, emphasis in the original)

Two main aspects appeared in this first proposal: the emphasis on "lower processes" accessed via "physical-stimulus cues" and the question of the "encoding system" that would facilitate "the new association and relationships" involved in learning. The first aspect of the problem was connected to Engelbart's project of "increasing the effectiveness of the individual's use of his basic capabilities," translated this time in terms of the relative complexity of the brain processes associated with each kind of cue. The emphasis on direct physical stimulus represented Engelbart's decision to consider somesthetic perception as the most direct—and therefore simplest or lowest—process to be pursued for such a project. In this first project, Engelbart did not justify this decision otherwise than by talking about the huge list of potential activities—moving the fingers, arms, or even legs—that would be amenable to the automatic teaching techniques that he proposed. He did go as far, however, as giving piano playing or dancing, "quite sophisticated physical skills," as examples of such activities.

The second aspect, the question of the "encoding," however, went further than a mere automatization of teaching techniques, that is, further than a didactic application of the basic principles of the augmentation framework. Here, Engelbart was already thinking about subsequent applications of these principles, once the mechanisms were learned and the processes in place. These applications involved new means of communication between the user and the computer that would be based on such newly learned physical skills:

> It is also intriguing to consider the possibilities for applying such a skill if it becomes easy and automatic to teach. A very direct, man-to-machine communication link is handily available. . . . Furthermore, it seems highly likely to me that, once this skill has been developed to a reasonable extent, these cueing signals that are no longer needed to help the man link a character stimulus to a key-combination finger response could become a means of receiving electrically carried information. (Ibid., 4)

Using the "standard teletype five-bit code" that had been developed as telegraphy evolved beyond simple Morse code (five is the smallest number necessary to encode the roman alphabet in binary code—$2^5 = 32$), Engelbart proposed to develop the physical skill of operating a "five-key binary keyboard for the encoding of alphabetic and numeric information" (ibid., 4, see Figure 2–1). The device he developed to do this was the original version of what became known as the "chord keyset." With it, the user wouldn't enter information sequentially, by pressing one key after another, as on a typewriter keyboard, but would hold down combinations of keys, the way a piano player does when playing chords.

Moreover, the computer in turn could communicate tactually with the user. This vision of two-way somatic communication was virtually coeval with Engelbart's efforts to think about human-computer interfaces and human-computer coevolution, as his notebook from the period reveals:

> 9.22.60 Some notes on physical-skill self instructional devices and techniques. These relate back to ideas of six to ten years ago, when I used to speculate on using computer-like controls to provide a signal to different locations on (or in) a human, which his system has learned to interpret as explicit motor-response cues. Purpose would be to guide human through complex "response" actions which he is trying to learn as response to new stimuli. e.g. typing . . . where each finger is to go . . . if could train to react automatically to electric impulse stimuli in direct ??? basic finger, hand, arm motions. . . .

In a second proposal, entitled "Man-Machine Experiments" (an unsolicited proposal to the Psychological Sciences Division of the Office of Naval Research, dated March 15, 1962), Engelbart carried this idea of a new kind of man-machine communication based on somesthetic processes further. He presented "two different ideas involving man-machine information handling. . . . One idea concerns the direct use of binary signaling between man and machines and involves interesting possibilities in both equipment and techniques. The other idea concerns the development of techniques for automating the

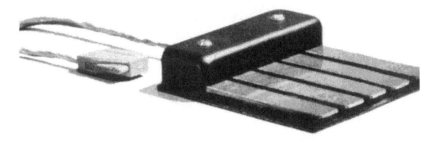

Figure 2-1. Engelbart's Chord Keyset. Source: Engelbart (1988), p. 200.

teaching of psychomotor skills" using the chord keyset, with its tactile feedback of information, rather than the standard typewriter keyboard. In this second proposal, he anticipated the following areas of exploration:

1. Develop a five-key handset suitable for conveniently selecting the thirty-one transmission codes. See how usable this is for "typing" general text—what rates can be achieved, how liable to error the technique is, how much fatigue develops in its use—all in comparison to work on the standard typewriter keyboard.

2. Make keysets for both hands. See how much transference of skill seems to occur from a trained hand to a new hand. See whether speed is increased by using both hands in the alternate mode of typing.

3. See what skill can be developed for reading the five-bit code directly from a dot or punch pattern, and whether this skill facilitates operational activity. . . .

4. See what skill can be developed for reading binary tactile signals corresponding to the transmission code applied directly to the fingers. . . .

5. Experiment with keysets that can "move with the hand" to free the user from having to stay in a fixed position, and perhaps to free his hands for (nondistracting) other activity. A type of glove might be used, or individual finger caps wired to the recording or typing mechanism (perhaps by cabling that goes up the arms and to the mechanism in an unobtrusive manner). Drumming the fingers on any hard surface could actuate the keys, so that the hands could be used freely for other purposes without losing the availability of the transmitting means. Development of a symmetrical two-handed transmitting skill would further increase the operational freedom of the hands.

In the time between these two proposals, Engelbart refined his ideas, got better acquainted with the relevant literature, and most crucially, met a couple of colleagues at SRI who were to embark with him on the project. The first was Philip H. Sorensen, a senior psychologist from the SRI Behavioral Sciences Research Program, and the second was James C. Bliss, a young research engineer from the SRI Control Systems Laboratory. Sorensen was the education specialist of the group and provided the academic background for the teaching part of the second proposal. Bliss, who had joined SRI in 1956, had taken a leave of absence from 1958 to 1960 to obtain a Ph.D. at MIT in the Sensory Aids Research Group. He was a somesthetic communication specialist whose thesis was entitled "Communication via the Kinesthetic and Tactile Senses." By 1962, he already had published on the topic and certainly had some influence on Engelbart's second proposal.[1] For instance, Bliss had carried out experiments at MIT on "information presentation to the kinesthetic sense," involving an eight-key information display for the fingers, excluding thumbs.

Before he could get much further, however, a fundamental question arose concerning what he in fact was proposing. The issue is clear enough from simply looking at the experimental devices. (See Figure 2–1.) They look a lot like rudimentary keyboards, and keyboards already had been developed well beyond the rudimentary stage as input devices. Was Engelbart in fact proposing something new, or was he harking back to a technology that already had been discarded?

The answer to both questions is "Yes." Innovation sometimes depends on revisiting previously discarded alternatives and employing them in new contexts. In 1992, thirty years after Engelbart's first experiments with the chord keyset, I first saw the device on Douglas Engelbart's desktop and took my first lesson in operating it from its inventor. I immediately realized that I was using one of the most efficient tools that I ever had the opportunity to encounter. As I eventually discovered, its value as an input device had been well recognized since the nineteenth century. Engelbart was able to ignore its subsequent eclipse and see how it could serve his purposes for user-machine communications in a way that what had become the standard, ubiquitous input device, the QWERTY keyboard, could not. What he was unable to ignore, however, was the hegemony of the QWERTY keyboard.

"RE-INVENTING THE HIGH-WHEEL BICYCLE WITH GOVERNMENT FUNDS"

The charge that, at this early stage, Engelbart was simply returning to an obsolete and discarded technology was made by one of his sponsors, Harold Wooster, director of the Information Sciences Directorate of the Air Force Office of Scientific Research at the time of Engelbart's second proposal. In a letter to Engelbart dated October 18, 1962, Wooster criticized Engelbart's proposal to use the chord keyset and his lack of understanding of the lessons of history, specifically, the history of input devices used in telegraphy. According to Wooster,

> there is a straightforward historical evolution from five-key devices to single keys to full typewriter keyboards in telegraphy. What you are proposing is essentially

a telegraphic problem—the translation of finger motion into a code—and I suspect that the telegraphic art has thoroughly explored the pros and cons at each stage of its evolution—and that there is very little that is new that can be done with fingers and keys.

It would seem to me that there are only two possible classes of devices (aside from light-pen) for putting alpha-numeric information into a computer in the system you envisage; keyboard devices, which perform the coding automatically, or key devices, in which the operator has to do the coding. Keyboard devices seem to me to have many advantages, not the least of which is the short familiarization period required—and the fact that the skill required to operate a keyboard is a transferable skill.

Key devices, on the other hand require learning a code. I rather suspect that if a code must be learned, Morse code with a single key is as good as any. . . . Most of the advantages you cite for the 5-key set, such as operation with either hand or rhythmic operation with either hand, certainly apply equally well to single Morse key—try talking to some CW hams.

Let me summarize my position on this proposed line of experimentation. The principal advantage of your five-finger system to me has always been its novelty. I now find that it is not new at all, but somewhat over 100 years old; that it is not something being tried for the first time, but rather an old and abandoned state of the telegraphic art. I have no objection to antiquarianism as a hobby—restoring and learning to ride a high-wheel bicycle could be fun—but re-inventing the high-wheel bicycle with government funds is something else again.

If the keyboard can do the coding, why force the user (or "operator," to borrow from the vocabulary of telegraphy) to do it, and to have to learn the code in order to do so? Wooster thus objected to Engelbart's approach in the way many of his sponsors and colleagues would object to it at a later stage: Let the machine do the work! Very early then, and without even a computer in the picture yet, Engelbart was confronted with the controversy that he would find himself submerged in with the proponents of Artificial Intelligence: Whom or what do you want to augment?

But Wooster's critique was even stronger than this, since he added that if the operator were to do the coding, Engelbart's solution could still not be acceptable, relying as it did on "an old and abandoned state of the telegraphic art." Wooster believed in a process of "straightforward historical evolution" in technology that once and for all sent the chord keyset to the cemetery of discarded ideas. The result of this process, of course, meant that a general problem, "input entry," had been solved in a specific context, telegraphy, and the solution developed in this context, the standard keyboard or Morse code, therefore applied in any other specific context where the general problem occurred. Engelbart, in his answer, dated November 7, 1962, was prompt to stress the obvious differences between the context of nineteenth-century telegraphy and the context of his own experiment:

> The typewriter keyboard is not a competitor for the five-key handset in the systems we are interested in, where being able to transmit with one hand (without looking) is a critical feature. Other one-handed transmitting means are acceptable contenders, of course. If we can find good evidence in the literature that, under conditions relevant to those of our systems, Morse is faster and more desirable for system usages we have in mind, then we should give it consideration. However, I rather doubt that a coding system which requires a set of serial operations of one key to encode a character that without [sic—"with our"] keyset is encoded by one stroke of the hand would likely be a serious speed contender. And Morse code has a serious disadvantage in the basic difficulty for its automatic detection and code conversion (for human transmission) into any form that our system can accommodate for storage and outputting to printer or display. It can and has been done, but it would be enough more expensive and complicating to make its system desirability rather poor. . . . In short, I am rather dubious about finding something in the literature that will preclude considerable value to our direct empirical approach of seeing how this five-key system of communication actually does seem to work out for one experimenter in man-machine system—a system that will be much different from those in which the history of telegraphy would show five-bit direct transmission to have been used and evaluated.

The first component of Engelbart's answer was "logical": the chord keyset should in principle be faster, since chording does in parallel, "in one stroke of the hand," what Morse does serially on one key. The second was "pragmatic" and involved "the basic difficulty" that Engelbart had noted earlier when he had first thought of the experiment, as his notebook entry for September 22, 1960, testifies: "Could do similar job with Morse-code teacher, but don't have a Morse decoder-to-typewriter device." To get such a device, of course, would have increased the cost of the project. But Engelbart also used one other line of argument in his reply to explain his denial of Wooster's critique:

> If all the five-wire systems faded out before the development of automatic means for receiving, decoding, and printing out the message were pushed, then historical continuity and the prevalence of the typewriter as a flexible printing device, and its natural and compatible facility for keyboard transmission, *could* have caused the complete overlooking of the possibility for using five keys and a synchronous commutator (borrowing the latter from the teletype transmitter) to effect the transmitting.

This line of argument summarized Engelbart's view of the history of input devices, a view quite different from the linear, "progressive" argument developed by Harold Wooster. A solution discarded at a certain point of time could reappear once the context had changed. But this line of argument was only hypothetical in Engelbart's answer, and would have required a thorough examination of the historical record, an inquiry that, later in his answer, he in fact promised Wooster he would assign a graduate student to undertake. The result of that inquiry, if it ever took place, is now long forgotten. However, it can be repeated. When it is, the innovative use to which Engelbart was proposing to put this "old" technology becomes clear, as does the inertia exerted against such innovations by technology already in place.

If one simply consults the documents available to both Engelbart and Wooster at the time of their disagreement, it becomes apparent how each could believe his own position was warranted. One of the documents that Harold Wooster quoted to Engelbart to defend his position, the "Telegraphy" entry in *The Oxford History of Technology*, does not actually provide any straightforward backing for Wooster's position. The nearest thing to support for the contention that the chord keyset was an obsolete telegraphic device comes from the few paragraphs about William Fothergill Cooke and Charles Wheatstone's first patent for a "five-needle telegraph," a five-unit code device for transmitting the alphabet, rather than Morse code:

> Wheatstone himself particularly favored the use of letter-indicating telegraphs, and the original five-needle instrument of 1837 was of this type.... His ABC telegraphs ... remained popular for many years, particularly where traffic was light and where the telegraph had to be operated by unskilled persons. In regular telegraph offices, however, where trained operators were employed, it was soon found that a predetermined code formed a far quicker way of operating; in time it became almost universal. (Garratt 1958, 658)

This, however, did not provide any explanation or interpretation of why five-wire systems "faded out." In Wooster's letter, he claimed their disappearance was exemplified by the fate of the "Baudot system." In 1874, Jean-Maurice-Émile Baudot patented a system designed to replace the dots and dashes entered by a single key in Morse code with five-unit combinations whose 32 possible permutations not only allowed all the letters of the alphabet to be encoded and transmitted, but also accommodated the encoding and transmission of punctuation and machine-control functions. The operator encoded messages using a keyboard similar to a piano's. In 1894, Baudot also developed a system for the simultaneous ("multiplex") transmission of a number of telegraphic messages over the same circuit. It is by no means clear, however, that the Baudot system could be said to have faded out at all.

Another reference available to Engelbart and Wooster, Percy Dunsheath's *History of Electrical Engineering* (1969 [1962]), deals with the encoding and the comparative values of Morse and five-unit codes only in the context of

Figure 2-2. Cooke and Wheatstone's Five-Needle Telegraph, 1837. Source: Garratt (1958), p. 657.

"automatic working" for the reception of the message. The encoding problem, "the need to translate code messages into straight Roman script," was "recognized by [Edward] Hughes as early as 1854," and embodied in Hughes's system for printing out in alphabet form messages sent in Morse code, a system that "was widely employed over fifty years." The Hughes transmitter also had a keyboard "similar to that of a piano" (ibid., 223, 224).

Multiplex arrangements for telegraph transmission enjoyed an inherent speed advantage over single-key Morse telegraphs, according to Dunsheath: "a manual key operator could transmit at the rate of 30 to 40 words a minute, but the current in an ordinary telegraph line could rise and fall much more rapidly than was necessary for this speed" (ibid., 225). Multiplexing technologies took advantage of this to drastically increase throughput. And five-unit codes and keysets maximized the advantages of multiplexing:

> Before the multiplex system was brought to complete success it was necessary to substitute a more satisfactory code in place of the dots and dashes of the Morse code and this was achieved by the five-unit code. In this code there is no discrim-

ination on duration of the elements of current as between dots and dashes but only in direction, either "spacing" or "marking." All characters occupy the same length of time in transmission and consist of five units so that by arranging these in different ways 32 combinations are obtained. (Ibid.)

Thus, sources available to Wooster and Engelbart seem to contradict Wooster's position that "a straightforward historical evolution from five-key devices to single keys to full typewriter keyboards in telegraphy." Dunsheath supports Engelbart's claim that five-unit code is faster than Morse code. Its relative speed advantage over Morse code, or over the standard typewriter keyboard, however, proved not to be the decisive issue.

It is true that pianolike keyboards and five-key sets practically disappeared in telegraphy in favor of the QWERTY keyboard. On that point, Harold Wooster was correct. The reason for this change, however, was not the progressive development of technology that Wooster took for granted. Instead, it involves the genesis and spread of a new, pervasive work practice, an "incorporating practice," in Katherine Hayles's terms, "an action that is encoded into bodily memory by repeated performances until it becomes habitual," in this case, touch typing (Hayles 1999, 199).

> When we say that someone knows how to type, we do not mean that the person can cognitively map the location of the keys or can understand the mechanism producing the marks. Rather, we mean that this person has repeatedly performed certain actions until the keys seem to be extensions of his or her fingers. . . . This is [Paul] Connerton's point when he writes that the meaning of a bodily practice "cannot be reduced to a sign which exists on a separate 'level' outside the immediate sphere of the body's acts. Habit is a knowledge and a remembering in the hands and in the body; and in the cultivation of habit it is our body which 'understands.'" (Ibid.)[2]

How and why touch typing became the norm, in turn, involves the prior hegemony of another incorporating practice: the use of Morse code in telegraphy.

The rise to ubiquity of the QWERTY keyboard and the eclipse of the five-unit keyset began when telegraphers confronted the same problems that Engelbart confronted when trying to develop a user-computer interface. Donald Murray, inventor of the Murray Automatic Printing Telegraphy system for remotely setting type on Linotype machines from telegraphic input, as well as of improvements on the Baudot multiplex telegraph, summarized the form these problems took at the turn of the century and described the technology available to deal with them in two pathbreaking papers, "Setting Type by Telegraph" (1905) and "Practical Aspects of Printing Telegraphy" (1911), presented to the American Institution of Electrical Engineers.[3] Telegraphers needed "to set type at a distance . . . [and] to bring a particular type to a particular printing point in the shortest possible time . . . over a single telegraph wire" (Murray 1905, 555). Solving these problems required the same things that Engelbart needed for his project: an appropriate interface, that is, an input device between the operator and the transmissions of the telegraph system, and some kind of code to translate this input into a signal. At the other end, the decoding of the signal and the setting of the type would be performed automatically by a telegraph printer.

These needs were met in Engelbart's interface by the chord keyset and "standard teletype five-bit code." The chord keyset and five-bit code likewise very well could have served the ends that Murray specified. Even though they were actually inherent in the multiplex telegraph system and therefore were in widespread use by the beginning of the twentieth century, however, they were abandoned in favor of another input device and code. They were abandoned because engineers were forced to adapt the solution of these problems to the existing work practices of telegraph operators.

In the first of these papers, which Donald Murray read to the Institution of Electrical Engineers on February 23, 1905, he distinguished between the "manual signaling" to which Morse telegraphers were accustomed and "machine telegraphy":

> For manual signaling of all kinds, the arrangement upon which the Morse alphabet is built is not only good, but it is practically the only arrangement possible. There are only two different time intervals, namely 1 unit and 3 units. For manual signaling, intervals of 2 and 4 units are not sufficiently distinct from 1 and 3. With machine telegraphy, on the other hand, time can be divided with great accuracy, and the use of more than two time intervals presents no difficulty. (Ibid., 563)

Of course, both manual and automatic signaling supposed the manual input of text at some point. In the Morse system, however, the text was translated into a signal by the operator through the operation of a single key that input the signal as a series of dots and dashes, while in the printing telegraphs such as those advocated by Murray, the operator input text on keyboard, and the system translated it into a signal using the five-unit code. For this purpose, Murray contended that "unquestionably the best alphabet for machine telegraphy is that used in the Baudot and Murray systems. It is the shortest of all practicable telegraph alphabets, in fact the shortest possible, and it is an equal-letter alphabet, consisting of five units per letter" (ibid., 564).

One could of course consider a third alternative, where the operator input directly the type as a five-unit code. This is exactly what Engelbart proposed over fifty years later. But in 1905, this alternative could not be considered feasible. The reason direct input of the five-unit code would have to be rejected, Murray said, was that "the Morse alphabet . . . has been in possession of the field so long, and telegraph officials in English-speaking countries are so saturated with Morse traditions, that it would be impossible to introduce a new alphabet if the operators had to learn it" (ibid., 563). However, "fortunately with machine telegraphy it is not the case. All the operator has to do is to learn typewriting" (ibid.).

This was because typewriting was in accord with existing practices that made telegraphers efficient—especially in terms of their ability to input text without looking at their input device, which Engelbart also claimed was an important criterion for his system later in the century. But for Murray, the only clear way to do that seemed to be via touch typing on a keyboard, not with a five-key keyset. In his second presentation to the Institution of Electrical Engineers, on May 4, 1911, Murray noted that

> with codes and cipher messages it is absolutely essential that the operator shall keep his eyes fixed on the message all the time that he is sending, if he is to work rapidly and accurately. With the Morse key and sounder it is an easy matter for an operator to keep his eyes on the copy. With a typewriter keyboard, on the other hand, it would appear at first glance to be very difficult to work without looking at the keyboard. Experience has shown, however, that there is no real difficulty, and that in one month, with proper training, an operator can become an expert in "touch writing" on a typewriter keyboard. (Murray 1911, 493)

Actually, the facility with which telegraphers could learn touch typing on a keyboard was long established. In 1869, when E. Payson Porter, "the dean of American telegraph operators," then employed at the Chicago office of the Western Union Telegraph Company, met Christopher Latham Sholes, one of the principal nineteenth-century innovators responsible for the modern typewriter, he "astonished the inventor by the rapidity with which he manipulated the keys at first sight":

> His skill was due to the fact that he had formerly worked a House telegraph printer. Sholes, of course, was delighted. He promised Porter the finest machine he could make, upon condition that he could receive on the typewriter as fast as any telegrapher could send a message. In due time the machine arrived in Chicago, and Porter thus describes the demonstration which followed. "A [Morse] sounder and key were placed upon the table and General Stager was the first to manipulate the same for me to copy, which I did readily. Colonel Lynch then attempted to 'rush' me, and failing to do so, an 'expert' sender was sent for from the operating room. A thorough trial of my ability to 'keep up' resulted so satisfactorily that the typewriter was taken into the operating room." (Herkimer County Historical Society 1923, 45–46)

By 1869 then, or a good five years before there ever was such a thing as a successful commercial typewriter, the partnership between telegraphy and typewriting (or, as telegraph operators called the typewriter, the "mill") was well established.[4]

Training telegraph operators to touch type efficiently would be necessary whether they were to use the five-key chord keyset or another kind of keyboard. Murray also reconsidered the alternative of using the five permutations of keys in the Baudot system to input text directly, the model Engelbart was to embrace. But he, too, noted that this solution "would have the drawback that the operator would have to learn the permutations, the operator and not the machine then doing the translation," although "it would have the advantage that the operator could keep his eyes on the telegram as easily as with the Morse key." Murray even noted that two sets of these permutation keys can be used, "one set for the five fingers of each hand, to be worked alternately" But he concluded that "with properly trained operators the typewriter keyboard is undoubtedly the best" (Murray 1905, 580).

> There is much misconception about the speed of manual operation of keys and keyboards. In reality it is much below what is generally supposed . . . there is no space in this paper to do more than point out that the average speed on a typewriter keyboard is not more than about 120 letters (20 words) per minute. . . . The remedy, as already mentioned, is to train the operators to write without looking at the keyboard. It is possible that in this way the average speed may reach about 180 letters (30 words) per minute, or about double the average speed of a good Morse operator. (Ibid.)

The fading away of the chord keyset, then, has to be understood not in terms of some vision of technological progress, but in terms of the rise to hegemony of a particular kind of work practice—touch typing, and the technologies developed to implement it—via its incorporation, understood in the literal sense of the term, as having become encoded into bodily memory.

QWERTY

Although the fate of the chord keyset and the five-unit code thus ultimately was sealed in the early twentieth century by the emergence of touch "typewriting," what exactly "typewriting" was going to be, had not yet been fully determined. The evolution of typewriting was far from complete when Murray made the connection between telegraphic practice and typewriting in 1905. It was by no means clear yet what a typewriter should be like or how it should be operated. In particular, it was by no means clear that touch typing had to be touch typing as we know it today, on a QWERTY keyboard. Many early typewriters in fact employed chord keysets. It took the emergence of touch typing on a QWERTY keyboard as an incorporating practice to settle

that issue and to finally seem to banish the chord keyset to the museum of obsolete technologies.

QWERTY keyboards, chord keysets, and, indeed, Morse telegraph keys all
share an essential characteristic: the unlinking" of the hand, eye, and letter.
Focusing on the typewriter, Friedrich Kittler, in his impressive *Discourse Networks, 1800/1900*, notes:

> In typewriting, spatiality determines not only the relations among signs but also
> their relation to the empty ground. . . . Whereas handwriting is subject to the
> eye, a sense that works across distance, the typewriter uses a blind, tactile power.
> Before the introduction of John T. Underwood's "view typewriter" in 1898, all
> models (much to the disadvantage of their popularization) wrote invisible lines,
> which became visible only after the fact. . . . Underwood's innovation unlinks
> hand, eye, and letter. . . . Circa 1900 several blindnesses—of the writer, of writ-
> ing, of script—come together to guarantee an elementary blindness: the blind
> spot of the writing act. Instead of the play between Man the sign-setter and the
> writing surface, the philosopher as stylus and the tablet of Nature, there is a play
> between type and its Other, completely removed from subjects. Its name is in-
> scription. (1990 [1985], 195)

More recently, Mark Seltzer has revisited Kittler's thesis to stress that "the
typewriter, like the telegraph, replaces, or pressures, that fantasy of continuous transition [from nature to culture] with recalcitrantly visible and material
systems of difference: with the standardized spacing of keys and letters; with
the dislocation of where the hands work, where the letters strike and appear,
where the eyes look, if they look at all" (1992, 10). Kittler's and Seltzer's interpretations of this unlinking, however, stress discontinuity at the expense of
continuity and collateral influence, and therefore they tend to miss how the
characteristics of the new "agencies of expression" (to borrow one of Seltzer's
phrases) already were to be found elsewhere.[5] Something in the typewriter
keyboard will always allude to the piano, no matter how decades of use might
prevent this analogy from being noticed. Likewise, something in the Morse
telegraph key also points straight to the typewriter keyboard. In fact, one of
the principal innovators in the invention of the typewriter, Christopher
Latham Sholes, used an old telegraph key in an early demonstration model to
illustrate how his typewriting machine would work.

Indeed, the piano keyboard and the Morse key first performed Kittler's
"unlinking" long before the typewriter's soon-to-be-standard QWERTY keyboard. The piano keyboard is the paradigmatic chord keyset, and everyone
who plays with any facility plays by "touch," whether they are reading notes
from a score or improvising, just as much as a touch typist works by touch on
a typewriter keyboard. And as Donald Murray pointed out, the ability of the

Figure 2-3. Francis's Machine, 1857. Source: Herkimer County
Historical Society (1923), p. 27.

telegraph operator to transmit messages by touch, without looking away from
the text being entered, seemed to be the defining characteristic of the telegraph's operator-machine interface.

The Morse telegraph's single key makes it a special case, but there is no fundamental difference in principle, with respect to touch typing, between chord
keysets and what has become the standard QWERTY keyboard. And in actual
fact, over the long history of efforts to develop a typewriting machine up to
1873, when the Remington Model 1 stabilized the form of data entry with the
standard QWERTY keyboard, attempts to develop both typewriters and automatic and/or printing telegraphic systems favored neither model (Herkimer
County Historical Society 1923, 22). Instead, they focused on both, with
pianolike chording and keyboard or letter-indicating systems almost equally
popular.

Many of the early devices in both technologies used piano keyboards that
provided the opportunity to chord data entry. In 1774, for example, Georges
Louis Lesage, a Frenchman living in Geneva, made the "first serious attempt at
producing a static electricity telegraph. He employed 24 wires communicating
with 24 simple electrometers with pith balls each identified as one of the letters
of the alphabet. At each end the wires were arranged horizontally as the keys
on a harpsichord" (Dunsheath 1969 [1962], 69). In 1857, Dr. Samuel W. Francis of New York was granted a patent for a machine "the keys of which re-

Figure 2-4. The Sholes, Glidden, and Soulé Machine, Patent of June 23, 1868. Source: Herkimer County Historical Society (1923), p. 47.

sembled those of a piano, and the types, which were arranged in a circle, printed at a common center. It was said of the Francis machine that it printed with a speed *exceeding* that of the pen, a degree of praise not accorded to any of its predecessors" (Herkimer County Historical Society 1923, 26, emphasis in the original). The typewriting machine that Christopher Latham Sholes, Carlos Glidden, and Samuel W. Soulé patented on June 23, 1868, also had a keyboard resembling a piano's, as did Edward Hughes's type-printing telegraph of 1854.

Although it was the keyboard-entry machines that prevailed, the image of the piano chord keyset as an entry device nevertheless exerted a strong hold. In the typewriter design patented by John Pratt of Centre, Alabama, on August 11, 1868, Pratt's keys look more like telegraph keys than piano keys. When his "Pterotype" was described in an article in the *Scientific American* of July 6, 1867, however, the article announced that "the weary process of learning penmanship in the schools will be reduced to the acquirement of writing one's own signature and *playing the literary piano*" (ibid., 109, emphasis in the original). Sholes, Glidden, and Soulé worked with both piano and keyboard models in the 25 to 30 experimental versions of the "Type-Writer" they built between 1868 and 1873, and it was far from clear which input device would prevail in the end, although their 1873 machine strongly resembles the now-familiar form of the Remington shift-key typewriter of 1878.

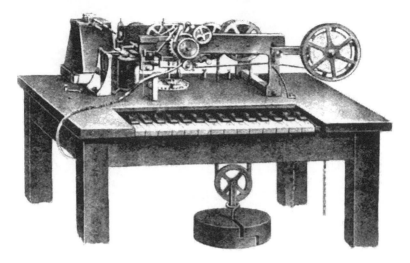

Figure 2-5. Hughes's Type-Printing Telegraph. Source: Crotch (1908), 2.

There also was no "natural" connection between touch typing and the development of the QWERTY typewriter keyboard over its long history, both in its own right and in association with telegraphy. Until 1900 at least, most typists still looked at the keyboard, at the site where their hands were working, and I am tempted to say they still do so even now.

The reason why the QWERTY keyboard became standard was simply that "touch typing" and "all-finger typing" required a standard keyboard. QWERTY became that standard—not out of any inherent superiority in it as a technological innovation, but as a result of the stochastic nature of technological evolution. It was the keyboard employed by C. L. Sholes, and when Sholes and his backers went to Remington to secure mass production of their Type-Writer, which appeared in 1874, it was the keyboard that was used. Because it was in use, it was used by serious competitors of Remington in subsequent years, whose innovations lay in the machine itself, not the machine-user interface. It became the standard because it became the standard. Something had to.

Contrary to myth, Sholes had not invented the QWERTY keyboard in a diabolical attempt to slow down typists to prevent overloading his primitive machine. The machine was designed with the letters on the ends of typebars that were arranged in a circle and that swung up to print a letter on the back of the paper. Typebars too close to each other would tend to clash and lock up the machine if activated sequentially, which certainly would slow the typist, but which was a mechanical design problem, not a problem of the machine-user

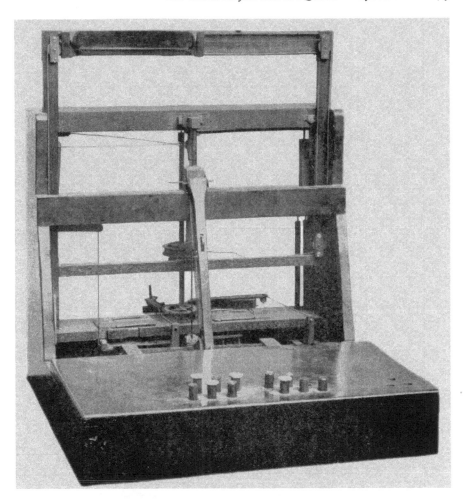

Figure 2-6. John Pratt's Typewriter, Patent of August 11, 1868. Source: Herkimer County Historical Society (1923), p. 28.

interface. Sholes solved it by arranging the letters so that letters he believed frequently to occur in sequence would have typebars far apart.

Touch typing and the QWERTY keyboard thus evolved together, symbiotically, as an instance of the sort of coevolution the cyberneticists later would identify. It was a slow process. Mrs. M. V. Longley first proposed a system of touch typing at the First Annual Congress of Shorthand Writers held in Cincinnati in 1882, yet a comprehensive survey of schools all over America conducted by the Remingtons in 1901 found that only half of the schools "had already begun instruction by the touch method" (ibid., 112–13). And as Donald

Figure 2-7 (above). The Sholes and Glidden Machine of 1873. Source: Herkimer County Historical Society (1923), p. 55.

Figure 2-8 (below). The Remington Shift-Key Typewriter, 1878. Source: Herkimer County Historical Society (1923), p. 83.

Murray worried, the diffusion of touch typing was still very much considered a problem in 1905 and 1911. But they did become standards in the end.

To do so took a series of developments, including further technological innovations in typewriter design, the promotion of efficient touch-typing methods, and the institutionalization and regularization of touch typing in schools preparing people for the workplace. Typebars that swung up from in front, allowing the typist actually to see what was being typed, shift keys to permit the typing of both capital and lowercase letters, and lighter, faster keyboards simultaneously were required by and aided the dissemination of touch typing.

But "touch typing" was itself not a single, settled practice. Sholes originally had assumed that the pinkie and ring fingers of each hand are too weak to work a keyboard, and for years afterward, four-finger and even two-finger touch-typing schemes that allowed typists to use whatever finger-key combinations they wished dominated the scene. When Mrs. Longley's *Remington TypeWriter Lessons* was published in 1882, it was the first printed system for teaching the all-finger method (ibid., 111).

A network of Remington agents and business college educators provided the professional medium for the diffusion of touch typing, among them H. V. Rowell, the manager of the Remington's Boston office, and W. E. Hickox, who took up this method at Rowell's suggestion and began teaching it at his private shorthand school in Portland, Maine (ibid., 112). From there, touch typing spread in the eastern part of the United States and eventually to the Midwest in the 1880's. Thus, the interests of the typewriter manufacturers and those of business educators came to coincide in disseminating the practice of touch typing as we now know it, to the extent that the Herkimer history of the typewriter claims that "the whole modern system of commercial education is a creation of the writing machine" (ibid., 79). Remington and the other manufacturers were indeed crucially in need of such an education system, for they had to supply the operator along with the machine. In 1923, the Herkimer history could conclude,

> This necessity of supplying the operator led to the growth of another distinctive feature of the typewriter business, namely the free employment departments for stenographers and typists, maintained for the service of typewriter users. The yearly total of stenographers placed in position by these departments has grown to enormous figures. More than one typewriter company today places upwards of one hundred thousand typists per year in positions in the United States alone. (Ibid., 78)

The way in which touch typing on the QWERTY keyboard achieved hegemony has been well noticed by historians and economists who have tried to explain the persistence of the QWERTY standard in spite of its alleged inefficiency. Paul A. David, in a landmark paper on the topic, has argued that "touch typing gave rise to three features of the evolving production system which were crucially important in causing QWERTY to become 'locked in' as the dominant keyboard arrangement. These features were *technical interrelatedness, economies of scale,* and *quasi-irreversibility* in investment. They constitute the basic ingredients of what might be called QWERTY-nomics" (1985, 334). In all three of these features, David stresses "software over hardware," or "the touch typist's memory of a particular arrangement of the keys" over this particular arrangement of the keys, and concludes "this, then, was a situation in which the precise details of timing in the developmental sequence had made it profitable in the short run to adapt machines to the habit of men (or to women, as was increasingly the case) rather than the other way around. And things have been this way ever since" (ibid., 336).[6]

Thus, it was by institutionalization as an incorporating practice that the QWERTY standard became established. The establishment of a commercial education network favoring the QWERTY was the decisive factor, the source of the "historical accident" that governed the stochastic process that secured forever the supremacy of the QWERTY. It is indeed because of such an "accident" that the six or seven years during which Remington enjoyed the early advantage of being the sole owner of the typewriter patent also saw its selling agents establish profitable and durable business associations with the commercial education business. These early business ties soon gave place to an organized and institutional network of associations that secured Remington's position in the typewriter business.

The Herkimer history credits William O. Wyckoff, Clarence W. Seamans, and Henry H. Benedict with envisioning this symbiotic relationship and the persistence to carry it forward. Remington had made them marketing agents for the typewriter for the entire world (Herkimer County Historical Society 1923, 85), and in March 1886, they acquired the ownership of the patent of the typewriter. When their firm started to bring the Remington typewriter to European markets, what had begun as an informal but fortuitous harmony of interests became an explicit business plan. To provide operators for their machines, they founded Remington-owned schools to teach QWERTY touch typing.

> One development of the typewriter business in nearly all foreign countries is totally different from anything known in America [where] the typewriter companies and commercial schools, though each is a necessity to the other, have grown up as distinct and separate institutions. This may be accounted for by the fact that the germ of our modern commercial school system existed in a few so-called "business colleges" before the day of the typewriter. . . . If the task of getting operators during the early days of the business was a difficult one in America, in

the other countries it was formidable. It soon became evident that the problem could be solved only in one way, by the founding of schools of shorthand and typewriting, owned and operated by the typewriter company itself. This was the origin of the Remington system of commercial schools, which were established by the company or its selling representative in practically every country on earth, with the one conspicuous exception of the United States. (Ibid., 96)

In the United States, in addition to private business colleges and instructional schools, the YWCA began teaching touch typing on QWERTY keyboards as a way of fitting women for work in the modern world, and public schools soon followed suit. Thus, the development of an educational and industrial network of entrepreneurs, beginning in the earliest days of the diffusion of the typewriter, permitted the symbiotic coevolution of touch typing and the QWERTY keyboard. By World War I, both were well established.

When, in 1962, Engelbart proposed to go back to a five-key handset to "communicate" with a computer, he was in fact correct that the history of telegraphy had established the five-unit alphabet, Engelbart's "standard teletype five-bit code," as the simplest and most efficient alphabet for machine transmission over a wire. This was the consensus among telegraph operators and electrical engineers. The supremacy of the five-bit code actually lasted until 1966, when the American Standard Code for Information Interchange (ASCII) was established. ASCII consists of seven bits, which allowed 128 different coded letters or symbols, as compared to 32 for the Baudot code. Code speeds of 150 words per minute were possible with teleprinter systems using ASCII, as compared to 75 words per minute for those using the Baudot code.[7] However, Engelbart was wrong in assuming that in 1962, with the QWERTY keyboard long established as the norm for machine-user interfaces, the mere efficiency of the five-bit code implied that the human users (or operators) could—or would—willingly learn it and perform the translation with the help of a chording input device, abandoning the QWERTY keyboard. Here again, Harold Wooster was correct: that learning process presented an impossible task.

In fact, however, the history of the two devices never really established that chording keysets were outperformed by keyboards. That was not the basis on which one technology prevailed and the other was discarded. Instead, an early process of selection in one context, that of typewriting and teleprinting, together with the diffusion of the incorporating practice of touch typing, determined the outcome. In the different context of electronic computing fifty to one hundred years later, the performance advantages of the five-bit devices that Engelbart employed still existed. Although the QWERTY keyboard layout has been severely criticized since the 1930's at least, with the invention of the Dvorak keyboard and its supposed efficiencies, no other type input device ever has managed to challenge its supremacy.[8] As Jan Noyes (1983a, 278–79) puts it in "The QWERTY Keyboard: A Review":

> Rearranging the letters of the QWERTY layout has been shown to be a fruitless pastime, but it has demonstrated two important points: first, the amount of hostile feeling that the standard keyboard has generated and second, the supremacy of this keyboard in retaining its universal position. . . . The design and the layout of the QWERTY keyboard are not optimal for efficient operation. However it is not feasible to modify the standard keyboard and hence improve, because of confounding factors pertinent to QWERTY's situation. In 1981, the amount of commercial, financial and skill investment in the QWERTY keyboard is of greater importance than the fact that it is not the most efficiently designed layout.

This is in effect confirmation of J. C. R. Licklider's later recollections "on early history":

> There's a long-standing debate about the qualities of keyboards. I think that one of the great inventions was Doug Engelbart's invention of the one-handed keyboard. But there's an awful lot of human factors and ergonomics wrapped up in that. In fact very few people—maybe Doug is the only one—very few people use one-handed keyboards. It has to be based on a stenotype-like keyboard scheme with multiple finger pressings. It takes a good bit of learning. It's very valuable after you've learned it, but I sort of conclude that people who are buying computers, especially personal computers, just aren't going to take a long time to learn something. They're going to insist on using it awfully quick—easy to use, easy and quick to learn. (Licklider 1988, 119)

Engelbart was unconvinced by Wooster's criticisms, and Harold Wooster, in turn, did not fund Engelbart's early proposals at SRI, although he did fund subsequent proposals for the project to augment the human intellect. As Engelbart carried on with his project, however, convinced that he was right, he not only built chord keysets, but made them integral to his oN-Line System (NLS), the computer system that emerged from the innovations of the augmentation project. Engelbart did not want to accommodate his technology to the way people work—he wanted to use that technology to change the way people work, and to him, the chord keyset offered the best way to do that.

As a replacement for the QWERTY keyboard, Engelbart's chord keyset nevertheless faced overwhelming odds against acceptance, even though it promised not only greater efficiency, but a direct, psychomotor, tactile, two-way interface between user and machine that seemed to have the potential for transforming what the user could do and be. Another prosthesis for the augmentation of the human intellect from Engelbart's SRI lab, however, eventually enjoyed considerably more success, this time as a supplement to the QWERTY keyboard: the mouse.

CHAPTER THREE

The Invention of the Mouse

The problem of the dialogue between the individual and society, which has come up in connection with the question of intelligence and instinct . . . is nothing other than this capacity human beings have of distancing themselves from their environment, both external and internal. This detachment, which expresses itself in the separation between tool and hand and between word and object, is also reflected in the distance society creates between itself and the zoological group. . . . The most striking material fact is certainly the "freeing" of tools, but the fundamental fact is really the freeing of the word and our unique ability to transfer our memory to a social organism outside ourselves.

— ANDRÉ LEROI-GOURHAN, *Gesture and Speech*

In his earliest actual description of his Framework for the Augmentation of Human Intellect, Douglas Engelbart had the reader imagine the operation of the system by a character named "Joe":

Joe has two display screens side by side, but one of them he doesn't seem to use as much as the other. And the screens are almost horizontal, more like the surface of a drafting table than the near-vertical picture displays that you had somehow imagined. But you see the reason easily, for he is working *on* the display surface. . . . Some of the time Joe is using both hands on the keys, obviously feeding information into the computer at a great rate . . . you see that each hand operates on a set of keys on its own side of the display frames, so that the hands are almost two feet apart. But it is plain that this arrangement allows him to remain positioned over the frames in a rather natural position, so that when he picks the light pen out of the air (which is its rest position, thanks to a system of jointed supporting arms and a controlled tension and rewind system for the attached cord) his hand is still on the way from the keyset to the display frame. When he is through with the pen at the display frame, he lets go of it, the cord rewinds, and

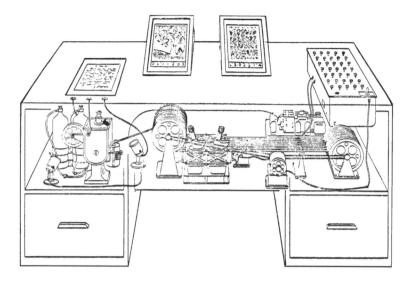

Figure 3-1. Memex, Front View. Source: Bush (1991 [1945]).

the pen is again in position. There is thus a minimum of effort, movement, and time involved in turning to work *on* the frame. That is, he could easily shift back and forth from using keyset to using light pen, with either hand (one pen is positioned for each hand), without moving his head, turning, or leaning. A good deal of Joe's time, though, seems to be spent with one hand on a keyset and the other using a light pen on the display surface. (1962, 74–75, emphasis in the original)

This conceptualization, in addition to employing two chord keysets, also used two other input devices: the light gun and the tablet. The idea of working directly on twin display surfaces or tablets came from the conjunction of one previous representation of the computer, Vannevar Bush's Memex, with the ancestor of pointing devices, already well diffused in radar technology, the light gun. Engelbart was familiar with both of these devices. And although Bush conceived the Memex as a machine for expediting the individual association of ideas and Engelbart conceived of his project as furthering their intersubjective connection, physically, the machines they at first envisioned had a lot in common. In the original 1945 paper, "As We May Think," Bush wrote:

Consider a future device for individual use, which is sort of a mechanized private file and library. . . . It consists of a desk, and while it can presumably be operated from a distance, it is primarily the piece of furniture at which he works. On the top are slanting translucent screens, on which material can be projected for convenient reading. There is a keyboard, and sets of buttons and levers. . . . On the top of the memex is a transparent platen. On this are placed longhand notes,

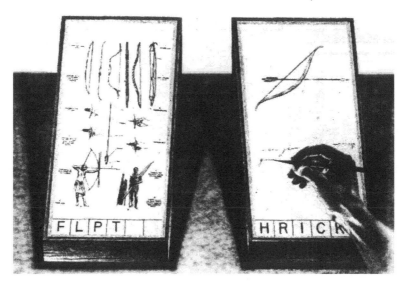

Figure 3-2. Memex's Twin Screens. Source: Bush (1991 [1945]).

photographs, memoranda, all sorts of things. When one is in place, the depression of a lever causes it to be photographed onto the next blank space of the memex film, dry photograph being employed. (Bush 1991 [1945], 102)

From this original shared conception, Engelbart characteristically evolved his vision of the personal computer and its user interface in a completely different direction. Not only did he invent what we today know as the mouse, more significantly for the history of the personal computer, he also began the process of inventing the person who would use the personal computer.

FROM "SKETCHPAD FEATURES" TO INPUT DEVICES

At the same time that Engelbart was putting together his ideas for an Augmentation Research Center in his 1962 report and starting to explore systematically the multiple dimensions of the augmentation process, J. C. R. Licklider was summarizing the agenda for further research into the human-computer symbiosis that he had envisioned. In a paper called "On-Line Man-Computer Communication," Licklider and Welden Clark defined "five immediate problems" or "essential steps" to be carried out. The second dealt with input-output devices: "Devise an electronic input-output surface on which both the operator and the computer can display, and through which they can communicate, correlated symbolic and pictorial information. The surface should have selective persistence plus selective erasability; the computer should not have to spend a large part of its time maintaining the displays. The entire device should be inexpensive enough for incorporation into a remote console" (1962, 121).

In a subsequent contribution, a report to the Council on Library Resources written during the final months of 1963, Licklider provided the grounding vision for research into input-output devices in the years to come.[1] There, Licklider laid out a wish list for a visual user-machine interface, estimating each item's degree of importance by a number on a scale from 0 to 10:

> We should like to have: a color display (4) if possible, or, if not, a black-on-white display (7) with at least eight gradations of brightness (5) and a resolution exceeding 400 (4), or 200 (6) or, at any rate, 100 (9) lines per inch. Each element of the display should be selectively erasable by the computer program, and also either directly or indirectly by the operator (9). The display should have controllable persistence (6) and should be free of flicker (9). There should be a way to capture any frame of the display in the form of "hard copy" (9), and the hard copy should be coded automatically for machine filing, retrieval, and redisplay (7).
>
> The display should provide the set of features called "Sketchpad" features (10), which assign to the computer those parts of sketching and drawing skill that involve much practice and precision, and leave the man responsible mainly for expressing the essential structure of the concept he desires to represent. (Licklider 1965, 94)

This first set of desiderata concerned the display system, realized up to that point by the oscilloscope screen. But Licklider's wish list exceeded then-current specifications of the oscilloscope screen, in terms of both form and function. Concerning the form of the display, he gave the most important rating (9) to a resolution of at least 100 lines per inch (in modern terms, 100 dots per inch). However, he attributed the most important rating (10) to the functional features of the system that he called "Sketchpad" features.

These were part of Ivan Sutherland's system design at the MIT Lincoln Lab on the TX-2 computer for his doctoral thesis (Sutherland 1963).[2] Sketchpad was the most important ancestor of today's Computer Aided Design (CAD) applications. The Sketchpad Input/Output system included an x-y point plotter display that allowed the user to produce graphic images on a screen. It was equipped with both a light pen and a control board with a series of buttons, toggle switches, and analog knobs. The user could interactively produce images with "a combination of switch settings, knob positions, button-pushes and pen flicks" (Norberg and O'Neill 1996, 126).[3]

Most researchers of that period consider Sutherland's project as the most valuable Ph.D. dissertation ever written in computer science. Sutherland's Sketchpad system certainly revolutionized research on human-computer interaction. Engelbart was aware of Sutherland's work before it was formally introduced to the computer science community in 1963. In a section entitled

"Other Related Thoughts and Work" in his 1962 report, Engelbart wrote: "we understand that another graduate student there [at MIT], Ivan Sutherland, is currently using the display-computer facility on the TX-2 computer at Lincoln Lab to develop cooperative techniques for engineering design problems."

Producing and manipulating graphical images on a screen, the essence of what Sketchpad did, was crucial to Engelbart's project for the fourth and final stage in the evolution of human intellect, "automated external symbol manipulation." These Sketchpad features, in Engelbart's vision, were to be made available "by means of special cooperative technological devices . . . a computer, with which we could communicate rapidly and easily, coupled to a three-dimensional color display within which it could construct extremely sophisticated images with the computer being able to execute a wide variety of processes upon parts or all of these images" (Engelbart 1963, 25).

The chord keyset would make "feeding information into the computer at a great rate" possible for users like "Joe," but for the Framework for the Augmentation of Human Intellect, Engelbart also needed a device for manipulating symbols on a display screen. There were a number of existing ways to think about how to develop input-output hardware to achieve this.

> For presenting computer-stored information to the human, techniques have been developed by which a cathode-ray-tube . . . can be made to present symbols on their screens of quite good brightness, clarity, and with considerable freedom as to the form of the symbol. . . . On displays of this sort, a light pen (a pen shaped tool with a flexible wire to the electronic console) can be pointed by the human at any symbol or line on the display, and the computer can automatically determine what the pen is pointing at. . . .
>
> Much cheaper displays can "draw" arbitrary symbol shapes and diagrams on paper. . . . Also special typewriters . . . can type out information on a sheet of paper, as well as allow the human to send information to the computer via the keyboard. But these two types of devices do not allow fast and flexible re-arrangement of the symbols being displayed, which prove to be an important drawback in our current view of future possibilities for augmentation.
>
> For communicating to the computer, considerable freedom exists in arranging push buttons, switches, and keysets for use by the human. The "interpretation" or response to be made by the computer to the actuation of any button, switch, or key (or to any combination thereof) can be established in any manner that is describable as a structure of primitive computer processes—which means any manner that is explicitly describable. The limitation on the flexibility and power of any explicit "shorthand" system with which the human may wish to utilize these input devices is the human's ability to learn and use them. (Engelbart 1962, 68–69)

Characteristically, in approaching this problem, Engelbart was still thinking in terms of its human side, in terms of inscribing and incorporating practices, rather than merely in terms of hardware. There were, however, two existing hardware devices available to Engelbart at the time of the actual implementation of the symbol manipulation necessary for his augmentation system: the light pen and the tablet. Each device had both advantageous features and drawbacks. As these devices evolved, they framed the possible ways to think about solving this problem.

"This thing we built, called the mouse—it just happened," Engelbart explained later when asked, "How did you get from the Framework to the specific products that came out so early in the project?" The chord keyset and the mouse "were just two fairly simple things to start with." The mouse "wasn't a very high priority," in fact. NASA was funding Engelbart's research at the time, "and they wanted something that wasn't just melded into the rest of it," something distinct from his IPTO-funded projects. "So I said, 'Well, let's go after some screen-select devices, that's a good project.' . . . With the mouse, we were trying to create something different" from both the light pen and the tablet (Engelbart 1996). But what they created drew on functions that had been developed in both of these technologies.

INPUT DEVICES: THE LIGHT PEN

The light pen was developed first, principally on the East Coast, within the formative Artificial Intelligence community. The light pen emerged as a descendant of the light gun, which was first developed in 1948–49 by the Whirlwind laboratory's technical director, Robert Everett, and developed further and used in the context of the Cape Cod system, the precursor of the SAGE (SemiAutomatic Ground Environment) radar system from 1954 on (see Ross 1988).[4] It was used in the SAGE system to select a specific blip on the radar screen for tracking.

"SAGE involved the first extensive use of CRTs [cathode ray tubes]. . . . Early CRT consoles had a display generator: an interface that connected a terminal to a computer and converted the information passed between them. The viewing screens were typically round and ranged from sixteen to twenty-four inches in diameter" (ibid., 64–65). The light gun was a crucial part of this interface. It was the first display-selection device that allowed a direct, real-time connection between the computer and a cathode ray tube display. Douglas Ross, a member of the Whirlwind team beginning in 1954, described the light gun as follows:

> It was shaped like a backward pistol, with a sight close to your trigger finger knuckle and a wire out of a barrel that extended back over your hand. The barrel contained a photo-multiplier tube, and the wire connected to an "si" [select input]

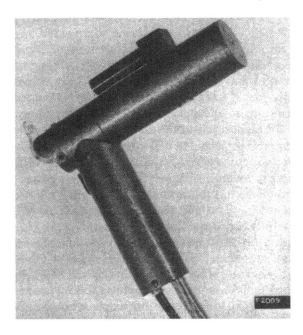

Figure 3-3. The Whirlwind Light Gun. Source: Goldberg (1988), p. 65.

line of the computer. If a displayed spot was in the sight when the trigger was pulled, that would set an *activate bit* (one-time, read-only) so that a suitable "si, rd [read]" sequence, following the "si, rc [record]" that displayed the spot (but before any other spot was displayed) said that the operator had selected that spot from all the others in the display. (Ibid., 64–65)

At the MIT Lincoln Laboratory in 1957, Ben Gurley and C. E. Woodward developed an early version of a light pen, a smaller version of the light gun (Gurley and Woodward 1959), and by 1959, there were at least thirteen different companies manufacturing consoles featuring such a device (Licklider and Clark 1962, 113). By 1964, the light pen was commonly used in early computer graphics and time-sharing systems, such as the Kludge system, a display system developed at MIT Electronic Systems Laboratory as part of the CAD project headed by Ross. It was also used later on Ivan Sutherland's Sketchpad on the TX-2 computer.

As it appeared in Sutherland's 1963 design, the Sketchpad's stylus was the most recent descendant of the original Gurley and Woodward design at MIT. Robert Stotz, a member of the Electronic Systems Laboratory, described it as "a hand-held cylinder with a photocell mounted inside at one end and a wire leading back to the computer at the other" (1963, 323). The stylus therefore could operate on the classical radar principle employed by the light gun and "recognize" any spot displayed on the screen. But it could also fulfill the drawing functions necessary to human-computer graphic communication:

> In Sketchpad the light pen is time shared between the functions of coordinate input for positioning picture parts on the drawing and demonstrative input for pointing to existing picture parts to make changes. Although almost any kind of coordinate input device could be used instead of the light pen for positioning, the demonstrative input uses the light pen optics as a sort of analog computer to remove from consideration all but a very few picture parts which happen to fall within its field of view, saving considerable program time. (Sutherland 1963, 333)

This analog part of the system was augmented by a variable-focus lens mounted in front of the photocell, giving the pen a variable field of view ranging from two-thirds of an inch down to one-sixteenth of an inch in diameter. The tracking ability of the computer with respect to the motion of the pen on the screen was the mathematical computation of the center of gravity of several divergent points at the edge of the field of view, known as "the four arms cross" principle (Stotz 1963, 324; Ninke 1965, 844). This mathematical computation was at the core of the "inking and marking" operation of the pen, and was carried out in an iterative manner, each iteration requiring from 1 to 3 milliseconds:

> To initially establish pen tracking, the Sketchpad user must inform the computer of an initial pen location. This has come to be known as "inking-up" and is done by touching any existing line or spot on the display, whereupon the tracking cross appears. If no picture has yet been drawn, the letters INK are always displayed for this purpose. Sketchpad uses loss of tracking as a "termination signal" to stop drawing. The user signals that he is finished drawing by flicking the pen too fast for the tracking program to follow. (Sutherland 1963, 334)

The Sketchpad stylus fulfilled the basic characteristics Licklider had specified for a light pen: it "resemble[d] an ordinary pen or pencil in size, shape, weight, and feel" (Licklider 1965, 94).

The stylus of the Sketchpad system thus linked the hand and eye of the user with the display on the screen. We could say that the pen functioned as both an eye on a wand and a pen on the screen. As such, it reversed the trend in the history of input-output technology, from the telegraph to the typewriter, that led to an unlinking of what the hand does from what the eye sees. But it could be a pen on the screen only when the eye on the wand had seen something on the display, "any existing line or spot." In other words, the light pen was first of all simply a light-sensing device. This sensing ability was cleverly used in Sketchpad with the introduction of "light buttons" to display control functions directly on the screen, instead of putting them on function keys on the keyboard.[5]

Since the original design of the light gun, the sensing mechanism had consisted of a photocell circuit designed to respond to the initial (blue) flash of the spot lit up on the fast phosphor layer of the scope face. It was insensitive to the yellow persistence of the flash, the output actually observed by the human eye. With such a design, the bandwidth[6] of the system was limited, since

> the light pen output for a given pulse is determined by the combined time responses of the light-producing mechanism in the phosphor, the light-detecting mechanism in the light pen, and the pen amplifier. Each of these responses is characterized by a delay in buildup and a delay in decay, with the result that the pen output corresponding to a single narrow square pulse of beam current is a delayed and much broadened pulse with a long tail. (Haring 1965, 847–48)[7]

At the Joint Computer Conference of the American Federation of Information Processing Societies in the fall of 1965, Douglas R. Haring presented a solution to this design problem in the form of a "beam pen" from the MIT Electronic Systems Laboratory's contribution to Project MAC. This device was designed to detect the electron beam that caused the initial blue flash on the screen, rather than either the flash itself or its persistence in the phosphors. From a light-sensing device, the pen became an electron-sensing device. The obvious gains of speed allowed by the system (Haring reported a period of 3.5 microseconds), however, were countered by a lesser resolution of the beam pen compared with the classic photosensitive pen.

There was thus a continuous and cumulative stream of innovative work on what Licklider called the original "oscilloscope-and-light-pen schema" being done at MIT since the original radar work of the late 1940's. But by 1964, one aspect of the design of the input device was still open. The light pen might be used to communicate with the computer via a screen, but existing oscilloscope screens obviously were inadequate for the task. On the West Coast, focusing on the screen as the central aspect of the visual input-output device led to an entirely different schema for user-machine input and output: the tablet.

INPUT DEVICES: THE TABLET

Licklider had summarized the kind of screen he thought was needed for an interface thus:

> The oscilloscope-and-light-pen schema of the next decade should have a hard, tough surface upon which both the user and the computer can print, write, and draw, and through which the user's markings will be communicated to the com-

puter. Even when this surface is flush with the top of a desk, no "electron gun" sticks down through the desk and bumps the user's knees. The mark appears on the surface, of course, and not on a lower subsurface: there is no explosion screen and no parallax.

Ideally, the user and the computer should make their marks in precisely the same coordinate frame, so that it will not be necessary to compensate for poor registration. It is easy and natural to designate part of an observed pattern by pointing to it or touching it directly with fingertip or stylus. Since the computer must act upon designations made by the pointing or touching of patterns displayed on the screen, it seems to us important to have the frame of reference for sensing correspond precisely to the frame of reference for displaying. It may be easier to develop equipment in which the user and the computer make their marks on different screens, but whether that is a satisfactory arrangement should be evaluated carefully. (Licklider 1965, 94–95)

Efforts to develop "equipment in which the user and the computer make their marks on different screens," that is, equipment in which, as on a typewriter keyboard, what the hand does and what the eye sees were again unlinked, in fact had started in the mid-1950's, with the design and operation of JOHNNIAC, a Princeton-class computer built at RAND between 1950 and 1953 and named after John von Neumann, and the work of Allen Newell, Herbert Simon, and Cliff Shaw at RAND on JOSS, the JOHNNIAC Open Shop System, between 1960 and 1964. JOSS's main application was a "helpful assistant" in the Artificial Intelligence tradition designed for mathematicians, an "open-shop" experiment in on-line communication.[8] "Open shop" in this context meant that JOSS was directly available to its users, who for the first time in computing history were not programmers or computer scientists: they were mathematicians at RAND. JOSS "was designed to give the individual scientist or engineer an easy, direct way of solving his small numerical problems without a large investment in learning an operating system, a compiler, and debugging tools, or in explaining his problems to a professional computer programmer and in checking the latter's results" (Shaw 1964, 455).

Human-machine communication was the common thread at RAND for both JOSS and Keith Uncapher's GRAphical Input Language (GRAIL) project.[9] Both systems were totally user-oriented. GRAIL's 1964 project report, for instance, stated that "it will not force upon the user language devices which are inefficient for his purpose. The system's efficiency will be subordinate to the user's need" (cited in Norberg and O'Neill 1996, 124).[10]

In 1961–62, Thomas O. Ellis and M. R. Davis had designed and directed the construction of a multiple-typewriter communication system for JOHNNIAC that was necessary to JOSS's operation. It consisted of ten remote consoles equipped with IBM model 868 electric typewriters augmented with switch and indicator boxes and available for either off-line or on-line time-shared work. The only input device was the typewriter keyboard, a slightly modified QWERTY keyboard with switches for power, on/off, ready, and in/out and with several indicator lights marked "power," "enable," "ready," and so on. The only output was a hard-copy "report-quality" typewriter printout (Shaw 1964). This typewriter output became the metaphor that governed the development of another device designed and built by Davis and Ellis during the GRAIL project in 1963–64, the RAND tablet.

The RAND tablet was completed in 1964 by a group managed by Ellis and directed by Uncapher, with funding from ARPA. The GRAIL design team included Bill Sibley (software), together with Tom Ellis and Ray Clewett (hardware). According to Uncapher, "Ellis, a very good engineer, did most of the design of the tablet. Clewett designed the stylus with the help of Tom Ellis. It was a nightmare to do it right ... it was the best stylus around, by an order of magnitude" (1993). It was also essentially different from the light-pen stylus developed on the East Coast. The tablet's design, its developers claimed, was closer to what Vannevar Bush had in mind for his Memex machine. But they also saw it as an improvement on the original Sketchpad concept.

In the first report on the device, "The RAND Tablet: A Man-Machine Graphical Communication Device," Davis and Ellis explained that "early in the development of man-machine studies at RAND, it was felt that the exploration of man's existent dexterity with a free, pen-like instrument on a horizontal surface, like a pad of paper, would be fruitful. The concept of generated hand-directed, two-dimensional information on a surface not coincident with the display device (versus a 'light pen') is not new and has been examined by others in the field" (Davis and Ellis 1964, 325).[11]

The allusion to "others in the field" who had confirmed their interest in a tablet device was a reference to Bush. But both the reference to "a paper pad" and the allusion in their own title to Sutherland's Sketchpad, which he identified as a "man-machine graphical communication system," suggest that Davis and Ellis also meant they believed that Sutherland's system should be based on a tablet, rather than a light pen.

Keith Uncapher confirmed that Sutherland's influence was obvious on the GRAIL group:

> Ivan Sutherland's thesis was a revelation of the kind of things that could be done with graphics. We naturally thought about the output and the input. ... We thought about the concept of writing while looking at a screen, and how to communicate with hand-printed characters. We first looked at a screen superimposed, a metal screen on the face of the CRT, and operate that way. The problem is the resolution is lousy and the person's hands were in the way. We said well, lots of people had tried the writing surface displaced from the viewing surface, including

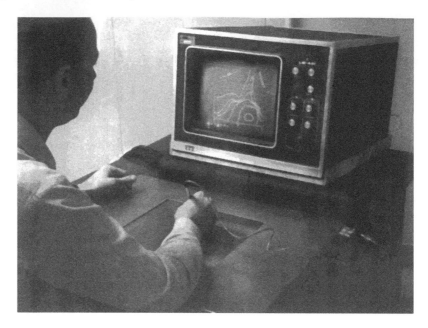

Figure 3-4. The RAND Tablet. Source: Davis and Ellis (1964), p. 2.

> Licklider, who did some of the pioneering work at MIT . . . what we decided is to
> have a stylus as much like a ball-point pen as possible, and the feedback loop, the
> only one, would be on the CRT itself. (1993)

The RAND group thus shifted the focus of the device away from a stylus linking hand and eye, the eye on a wand in light-pen devices, and back toward a
"writing surface displaced from the viewing surface," as in their typewriter
metaphor. The feedback loop on the screen resulted from the multiplexing of
"the stylus position information with the computer generated information in
such a way that the oscilloscope display contains a composite of the current
pen position (represented as a dot) and the computer output" (Davis and Ellis
1964, 325). The display screen was conceived as a two-dimensional space with
an x and a y axis, and the separate tablet was responsible for the generation of
a 10-bit x and a 10-bit y stylus position information. The original tablet was
essentially a very sophisticated printed-circuit board, 10.24 inches long by
10.24 inches wide, with extremely fine lines.[12]
    The RAND device can be described as a capacitative (or electrostatic) trans-
ducer, "a device that converts input energy into output energy, the latter usually differing in kind but bearing a known relation to input."[13] The stylus po-

sition controlled by the hand gesture of the user, the input energy, is translated into twenty bits of electrically coded information, the output energy, thanks to the displacement of the stylus on the electric grid of the tablet. According to M. H. Lewin, "the pen in this case is merely a metallic electrostatic pickup connected to a high input-impedance amplifier." Or as he also put it, both the RAND tablet and the light pen "utilize the pen as a signal pickup and the writing surface as the signal generator" (1965, 831).

Thus, instead of an eye on a wand, the RAND stylus was an electrostatic-sensitive finger leaving traces on the tablet that appeared elsewhere, on the CRT display. In each case, the signal generated by the writing surface was of a very different nature: light for the light pen, electric current for the tablet.[14] But more importantly, the nature of the feedback loop is what finally separates the two. As Kittler would have it, because the tablet unlinks the hand and the eye, its feedback loop relegates the eye to a secondary role,[15] while the light pen does not.

The "directness" of this solution, which was presented as an advantage at the time, also meant that the tablet handled only the problem of communication from the user to the computer, delegating to the CRT screen communication in the other direction, from the computer to the user. The fact that the only feedback loop from the computer to the user was on the CRT screen meant that users needed to get used to this unlinking. Licklider reported that "on the basis of early experience, the RAND people say that the separation of the computer's display from the user's tablet is not a source of serious difficulty" (1965, 96). That is not surprising, since touch typing on a QWERTY keyboard as an incorporating practice long had accustomed potential users to the unlinking of eyes and hands.

The main application of the GRAIL project was programming flow-charting, producing precisely drawn boxes for flow charts from the loosely drawn ones the programmers sketched, allowing them to nest subroutines to any depth. The tablet also was supposed to allow real-time computer recognition of hand-printed text. Two major dedicated applications were developed during the 1960's: a helpful application for cartographers and BIOMOD, a biological modeling application (Clark, Groner, and Berman 1971). The work was initially funded by the Air Force until ARPA picked it up in 1969. Probably ten tablets were used inside RAND, and two more were sent for beta testing (Uncapher 1993).

The most serious difficulty encountered by users and GRAIL's biggest problem was one that would persist for some time. Keyboards as input devices not only unlink hand and eye, they intervene between computer and user. Ideally, the interface between the two should seem to disappear—the user of the tablet, for example, should be able simply to write on it, as if on a tablet of paper.

> The matching of input-output capabilities is an important consideration. For if both man and the machine have equal freedom in dealing with the contents of the display, the CRT face can be considered a common working surface. In fact it may suffice for all man-machine communication. The next step is to eliminate the middleman. That is, to create a software-hardware system in which the man apparently creates and manipulates the contents of the display directly and naturally without reference to an intermediary (the machine). The contents of the display should represent, in a very real sense, the problem at hand; allowing the man to feel that he is dealing directly with his problem. (Ellis and Sibley 1968, 124)

The pursuit of this ideal ran afoul of problems with the algorithm for character recognition when users tried to input text via handwriting on the tablet (Uncapher 1993; Groner 1966). According to Sketchpad operational goals, this was not supposed to be a problem because such pen devices were supposed to be part of an almost purely graphical human-computer communication system, not a text-based system, and there simply was not supposed to be any text involved at all. Sutherland actually introduced his graphical system by stating that "the Sketchpad system, by eliminating typed statements (except for legends) in favor of line drawing, opens up a new era of man-machine communication" (Sutherland 1963, 329). It was a design dead end at that point, however, to consider that the same input device could be the device of choice to enter both graphics (line drawing) and text (character recognition).

The storage needed for refreshing the screen was a problem, as well. The GRAIL project team had reached an agreement with IBM in which IBM supplied some hardware, including a storage disk for refreshing display screens, constantly updating what would appear on them as a user made marks on the tablet. This early disk was six feet in diameter and had a gyroscopic effect so powerful that researchers joked it "stabilized the RAND building" in earthquake country. The necessity of refreshing the display screens was central to the design and the hardware was so cumbersome and in such an early stage of development that in the end, RAND agreed not to distribute the tablet. In fact Uncapher (1993) told me that they "couldn't even show the hardware to anybody."

Originally, Engelbart wanted simply to begin by using the RAND tablet for symbol manipulation. In the end, what he developed could be called both a lightless light pen with wheels that manipulates symbols on-screen and a tabletless tablet that retains the separation between hand and eye: the mouse. "These tablets that people have made now, the tablet is sort of alive and you put a stylus on it and the computer senses it and can control the cursor," he said in 1996. Well, the very first of those was being developed at RAND Corporation and we thought that they could probably loan us one. But they said, 'Well, we don't have that many.' We said, 'Alright.'" (Engelbart 1996)

THE PLANIMETER AND THE MOUSE

Engelbart's invention of the mouse was based on a well-known engineering principle, the planimeter, and the only problems it raised were problems of implementation. Basically, the mouse function was the same as the light pen's in Sketchpad, but implementation concerns gave it its now-familiar shape. The space needed for the wheels that control a cursor's movement over the screen made a pen shape impossible. Initially, Engelbart thought of it instead as a "bug." At the same time, it did what the GRAIL tablet he could not obtain did. It allowed a hand poised over the desktop to initiate movements on the screen. As Engelbart envisioned it, the "bug" also could carry a set of keys or buttons, which could make it function as a chord keyset, as well.

The basic technology employed by the mouse had a long history, and as with the chord keyset, Engelbart's innovation consisted in part of being able to imagine—in a moment of alienation from what everyone else was discussing, as he recounts it—a new use for an old technology:

> I remember sitting at some graphics conference and just feeling at a wall because everybody was talking and I'm not skillful at all in getting them to listen to me. So a lot of times out of frustration I'd start talking to myself. I remember thinking, "Oh, how would you control a cursor in different ways?" I remember how my head went back to a device called a planimeter that engineering uses. It's a little simple mechanical thing. . . . I saw that used when I was a senior and I was fascinated. (Engelbart 1996)

The conference was the Reno November 1963 Graphics Conference. Excerpts from Engelbart's notebooks, the first entries concerning the mouse, dated November 14, 1963 read:

> 85. How about earlier idea of counting impulses from X+Y displacement points? Early system could ??? line on 140. Later could have hardware integrator. 86. Separate possibility of a "bug" instead of a stylus. Bug being something that does not fall if you take hands off—just stay where you left it. Much better for coordination with the keyboard. Also easier (more natural space) . . . 101. 3-point bug—a drop point and 2 orthogonal wheels.

And the next entry dated of the following day: "113. Bug could carry 5-keyset or other control switches." Note the indication saying that the "bug" differs from the stylus in that it "does not fall if you take hands off" in relation to the

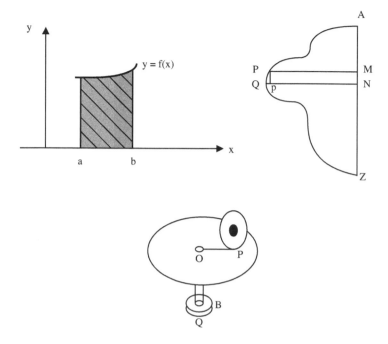

Figure 3-5 (above, left). A Mathematical Representation of the Integral.

Figure 3-6 (above, right). Maxwell's Illustration.

Figure 3-7 (below). The Operating Principle of the Planimeter.

Licklider proviso that the light pen should "return to its resting place whenever the operator releases it" (1965, 94).

The "hardware integrator" was the planimeter. Much of modern computing started with work on analog computers as a means to mechanize the computation of the integral *S*, described mathematically as follows:

> If *S* is the area bounded by a simply closed curve, then *S* is expressed mathematically as the integral of the function $f(x)$ describing the curve between the position *a* and *b* on the *x* axis, or

$$S = \int_a^b f(x)dx$$

The operating principle of the planimeter seems to have been discovered in 1814 by the Bavarian engineer J. H. Hermann and later by Tito Gonnella in Florence in 1824, but neither was able to implement it successfully. This was achieved around 1836 by one Swiss engineer, Oppikofer, and improved by another, Welti, in Zurich, in 1849 (Bromley 1990, 166–71). Then, around 1855, James Clerk Maxwell reinvented the planimeter, discussed it with James Thomson, who in turn produced one himself, and used it with his brother William Thomson (later Lord Kelvin) in a tide-calculating machine (Goldstine 1972, 40; Bromley 1990, 172–77). Maxwell described the mechanical integrator, the fundamental idea behind the planimeter, as follows:

> In considering the principles of instruments of this kind, it will be most convenient to suppose the area of the figure measured by an imaginary straight line, which, by moving parallel to itself, and at the same time altering in length to suit the form of the area, accurately sweeps it out.
>
> Let AZ be a fixed vertical line, $APQZ$ the boundary of the area, and let a variable horizontal line move parallel to itself from A to Z, so as to have its extremities, P and M, in the curve and in the fixed straight line. Now, suppose the horizontal line (which we shall call the generating line) to move from the position PM to QN, MN being some small quantity, say one inch for distinctness. During this movement, the generating line will have swept out the narrow strip of the surface, $PMNQ$, which exceeds the portion $PMNp$ by the small triangle PQp.
>
> But since MN, the breadth of the strip, is one inch, the strip will contain as many square inches as PM is inches long; so that when the generating line descends one inch, it sweeps out a number of square inches equal to the number of linear inches in its length.
>
> Therefore, if we have a machine with an index of any kind, which, while the generating line moves one inch downwards, moves forward as many degrees as the generating line is inches long, and if the generating line be alternately moved an inch and altered in length, the index will mark the number of square inches swept during the whole operation. By the ordinary method of limits, it may be shown that, if these changes be made continuous instead of sudden, the index will still measure the area traced by the extremity of the generating line.
>
> We have next to consider the various methods of communicating the required motion to the index. The first is by means of two discs, the first having a flat horizontal rough surface, turning on a vertical axis, OQ, and the second vertical, with its circumference resting on the flat surface of the first at P, so as to be driven round by the motion of the first disc. The velocity of the second disc will depend on OP, the distance of the point of contact from the center of the disc; so that if OP be made always equal to the generating line, the conditions of the instrument will be fulfilled.
>
> This is accomplished by causing the index-disc to slip along the radius of the horizontal disc; so that in working the instrument, the motion of the index-disc is compounded of a rolling motion due to the rotation of the first disc, and a slipping motion due to the variation of the generating line. (1965 [1855], quoted in Goldstine 1972, 40–43)

Vannevar Bush had experimented with the principle of the planimeter in his 1913 master's thesis at Tufts College. He used a disc integrator as the key mechanism in the device that earned him his degree: the Profile Tracer, an automatic instrument for recording terrestrial profiles (Owens 1991, 29). The Profile Tracer was the first device that Bush created on this automated principle—turning motion to graphics. It was soon to be followed by Bush's multiple experiments with integrators in his differential analyzers.[16] The integrator and its engineering principles would become fundamental to later analog computers such as Bush's analyzers,[17] but also to most digital graphical display and position-indicator technology: the integrator is in fact the operating principle of most position-indicating transducers.

Bill English, an electrical engineer who joined Douglas Engelbart in 1964 after earning his master's at Stanford, took charge of the project of developing a planimeter-based input device for manipulating symbols on a computer display. The first report of the mouse appeared in a July 1965 report to NASA-Langley written by English, Engelbart, and Bonnie Huddart, and entitled "Computer-Aided Display Control" (Contract NAS-1-3988, report NTIS N66-30204). The "screen-select devices" that they began by considering took into consideration the continuing hegemony of the QWERTY keyboard. Engelbart recalls saying:

> Here's one of the devices we could pick. I want it to be in context, so that you're making the selection in a context that we'd be thinking and working with, where you assume that the keyboard is still an important part of it. At the outset it's text. So that steered us into the kinds of things to select. I wanted it so that it wasn't just how fast you could find a spot and get there—this includes accessing a device, pointing, the errors you could make—not just doing it fast. (Engelbart 1996)

Contrary to the light pen or the tablet schema, the mouse design assumed that the surface on which the user moves the mouse is not a primary component of the system. The "bug" referred both to the artifact *and* to the cursor on the screen. Engelbart's project thus was very close conceptually to Ellis and Sibley's goal of "allowing the man to feel that he is dealing directly with his problem." To give the same name to both these elements, one in the concrete world of the user and the other in the symbolic world of the computer, surely meant, as Ellis and Sibley would put it, that the user could work on problems "without reference to an intermediary," without the interface seeming to intervene. From this perspective, using the mouse is analogous to pointing with a stylus on a screen, except that the hands of the user are not in the way of his or her eyes, the mouse does not fall when the user types on the keyboard, and most importantly, the mouse is the signal generator, contrary to the preexisting input devices such as the light pen and the tablet, where the writing surface was the signal generator.

So actually, when the user employs a mouse and a chord keyset combination, he or she can alternatively input both text and graphics without looking at his or her hands, freeing the eyes to contemplate the results of these hand gestures turned into graphical symbols, in real time. As in the RAND tablet schema, the only feedback loop is on the screen. But contrary to this schema, the bandwidth of the mouse is independent of the dimensions of the desktop surface (the mouse pad). As in the light-pen schema, the information bandwidth of the mouse is determined in part by the resolution and the dimensions of the display with which it is used. The first design of the mouse, however, where two wheels connected to two potentiometers (capacitive transducers) served as the position indicator, depended on the relationship between the diameters of the wheels and the resolution on the screen:

> They [the first mice] were big, because at that time we used potentiometers and analog to digital converters and since you only got one revolution out of the potentiometer, you had to choose the wheel size that gives you the right ratio of mouse motion/screen motion. That determines the size of it. . . . Part of the job was picking the wheel diameter because that is the way you control the resolution on the screen. And the other thing was the fact that since you had two wheels 180 degrees one to the other, one always had to slide, so you had to get the right radius on the wheel depending on which surface you were working on. I spent quite a good time on that, getting the wheels right. (English 1992)

"Once you had your hand on any of them, they were all accurate, with a little bit of skill, at picking something," Engelbart later recalled. "It would sit there and be where you left it. You didn't have to pick it up and you could put buttons on it, which helped" (Engelbart 1996). In the documentation for the first patent of the mouse, the "summary of the invention" still shows evidence of this first analog design, even if some digital alternatives were already available at that time.

> One subject of the invention is to provide an X-Y position indicating control mechanism for controlling indications of positions on a cathode ray tube (CRT) display, by movement along a surface which can be other than the face of the CRT.
>
> Another object of the invention is to provide a position indicator control which transmits signals defining its position on a surface, and which is connected by only a cable to the apparatus which acts upon such information.
>
> Still another object of the invention is to provide a simple and improved X-Y position locating device.

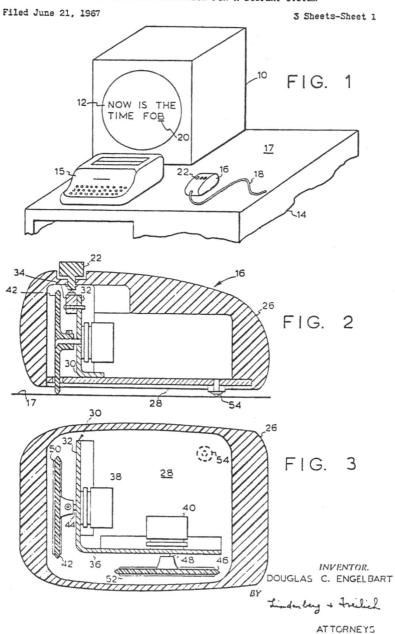

FIG. 1

NOW IS THE
TIME FO<u>R</u>

FIG. 2

FIG. 3

INVENTOR.
DOUGLAS C. ENGELBART
BY
Lindenberg + Frelich
ATTORNEYS

Figure 3-8. Illustrations for the Original Patent of the Mouse.

The foregoing and other objects are realized by an X-Y position indicator control mechanism comprising a small housing adapted to be held in the hand and having two wheels and an idler ball bearing for contacting the surface on which it rests. The two wheels are mounted with their axes perpendicular to each other and each wheel is attached to a potentiometer or other means for indicating its position. The position indicator control is held by the hand and moved over any surface, such as a desk top (or even may be moved by the feet). As the indicator control is moved, the two wheels rotate and the resistance of the potentiometer changes. Electrical leads connected to the potentiometers trail behind the indicator control and connect to a computer which continuously monitors the indicator control's position. The computer causes the CRT to display a symbol, or cursor, such as a short line on the CRT screen to define a position on the screen about which changes or the like may be made, the cursor position changing in accordance with movement of the X-Y position indicator control. Buttons are provided on the indicator control housing for closing switches to send pulses through additional wires trailing behind the indicator control to signal for a change in the displayed information. For example, one button on the indicator control may be used to cause the erasure of a small area directly above or following the cursor. New material may then be inserted in place of the material erased in accordance with the programming of the computer, as by typing in letters.

While a potentiometer may be connected to each of the two wheels on the indicator control, other devices can be used for generating signals indicating rotation of the wheels. One such device is a shaft position encoder which produces a digital output corresponding to the angular position of the wheel. While such an arrangement provides a direct digital output, instead of an analog output which must be digitally converted to be used by the computer control in the CRT display, the output from a shaft encoder necessitates a larger cable. Still another means for indicating position of a wheel is an incremental encoder and counter. An incremental encoder generates an up indicating pulse each time the shaft moves by a certain increment of rotation in one direction and generates a down indicating pulse when the shaft moves in the other direction. These pulses are transmitted to an up-down counter, which provides a digital output equal to the sum of the up inputs minus the sum of the down inputs. (United States Patent Office # 3,541,541, patented November 17, 1970)

For Engelbart, the mouse, like the chord keyset, was part of an effort to optimize basic human capabilities in synergy with ergonomically and cognitively more efficiently designed artifacts. The coupling of these processes was a very concrete thing for Engelbart. He wanted to allow the user to have one hand on the mouse and one hand on the keyset so that very few keystrokes were needed to issue a command (or, in his words, to "couple") to explicitly computer processes. His first fully realized user-computer interface was the keyset used together with the mouse. To this day, Engelbart still claims that it was actually faster than today's menus. The keyboard was merely a secondary device, and

was to be used if the user needed to enter a relatively longer string of characters, such as words and sentences.

With the QWERTY keyboard and the teletype terminal available in the
1950's for human-computer communication, the body of the user was employed only as a medium to transfer manipulated symbols from the user to the
machine. In this sense, the keyboard did not differ from the punch card as a
communication medium between human and computer. The user's hands and
eyes were limited input and output devices in the human-computer interface.
In developing the mouse and the chord keyset in the early 1960's, Engelbart
and his group at SRI made a quantum leap in human-computer interaction:
the introduction of the body as whole as a set of connected, basic sensory-
motor capabilities. As we will see, the experiments that the group conducted
with these interface devices were not limited to the hands and the eye, but involved many other parts of the body, including the knee, the back, and the
head as potential sensory-motor ways to control a pointer on a screen. The
chord keyset and the mouse represented Engelbart's first and basic effort to develop an interface that, in the literal sense of the term, incorporated the body
of the user into the prosthesis that linked user and computer. The chord keyset consolidated the inputting of characters in the hand, while the mouse was
a step toward translating the gestures of the user into the graphical space of the
computer.

Together, these two devices equipped the user with learning prostheses enabling the bootstrapping process to start. They also show the extent to which,
in pursuit of "automated external symbol manipulation" for the augmentation
of human intellect and the coevolution of humans and machines, Engelbart
took the word "manipulation" in the strictest sense possible. Used in conjunction, these two devices liberated the hands of the user from the keyboard
in favor of more "natural" ways for humans to use their computers.

This was the rationale for the earliest implementation of the personal interface. In this perspective, the interface composed of the chord keyset and the
mouse inscribes the user for whom Engelbart intended it. And for Engelbart
the coevolution of its users with the technology remained the basic point. Users
were not supposed to be employing the computer as a tool for merely entering,
storing, retrieving, and manipulating data. They were supposed to employ it
as a new way to think—to see the relations between their fingers and what new
things those relations could produce, to use Gregory Bateson's example, not
just to stare endlessly at the fingers themselves, a sight they already knew like
the back of their hand. From the start, Engelbart wasn't just envisioning new
technology, he was envisioning new users of technology. As with most technological innovations, the development of the chord keyset and then the mouse
entailed inventing the kind of people who most fruitfully could use them.

CHAPTER FOUR

Inventing the Virtual User

For now we see through a glass, darkly; but then face to face: now I know in part; but then shall I know even as also I am known.

— P A U L , 1 Corinthians 13 : 12

According to Brenda Laurel and to many other interface designers, "human-computer interface design is an ad hoc discipline," and its history is the result of a number of ad hoc decisions and implementations (Laurel 1990, xi, xii). As Laurel also says, "many people today equate the interface with the screen" (ibid., xi). It was not ever thus, however. Several models of the interface emerged through time, ending in a notion of the interface as a surface, a place or space of contact between the human user and the computer.

The problem of how to imagine the user-computer interface remained a vexed one for some time. Only slowly, as the result of the decisions and implementations made in the community of the interface designers, did the screen come to be taken for granted as the location of the user-computer interface. These decisions and implementations resulted from the dialectical relationship between technological innovations and the conceptions of their uses—and their users—entertained by their designers. Technological innovators such as Douglas Engelbart also invent the kind of people they expect to use their innovations.

THE PROBLEM OF THE INTERFACE

In her remarkable *Computers as Theater*, Brenda Laurel gives a telling illustration of how the accumulation of decisions in one particular setting addressed the problem of conceptualizing the user-computer interface. Laurel recounts how in the early 1980's she and the participants of a seminar at the Atari Company, where she was then working, attempted to define the interface. They rapidly dismissed the simplest model (Figure 4-1), represented as a shadowed rectangle between the user and the computer, one that simply "encompasses what appears on the screen, hardware input/output devices, and their drivers" (1991, 12–14).

This overly simplistic model of the interface was dismissed as "pre–cognitive science": "In order for an interface to work, the person has to have some idea about what the computer expects and can handle, and the computer has to incorporate some information about what the person's goals and behaviors are likely to be. These two phenomena—a person's 'mental model' of the computer and the computer's 'understanding' of the person—are just as much a part of the interface as its physical and sensory manifestations" (ibid., 12–13). The model that encompasses the "mental model" of the computer and the computer's "understanding" of the person, is represented in Figure 4-2. Once the "pre–cognitive science" model of the interface is dismissed, and once the idea that the interface is just "what appears on the screen," plus "hardware input/output devices, and their drivers" is overcome, the "conceptual interface" becomes part of the interface. The user and the computer must have some kind of "understanding" of each other.

This model, however, suffers from what Laurel and her colleagues called the problem of "horrible recursion": "If you are going to admit that what the two parties 'think' about each other is part of what is going on, you will have to agree that what the two parties think about what the other is thinking about them must perforce be included in the model. . . . This elaboration has dizzying ramifications" (ibid., 14).

Facing this "nightmare," the seminar turned its attention to "more manageable concepts." They settled on a simpler concept of the interface: "How humans and computers interact." Figure 4-3 represents this model, where "the interface is that which joins human and computer, conforming to the needs of each." Laurel concluded that this representation "avoids the central issue of what this all means in terms of reality and representation," and that "when we have such trouble defining a concept, it usually means that we are barking up the wrong tree."

There is no need, however, to stake out a position that requires avoiding so central an issue. The computer represents the designer. This is because in the early stages of development of the interface, the designer represents the user. The computer comes to learn about the user from the representation of the user that the designer of the interface embodies in its design. The interface thus is the representational space where the designer constructs the user. The first step in understanding how the interface functions as a representational space is the

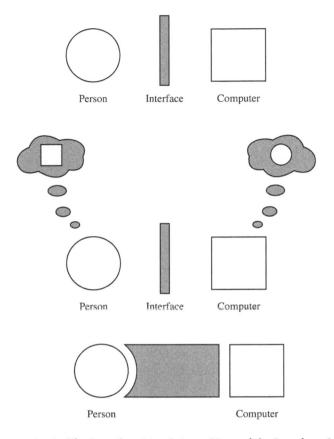

Figure 4-1 (top). The Pre–Cognitive Science View of the Interface. Source: Adapted from Laurel (1991), p. 12.

Figure 4-2 (middle). The Mental-Models View of the Interface. Source: Adapted from Laurel (1991), p. 13.

Figure 4-3 (bottom). A Simple Model of the Interface, ca. 1989. Source: Adapted from Laurel (1991), p. 14.

realization that human and nonhuman agents in the interface, like characters in a play, cannot be separated from the plot itself, and vice versa.[1] Like many technological innovations, the human-computer interface entails entire narratives of interaction.

If the narrative's plot is convincing, the medium becomes transparent: user and designer agree on the "truth" of the representation, and consequently it appears "real." As Alan Kay puts it, the relationship between what the users see on the screen and what they think they manipulate is better seen as an illusion, rather than as a metaphor such as a "desktop"—that is, as a relationship between what the users visualize and their internal models of action. Designing this illusion is designing the user interface.

When, for instance, a user is creating a document in the desktop environment of a personal computer, he or she manipulates an iconic representation of this document that is designed to stand for the document in the user's internal model of action—moving it from one place to another, for example. For most users, moving the icon of a document on the desktop is a quite straightforward action, similar to but different from moving the "real" document on a "real" desktop. The difference lies in the "false residual" that metaphor encourages them to ignore—or so says the metaphorical conception of what is happening. But if the users visualize this action in a way that conforms to their internal models of action, the residual difference between the "real" and what the user does disappears. Instead, it is an illusion, and the role of the designer is to make the users believe that what they do when they move the document's representation is what they do when moving the real document.

Developing a plot that functions in this way involves representations of the user. The user is at first a virtuality to be invented by the designer and realized along with the technology. Or to put it the other way around, technological innovation initially entails a script that defines specific characters as its users, independent of any real actors who might take those parts.[2]

This stage of technological innovation is in fact endemic to the methods of scientific investigation since the Enlightenment. Steven Shapin and Simon Schaffer characterize those methods as "virtual witnessing": "the production in a *reader's* mind of such an image of an experimental scene as obviates the necessity for either direct witness or replication. Through virtual witnessing the multiplication of witnesses could be, in principle, unlimited. It was therefore the most powerful technology for constituting matter of fact" (1985, 55).

The invention of the user as a virtuality via virtual witnessing in Engelbart's ARC lab thus involved the development of the "script" before any "real user" validated it. It involved not real users, but the imagined users who resulted from the thought process of the designer anticipating the potential use of the design. The virtual user is thus also a reflexive user, a product of the designer's own mental representations. These allow the designer to speak and act in place of this user-to-be—the imagined user resulting from the thought process of the designer anticipating the potential use of his or her design.

The reflexive user is reflexive in yet another sense of the word: quite often, the designer's representation of the user is some sort of distorted representation of the designer himself or herself. In the process of inventing a virtual user, the designer often reflects on his or her own experience as a user and claims "I am the user": "The user, c'est moi." Or, as Donald Norman puts it, "designers often think of themselves as typical users" (1990, 155). The reflexive user thus literally embodies the virtual user. The body of the designer represents the least common denominator between the designer and the real user to come.

The virtual user is progressively shaped and transformed via virtual witnessing in order to control the process by which the real user comes into being. But that control is temporary, and in the end is bound to be eluded when the virtual user inevitably is replaced by a separate, living entity—the real user. At the heart of the process by which the personal interface came into being, then, was a dialectic of control and uncertainty that characterizes the innovation process.

INVENTING THE VIRTUAL USER

The question of the user at first seemed to pose no serious challenge to the implementation of Douglas Engelbart's Framework for the Augmentation of Human Intellect. The experiment was considered to be a learning experience, an experience of "bootstrapping" for the programmers that would lead to learning that would produce profound coevolutionary changes for both humans and machines. In this process, the first to learn was thought to be the designer, who envisioned the virtual user, reflexively, in his own image. Douglas Engelbart was the designer of the system, and the user was soon described in his own idealized image: what he called the intelligence worker, or later the "knowledge worker."

The Bootstrap Group

The initial figure of the virtual user had been implicit in the plan since the original 1962 augmentation report: Who would be the most likely intelligence worker to envision using a computer if not a computer programmer? There was a ready-made set of justifications for this plan: "The experimental work of deriving, testing, and integrating innovations into a growing system of augmentation means must have a specific type of human task to try to develop more effectiveness for, to give unifying focus to the research. We recommend the particular task of computer programming for this purpose—with many reasons behind the selection that should come out in the following discussion" (Engelbart 1962, 116).

These reasons are numbered from 1 to 9 in the text and can be grouped along two main axes: experimental reasons (1 to 6) and fundamental reasons

(7 to 9). The experimental reasons given by Engelbart refer to the special status of the computer programmer for experimental purposes:

1. The programmer works on many problems, including large and realistic ones, which can be solved without interaction with other humans. . . .

2. Typical and realistic problems for the programmer to solve can be posed for experimental purposes that do not involve large amounts of working and reference information. . . .

3. Much of the programmer's working data are computer programs . . . which have unambiguous syntactic and semantic form so that getting the computer to do useful tasks for him on his working data will be much facilitated—which helps very much to get early experience on the value a human can derive from this kind of computer help.

4. A programmer's effectiveness, relative to other programmers, can probably be measured more easily than would be the case for most other complex-problem solvers. For example, few other complex solutions or designs beside a program can so easily be given the rigorous test of "Does it actually work?"

5. The programmer's normal work involves interactions with a computer (although heretofore not generally on-line), and this will help researcher use the computer as a tool for learning about the programmer's habits and needs.

6. There are some very challenging types of intellectual efforts involved in programming. Attempting to increase human effectiveness therein will provide an excellent means for testing our hypothesis. (Ibid., 116–17)

These experimental reasons describe programmers as ideal intelligence workers: they are autonomous and creative. Moreover, the input ("working data") and output ("complex solutions or designs") of their work are both computer programs, and this, according to Engelbart, would create ideal experimental conditions. The fundamental reasons, however, deal more directly with the benefits of using computer programmers as the template for constructing new kinds of users for the new technology. They would form a vanguard, "the bootstrap group," that would spearhead the crusade:

7. Successful achievements in evolving new augmentation means which significantly improve a programmer's capability will not only serve to prove the hypothesis, but will lead directly to possible practical application of augmentation systems to real-world problem domains that can use help.

8. Computer programmers are a natural group to be the first in the "real world" to incorporate the type of augmentation means we are considering. They already know how to work in formal methodologies with computers, and most of them are associated with activities that have to have computers anyway, so that the new techniques, concepts, methods, and equipment will not seem so radical to them and will be relatively easy for them to learn and acquire.

9. Successful achievements can be utilized within the augmentation-research program itself, to improve the effectiveness of the computer programming activity involved in studying and developing augmentation systems. The capability of designing, implementing, and modifying computer programs will be very important to the rate of research progress. (Ibid., 117–18)

The initial conceptualization of the computer user as a knowledge worker in the guise of a computer programmer had ramifications that are best seen in the way that Engelbart's lab proceeded to test the mouse and other pointing devices. The decisions made at this early stage in many ways established a dynamic that ran counter to the avowed goals of Engelbart's crusade.

Black-Boxing the User

Trevor Pinch has argued that "it is not enough to show that a technological artifact like a television set can be given different meaning by different social groups: What has to be shown is that every working of the TV set can be subject to sociological analysis. Testing, in that it establishes workability, is an important test case." "What is at issue in such tests is not so much the projection from 'test' to 'actual use' of the *machine*, but the projection from test to actual use of the *user*" (1993, 26, 36).

In the sociology of technology, the projection of a representation of the user via testing has sometimes been called "black-boxing the user."[3] Much of the uncertainty in the process of developing a technological innovation resides in the potential differences between what the designer envisioned the virtual user to be and what the real user actually becomes. The testing phase is a central moment in the process of technology development, a moment when the representations of the user are developed, challenged, and altered through various experiments, procedures, and measures. Many of the efforts of the designer involve trying to make the representation of the user, the virtual user, as robust as possible to accommodate these possible changes—to create something that would support many different kinds of outcomes. And indeed, in testing, the user envisioned for the mouse kept changing.

The kind of testing involved in the invention of virtual users is "prospective testing," testing to "find if the design is feasible, whether the technology works as specified in the design, whether different components can be integrated, and to monitor the performance for a range of putative uses" (ibid., 27). At ARC, prospective testing of the mouse included testing it with other input devices (other transducers) to establish the performance and utility of the technology in comparison with alternative devices fulfilling the same function and testing it to establish the performance and utility of a specific design in comparison with alternative designs. Bill English, assisted by Roger Bates and Melvyn

Berman, carried out the comparative testing phase as an extension of the NASA project that got funding in 1963:

> We were looking for the best—the most efficient—device. We approached NASA in 1966, and said, "let's test them," and determine the answer once-and-for-all. With NASA funding, the team developed a set of simple tasks, and timed a group of volunteers in doing those tasks with the various devices. For example, the computer would generate an object in a random position on the screen, and a cursor somewhere else. We timed how long it took the users to move the cursor to the object. It quickly became clear that the mouse outperformed all the others. Devices like the light pen simply took too much time, by repeatedly requiring the user to pick up the pointer, and reach all the way to the screen—very tiresome.[4]

The results of this phase of testing appeared in a March 1967 paper authored by English, Engelbart, and Berman. The mouse was compared with alternative devices already well established in the market, devices that it was supposed to replace. Several pointing devices were tested, including the mouse, a light pen manufactured by Sanders Associates of Nashua, New Hampshire, a tablet, the Grafacon, manufactured by Data Equipment Company, and a joystick manufactured by Bowmar Associates. The performances of these devices were compared "under conditions similar to those that the user would encounter when actually working on-line" (English, Engelbart, and Berman 1967, 7).

The design of these experimental tests assumed that the user "must interpose a screen-selection operation into his on-going working operation" (ibid., 5). Engelbart and his colleagues assumed here the classic "operator-operand" sequence of interaction, where the user first enters the command (operator) and then designates (selects) the element (operand) on which the command is to be performed.[5] For Engelbart and his colleagues, the most important of the results obtained in their tests seemed to have more to do with the "human factors" involved in the design than with the performance of users with the different devices:

> Tests and analysis to determine the best display-selection techniques for a computer-aided text-manipulation system reveal that the choice does not hinge on the inherent differences in target-selection speed and accuracy between the different selection devices. Of more importance are such factors as the mix of other operations required of the select-operation hand, the ease of getting the hand to and gaining control of a given selection device, or the fatigue effects of its associated operating posture. (Ibid., 5)

The authors acknowledged in the paper that their results seemed "disappointingly nonspecific," but turned this disappointment into an "important lesson": "it seems unrealistic to expect a flat statement that one device is better than another. The details of the usage system in which the device is to be embedded make too much difference" (ibid., 14).[6]

One of the components of the "usage system" is of course the user. Numerous statements in the paper dealt directly with the user, starting with the assumption that the "usage system" was functionally centered on "text manipulation." The first assumption regarding the "general situation faced by the user of the on-line system" was that "the user has generally been entering information on the typewriter-like keyboard" (ibid., 5). If long strings were still to be entered on a standard "typewriter-like keyboard," "text manipulation," however, was to be carried out with a system whose interface would not rely on such a keyboard. Instead, the chord keyset and the mouse would provide the user with all the functions he or she needed to manipulate text. In this perspective, the most important characteristic of the virtual user for the design of the experiment was the degree of experience that real test subjects had with various other devices:

> We try to do naive users as well as experienced users. So experienced users were within our group. And since we had a completely abstract design of an experiment on the screen, with various sizes of targets, we brought in people who had nothing to do with the project, other people at SRI. . . . We picked a range, there were scientists and engineers and secretaries, people of that sort, to run the experiment on pointing devices. And we plot learning curves as people repeatedly run the same questions, to see how quickly they learn as well as how well they behaved from the start. (English 1992)

There were eight "experienced subjects" who were already somewhat familiar with the on-line system"[7] and "three inexperienced subjects who had never before used either the system or the particular devices being tested" (English, Engelbart, and Berman 1967, 9). The testing procedure was different for both groups of users, and so were its results. The experienced subjects found the mouse both faster and more accurate than the other devices, while the inexperienced subjects tended to perform better with the light pen. This seems to mean that there was indeed some learning involved in the unlinking of the eye and the hand. The authors stressed the point that "the light pen exploits one's inherent tendency to select something by straightforwardly 'pointing' at it rather than by guiding a bug across a screen toward it from a remote control" (ibid., 13).

The "important, general conclusion," of the study, however, was that only experienced users provided the basis for an adequate assessment of the technology and that "the relative value of different schemes cannot be judged on the basis of their appeal for inexperienced users" (ibid., 14). This seems paradoxical, but in fact it is not, although the apparent paradox highlights an important point. The purpose of Engelbart's augmentation quest put the learning experience at its center. But Engelbart and his crew started by defining the virtual user in terms of someone who did not need to learn how to employ the technology—as an already trained, reflexive user, in fact. To test any technology, however, one has to assume that its user is able to use it appropriately, that its user is "an experienced user." So at the start, the character of the user written into the script for the mouse and projected via the testing's black boxing was not just the reflexive user, the intelligence worker, but someone who already embodied a particular incorporating practice, the use of "a remote control" in place of "straightforwardly pointing." [8]

This was a crucial step. The manner in which user was constructed in the process of developing the technology proscribed him or her from being otherwise. It *then* served as a justification for this very same construction. And the figure of the user that developed was the result of a long history of such decisions and such virtual witnessing. Decisions are choices between alternatives, and their products are not the only ones possible. Out of such early decisions as these, the figure of the virtual user, and then of the real user, began to evolve alongside, and often in tension with, the technology and the vision of its creator.

From the start, the user of the personal computer thus was imagined in terms of an existing incorporating practice. As the history of the QWERTY keyboard shows, it is not familiarity with a given practice in dealing with a technology per se, however, but the diffusion of the practice that tends to determine the success of the technology. What remained to be seen was what exactly the incorporating practice involving use of "a remote control" would be. It didn't even necessarily have to involve the hand.

In the process of using what they had designed, which was one of the characteristics of the first phase of the reflexive bootstrapping process envisioned by Engelbart, the members of the laboratory progressively tested and refined the original design of the mouse. For instance, Engelbart noted recently [9] that the very first mouse they had built had the cord coming out the back, and he added "It wasn't long before we realized that it would get in the way, and then we changed it to the front." But there were other directions that they also explored in envisioning a virtual user for this technology, among them the "knee-control" design and the question of the numbers of buttons on the mouse.

The "knee-control" was an alternative design for the mouse that was supposed to be used under, rather than on the desktop. Movements of the user's knee controlled the device and the "bug" on the screen: a sideways movement of the knee controlled the cursor in the horizontal dimension of the display, while an up-and-down movement controlled its vertical dimension. Engelbart recently explained the genesis of this design, "That 'knee-control' device was

Figure 4-4. The Knee Control. Source: Engelbart (1988), p. 197.

based on my observation that the human foot was a pretty sensitive controller of the gas pedal in cars. With a little work, we discovered that the knee offered even better control at slight movements in all directions. In tests, it outperformed the mouse by a small margin" (ibid.).

The knee-control device was tested along with the other input devices, but with inexperienced users only, since the device was designed at the time of the testing experiments, leaving no time for the experienced subjects to get acquainted with the device. However, a few individual check tests were conducted with these experienced users, and this time, again, the results provided by the experienced and the inexperienced subjects were contradictory:

> In these tests [with experienced subjects] the knee-control appeared both slower and less accurate than the light pen and mouse. . . . Inexperienced subjects found the knee control to be the fastest device. Undoubtedly the main reason for this was that the knee control, unlike the other, has no access time (if the access time is subtracted from the total times measured for the other devices, the knee control no longer shows up so favorably). (Ibid., 5)

The question of the access time, measured as the time necessary to move the hands off the keyboard to hold the device, appeared indeed as a crucial criterion for the comparative testing of the various input devices. The light pen, for instance, was criticized for its poor performance in access time: the authors insisted that, even though they had made no measurements, they had found, from observing the subjects at work, that "a good deal of time was consumed in reaching from the keyboard to grasp the light pen" (ibid., 13).

The argument in favor of the knee control was that it liberated both hands from selection operations. However, this argument appeared not to be sufficient to assure a subsequent diffusion to the device. Here again, the drawbacks of the device for experienced subjects were more important than its advantages for inexperienced users. Here again, the incorporating practices that experienced subjects brought to the testing exerted their power over the decisions affecting the ultimate design of the pointing device. Engelbart told me that they tried other alternative designs as far-fetched as the knee control: a head-mounted mouse, a back mouse, a foot mouse (1992). Even if some of these designs seem quite surreal now, they merely represented systematic attempts to imagine ways to use the possibilities provided for instrumentation by the human body.[10]

At ARC, the question of the number of buttons was never problematic: from the start, Engelbart had assumed that the "bug" should carry five buttons, like a chord keyset. After some preliminary testing however, the number of buttons was reduced to three: two buttons that had been located on the sides of the mouse disappeared after a period of use in the laboratory. The reason for this, however, had nothing to do with inventing the virtual user. Engelbart summarized this decision in the following fashion: "People have asked me, 'How did you decide on three buttons?' Well, it was all we could put on. That was all there was room for" (1996).

A Mouse in a Maze

What Engelbart had in mind, in conceiving a system in which the mouse played a part, however, was a user interface—and a user—that went well beyond the mouse and beyond anything its real users now do. The mouse and chord keyset were merely part of what is called a "marking interface," an interface in which the "user's input is in the form of a stream of x,y coordinates that could be called digital ink" (Baecker, Grudin, Buxton, and Greenberg 1995). As Engelbart put it, the feedback loop is still on the screen, and the information bandwidth of the input device is determined by the display system. However, the necessity of this visual feedback loop is not absolute. Engelbart still had in mind an input and feedback loop that was purely tactile, that depended not on the QWERTY keyboard and mouse or mouse and chord key-

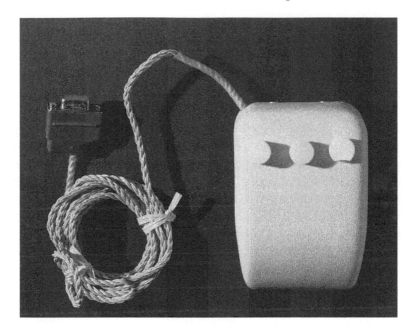

Figure 4-5. Front View of an Early Three-Button Mouse. Photo by the author.

set, but on one of the fundamental human ways of communicating, the gesture. As William Buxton points out,

> many people use the term "gesture" to refer to the marking interfaces. . . . While
> every mark requires a gesture in order to be articulated, it is worthwhile to rec-
> ognize that it is the resulting mark and not the gesture, that is used as input to the
> system. There is a distinct class of system in which it is truly the gesture itself
> which is recognized. Typically, such systems leave no marks, and produce more
> dimensions of input than the x,y point stream of marking input. One of the most
> common ways to capture manual gesture is by instrumenting the hand. The main
> technique used for this is a special glove which is equipped with a number of sen-
> sors which provide the system with information about hand position, orientation,
> and flex of the fingers. (Ibid.)

As early as 1962, Engelbart envisioned a keyset that can "move with the
hand," "a type of glove," or "individual finger caps wired to the recording or
typing mechanism." But the development of such input devices would require
the coevolution on the human side that Engelbart also envisioned.

In 1986, Buxton concluded that "the main limiting factor, restricting the
range of available gestures in our repertoire is the sorry state of current practice in input"—that is, in users (Buxton 1986). In 1986, too, in a retrospective

exhibition of the advances of the ARC project, Douglas Engelbart also concluded that "the technology side has grown way out of proportion, in my view, just stupendously so . . . but all we have to do is turn and look at ourselves to realize that our culture has not yet understood that the human side is open for progress and change" (Engelbart, quoted in Goldberg 1988, 233).

One way Engelbart sought to exert influence over "the human side" was by developing what he called "the augmented knowledge workshop," "the place in which knowledge workers do their work" (Engelbart, Watson, and Norton 1973, 9). This application of the bootstrapping principle was used between 1965 and 1968 to add another dimension to the ARC lab's conceptualization of the virtual user.

Engelbart believed that the activity of the knowledge worker actually involves "core" processes that for the most part are not themselves highly specialized: "a record of how this person used his time, even if his work was highly specialized, would show that specialized work . . . while vital to his effectiveness, probably occupied a small fraction of his time and effort" (ibid., 10). If so, that meant knowledge workers didn't have to be isolated from each other, segregated by the specific demands of the software necessary to their individual tasks. Instead, they could use a common interface and be connected into a network that would link the user with other users. Envisioning the user as a knowledge worker and conceptualizing the knowledge worker in this particular way allowed Engelbart to begin to see a way in which one central aspect of his crusade could be realized. Instead of the artificial intelligence project's aim of creating a cybernetic "colleague" who would supplement an individual user's creativity, Engelbart could begin to develop ways that computers could allow users to share and shape knowledge intersubjectively and collectively. The technological manifestation of this conception of the virtual user was ARC's oN-Line System, NLS.

If software development could be allowed to proceed like natural evolution, by means of "semi-random growth," the result would be several problems that the coevolution of software along with the virtual user as a knowledge worker in an augmented knowledge workshop would solve in advance:

(1) Repetitive solutions for the same functional problems, each with the skewed perspective of a particular special applications area for which these problems are peripheral issues,
(2) Incompatibility between different application software systems in terms of their inputs and outputs,
(3) Language and other control conventions inconsistent or based on different principles from one system to another, creating unnecessary learning barriers or other discouragements to cross usage. (Ibid., 10–11)

The conception of the virtual user as a knowledge worker who shares core processes with others in an augmented intelligence workshop allowed a "coordinated set of user interfaces principles" to be introduced in the development of NLS. While each specialty within the workshop or within a specialized application might have its own specific vocabulary and commands, a consistent language and control structure could be made available throughout the system. The user who learned to employ this structure for a specialized core activity also would "learn to use additional functions by increasing vocabulary" (ibid., 11). Engelbart later remembered his basic thinking in the following fashion:

> For any such application program, there are two facets: an interface process and the actual process that does the substantive work—two different parts. Let's think about them as two distinct but related design issues. For instance, I don't want the smart programmer who knows all about how this program works internally to think that he's the one to tell the world how to interface with it. By 1968 we had begun evolving the programming language so that it was different for each part, and we could actually think and design for [the] two separate modules. . . . The next step was to ask, Why, for each different application package, should you have a different front end? Front ends should be universal things . . . to serve multiple (or all) applications for the user. So our language ideas were evolving to handle this approach. (Engelbart, quoted in Goldberg 1988, 221)

NLS was designed as a collection of what we would think of today as applications (then called "subsystems") for given functions. When the user went inside these subsystems, there was a collection of commands, most of them character-stroke commands. These commands were input as chords on the keyset. Certain kinds of commands did certain kinds of things no matter where you were. They were consistent throughout the whole system, although some other commands were specific to certain subsystems.

The problem with this vision was not with the vision itself, which has been realized in many forms, from the graphical user interface and the architecture it shares with specific program interfaces to the linking of computers into networks. The problem was that it relied, for its implementation, on practices that, while by definition were assumed to be familiar to the reflexive virtual user that Engelbart and his lab were contemplating, also were radically at odds with the incorporating practices regnant in the world of real users. On the basis of the virtual user they had constructed, Engelbart and his crew were developing what is known as a modal interface, and real users were accustomed to working modelessly.

A mode is a particular state of a system. In a stick-shift car, for example, one can change gears only when the pedal is down, that is, when the car and its clutch are in a certain mode. In computing, most early text-editing systems had at least two modes: an input mode, in which the user could type new symbols, and an edit mode, in which the same symbols would trigger commands. For instance, in the input mode, hitting the "d" key would input a "d." In the edit mode, it would send the Delete command.

The architecture of NLS multiplied such discrete states or modes into so many exclusive conditions of the user's activity. To tap into the functionality of a given command, the user needed to establish a certain configuration of preliminary commands to put the system in a specific mode in which the needed command was available. In such a system, the user had to memorize where he or she was in the hierarchy of commands and modes. The interface was a kind of maze, often requiring backtracking to access new functions and commands.

The mouse and the chord keyset were devoted to the material interface process, and learning to use them was supposed to lead to a considerable increase in the speed of the interaction, since it would proceed through the incorporation of the commands and the architecture in the body of the user. For Engelbart, this somesthetic process was the core of the interface, thereby transforming the two devices into "wings" allowing the user to "fly" through the maze of the system (Engelbart 1992). In this representation, the mouse and the chord keyset were prosthetic extensions of the body of the user. But it is not difficult to see how such a user could come to view an input device called a "mouse" ironically. The modal architecture could make its user into a mouse in a maze.

As Larry Tesler, one of the most important researchers at Xerox PARC, began to see in 1973, modal interfaces were at odds with existing practices, and Engelbart's virtual user was in an important way different from potential real users:

> It started . . . when I began work . . . on the design of interactive systems to be used by office workers for document preparation. My observations of secretaries learning to use the text editors of that era soon convinced me that my beloved computers were, in fact, unfriendly monsters, and that their sharpest fangs were the ever-present modes. The most common question asked by new users, at least as often as "How do I do this?," was "How do I get out of this mode?" (Tesler 1981, 90)

As reflexive users, however, most of Engelbart's colleagues accepted the premise of the modal interface, and they have reported to me that the chord keyset did not raise special problems for them. Some of them told me that they learned to use it in a couple of hours, and that the results were remarkable: "To see somebody who really knew how to use the system, it was pretty amazing. Even if you knew ahead of time what they were going to do, you could not follow what they were doing. It was going that fast" (Andrews 1996). The learning was incremental and based on practice with the device: if you could spend a couple of hours learning it to get proficient enough to start using it, then you could get good at it.

By defining the virtual user reflexively, as programmers much like themselves, the knowledge workers at the ARC lab had been led into technological implementations that were supposed to be part of a coevolutionary transformation of humans and machines, but that threatened instead to become an evolutionary dead end. That may not necessarily be surprising. At the time, Engelbart was still very much the outsider, isolated at SRI and struggling to express his "crusade" in a way that would be both comprehensible and attractive to his coworkers.

Engelbart's vision made his laboratory an incubator for ideas, a place where cutting-edge work could be done, and this attracted young people with the same visionary bent. This emphasis on vision and the relative young age of most of the "knowledge workers" ended up creating a growing community of "misfit system builders" prone to "maverick and innovative thinking that usually go together" (ibid.). Using it as a model for a community of virtual users, however, was not, perhaps, the most realistic way to proceed.

Engelbart, however, was not interested in accommodating people's existing work practices in his conception of the virtual user. The design of the interface combining the chord keyset and mouse was intended to produce a scaling effect, producing a qualitative transformation in people and their practices by means of the quantitative increases in speed that experienced users actually had achieved. It was this goal that drove the whole concept of the interface— and making the design serve the end of coevolutionary transformation was the complete opposite of the idea of making the system simple to learn and use. For Engelbart, the modal nature of NLS wasn't a problem, it was one of its central features.

████████████

CHAPTER FIVE

SRI and the oN-Line System

I don't know who invented water, but it wasn't a fish.   — ALAN KAY

The beginning of the construction of the personal interface at SRI started with the process of staffing the laboratory, which grew between 1964 and 1967, to reach a peak of approximately thirty people. The evolution of funding first through NASA and then through ARPA-IPTO (mostly thanks to Robert Taylor) permitted such an evolution. The staffing process occurred in tune with the growing achievements of the laboratory:

> For a while it was hard, until '65 and '66 when we started getting some that were really accomplished. Then we started to get guys fresh out of school who really had lots of experience and were going to graduate school and really wanted to learn about everything—a few people like that. . . . It was hard until we started getting stuff on the screen that was really unique. . . . So by the time we got to that point and started bringing people in, there was an excitement and a difference that could start attracting better people. . . . People had friends and they would call. People would show up. (Engelbart 1996)

Bill English was the first to join the laboratory, at the beginning of 1964. He received his M.S. at Stanford in 1962, in engineering, and he had come to know Engelbart through his work in magnetic core memory. Approximately at the same time, Dave Hopper and Roger Bates joined the group. English and Bates worked on the hardware and were mostly responsible for the implementation of the mouse, while Hopper was working on software. Young people like Don Andrews felt that "exciting stuff" was carried out at ARC. For most of them, "even then it was apparent that Doug's vision was beyond what people could do today and tomorrow" (Andrews 1996).

Such a staff did not fit in the SRI organization at all, and Engelbart soon experienced growing problems with SRI management. While the usual practice at SRI was to sell approximately 80 percent of the time to agencies making funding grants and to spend the rest of the time writing new funding proposals, Engelbart concentrated on his vision and allocated all of his resources to the project, without spending any of his funding on overhead:

> There was this sort of negative aura about stubborn, uncooperative me and my lab. I just got a hopeless feeling about trying to communicate to any of them [SRI management people] what was different in what I was trying to do. . . . That drags up all kinds of indigestion-producing things. . . . I was immersed in my own dream about things. I was really naive about a lot of the world, about management issues and problems that they had to face. I really didn't pay enough attention to the communications and to the basic everyday politics of trying to make sure that people understood or that you were putting on a good image. . . . The whole structure of what they [other labs at SRI] were doing was so different that right at the outset it makes it very hard to compare. Here I had this long-term perception and dream and went on to pursue it, and my picture was that I was getting the money and I was hiring people who would help me pursue it. (Engelbart 1996)

As Engelbart said, "people would show up." The connections to the laboratory occurred according to both friendship and professional networks. At a time when there was no such thing as an established community in computer science, but when this community first was structuring itself thanks to the then-emerging ARPA-IPTO efforts, the Bay Area, and especially the Stanford and Berkeley campuses, seemed the place to be for many young people aspiring to a career in computing on the West Coast.

That atmosphere of innovation was what attracted some of the first students to join Engelbart's laboratory from the University of Washington, for example. Jeff Rulifson started in Engelbart's laboratory in January 1966, thanks to a connection to the laboratory via Chuck Kirkley, a close friend of Rulifson's at the University of Washington. Kirkley had been working for Engelbart as a consultant in 1965, then had gone back to the University of Washington and convinced Rulifson and later Andrews to join the laboratory. Another friend from the University of Washington, Elton Hay, was also working for Engelbart at that time. Rulifson was chief system programmer while he was an undergraduate, although the University of Washington had no computer science department at the time. He went to the 1965 Fall Joint Computer Conference of the American Federation of Information Processing Societies in Las Vegas where he met the Project GENIE people (Lampson, Deutsch, Pirtle) and Engelbart and English (via Kirkley). Although Engelbart did not have anything operational at that point, Rulifson got very excited by this meeting. He hung out for three days with them and did not go to anything else at the conference. He then flew back to SRI with Engelbart and called his wife to announce to her that they were moving to California (Rulifson 1996).

At that point (early 1966) the CDC 160A, a small, 12-bit minicomputer, and the CDC 3100, a 24-bit minicomputer, were operational in Engelbart's laboratory. Butler Lampson and Peter Deutsch, then students at UC Berkeley (where it was Deutsch's sophomore year), had come to the laboratory the summer before as interns and had produced a lot of code. Jeff Rulifson's job was to bring up the first real display-based system on the CDC 3100, a batch system that was shared with other people at SRI. Everything was written from scratch, including the very first on-line editor.

Don Andrews, another ex-undergraduate student from the University of Washington, also joined Engelbart's group in October 1966 while he was in his second year of graduate school at Stanford in the Computer Science Department. The CDC 3100 was one of the very first advanced interactive systems, but it was an off-line system and thus unsuitable for the networked core knowledge workshop that Engelbart envisioned. The user would sit at a Model 33 teletypewriter, and the programs and data processed in batches were stored on tape. Together, Jeff Rulifson and Don Andrews redesigned the CDC 3100 system, its file structure and the MOL procedures for manipulating its file structure. MOL was a subset of a C-like language that was created in the laboratory. Don Andrews wrote the compiler.

In total, I have been able to count 133 people that worked for, or were closely related to ARC. In 1969–70 the laboratory had a total staff of 32 people, including 25 full-time staff members. (See the Appendix for a complete list.) These are the people who provided Engelbart with a realization of his earliest model of the user as an intelligence or knowledge worker. To Engelbart, his staff of "professionals" (hardware and software engineers) and "clerks" represented the first level of his bootstrap community. He gave much thought to the practical organization of the work and kept a close eye on the social dynamics at work in the laboratory. In his mind, the laboratory was as much a social as a technological experiment.

The spatial organization of the laboratory was unusual for the time: everybody had a private office, but all the work was done in a bullpen area, a common space (the terminals were movable, etc.). Engelbart believed that open space fosters communication, and he organized the space according to his own conception of "social ergonomics." Even if some of Engelbart's staff shared the feeling that "it was both exhilarating and absolutely maddening to work in such an environment" (Wallace 1996), most would have agreed with Jeff Rulifson's expression of the overall atmosphere of the laboratory: "People on board knew, deep in their hearts, that something very serious was going on . . . that they were doing something that was going to change the world. But the amazing thing is how much unrecognized it was outside" (Rulifson 1996). The nature, and especially the consequences of Engelbart's conception of his lab as itself part of his crusade, as also a social experiment, however, were not at first all that apparent. As one of the staff members told me, "from 1962 up to 1969 or 1970, they were just so busy building the stuff that Doug did not get the chance to screw around" with the social side of the experimentation (Wallace 1996). Much of that time, they were building NLS.

BUILDING NLS, 1966–1968

In mid-1967, thanks to renewed support from ARPA-IPTO (a new grant of $565,500 for equipment) and especially from its then-director, Robert Taylor, the laboratory acquired its first time-sharing computer, an SDS 940 from Scientific Data Systems of El Segundo, California. The 30-day acceptance period for the computer began on July 5, 1967.[1] The 940 operating system had been designed and implemented in 1965 by the Project GENIE at UC Berkeley, whose staff included Butler Lampson and Peter Deutsch. The design of this system proved crucial for the building of NLS. Even though they never worked directly for Engelbart at ARC, Lampson and his colleagues created the hardware that allowed Engelbart to implement NLS at ARC. Central to their contributions was the development of paging techniques for memory addresses that allowed time-sharing by multiple users in a way that permitted Engelbart to realize his vision of the core knowledge workshop. These innovations made it possible to realize his goal of users working cooperatively over a network of computer terminals.

Time Sharing and the Core Knowledge Workshop

As I have said earlier, both Butler Lampson and Peter Deutsch had been summer interns at ARC in 1965, where they had worked for Engelbart with Bill English, Roger Bates, Dave Hopper, and Elton Hay, who was on board as a consultant. At that time, ARC was moving from using the CDC 160A, their first computer, to the 24-bit CDC 3100, but both were single-user computers. Peter Deutsch's task was to build programming tools for the CDC 3100, a complete semi-interactive assembly-language programming environment. Butler Lampson had built a SNOBAL system for Project GENIE, and Engelbart had decided that it was what he needed for programming part of NLS on the CDC 3100. This code was never used as such (some reported to me that it never was operational), but it started a relationship that would prove to be crucial for the building of NLS.

Butler Lampson was born in 1943 in Washington, D.C. He did his undergraduate studies at Harvard (B.A. in physics), where he met Peter Deutsch, and many of the people working on Project MAC there, the Machine Aided Cognition and/or Multiple Access Computer. He joined Project GENIE at UC Berkeley in late 1964 after his graduation from Harvard, when he enrolled in the Ph.D. program in physics. At that time, Peter Deutsch was a freshman at Berkeley who had just started working at Project GENIE. Chuck Thacker, another influential member of the project team, arrived at Project GENIE at the beginning of 1967 (he also graduated with his B.A. in physics from Berkeley in 1967). The hardware was done by Melvin W. Pirtle, a staff member who, along with Wayne Lichtenberger, an associate professor, was in charge of the project on a daily basis. Professors Harry Huskey and David Evans were officially in charge of the project as IPTO contractors.

Project GENIE had been running for approximately a year at that time, with a grant from ARPA to develop a time-sharing system. It was conceived by Licklider as a smaller-scale counterpart to Project MAC. It corresponded to the second step in Licklider's ARPA-IPTO goals: moving toward the creation of a time-sharing industry. (The first goal was "to actually learn how to do it.") The program was intended to overcome the general feeling of reluctance about time sharing in the emerging computing industry in the late 1960's:[2]

> Manufacturers were extremely skeptical about the commercial market for time sharing . . . this was not something that the mainstream customers understood, it was this crazy thing that ARPA had been sponsoring, and it was the government had a lot of money to piss away . . . yes, if the government insisted on giving you money to do this crazy thing the government wanted to do, maybe they would take some of it, but they did not really think that you could sell a lot of these machines and make money. So they were very very reluctant to get into this business. (Lampson 1997)

For realizing this goal, a system like CTSS, the Compatible Time-Sharing System, which had been designed and implemented on an IBM 7090 modified for time sharing at the MIT Computation Center by Fernando J. Corbató and his staff, was "totally useless": nobody could afford to make another one.

CTSS, whose system allowed 21 teletype users, had become operational in May 1963. It was radically innovative work and provided the standard for further time-sharing systems (Wildes and Lindgren 1986, 345). At the same time that CTSS was developed, in early 1962, J. C. R. Licklider, then vice president of Bolt, Beranek, and Newman, John McCarthy, Edward Fredkin, and Sheldon Boilen were the principal investigators in the development of another influential time-sharing system on the East Coast.[3] These two systems, developed and implemented before Project GENIE even started, provided the innovative references for the work that afterward went on there. But it was the engineering optimization effort that was special at Project GENIE. According to the objectives stated by Licklider, Lampson says:

> Our goal, which was actually achieved, was to take a solidly designed off the shelf computer and make modifications to it that were small enough that it would be possible subsequently to persuade a manufacturer to sell that system. And that's what they did. It was fairly hard to persuade them [Scientific Data Systems] to do it, but in fact 50 or 60 of those machines were sold. They were the first general purpose time-sharing machines that you could actually buy. (Lampson 1997)

Thus, Project GENIE proved to be a very successful enterprise. The "solidly designed off the shelf computer" they chose was the SDS 930, a batch-processing computer. Their SDS 930 was delivered in September 1964, and the new time-sharing operating system prototype, the 940, was operational in April 1965 and was demonstrated at the AFIPS Fall Joint Computer Conference in Las Vegas in November of the same year (Lichtenberger and Pirtle, 1965).[4] The memory system had a unique variable-priority access system that was the subject of Mel Pirtle's Ph.D. thesis. The system software was all written in a C-like language that they invented for the purpose, based on another C-like language that they had developed at Project GENIE. They also wrote a compiler for it.

Here again, the representation of the virtual user of the SDS 940 was reflexively based on its designers' experiences as users of earlier systems. Most of them were in their twenties at that time and had had opportunities to use earlier single-user "interactive computers" such as the TX-0 and the TX-2. Peter Deutsch, for instance, was famous for his "hacks" on the TX-0 at MIT when he was thirteen years old (Levy 1984a, 30–31). This "generational thing" was crucial. Like Ivan Sutherland, Peter Deutsch, Butler Lampson (and also Alan Kay and Larry Tesler) were all Baby Boomers, the first generation to grow up with computers, the first personal users, working and playing on huge multi-million-dollar computers as if they were their own:[5]

> The SDS 940 was a system that actually came out more or less the way we anticipated . . . we had a fair sense from experience with machines like the TX-2 and CTSS and so on . . . we had a pretty fair sense of the kind of things that a person sitting at a character-oriented terminal connected to a reasonable size computer with a file system could accomplish . . . you know, everything ranging from word processing, document production, scientific computing, a whole set of general-purpose programming and application tasks. The goal of our project, as I said, was to make it feasible to do those things on a substantially cheaper machine. So I think for the most part, that system did not involve a lot of significant innovation in the relationship between the user and the machine. It was more a technology

exercise to show how you could redo the implementation and get the same effect for much less money. (Lampson 1997)

One thing that was distinctive about this user interface was the strong emphasis on trying to make the system as interactive as possible. In Butler Lampson's words, "In the 940 system, we tried pretty hard to preserve one of the characteristics of the 'not personal' personal computers of the day, like the TX-2 or the PDP-1, which was that because the user's program was always running on the bare hardware on these systems, you could interact with every character" (Lampson 1997).

This is what Lampson referred to as "a character-oriented terminal," an early model of interactivity developed on the earliest machines constructed on the East Coast that differed from later, statement-based systems. On the TX-2 or the PDP-1, since there was only one user at a time, all the computing power was always available to the user. The operating system, the program managing the input and output devices, was minimal, and the interaction with the user was quasi-instantaneous. In the other early time-sharing systems such as the CTSS, on the other hand, because the computing power was shared among different users, each had to issue commands to the computer. It was thus easier to implement a model of interaction in which the computer would react to statements typed at the on-screen prompt in the manner that became widely disseminated with the advent of DOS, creating a "dialogue" between the user and the system.

The decision to use a character-based model of interactivity for a time-sharing system required a serious effort to develop the requisite hardware in order to reinvent and reimplement the earlier model of the single-user computer as exemplified by the TX-2 as a time-sharing system on the SDS 930. According to Butler Lampson, this was a consequence of the technological state of the art of the time, when "there was this very strong symbiosis between what you could do in hardware and what you could do in software, because typically the hardware that you could buy off the shelf was hopelessly inadequate in some major way" (Lampson 1997).

The major contribution of the Project GENIE engineering optimization effort consisted in retrofitting the SDS 930 to install a memory-paging technique for multiple users addressing the computer's memory. In order to have a working time-shared system, you need some way to share the memory of the physical computer among the different time-sharing users. Project GENIE was one of the first to use the paging technique that was invented by the people who built the Atlas computer in England. This technique simulates a distinct address space for each user and then materializes pieces of those address spaces using the physical memory that is available. That is done in units called "pages." CTSS and the earliest time sharing systems did not use paging, but anything that was implemented after 1963 adopted this technique in one form or another.[6] On the 930, this was mainly implemented by Melvin Pirtle.

The paging capability on the 940 later proved crucial for Engelbart's purpose because it enabled him to allow each of his ten or so users to run a fairly complicated program. In addition to making it possible to give each user an individual address space, paging also offered the possibility to store the program only once in the physical memory. That, too, was crucial for Engelbart's purpose, because in his design, every user would be using the core knowledge workshop, that is, would be running NLS. It was very important to him to be able to share all the code of NLS among all the different users, unlike many applications in time sharing, where the notion was that everybody would run a different program. Moreover, the relative cheapness and reliability of the SDS 940 was also important, since Engelbart did not have much money to spend on hardware.

One member of ARC insisted on the importance of paged memory for creating NLS: "The whole file system and the whole way NLS really worked inside . . . was all based on the single feature that was both on the 940 and the PDP-10, which was 'copy on write.' You'd map all the pages in it [the memory] and if you actually wrote into one page, the underlying hardware automatically copied that page and fixed the maps" (Wallace 1996). This copy-on-write "hack" meant that the page would remain shared when "read" or "execute" references were made to it, and if a process tried to write to it, a copy would be made and the process map adjusted to contain the copy.[7] This hack made the paging technique even more efficient and was part of the legacy of Project GENIE's work.[8]

Interfacing with NLS

Memory paging laid the foundation for creating a system of networked personal workstations, but it required further innovations from Engelbart and his crew at SRI to materialize his vision of a personal user interface for NLS. This required overcoming the shortcomings of existing technology. There were two main ways to interface with NLS, through teletypes, for the purpose of communications over the ARPANET, and through display terminals or consoles in the "special device channel."

The teletype terminal, a distant offspring of research in type printing for telegraphy, had been the standard interface for time-sharing systems since the early 1960's. It was basically a typewriter transformed for telegraphy input and printing, accurately described by Steven Levy as "a typewriter converted for tank warfare, its bottom anchored in a military gray housing" (Levy 1984a, 28). As John McCarthy recollected:

> My first attempts to do something about time sharing was in the fall of 1957, when I came to the MIT Computation Center on a Sloan Foundation fellowship from Dartmouth College. It was immediately clear to me that the time-sharing IBM 704 would require some kind of interrupt system. I was very shy of proposing hardware modifications, especially as I didn't understand electronics well enough to read the logic diagrams. Therefore, I proposed the minimal hardware modification I could think of. This involved installing a relay so that the 704 could be put into trapping mode by an external signal. It was also proposed to connect the sense switches on the console in parallel with relays that could be operated by a Flexowriter [a kind of teletype based on an IBM typewriter].[9]

The Flexowriter, a teletypewriter made by a company called Friden, could punch paper tape or type the contents of a paper tape.[10] Its use in connection with computing originated with the Whirlwind project in the mid-1950's. Doug Ross reported at the History of Personal Workstations Conference that direct keyboard input on a Flexowriter "was not used for Whirlwind until Summer of 1956, which led to later time-sharing projects at MIT" (1988, 83–87). He found the origin of this use in a memo dated December 14, 1955, where he wrote:

> To augment the Manual Intervention facilities mentioned above, it is suggested that the Flexowriter presently attached to the AFAC 1103 computer be connected to act as both a keyboard input and mechanical tape reader input device. This method is considered preferable to the purchase of special keyboard input devices at this time because, again, it should be very inexpensive, and will give considerably more flexibility than any commercially available keyboard of another type.

Flexowriters and other types of teletypewriters (or printers) were indeed used on most time-sharing projects of the early 1960's, but very often against the better judgment of teletype manufacturers. Kenneth Olsen, for instance, still considers that their decision at Digital Equipment Corporation (DEC) to use a teletype printer in the design of the PDP-8 was a "gamble," and perhaps even a gamble of major significance for the development of personal computing:

> We also standardized a teletype printer which was not designed for continuous use. We very formally made the decision that we would gamble on that teletype and work hard to make it reliable enough for continuous use. That one gamble, and that one small success, probably was a key part in the introduction of mini-computers and personal computers. . . . Printers before that were very expensive. You could not have an inexpensive machine just because of the printer. That machine was quite an expensive, very cleverly designed, but made for offices where

it was used intermittently. Computer users are continuously at a very high rate [sic]. And so it was a very important development in the history of computers from our point of view. It was a bold thing. Because teletype [manufacturers] said, don't do it. It's not designed for this. In time they appreciated it and together we made it reliable enough for this use.[11]

Robert M. Fano remembered that he participated in a delegation that attempted to persuade the Teletype Company, in Texas, to produce a teletypewriter with lower-case letters (the Flexowriter only had upper-case printing): "Well, the chief engineer was rather opposed to it. He said we made a market survey and the market survey came in saying that nobody knew what to do with lower-case characters, so we're inclined not to do that." [12] According to Fano, the delegation eventually managed to persuade them, leading to the release of the Teletype models 37 and 33. The latter soon became the standard teletype terminal for time sharing, still remembered to this day in the rather cryptic TTY33 acronym well known to most UNIX users.

Engelbart and his staff started with the Teletype Model 33 terminals for the NLS, moved to the faster Model 37 (with an operating speed of fifteen characters per second compared to ten for the Model 33), and later switched to the General Electric Terminet-300 and the Computer Transceiver Systems Execuport, a portable terminal.

However, by the mid-1960's, the teletype interface was already considered as a technology worth replacing for interactive graphic work with computers. In his agenda-setting study for the Council of Library Resources, J. C. R. Licklider (1965, 98) saw in the "familiar teletype-writer" the first instance of his "typewriter schema." Everything he had to say about the teletypewriter characterized it implicitly as an alternative to be transcended: "compared to most other man-computer communication devices, it is rugged, reliable, and inexpensive. However, it has no lower-case letters, it is slow, and it has a strange 'touch' for anyone accustomed to office typewriters."

Even if they still relied mostly on the teletype interface model, most time-sharing projects of the early 1960's attempted to introduce some sort of display for interactive graphic computing work. For Wes Clark, it became clear at that time that "you have to be oriented toward interactive use of machines before you realize that CRT display is the one essential thing that you must have for wide-band presentation of information, no matter what else you have" (quoted in Goldberg 1988, 398). "I tried to point out that it was going to be very hard to do real-time work, or even non-real-time, but display work, for displays. You see, the image in mind was that of a typewriter, or teletype machine actually, as the principal means of interacting with this time-sharing machine. And that's very limited" (Clark 1990).

Engelbart also understood in the early 1960's that the Flexowriter was a thing of the past. Since the earliest expression of his Framework for the Augmentation of Human Intellect, he had insisted on the seminal importance of visualization: "another significant step toward harnessing the biologically evolved mental capabilities in pursuit of comprehension and problem solutions came with the development of the means for externalizing some of the symbol-manipulation activity, particularly in graphical representation" (Engelbart 1962, 23). In the 1969 implementation of the system, the teletype interface, called TODAS for "Typewriter-Oriented Documentation-Aid System," was actually considered as a "typewriter counterpart to NLS," not part of the oN-Line System itself. Even if it shared most of the capabilities of NLS, it lacked an analog cursor device—the mouse. It was simply designed and implemented in order to provide access to the ARPANET Network Information Center hosted in the laboratory.

The teletype terminal certainly was not an adequate interface device for implementing the character-based model of interactivity that the SDS 940 made possible, since it relied on a statement-based model of the dialogue between the computer and the user. In the progressive implementation of the system, the teletype interface thus took a secondary role from the start, restricted to the execution of tasks that did not require the rapid display response of NLS. A second kind of interface, called "the special devices channel," assumed the principal role. It was basically a display-terminals system organized around NLS consoles equipped with CRT displays and the input devices that had been designed in the laboratory, the chord keyset and the mouse.

The earliest models of single-user computers, the TX-o, the TX-2, and the PDP-1, all had point-plotting displays ten inches by ten inches and 1K point resolution (Bell 1988, 29–30). A point-plotting (or writing) display is a cathode ray tube (CRT) display whose electron gun creates images by lighting up individual points specified by a software instruction. The origin of such a display in computing dated back to the Whirlwind radar project, which was "first and far ahead in its visual display facilities. One form of information output was a cathode ray tube capable of plotting computed results on airspace maps" (Redmond and Smith 1980, 216).

During the 1960's, point-plotting displays were progressively replaced by line-drawing displays (also known as calligraphic or vector displays) whose electron guns were now able to draw entire lines from two points. Newman (1976, 1321) reported that "the majority of interactive graphic techniques developed since the early 1960s have been oriented towards the display of line drawings . . . the engineering designer, who has become one of the more common users of interactive graphics, is accustomed to line drawings." Both point-plotting and line-drawing displays did not require huge computer memory, since the computer needed to maintain only a display list instead of storing a picture of the screen. To appear "flicker-free"[13] the displayed picture needed to be refreshed (that is, repeated) on a regular basis, but the memory required was relatively small, since the information to be displayed could be stored in any order.[14] However, these displays were equipped with complex internal electronics (mostly for the display generator)[15] and were usually built to individual specifications, which made their price usually quite high, between fifteen and twenty thousand dollars for a display of average size and resolution.[16] Here is how a member of the Stanford Artificial Intelligence Laboratory remembers their display problem in the mid 1960's:

> When our PDP-6 computer arrived in June 1966 it came with a number of Model 33 Teletypes. We had wanted to use displays instead but encountered substantial delays in getting them. You couldn't buy displays "off the shelf" in those days—you had to draw up a specification and get someone to design a system that would meet it. We tried to interest Philco in bidding, given that they had built some displays in 1964 that worked pretty well in the Zeus time-sharing system at Stanford, but Philco was no longer convinced that displays would "catch on" as part of computer systems. After another manufacturer contracted to build the displays, then defaulted, we finally got Information International Inc. (III) to build some.[17]

However, by the mid-1960's, another kind of display started to be considered for computer output: video monitors, that is, TV sets without the reception circuitry. These displays, also commonly called raster-scan displays, produce the picture by scanning the screen sequentially, row by row, at a regular interval. All the while, the gun fires at only those points on the rows (called picture elements, or pixels) that need to be illuminated. Although they were mass-produced for the television industry and therefore relatively cheap in comparison with vector displays, raster-scan displays had the disadvantage of requiring a significantly larger memory to operate them: the display file for a raster-scanned CRT must normally be arranged as a matrix of intensity values stored in a large frame buffer. The information in a frame buffer is basically an unencoded video image and therefore requires a bulky and costly amount of memory. In the mid-1960's, the price of computer memory made it rather expensive. In 1976, William Newman still considered that "there are three main problems associated with raster-scan CRT displays: the size and cost of the frame buffer, scan conversion, and quantization effects. At present none of these problems has a satisfactory solution" (1323).

One solution that would decrease the size and cost of the frame buffer was to encode the video image in order to save space in the memory. This required designing and implementing a display processor capable of processing the information and passing it to the CRT. Newman (1976, 1323) considered that the most attractive design solution "was to encode the image as the original line segments contained in its definition. We then have a display file identical in form to that used with a line-drawing CRT and can employ the same software." However, this solution created a new problem: the processor should be designed to be able to perform the scan conversion in real time for interactive use: "to pass over the display file 25 or 30 times a second, converting it into a video signal" (ibid.). Again, in 1976, Newman considered that "no complete solution to the real-time scan conversion problem has been demonstrated to date."

By 1967, then, Engelbart was facing a display dilemma: neither the vector displays nor the raster-scan displays could be a solution, assuming his level of funding. The first were too expensive, since the twelve displays he needed would have eaten more than half of his hardware budget, and the second required too much memory for the frame buffers and were therefore also too expensive.[18] Engelbart and his staff finally decided to use raster-scan displays,[19] but in quite an original way to solve the real-time scan conversion problem. The solution they designed was more in the tradition of *bricolage*—tinkering—than of state-of-the-art engineering (see Figure 5-1):

> The computer and display drivers time-shared their attention among multiple, 5-inch CRTs, which happened to be the most economical size for a given percentage of screen resolution. In front of each CRT we added a commercial, high-quality video camera, mounted with a light shroud over the camera lens and CRT screen. The resulting video signal, amplified and piped out to our laboratory, drove the video monitors that were our workstation displays. Two display generators, each driving up to eight CRTs, implemented with vacuum-tube technology, were both bulky and very costly. It took one and a half people to keep those things running all the time. The stroke-generated characters and vector graphics allowed us to have flexible, mixed text and graphic document presentations. (Engelbart 1988, 197–98)

Their solution was clever, if not straightforward. The twelve five-inch CRTs that they used were line-drawing displays, but the final outputs at the terminals were presented on video monitors, via a closed-circuit television network. Thus, whatever was shown on the line-drawing displays was also shown on the video monitors. This setup had several advantages, starting with its low cost (approximately fifty-five hundred dollars per console). But it also gave the opportunity to display and combine information from a variety of sources, including live video feeds. Moreover, for purposes of collaboration, the information from one of the five line-drawing CRTs could be fed to various video monitors at the same time. Engelbart and his staff therefore in this way managed to

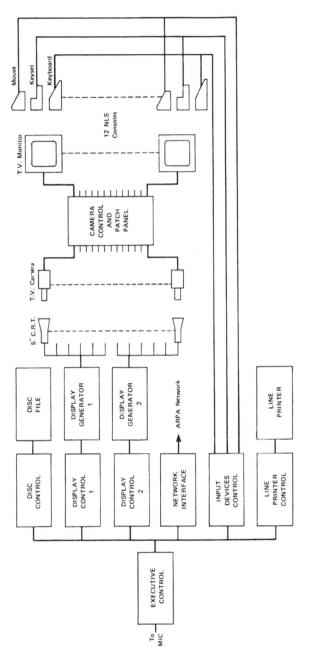

Figure 5-1. The Special Devices Channel. Source: Engelbart et al. (1970), p. 7.

extend the principles of time-sharing: in NLS, not only was the computer time-shared, but so were the displays.

Of course, these video monitors were not really integrated as computer displays in NLS, and some of their original qualities or potentials were lost, since they simply mirrored information presented on line-drawing displays. For instance, Stan Augarten reports that:

> Because of their technical characteristics, video monitors and line-drawing displays produced different images. The latter excelled at line drawings, or stick figures, but did a poor job with solid surfaces, depicting them only in the form of a series of parallel lines, which took a long time to draw (and redraw, if the image had to be changed). But its imagery was sharp and clear. A video monitor, on the other hand, didn't do a good job with line drawings, but excelled at solid surfaces, representing them in the form of swaths of pixels that were automatically illuminated (or not) with every sweep of the electron gun. Moreover, it did a great job with certain special effects . . . such as overlapping surfaces, which were all but unattainable on line-drawing displays. All in all, video monitors produced the best graphics.[20]

At the time, when computer terminals were equipped with displays, they tended to look like military or industrial equipment, showing very few concern for user comfort: "most consoles looked like submarine battle stations, with the CRT and keyboard fixed in position in metallic cabinets painted in institutional gray or beige" (Augarten, forthcoming). As they had with the invention of the pointing device, Engelbart and his staff explored the various opportunities for a more ergonomic design, which their display system and the separation of the input devices made possible. This concern for the design of the consoles translated into innovative designs such as the "yoga workstation," which required the user to sit or kneel on the floor, and the "Herman Miller console," which instead of a desk, used a tray appended to the user's chair to hold the chord keyset, keyboard, and mouse (see Figure 5-2).

The Beginning of Computerized Hypertext

Engelbart considered NLS to be principally "a highly sophisticated text-manipulation system," not a text-entry device. As such, graphical capability was a crucial element of the system for visualization purposes, although it was restricted to simple line drawings. "Continuous use of NLS to store ideas, study them, relate them structurally, and cross-reference them results in a superior organization of ideas and a greater ability to manipulate them further for special purposes, as the need arises—whether the 'ideas' are expressed as natural language, as data, as programming, or as graphic information" (Engelbart et al. 1970, 184). The emphasis once again was on relations, on structure, as

Figure 5-2.   The Herman Miller NLS Console. Source: Engelbart et al. (1970), p. 137.

in Bateson's formulation of what you see when you look at your hand. And the result was the invention of hypertext, linked relations between texts.

A "text" (or a "file") simply is any structured set of character strings (or "statements"). All text handled in NLS was in "structured-statement" form, a hierarchical arrangement of these character strings resembling a conventional outline. Each statement possessed identifying features such as a "number" (position and level in the structure) and a "signature," a line of text giving the initials of the user who created the statement and the time and date when it was done. The hierarchical structure applied to text manipulation resulted from the overall conception of the augmentation process, justified as such since the earliest statement of the project in the 1962 report:

> The fundamental principle used in building sophisticated capabilities from the basic capabilities is structuring—the special type of structuring (which we have termed synergetic) in which the organization of a group of elements produces an

effect greater than the mere addition of their individual effects. . . . We are developing a growing awareness of the significant and pervasive nature of such structure within every physical and conceptual thing we inspect, where the hierarchical form seems almost universally present as stemming from successive levels of such organization. (31)

In the same document, Engelbart defined five types of structure: mental structures, concept structures, symbol structures, process structures, and physical structures.

A mental structure is "the internal organization of conscious and unconscious mental images, associations, or concepts (or whatever it is that is organized in the human mind)" (ibid., 32).

A concept structure is the conscious and communicable part of a mental structure, where the concepts are seen as the "medium of exchange," "tools that can be grasped and used by the mental mechanisms." A concept structure, which can be consciously developed and displayed, can be presented to an individual "in such a way that it is mapped into a corresponding mental structure which provides the basis for the individual's 'comprehending' behavior" (ibid., 34). It is important to notice that concept structures are both conscious (reflexive) and devoted to communicative processes. We find here the expression of Engelbart's opposition between "associative" and "connective" processes, an opposition, as we have seen, that is deeply buried in his conception of language: "A natural language provides its user with a ready-made structure of concepts that establishes a basic mental structure, and that allows relatively flexible, general-purpose concept structuring. Our concept of 'language' as one of the most basic means for augmenting the human intellect embraces all of the concept structuring which the human may make use of" (ibid., 35).

A symbol structure is a representation of a concept structure. In the project of using a computerized system as a means for augmenting the human intellect, the basic idea was that with such a system, the human user no longer is forced to think in terms of the symbol structure that is stored in the system, as in print media, but can focus instead on the dynamic generation and transformations of displayed symbol structures.

A process structure, finally, is a complex organization of some of the fundamental components in such a human-machine interaction within what Engelbart called the Human using Language, Artifact, Methodology, in which he is Trained system:

> The fundamental entities that are being structured . . . seem to be what we would call processes, where the *most basic* of physical processes . . . appear to be the hierarchical base. There are dynamic electro-optical-mechanical processes associated with the function of our artifacts, as well as metabolic, sensory, motor, and

cognitive processes of the human, which we find to be relatively fundamental components within the structure of our H-LAM/T system—and each of these seems truly to be ultimately based (to our degree of understanding) upon the above mentioned basic physical processes. (Ibid., 31)

The process structures belong to a higher level, providing for the manipulation of concept and symbol structures in the service of the mental structures. As Engelbart put it, "whereas concept structuring and symbol structuring together represent the language component of our augmentation means, process structuring represents the methodology component" (ibid., 38).

Finally, a physical structure represents the artifact component of the augmentation system, insofar as its actual physical construction is concerned.

These different types of structures were considered mutually dependent, and their interdependence was seen as cyclic and regenerative. Although Engelbart never described them as such, one can safely infer that feedback mechanisms actually organized their relationships: "significant improvement in symbol-structure manipulation through better process structuring (initially perhaps through much better artifacts) should enable us to develop improvements in concept and mental-structure manipulations that can in turn enable us to organize and execute symbol-manipulation processes of increased power" (ibid., 39). This was precisely the kind of synergistic coevolution of human mental capabilities and technological "artifacts" that the founders of cybernetics hoped would take place.

As we have seen, the reference to "manipulations" is far from incidental in this description. Text manipulation involved three basic types of activity by the NLS user: composition, study, and modification. Composition was simply the creation of new text material as content for a file, and its basic command was "Insert." The mouse served as a pointer to indicate where the statement was to be inserted, and a CA [Command Accept] button (either on the mouse or on the keyboard) sent the instruction to refresh the display with the new statement included. Study, however, employed the most powerful features of the system, with operations such as jumping, view control, content analysis, indexing, and linking. Modification referred to the use of NLS editing commands such as Insert, Delete, Move, and Copy.

Here is a short description of the main NLS Study commands. It illustrates not only how the chord keyset, mouse, and, when necessary, the keyboard worked in NLS, but how NLS allowed users to create and modify links between texts—to produce hypertext relations, not just texts.

JUMPING: NLS files were described as early as 1962 as "scrolls," and the process of moving from one point in the scroll to another was called "jumping." Its basic command, issued from the chord keyset, was "Jump to Item" (ji). The mouse pointer was again active in the process, since after chording "ji" on the keyset, the user pointed with the mouse to any statement. Most of the Jump commands in the system, such as Jump to Successor, Jump to Predecessor, Jump to Up, referred to the hierarchical structure of the text.

VIEW CONTROL: The user was able to control the level of statements displayed in the hierarchical structure of the file ("level control"), but also the number of lines displayed per statement ("line truncation"). Level and truncation controls were designed so that the necessary specifications may be made with only one or two strokes of the keyboard or keyset.

CONTENT ANALYSIS: NLS allowed automatic searching of a file for statements satisfying content patterns specified by the user: content patterns could range from simple (e.g. the occurrence of a given character string) to complex (e.g. the order of occurrence of two or more strings).

INDEXING: Statements were indexed by named statements written in a special format (a keyword statement). Statement retrieval was fairly highly developed: the user could select keywords with the pointer and weight them (between 1 and 10) according to his or her interest. (When no weight was specified, the system assumed a weight of 1.) The system would then score statements according to these preferences and display nonzero scores in decreasing order.

LINKING: An NLS "link" was a character string in a statement indicating a cross-reference to another statement, whether in the same file or not. The text of the link was readable by both the user and the machine. The command "Jump to Link," followed by the selection of the link, displayed the reference statement. The use of interfile links allowed NLS users to construct large linked structures made of many files: hypertext.

THE MOTHER OF ALL DEMOS

By 1968, with the combination of the chord keyset, mouse, CRT display, and hypertext, Engelbart and his crew at SRI had concrete results to show the world. "By 1968 we had a marvelous system," Engelbart later recalled. "A few people would come and visit us, but we didn't seem to be getting the type of general interest that I expected." As a result, "I was looking for a better way to show people, so we took an immense risk and applied for a special session at the ACM/IEEE-Computer Society Fall Joint Computer Conference in San Francisco in December 1968"—the conference of the Association for Computing Machinery and the Institution of Electrical and Electronics Engineers.

Every book devoted to personal computing at some point reports this famous presentation, which Douglas Engelbart and his staff offered at the AFIPS Fall Joint Computer Conference on December 9, 1968, later dubbed "the mother of all demos" by Andries van Dam, as indeed it was, with the likes of Microsoft and Apple eventually building on the basis of innovations first introduced there. Reiterating such a pervasive generic formula in accounts of the history of the personal computer seems obligatory. In place of yet another recitation of one of the computer community's foundational tribal tales, however, here is Engelbart's own account of the first time that the personal interface was publicly presented to the world outside of the laboratory, assembled from recollections published in 1988 (Engelbart 1988, 202–6)[21] and an oral history interview that Henry Lowood and Judy Adams conducted in 1987 (Engelbart 1996).[22]

> What do you do to get people going on augmentation kinds of things? Maybe what we needed to do was to show a lot of people at once. I got the picture of what we could potentially do. What equipment can do for you, how you can put it together, has always been easy for me to perceive conceptually. I started out in engineering because I was interested in a lot of that. So I could picture how we could put it on. I also had this adventurous sense of, "Well, let's try it, then." It fairly often ended in disaster. Anyway, I just tried it out. I found out that the conference was going to be in San Francisco, so it was something we could do. I made an appeal to the people who were organizing the program. It was fortunately quite a ways ahead. The conference would be in December and I started out sometime in March, or maybe earlier, which was a good thing because, boy, they were very hesitant about this. They sent people twice to a site visit. One time they were going to cancel it all because one of them had been out at Langley, and somebody had proudly shown them a system that could already do what we were talking about. I said, "God, that's our system." Since they had sponsored us, we kept them a copy of it, and they every once in a while showed people (laughter). So they finally bought it.
>
> . . . Okay, we could do it. Actually, it really never would have flown if it weren't for Bill English. Somehow he's in his element just to go arrange things. Pretty soon, we had video channels from the telephone company all arranged. They'll come and put up the roof and before you know it, there is a co-ax running down, and they'll be up in the skylight with four dishes on a truck. We needed this video projector, and I knew they had one too. I think that year we rented it from some outfit in New York. They had to fly it out and a man to run it. The telephone installers were putting the other in. Pretty soon, by the conference time, I went up there and everyone was swarming all over. They had to make some special equipment, and a guy did it for us. We soon got the cameras out and I was working on how to script it and talking to everybody about how it ran. We knew we could get the video controls so we actually bought them. They weren't terribly expensive. There were boxes that you run two videos in and you turn some knobs and you can fade one in and out. With another one you can have the video coming in and you can have a horizontal line that divides them or a vertical line or a corner, in switching. It was pretty easy to see we could make a control station that could run

it. Bill had worked a lot as a stage manager or production manager for theatrical groups and he loved to do that, so he just made a very natural guy to sit there. He built a platform in the back with all this gear. The four different video signals came in and he would mix them and project them. (Engelbart 1996)

We set up to give an on-line presentation using a video projector pointing at a 20-foot screen. Brooks Hall is a large auditorium, and that video projector could put up our display images so you could read them easily from up in the balcony. The video projector we rented (built by a Swiss company, Eidophor) used a high-intensity projection lamp whose light was modulated by a thin film of oil, which in turn was modulated by the video signal. On the right side of the stage, I sat at our Herman Miller console.

We set up a folding screen as a backdrop behind me. I saw the same image on my workstation screen there as was projected for the audience to see.

We built special electronics that picked up the control inputs from my mouse, keyset, and keyboard and piped them down to SRI over a telephone hookup. We leased two microwave lines up from our laboratory in SRI, roughly 30 miles. It took two additional antennas on the roof at SRI, four more on a truck up on Sky-line Boulevard, and two on the roof of the conference center. It cost money—running that video projector, and getting people to help us do all of that, cost money; making the special I/O cost money; and leveraging special remote-presentation technology on top of our advanced, developmental laboratory technology created extra risk—and I was using research money. (Engelbart 1988)

That was a big part of the gamble. I was pretty sure that we were getting money from NASA and ARPA. It was a time when you are just sort of on a good friends basis and you interact. How much should I tell them? I got far enough so that they got the idea of what I was trying to do and they were essentially telling me, "Maybe it's better that you don't tell us" (laughs). They could get in trouble if the thing crashed or if somebody really complained about it. We had a lot of research money going into it and I knew that if it really crashed or if somebody really complained, there could be enough trouble that it could blow the whole program; they would have to cut me off and black ball us because we had misused government research money. I really wanted to protect the sponsors, so I would say that they didn't know. So that's the tacit agreement we had between us. As a matter of fact, I think Bill English never did let me see how much it really cost. (laughs) But I know it was on the order of $10–15,000, which would be like $50,000 nowadays, or the equivalent. A lot of money. (Engelbart 1996)

Back in our lab, we dismantled a number of the display units in our display system, so that we could use the cameras in San Francisco and SRI. We borrowed a few tripods and got some extra people to be camera people. One of our friends, Stewart Brand, who was at that time working on his first Whole Earth Catalog, helped as well. So it was really a group project; there were about 17 of us.

On my console on the stage, there was a camera mounted that caught my face. Another camera, mounted overhead, looked down on the workstation controls. In the back of the room, Bill English controlled use of these two video signals as well as the two video signals coming up from SRI that could bring either camera or computer video. Bill could select any of these four video images with optional mixing and frame splitting. We had an intercom that allowed him to direct the action of the people in our lab at SRI who were generating computer images or handling the cameras sending the video up from SRI.

We didn't use any specially made system capabilities; we were just using NLS the way it worked at that time. It had mixed text and graphics, so we could use those to display and represent things. We had the agenda in NLS, and we could run different parts and show diagrams; we could do things as examples. So it was a mix of things: here's the script and stuff to tell you about, and here's the way it runs; we could also bring other display screens or faces, from our SRI lab, in and out on the screen. At that time we firmly imagined that this was the way future conferences would be run.

"We could do screen splitting," Engelbart recalled. "This was the beginning of our demonstrating ways of structuring ideas." Asked "Was that common, that sort of presentation?" Engelbart replied "Absolutely not. No precedent we ever heard of" (Engelbart 1988, 1996). Instead, it became a precedent itself.

We wanted to show how the mouse works. The projected video showed Don Andrews controlling a cursor from our SRI laboratory by moving his mouse around. The superimposed video image of the display screen showed that the cursor would follow it exactly to show how the wheels worked. Remember, this was 1968—the first public appearance of a mouse. I could also show how the simultaneous use of mouse and keyset worked in such a way that the audience could watch my hands in the lower window and see the computer action in the upper window.

Then we brought in Jeff Rulifson to tell about how the software works. At the same time, his face could be brought in and out behind the display image that he was working with, demonstrating NLS's power for working with very explicitly structured software. He showed graphical diagrams that were embedded in the source-code documentation. During Jeff's presentation, Bill English brought the picture from a laboratory camera that caught the view of Jeff's keyset operation as he was manipulating his demonstration images—unconscious and unhurried—a nice way to show the fluid speed offered by combined mouse and keyset use.

Toward the end, we also showed that we could cut a "hole" in the screen and see Bill Paxton's face from SRI. For the computer-display part of the screen, we could switch back and forth between his work and mine; and we could also switch which of us was controlling all of this. (Engelbart 1988)

Engelbart and his crew put so much effort into creating this pathbreaking presentation that "we didn't think about giving out special publicity. A lot of people said, 'Oh God, we would have liked to have seen it!' I don't know how many people were there, but somebody has commented that there are more people who have claimed to have been there than were! . . . I keep being surprised when I run across people who really were there" (Engelbart 1996).

The auditorium "probably could have held 2,000 to 3,000 people," but Engelbart was too busy to notice how many came to the demonstration. "And nervous as hell," he added:

> So much swung on it and we had all this special technology to get it working in the first place. We had agreed that we would have some trial presentations captured on film, and that we would have that film standing by. But we just knew how the hell would we find our place in that film if everything crashed halfway into it? Every one we did was different. (Ibid.)

The effect of the demonstration, profound as it was, took a long time to register and ultimately eluded Engelbart's control.

> Some people came rushing up onto the stage, one in particular, Butler Lampson, who is a superbly intelligent guy, and at that time was at Berkeley, in '68. I don't think Xerox PARC started until the '70s and he moved down to the PARC. But anyway, he was just so excited and that was something pretty great. So I knew that there was a lot of enthusiastic reception about it right there. But basically I really was hoping that it would get other people seriously started in things like this, too, but it just didn't.
>
> . . . How much the sponsors over the next eight years kept supporting us because of the presentation, I have no way of knowing. But everyone else was still using linear files for years and years. The ideas of links were beyond them. I'm still very puzzled why there was sort of the dark ages for ten years where it just wasn't a topic. (Ibid.)

It was certainly quite an inspiring moment for a few people. Some people even joined the laboratory because of this presentation. This was the case for Charles Irby: "I went to that particular session not knowing what to expect, and I was completely blown away. I happened to find afterward the particular person who seemed to be in charge technically; his name was Bill English. I cornered him and said, 'This is really nifty and I think I can help you.' And he said, 'We're looking for a few good men. Why don't you come by?'" (quoted in Goldberg 1988, 185). The public debut of NLS, however, also proved to be the apogee of the ARC lab's augmentation project. Once Engelbart's crusade —and his crusaders—began to have to deal with the less committed and more skeptical computer users outside the lab, the fate of the project became increasingly less promising.

Engelbart lecturing at SRI, ca. 1970. (Courtesy of the Bootstrap Institute and Stanford University Special Collections)

(*above*) Mouse and chord keyset on the Herman Miller NLS console. (Courtesy of the Bootstrap Institute and Stanford University Special Collections)

(*below*) Early computer-assisted meeting, ca. 1968. Don Andrews sits at left. (Courtesy of the Bootstrap Institute and Stanford University Special Collections)

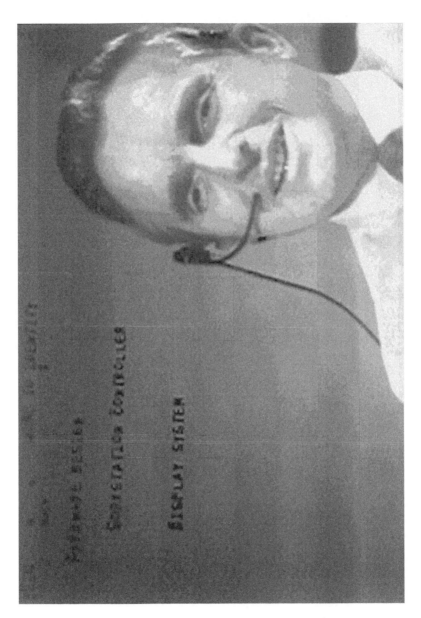

Screen shot of Engelbart during the 1968 Fall Joint Computer Conference demo, San Francisco. (Courtesy of Stanford University Special Collections)

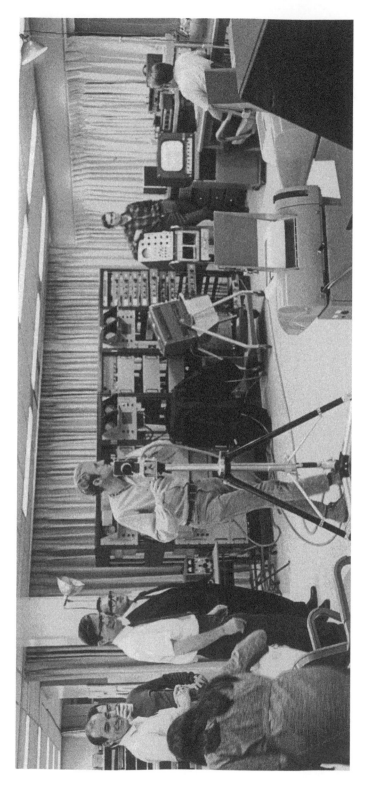

Behind the scenes at the 1968 Fall Joint Computer Conference demo. *Foreground*: Mary Church (back to camera). *Background, left to right*: Martin Hardy, David Evans, Ed Van de Reit, Dan Lynch (?), Stewart Brand (at the camera), Roger Bates, and Bill English (sitting). (Courtesy of the Bootstrap Institute and Stanford University Special Collections)

(*above*) Early NLS display set-up, using 5-inch CRTs and video cameras. (Courtesy of the Bootstrap Institute and Stanford University Special Collections)

(*below*) ARC workspace, ca. 1970. (Courtesy of the Bootstrap Institute and Stanford University Special Collections)

The yoga workstation was one of several experimental designs (ca. 1968).
(Courtesy of the Bootstrap Institute and Stanford University Special Collections)

Bill English, 1992. (Photo by the author)

Ted Nelson, 1993. (Photo by the author)

The Arrival of the Real User and the Beginning of the End

The History of every major Galactic Civilization tends to pass through three distinct and recognizable phases, those of Survival, Inquiry and Sophistication, otherwise known as the How, Why and Where phases. For instance, the first phase is characterized by the question How can we eat? the second by the question Why do we eat? and the third by the question Where shall we have lunch?

— D O U G L A S   A D A M S , *The Hitchhiker's Guide to the Galaxy*

Engelbart's work was based on the premise that computers would be able to perform as powerful prostheses, coevolving with their users to enable new modes of creative thought, communication, and collaboration providing they could be made to manipulate the symbols that human beings manipulate. The core of this anticipated coevolution was based on the notion of bootstrapping, considered as a coadaptive learning experience in which ease of use was not among the principal design criteria.

Augmentation research thus was essentially reflexive, research on research, and was aimed at "developing the means of extracting real user value from these computer aids, and then demonstrating the way we work and how we get this value" (Engelbart 1968, 23). Bootstrapping was more than the "use what you design" principle because it was centred on a representation of the user that was virtual and self-reflexive at first, but that developed along with the technology in successive iterative circles.

The 1968 San Francisco demonstration therefore was more than just a way to "get other people seriously started in things like this, too." From the point of view of the methodology underlying the Framework for the Augmentation of the Human Intellect, it was also a way to initiate the next bootstrapping circle, a strategic leap enrolling the next community of users in the crusade, those outside of the laboratory. For many observers and actors of that period, however, the demonstration instead has marked the acme of the evolution of the laboratory and the beginning of the end. The laboratory slowly went downhill afterward. The various figures of the user envisioned and realized after 1968 throw a powerful light on some of the reasons for that decline.

Problems with the relation between the envisioned virtual user of NLS and its real users first began to become apparent within the environment of the laboratory itself. The programmers of the system, in the course of their bootstrapping work, their coevolution with the system, had to adapt themselves to it—to become the kind of programmers the system demanded. They became something different than simply generic "programmers." As it was indeed intended to do, the technology inflected their identities, although not always in intended ways.

Certainly the most important of these adaptations came from the high emphasis that was put on structure in the system:

> The idea of structured text was very important. Using the structure was important to being able to clip in and flying that way . . . it forces people to change the way they do things. Many people don't like that way, they like a sort of free-floating approach to writing . . . many people never structure, some people after the fact. I personally like it: I use it all the time. . . . Anything I write, I do the structured outline and start filling in the words . . . It has to do with personal style more than anything. (English 1992)

The decision to emphasize structure indeed affected the way people wrote, be it text, in the literal sense of the term, or programs, a quite unique kind of writing. Engelbart had decided that all text in NLS should be presented in a structured form. This decision affected his staff in both a personal and a collective way. This feature of the system was deeply inscribed in its design, and some of the staff members felt strongly about it:

> One of the things that I think was a real limitation on the system was . . . the insistence on hierarchical information structures in documents. It's a powerful organizing methodology, but it's also limiting for certain kinds of things, and it caused this certain kind of stilted writing style, because you knew that people would cut out levels of detail and view it in different ways than you had originally sequentially wrote it. So it did affect the way people structured information, which is not all negative. (Irby 1992)

For Engelbart, "structuring conventions" were needed because of the complexity of the potential relationship made possible by a nonlinear structure of information. For him, the computer programmer, his first model of the user, ought to be a structured programmer. Everything that was produced in textual form in the laboratory, code or any form of "text," was to be structured and shaped by and with the practice of interactive computer support.

This computer assistance, in turn, was itself conceived on the basis of a certain model of interactivity in mind. The coevolution of NLS (the technological system) and its users (its designers and their community) had to start with some decisions (conventions), and these conventions, in Engelbart's mind, were constitutive of the community, as a community of practice. The realization of this vision rapidly shifted the actual focus of project from individuals working collaboratively in the core knowledge workshop created by NLS to groups working collaboratively *on* NLS. Nowadays, Engelbart's work is usually recognized as one of the very early models for computer-supported collaborative work (Grudin 1994; Taylor, Gurd, and Bardini 1997), but at the time of the design and implementation of NLS, the users collaborating were the designers of the system for collaboration, and the doubled emphasis on collaboration tended to subordinate the individual to the group or team, as this excerpt from an early report witnesses:

> One usage trend that has become evident during this period is a tendency for staff members who are working on a common problem to gather around an NLS console so as to have on-line access as a group to the working files that they are using in common. Even when working individually, group members frequently sit at neighboring consoles so as to be able to converse about related tasks in progress.
>
> This trend has been reflected, through bootstrapping, as an evolution of ARC goals from the augmentation of individuals to the augmentation of task-oriented teams. (Engelbart et al. 1970, 2–3)

Because of the highly original nature of the system, some of the practices also were unique to the ARC community and tended to separate that community from outsiders. Some astonished visitors reported that the ARC members had strange codes or habits, such as being able to communicate in a "weird" sign language. Some staff members occasionally communicated across the distance of the room by showing the fingers position of a specific chord entry on the keyset.[1]

One cement of this community of practice was the use of on-line computer support at a time when this was still pretty much arcane. This had quite important consequences on the ways Engelbart's crew worked as programmers. In Donald Wallace's words, they became "addicts" to a certain way of working, "users" in a less benign sense of the word:

> For a programmer, structured editors are wonderful. You can clip the views and only see the procedures, you can open up and see comments. In fact we got so addicted to it that we structured our code in such a way that you could not read the

goddamn stuff unless. . . . So for a person who lessoned into the NLS culture, this was an impediment to understand the code. . . . So we were seriously addicts with this stuff. So when we left NLS . . . the fix that we needed was the structured editor and structured editors have actually come back . . . the only thing that hasn't come back is clipped views and contents clipped views, and those would be very useful things . . . but you have to sort of have some NLS lineage or blood or something to even think about doing that. (Wallace 1996)

The effect of the technology on its users within the ARC laboratory at SRI thus was to draw them together into a group differentiated from other programmers outside, an elite cadre for Engelbart's crusade, to be sure, but also a group that courted isolation by its very commitment to that technology.

With the successive addition of real users outside the laboratory and the translation of the vision of the virtual user prompted by their addition, on the other hand, the qualities of the technology itself began to come into question among outsiders. Seen out of its context of origin—in which both the user and the technology were conceived in an interaction that, via the bootstrapping methodology, was considered as the object of inquiry—what was a necessity became a norm. The user, once tentatively and initially envisioned as a generic "computer person," now had to be one, and technology that was constructed to work in the laboratory became problematic in its operation when made available to a larger-scale network. The move to a larger set of users exemplified what was ironically enough a basic premise of Engelbart's vision: past a certain level, a quantitative change in scale becomes a qualitative change. But in this case, it was a change for the worse.

At the end of the 1960's, Engelbart thought that he had found in the ARPA community the next bootstrapping community, the converts to his crusade he was looking for when he created the 1968 San Francisco demonstration. Thanks to funding from Licklider at ARPA since 1963, Engelbart himself belonged to the community of contractors that formed the proto-network of innovators in personal computing. He found there a living expression of his "knowledge worker" model.[2] In 1967, following Larry Roberts's urging,[3] Engelbart volunteered to establish the ARPA Network Information Center (NIC) inside his SRI laboratory. Two major phenomena happened at that time. From the fifteen to twenty members at the ARC laboratory, the number of people involved in using the NLS technology over ARPANET, the predecessor of the Internet, expanded to an on-line community of approximately two hundred users at its peak. As Alan Kay puts it, after harping on the single string of his crusade for several years,

Engelbart, for better or for worse, was trying to make a violin. . . . Most of us at PARC had got to be users of NLS. Once you were willing to put in the effort, it

took about ten hours of really exercising the thing to get good. *If* you were willing to put in these ten hours of effort, and also you had to be a little bit adaptable.
You had to be a computer person. (Kay 1992)

Thus, the knowledge worker again became a "computer person," but this time
it was not the sort of computer person who had undergone the transformations of the bootstrapping enterprise within the community that had evolved
within the ARC lab at SRI, but real computer users. What had seemed the most
"natural" group of people to start augmenting now became the only group
augmented: the knowledge worker became a generic programmer again.

The growth of the number of potential users via the ARPANET quickly re-
vealed what some considered to be technological flaws in the system:

> The communication, in our lab [ARC at SRI], was very high performance . . . a
> quarter second response was not at all unusual. When you try to do that through
> 56 Kb lines going through several hops of the ARPA network, suddenly, it's slow.
> And so, I think that even though the fundamental ideas were appreciated by a lot
> of people in the community, the actual practicality of using it on a day-to-day ba-
> sis through the ARPANET just wasn't very good. (Irby 1992)

With this extended base of real users who were also working computer programmers, the adequacy of the hardware basis of the augmentation system began to be brought into question at a time when parallel evolutions in the technology made Engelbart's technological choices seem questionable. Since the
implementation of the augmentation framework in the mid-1960's, a new factor had changed the technological equation: the massive availability of relatively low-cost minicomputers, which made time sharing by users on large
mainframe computers less of a necessity. Users had less need to connect with one
central computer if they wanted to work either collaboratively or individually.

Since its beginning, the relationship between Engelbart and Licklider had
been one of mutual self-interest. Engelbart would get funded, and Licklider
would see the evolution of time sharing, one of his pet ideas. Originally, the
choice of a time-sharing system to support NLS had seemed natural and inevitable, since time sharing seemed to hold a potential second to none at the
time. But now that choice no longer was beyond question and indeed seemed
to be the source of fundamental problems, as became apparent when NLS began to be used in a different setting, the ARPA network. There, time sharing
didn't work very well. Yet Engelbart remained committed to it as the basis of
both NLS and the realization of his vision of collaborative work that NLS had
become. The results quickly proved devastating.

In a sort of a radical technodeterminist interpretation of what happened,
Alan Kay confirmed: "The destiny of Engelbart's system was not to run on
time sharing, because when you get a reasonable number of users on it you

start to get killed by response time problems and other things, and what's great about the tool goes away. . . . Engelbart did not want to go to minicomputers. He wanted to stay with time sharing, he wanted to put his system on PDP 10, move off the [SDS] 940." In Kay's view, the technology to which Engelbart had committed his project and his people was becoming outdated. "The result of that was in the summer of 1971, a whole bunch of Engelbart people just left, maybe half of the project. . . . NLS never recovered, it never happened further" (Kay 1992). Many of them left for Xerox PARC, taking "what's great about the tool" with them.

There is of course another way to look at the same problem, one that looks at the actors at this turning point and at their representations of their roles in the technological process, not at the process itself. This interpretation also emerged in my interviews, for example in the interview of Bill English, the co-inventor of the mouse at SRI in 1964 and also one of the first to move to Xerox PARC in 1971:

> There was kind of a schism developing between Doug and the rest of the staff in 1970. . . . NLS was pretty well working. . . . All these people who left were system builders. I was a system builder. And if it was done, if it was stable and we had finished it, what were we doing there? . . . It wasn't learning on the track how to build better systems. From the standpoint of both the hardware and the software, it was time to do it again. In this business you can't today continually evolve something. You've got to every now and then just say OK, let's start over . . . throw away, absolutely . . . that was the philosophy at PARC. That was never the philosophy at SRI. Strictly evolutionary. And again, I have to say that was driven by economics as much as anything, but Doug held on to that pretty tenaciously. When other people might want to make a break and do something different. Start again, that was certainly the PARC philosophy. Butler Lampson believed that. (English 1992)

To Douglas Engelbart, the justification of the decision to stick to the time-sharing technology was consistent with the augmentation framework. One goal of the project was iterative learning, the accumulated results of bootstrapping, and a major change in the hardware basis of the system would have meant the end of the learning experience as previously realized. In this sense, the system never could be finished, and the learning experience was endless. The emphasis on learning made the philosophy necessarily "evolutionary." The system was a whole, and you could not just take parts of it.

Charles Irby, another important member of the ARC team, proposed another explanation for the sociotechnical limits of bootstrapping and gave an alternative interpretation of the decision of some members of the team to move to Xerox PARC:

There is an interesting phenomenon here, that happens over and over again in this and I'm sure other industries. You develop something early on, way ahead of the infrastructure, basically. And as a result, you have to build a lot of the infrastructure yourself. And in so doing, you tailor the infrastructure to support what you are trying to do very well. And so you end up with a nice high-performance system that's kind of in synch with the psychomotor capability of the human being. And then you say, OK, that's fine, now we want to start rolling this up. But the infrastructure is not there. So you start making compromises in how you implemented this in order to, for example, use commercially available hardware, or commercially available communication networks. And all of this infrastructure that you originally built, that was tailored to what you wanted to do and hence delivered very good performance, starts diminishing. And you end up with a system that may deliver the functionality, but has lost the performance characteristics that are important to its successful use. Or it's lost reliability or some other aspect. And you end up delivering something that in your mind still has the inherent value because you have this legacy of experience with it, but to the new person walking up to it, seems very slow and clumsy. (1992)

Whatever the individual reasons might have been, at the beginning of the 1970's some of the most important members of the ARC team such as Bill English deserted the lab and decided to move ahead to the recently created Xerox Palo Alto Research Center. Figure 6-1 depicts these transfers and represents schematically the network of key people involved in the development of personal computing.

At Xerox PARC, the ARC renegades joined a group of some of the best computer scientists and designers of that period[4] and developed one of the first personal workstations, if not the first, the Alto. The first Alto was operational on April 1, 1973. It was principally the product of the vision of one man, Alan Kay. The Alto took Douglas Engelbart's innovations in a direction completely different from that envisioned by the Framework for the Augmentation of Human Intellect, a direction that ultimately led to the Apple computer and a much, much broader range of actual users.

FROM THE DYNABOOK TO THE ALTO

Alan Kay learned how to program computers in the Air Force in the early 1960's. He returned to college to study mathematics and in 1966 was admitted to the recently formed University of Utah graduate program in computer science. By 1969, Kay had both his Master's and Ph.D. from the University of Utah and an appointment as associate professor in the school's computer science department. In 1970, Kay spent a year as visiting lecturer at Stanford's Artificial Intelligence Laboratory, and Robert Taylor, after working for the

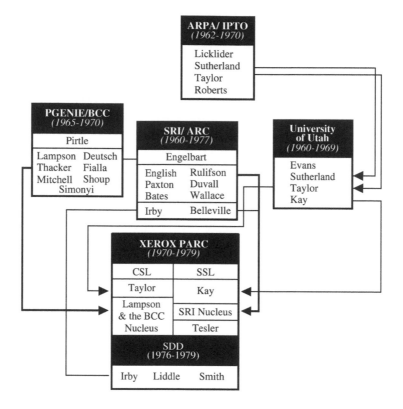

Figure 6-1. The Network That Developed the Personal Interface.

University of Utah for a couple of years, persuaded him to join the new Xerox Palo Alto Research Center, which he had been hired by George Pake to staff. After consulting for PARC for a while, Kay finally joined it in 1971 (Smith and Alexander 1988).

In his doctoral thesis, "The Reactive Engine," Kay had described a programming language and a computer called Flex. Flex would be

> an interactive tool which can aid in the visualization and realization of provocative notions. It must be simple enough so that one does not have to become a systems programmer (one who understands the arcane rites) to use it. It must be cheap enough to be owned (like a grand piano). It must do more than just be able to realize computable functions; it has to be able to form the abstractions in which the user deals. Flex is an idea debugger and, as such, it is hoped that it is also an idea media [sic]. (Kay 1969, 75)

At this stage, Flex encompassed hardware, software, and interface aspects. This representation evolved when Kay set up a research unit (the Learning

Figure 6-2. The Flex Machine. Self-Portrait, ca. 1968. Source: Kay (1993).

Research Group, LRG) within the System Science Laboratory of Xerox PARC (SSL). In the PARC scheme of things, SSL was in charge of creating user applications that operated on the hardware and software infrastructure base created by another PARC unit, the Computer Science Laboratory (CSL). In fact, SSL worked as a second computer lab inside PARC and corresponded to a broader strategy to seed SSL with Kay's influence to persuade PARC's management in the long run to reorganize and coordinate the resources of both laboratories (Smith and Alexander 1988, 71).

Following this strategy, Kay's Flex evolved both as a machine, the Dynabook, and as a language, Smalltalk. The Dynabook enriched the early vision of Flex on the basis of the computer as a medium: Kay described it as a "dynamic" medium "for creative thought . . . a self-contained knowledge manipulator in a portable package the size and shape of an ordinary notebook"— a notebook computer (Kay and Goldberg 1988 [1977]). Smalltalk took over the vision of Flex as a language accessible to nonexperts. But for the first time, it actually embodied a representation of a nonexpert user and gave that user an identity: it was a child.

From the very name of the language to the early applications of the system, such as a paint program, everything in Kay's "personal dynamic media" pointed to the child user. In a groundbreaking paper describing their efforts, Alan Kay and Adele Goldberg wrote:

> Considering children as the users radiates a compelling excitement when viewed from a number of different perspectives. First, the children really can write programs to do serious things. . . . Second, the kids love it! The interactive nature of

the dialogue, the fact that *they* are in control, the feeling that they are doing *real* things rather than play[ing] with toys or working out "assigned" problems, the pictorial and auditory nature of their results, all contribute to a tremendous sense of accomplishment to their existence. . . . Another interesting nugget was that children really need as much or more power than adults were willing to settle for when using a time-sharing system. The best that time-sharing has to offer is slow control of crude wire-frame green-tinted graphics and square-wave musical tones. The kids, on the other hand, are used to finger-paints, water colors, color television, real musical instruments, and records. If "the medium is the message," the message of low bandwidth time-sharing is "blah." (1988 [1977], 255–56)

Here began, in thought at least, a long series of Kay's experiments with children and computers, not to mention the ongoing vision of children as the most accomplished and demanding users of personal computers.

According to Alan Kay, PARC management refused support for his Dynabook project in the spring of 1972. But the idea was permanently in Kay's mind, and several months later, he managed to convince his colleagues at CSL, Butler Lampson and Chuck Thacker, especially, to build him "an interim Dynabook." Or, at least, that is the way it is represented in the journalistic historiography of the genesis of the personal computer. In fact, the Alto (the name of this "interim Dynabook" to be) was quite different from its never-born parent, the Dynabook. Instead, it corresponded to a further step in a chain of translations from Flex to the Alto.

This "interim Dynabook" resulted from the enrollment of Alan Kay's colleagues at PARC in his project and thus demonstrated a series of changes in the representation of the machine corresponding to the negotiations and interests of all these new actors in the game. Alan Kay acknowledged that when he said that it turned out to be "a vector sum of what Lampson wanted, what Thacker wanted, and what I wanted. . . . Lampson wanted a $500 PDP-10. . . . Thacker wanted a 10-times-faster Nova 800, and I wanted a machine that you can carry around and children could use" (quoted in Perry and Wallich 1985).

In this negotiation, one main feature of the Dynabook was lost: the Alto would not be portable. George Pake, a physicist and former provost of Washington University who had been hired in 1970 to establish and manage PARC, explained the reasons for this choice:

One major reason is that physical science has yet to generate the ideal affordable, low-power, light-weight rapid response display technology. Kay came to me on a number of occasions to plead for greater PARC investment in search of a new display technology. My response was that everyone had agreed for years that cathode-ray tube technology was too bulky and heavy, too expensive to build, and too extravagant in requirements for electric power. But until we had a really promising new idea, I did not see any sensible way to crank up PARC research toward a Dynabook display. Meanwhile, I said, there are many other research issues to be addressed—why not put aside the requirement for portability and see if you can configure a hardware-software system that is prototypical of Dynabook's workstation power? (Pake 1985)

In December 1972, Butler Lampson issued a lab-wide memorandum entitled "Why Alto" that described this new representation: "It would be nearly as powerful as the leading commercial minicomputer, include a remarkably rich display monitor, reside in a network of distributed machines, and, most important, be inexpensive enough for everyone to have his very own computer" (quoted in Smith and Alexander 1988, 85). In this memo, the representation of the personal computer was broadened, and Lampson coined a generic concept that had a bright future: "If our theories about the utility of cheap, powerful personal computers are correct," wrote Lampson, "we should be able to demonstrate them convincingly on Alto." If the new personal computer could be "nearly as powerful as the leading commercial minicomputer," there was a market for the personal computer "if it is inexpensive enough for everyone to own it."

In the process of developing such a computer, the central coevolutionary features of Engelbart's NLS, the chord keyset, with the demands it made on the user, faded into the background. It proved not to be "popular":

> The Alto keyboard was similar to that of a typewriter; it was not accidental that it lacked the cursor positioning keys and numeric keypad found on most personal computers today. In addition to the normal typing keys, it provided eight uncommitted keys that could be used by software as option or function keys. A five-finger keyset, which had been used successfully in Engelbart's NLS, was provided as an enhancement to the keyboard, but it required a trained operator for use, and never became popular as an input device. (Thacker 1988, 273)

The chord keyset was displaced by the easier to use "functional keys" or "uncommitted keys" of the Alto and many subsequent personal computers.[5]

The user envisioned for the Alto from the very beginning thus was not a programmer, but "everyone." However, "everyone" once again was first conceived reflexively, as a particular someone who was very much like an existing user of minicomputers, but someone who did not have the means to buy one of the costly minicomputers then available, such as the PDP-11 and the Nova 800. In other words, Lampson was claiming, a market for personal computers could be created from the minicomputer market if the product's cost was low enough to interest virtually anybody—below, say, the mythical $500 barrier.

The "utility of cheap, powerful personal computers," Lampson claimed, would be demonstrated if there was a "real user" who could manage to do something with it.

Demonstrating utility for a real user at Xerox PARC involved a return to bootstrapping and the reflexive definition of the user. Robert Taylor's formulation was simple and straightforward: "we use what we build." As Chuck Thacker, one of the most instrumental individuals in the creation of the Alto, put it:

> A strategy for carrying out work in experimental computer science was also adopted at this time. It was based on the idea that demonstrations of "toy" systems are insufficient to determine the worth of a system design. Instead, it is necessary to build *real* systems, and to use them in daily work to assess the validity of the underlying ideas and to understand the consequences of those ideas. When the designers and implementors are themselves the users, as was the case at PARC, and when the system is of general utility, such as an electronic mail system or a text editor, there is a powerful bootstrapping effect. (Ibid., 269, emphasis in the original)

Thus, the "bootstrapping philosophy" proposed by Douglas Engelbart at ARC during the 1960's ended up being put to use for very different ends than those envisioned by his crusade.[6]

To Engelbart, this appropriation of the bootstrapping methodology was a betrayal, and it masked a rejection of the main principle of the implementation of the augmentation framework: "I got a very very strong personal impression that the Xerox clan just totally rejected all that stuff. They take parts of the architecture, they take the mouse, they take the idea of the windows, all of that, but the rest of NLS they just rejected" (Engelbart 1992).

What they rejected was the coevolution of user and machine and the concomitant requirement that the user undergo the rigors of a learning process. Although Engelbart claimed that NLS was not designed exclusively for computer professionals, as we have seen, his first model of the user, the intelligence worker, found its expression in the staff of computer programmers that he assembled in the laboratory and in the community that developed there. The bootstrapping philosophy of design put a high emphasis on learning, and the system was designed and implemented accordingly. It made demands on its users, and Engelbart made no effort to make it "user-friendly."

> NLS is intended to be used on a regular, more or less full-time basis in a time-sharing environment, by users who are not necessarily computer professionals. The users are, however, assumed to be "trained" as opposed to "naive." Thus the system is not designed for extreme simplicity, nor for self-explanatory features, nor for compatibility with "formal" working procedures.
>
> Rather, it is assumed that the user has spent considerable time in learning the operation of the system, that he uses it for a major portion of his work, and that he consequently is willing to adapt his working procedures to exploit the possibilities of full-time, interactive computer assistance. (Engelbart et al. 1970, 173)

Engelbart put it this way when I interviewed him:

> What I feel is a very important thing is that the blind policy that it's got to be easy to learn is something that you say well for who? If it's for the first user, I say that's fine, but if that principle of design is welded in, and the provisions for the interface aren't adaptable to people as they want to learn to get more skills, so they can fly and maneuver better, then I say you're really doing your future a disservice. (Engelbart 1992)

The question of the ease of learning came to be translated later into the famous notion of "user-friendliness." For Engelbart, the ARC experience was a learning experience aiming at "augmenting" the user and was obviously at odds with a quest for user-friendly interfaces, or even, and more centrally, at odds with the research program of Artificial Intelligence. For Engelbart, PARC's decision to start over, using the bootstrapping process to develop user-friendliness, was equated with a rejection of the entire ARC experience and the central goal of the Framework for the Augmentation of the Human Intellect.

But the rejection in fact was not total. Most of my interviewees took part in setting up several ARC-PARC collaborative projects at the beginning of PARC in 1971.[7] In fact, some of the earliest members of the ARC laboratory to join PARC, Bill English and Bill Duvall in 1971, joined their efforts to create the PARC On Line Office System (POLOS) with the explicit purpose to implement NLS at PARC. The project was officially set up as a collaborative effort between the two institutions, and both Bill Paxton and Donald Wallace worked on the project from the SRI side before they, too, joined PARC.

Most of the PARC researchers agreed very early that the type of personal computing they wanted to explore could not just be done on a time-sharing machine: "you could prototype software that way but the future was in individual computers" (Deutsch 1996). The machine that came the closest to the specs that they wanted was the Data General Nova.[8] In a sense, the Nova served as a mental model for the scale of machine that later became the Alto. But in spite of this general agreement, there were quite a number of differences among them in respect to the best strategy to implement personal computing.

Bill English and the POLOS group first believed that the best way was to implement NLS or a subset of its functions was by setting up a network of Novas. The idea was to translate a time-sharing system such as the SDS 940 system or TENEX into a network of minicomputers in what they called a "migrating process design." The idea was to have a single application, the equivalent of the NLS core workshop, distributed over the network, with each individual machine in charge of a specific process, but all collaborating.

Robert Taylor also had brought to Xerox PARC the core group of engineers from the failing Berkeley Computer Corporation (BCC) in 1971, a company that Butler Lampson and his colleagues at Project GENIE had created when their work was done with the SDS 940 and when Xerox management, upon buying SDS, proved blind to the possibilities of time sharing.[9] Lampson joined PARC with seven other BCC people: Chuck Thacker, Peter Deutsch, Dick Shoup, Jim Mitchell, Ed Fialla, and Willie Sue Haugeland. Charles Simonyi came later, since he was going to school and was working for Pirtle at NASA Ames on the ILLIAC IV project. Mel Pirtle did not come, since he was wrapped up in closing BCC. Lampson and Roger Bates, another former member of ARC, designed a high-quality graphics-character generator to run the displays of the POLOS. However, the results of this design were not evaluated in the same way by the various researchers. For instance, Butler Lampson realized that "as time went on, it became very clear to us [the BCC people] that the system that they were putting together was going to be too clunky." Bill English and his colleagues could not agree with this assessment, since "they had plunged into this [project]." Lampson says they discovered after they had built the character generator that it was "painful to use" (Lampson 1997), and Peter Deutsch reported to me that POLOS "suffered from a combination of a sort of second-system syndrome and the fact that doing software on a network of microcomputers is just different from doing software on a time-sharing system. You had to do sharing in a very different way," and what would have been necessary "to replicate a . . . shared environment on a network of Altos, I don't think that any of us appreciated what that would take" (Deutsch 1996).

The project to implement NLS or parts of it at PARC was not dead yet, though. Bill Duvall, a former ARC member who had been very instrumental in POLOS, carried on with the implementation of a subset of NLS functions on a single Nova. This implementation was dubbed RCG, an acronym whose meaning is long lost now. But here again, the project was not necessarily considered a success by all, including by some of those who should have been the most sympathetic toward its goals. For example, Charles Irby, a former ARC member and later a leading researcher at PARC, recalled:

> The transfer of the technology was hampered a lot in my view, because Doug put so many constraints on what they could or couldn't do. I think [if] they'd . . . done a free flow of information, there would have been a much greater acceptance of it. But there was a prototype built of that technology at PARC by Bill Duvall, it was called UGH.[10] It only carried certain of the concepts forward, the simplest ones, basically the structured editing, outline editing, and file management, that was almost all there was in UGH. So all of the things having to do with the journal and tying and teleconferencing and integrating text and graphics and all that stuff was not part of the prototyping effort at Xerox. That was used by a small community and eventually disappeared. . . . It was initially implemented on a Data General

Nova. And then when the Alto was developed the prototype was also moved over to the Alto and there was also a small community of users.

The lack of agreement on the relative success of the various NLS implementations at PARC (POLOS, RCG, UGH) translated into a difficult climate inside Bill English's group, a part of CSL. According to Jeff Rulifson, who eventually had joined PARC after a short stay at the Stanford Artificial Intelligence Laboratory for his Ph.D., it created "a big split inside the group": Wallace, Duvall, and English on one side, and Larry Tesler and Rulifson on the other side. Tesler and Rulifson decided that "rather than pouring a lot of energy into building NLS over again, there were other interesting things to study" (Rulifson 1996). They wrote an internal Xerox paper describing what they called IT, for "Intuitive Typewriter." They decided that ease of use was important, and they realized that this was a "major schism with Engelbart." They finally decided to join efforts with the BCC nucleus and experiment with new interface designs on the Alto.

Under the influence of Butler Lampson, PARC added another principle to the bootstrapping design philosophy: "the one-hundred users ethic."

> Butler [Lampson] was pissed off at the bubble-gum-like stuff we had done in the 60's, including his own stuff. So when he came in, he sort of instituted a new ethic. It was basically that we would never build anything that isn't engineered for a hundred users. That was right at the edge. That was February 1971. . . . So when we decided to do the Alto, we had to build a hundred of them. . . . Butler was really incredible at this stuff, he really sort of forced everybody to be more real. (Kay 1992)

Forcing "everybody to be more real" was an accommodation to users as they are, not as they might be made to be, and combining it with the basic bootstrapping methodology spelled the end of the bootstrapping philosophy as envisioned by Douglas Engelbart. It meant tailoring the user interface to what the designers could find out about or imagine about how people actually do their work, not using the interface to force people to learn to do it in a new and better way. For his staff of "system builders" who moved to PARC, the 1970–75 period represented a transition between the implementation of the Framework for the Augmentation of Human Intellect via NLS and their first encounters and negotiations with "real users." The problem was to define what a "real user" could be, and the definition of what is "real" took on a very different meaning in the PARC context than it had at SRI.

SRI and ARC were research institutions; PARC was a research-and-development institution. The daily activities at the two institutions may have looked the same, but ARC was built on the idea of augmenting human intellect, while PARC was set up on the idea of developing a practical "architecture of information."

The idea of developing the architecture of information was subject to diverse interpretations during the 1970–75 period. Alan Kay could declare that "to make the stuff into products . . . wasn't the charter," while John Ellenby could say that he considered that "PARC's job is to develop the ideas on which we can produce a product scenario," and their colleagues could take positions all across the spectrum between those poles, from research to development. And as Charles Simonyi puts it, the bottom line was the "question of who we would be working with." In the end, however, the translation of the bootstrapping philosophy into a design principle defined by the hundred-user ethic was a first step toward defining PARC's activity not as research, but as product development.

This is clear from the nature of two different computer systems created at PARC during the 1970's: the Alto and the Star. The Alto was in effect the first personal computer. It looked like what we now expect of a personal computer: it was equipped with a bitmap display, a typewriterlike keyboard, and a mouse. Its display resolution was 606 pixels horizontally by 808 pixels vertically, and its cursor was "a small image, 16 pixels square whose contents and position could be controlled by software." The original Alto memory was 128 kilobytes of a main storage and a 2.5 megabyte cartridge disk. Its processor was microcoded and "shared between the emulation of a target instruction set and the servicing of up to fifteen additional fixed priority *tasks*, much of which were associated with the machine input-output devices" (Thacker 1988, 272–73). The Alto operating system was thus able to do multitasking. The original prototype of the Alto, introduced in April 1973, did not contain an Ethernet interface for networking, but it soon was equipped with one. Thacker reports that "Metcalfe and David Boggs worked on the network facilities during the summer and fall, and the prototype machines were exchanging packets by the end of 1973" (ibid., 279). The Alto was thus not just the first personal computer, but the first personal computer configured for distributed computing. But it was conceived and developed as a research project using the bootstrapping process to develop a more user-friendly machine "nearly as powerful as the leading commercial minicomputer" and "inexpensive enough for everyone to own it," with PARC researchers nevertheless the reflexively defined users.

By contrast, the 8010 "Star" computer system that Xerox officially introduced in April of 1981 was conceived of as a product from the start, designed as an "office information system" for the business world, bringing to ordinary users the personal distributed paradigm introduced with the Alto. Its main innovation, in this perspective, was the reorganization of the main characteristics of the Alto's graphic interface (windows, menus, buttons) under the umbrella of the "desktop metaphor." In the original memo introducing this meta-phor, on November 12, 1976, Dave Smith justified this decision as follows:

> The OIS [Office Information System] display environment is called a *desktop*. . . .
> A basic assumption in this note is that each user has his own personal OIS ma-chine and that a desktop is always (or nearly always) available on it. The principal motivation is to have the machine constantly ready to receive mail. A more ab-stract reason is that the OIS machine should be considered part of the office worker's resources, constantly available to him with its own identifiable network address, exactly like a telephone.

Although a specific microcoded processor was designed in-house for the Star workstation, the emphasis was put on software, and its designers actually con-sidered the Star more as "a body of software" than as a computer (Johnson et al., 23–24). They considered that "Alto served as a valuable prototype for Star. . . . Alto users have had several thousand work-years of experience with them over a period of eight years, making Alto perhaps the largest prototyp-ing effort in history" (quoted in ibid., 23).

The Alto thus was created by researchers as a tool they needed. The Star was created by developers as a product. The Alto was created in the research group within PARC, the Star was created by the System Development Division on the PARC campus. Charles Irby illustrates this point very clearly:

> There were two communities at Xerox. . . . The research community itself, while it included some people from SRI, included a much larger set of people from the general university environment or a few research labs. . . . They weren't very con-cerned with getting that out to the world at all. They were just really trying to work on a whole family of research topics, most of which didn't come to any-thing. . . . The second community was what later became the Office System Divi-sion and was originally called the System Development Division. That was the ef-fort founded by David Liddle, where he basically transitioned out of the research lab to form a group specifically focused on productizing, commercializing, creat-ing market-ready versions of some of these researches. . . . Basically, the environ-ment within SDD at that time was very much how do we take these raw ideas from these disparate groups that have no logical connections with each other and put them together into an integrated system that a user that has never been ex-posed to any of this stuff could actually apply it to useful business endeavors. . . . PARC is a location and is also an institution so people use the name interchange-ably for those two purposes, it's very confusing. . . . We [SDD] were colocated with the research center. (Irby 1992)

The Alto was created by young computer scientists coming from a university background (Alan Kay, Butler Lampson, Chuck Thacker). The Star was created by system architects from the computer industry, and especially by programmers brought in from Xerox Data Systems, the former Scientific Data Systems, after Xerox shut it down and incorporated it in SDD in 1977. It was directed by the second wave of people out of SRI (Charles Irby, Bob Belleville, etc.) (Johnson et al. 1989).

The Alto was first of all a necessary tool for the research people at PARC, but its development also was a bridge to a different conception of the user, from the programmer as reflexive user to "everyone," conceived as someone much like PARC researchers who would buy a minicomputer if it were affordable, finally to the nontechnical person as the potential user. Thus, the move was complete from the intellectual worker to the "naive user," although in the development of the Alto, both coexisted for a short time. But creating a user-friendly, commercially viable machine for "the avarage person" had beeen the goal from the start: "When we moved to PARC, we were at least thinking about the naive user. Xerox was a commercial company, and we were thinking we'd better build these systems so as the average person can use the technology. . . . I think the only model we had, again, were the people around us. Secretaries. We would look at the nontechnical people as the users" (English 1992).

By this point, the very utility of the bootstrapping methodology and the reflexive definition of the user were open to question: "in addition to limiting the expansion, it [bootstrapping] also forces a certain kind of myopia on you. Since you don't have users who have different viewpoints, different needs, coming in and criticizing what you've done, you just don't broaden it. As long as it's meeting your needs, as the bootstrap community, it's very hard to push it out" (Irby 1992). Taking its place at PARC was a methodology of interface design based on a "user model" and "task analysis." The result was a new set of principles for the design of the user interface[11] and a new look and feel: icons and menus.

This new methodology for the first time involved actual negotiations with "real users" over the kind of characters inscribed in the script of personal computing and the narrative that script was going to involve:

> Having the opinion, which it was all that it was, that the bootstrapping methodology had not worked well at SRI, I felt that it was necessary to expose this collection of designers that I was hiring to real users. So they knew that Sally looked like this, talked like this, knew this kind of concepts and didn't know other kinds of concepts. So all we did was develop a certain methodology where the designers were fanned out to various companies, and they would actually go and live there for a number of days, get to know the people, talk to them about what they did, come to understand their jargon, and try to abstract the concepts that they dealt with in doing whatever it is that they did. (Irby 1992)

Thus, the "real user" was born, and her name was Sally. On the machine side of the interface, her doppelgänger also came into being at the same time: the graphical user interface (GUI). Their fates, as always with this technology, were intertwined.

The Invention of Modelessness

There initially were two main philosophies of design and numerous representations of the user competing inside PARC's two principal organizational components, the Computer Science Laboratory and the System Science Laboratory. On the one hand, some PARC researchers, and especially the ARC renegades around Bill English, rooted for a distributed system, either a time-shared system or on a network of minicomputers, on which NLS and TENEX could run. On the other hand, in CSL, others, and especially Alan Kay and the BCC nucleus around Butler Lampson and Chuck Thacker, moved onward to develop the project of personal computing with the creation of the Alto.

It was in the framework of this second agenda, the agenda of personal and (secondarily) distributed computing, that the fate of the personal interface was realized. In the PARC setting, the evolution of the interface occurred with the invention of a new model of human-computer interaction defined in opposition to previous models, of which NLS eventually appeared as emblematic. This new model was the modeless interface, an interface rid of the modes that, as we have seen, characterized and, according to some, plagued previous interface designs, including that of NLS.

Like Jeff Rulifson, whom he had met at the Stanford Artificial Intelligence Laboratory, Larry Tesler was a member of Bill English's team inside SSL. With Rulifson, Tesler had decided that there was something more interesting to work on than simply doing NLS over again. As Butler Lampson mildly puts it, "The politics of this were quite complicated because Larry [Tesler] and Tim [Mott] were part of SSL but they did not buy this POLOS thing . . . and they wanted to use the Alto, but that was politically incorrect in SSL in 1973 and 1974. So what they did was to find another project to work on. That was their excuse to getting loose from POLOS and to be allowed to work on the Alto" (Lampson 1997).

This project was to help a Xerox publishing subsidiary, Ginn and Company, improve efficiency with the introduction of computer-assisted editing and printing. In early 1974, Bill Gunning, the former head of SSL,[12] at that time in charge of the technical liaison between PARC and the rest of Xerox, relayed Ginn's senior administrative editor Darwin Newton's demands to Bill English, who assigned this task to Larry Tesler. According to Tesler's own account, this assignment was a welcome one for English, too, since "[Tesler] didn't like the

POLOS architecture at all and [he] complained about it a lot. [He] was dis-ruptive. They were happy to move [him] to one side" (quoted in Smith and Alexander 1998, 105). To avoid diverting anyone else from the POLOS proj-ect, English proposed that Ginn hire its own person to help Tesler, and that person was Tim Mott. Taking over the work that Charles Simonyi[13] had done for the text-editing application of the Alto called Bravo, Tesler and Mott de-veloped a new application called Gypsy. But whereas Bravo was still a moded application, requiring the user to put it into insert mode to enter text, then shift to edit mode to edit it, Gypsy's design introduced menus. Here is how Mott summarized their experience with Gypsy for Ginn:

> Ginn needed fairly simple programs for word processing and page layout. . . .
> The POLOS application were modeled after NLS, which in turn was based on the
> [Vannevar] Bush paper [Memex]. They were really tools for organizing thought,
> not for editing and page design. While the word-processing functions were there,
> there was also lots of other stuff that Ginn would not have needed and were [sic]
> too cumbersome. I didn't think the editors at Ginn would take the time required
> to learn. My model for this was a lady in her late fifties who had been in publish-
> ing all her life and still used a Royal typewriter. . . . When it came time to begin
> instructing people about Gypsy, I went straight for the lady with the Royal type-
> writer, figuring if I could teach her, it would be clear sailing for the rest. After a
> few hours of coaching, she had learned enough to go off and use the system on
> her own. A few days later, she said that the quality of her work had improved be-
> cause she was always dealing with clean copy, and it was easy to make changes.
> She volunteered that she couldn't imagine having ever worked differently. (Mott,
> quoted in Smith and Alexander 1988, 110–12)

"The lady with the Royal typewriter" provided Tesler and Mott with their first and foremost model of a user who differed from them, the designers. It is worth noticing that Tim Mott's special position (he was hired by Ginn, not by PARC) and relative lack of technical experience[14] might have helped him tremendously here. He could not feel as if he knew more than the user about the task to be assisted by the computer, and he very much felt that he didn't know more about the computing applications themselves.

Two main characteristics defined this new model of the user: Sally was working on paper, on her Royal, but in the professional business of publish-ing, and she was a skilled touch typist. The somesthetic and cognitive learning processes of the NLS interface and its devices, and especially those of the chord keyset, were alien to her. Sally, "the lady with the Royal typewriter," once and for all validated Licklider's conclusion that the real users, "people who are buying computers, especially personal computers, just aren't going to take a long time to learn something. They're going to insist on using it awfully quick—easy to use, easy and quick to learn."

It is worth noticing, however, the regressive character of this identification of the user with some kind of lowest common denominator in terms of skills. Mott selected Sally with the Royal "figuring if I could teach her, it would be clear sailing for the rest." It was a concession to the hegemony of an existing technology that Engelbart had hoped to transcend, or at least to subsume— the typewriter's QWERTY keyboard.[15]

With that concession came others. It was at the level of the display screen that a new model of the human-computer interaction emerged at PARC, one in tune with Tesler's notion of modelessness. However, the graphical user interface, the GUI, that implemented the modeless interface also was characterized by a regressive concession to existing technologies, at least metaphorically. Sally would not only be typing, but typing on "paper" and moving around pieces of "paper" on a "desktop."

We have seen in a previous chapter the hack that Engelbart and his crew had to make in order to build their display system on raster-scan displays in the mid-1960's. In the early 1970's, however, the decreasing cost of the memory made it possible to use TV monitors for the display system in computing. Chuck Thacker and the CSL crew realized that[16] and decided to equip the Alto with a raster-scan display:

> The major departure from past systems was the machine's display. To emulate as many of the characteristics of paper as possible, we chose to provide a full bitmap, in which each screen pixel was represented by a bit of main storage, and to use raster-scanning rather than the lower-cost calligraphic techniques popular at the time. We were encouraged by the earlier experiences of a group in SSL, which had developed a character generator for a similar, but higher-resolution display. The display resolution . . . allowed display of a full page of text. (Thacker 1988, 272)

The Alto display screen recreated the standard 8½-by-11-inch sheet of paper, the standard for most American printed documents. And what was put on the screen—the symbolic interface—reinforced the reference to paper. Here, Alan Kay's team inside SSL, the Learning Research Group (LRG), played its part. Here is a classic treatment of Kay's "radical" move:

> In his own interface design, Kay strived for the clarity and breadth of a piece of paper. He finally cracked the problem by a sleight of the hand called overlapping windows. While Engelbart and his Augmentation workers had pioneered the window, the partitions they had in mind each staked out its own portion of the monitor. Not only was it difficult to keep straight which window one was working in, but the windows wound up competing for the extremely limited real estate on the screen. Kay's solution to this was to regard the screen as a desk, and each project, or piece of a project, as paper on the desk. It was the original "desktop metaphor." As if working with real paper, the one you were working on at a given

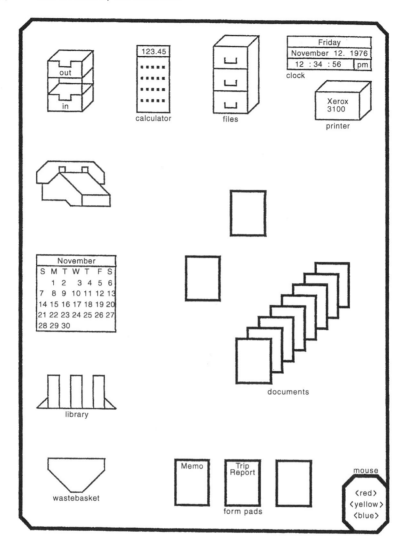

Figure 6-3. The Original Desktop, 1976. Source: Smith (1976).

moment was on top of the pile. . . . To move to the other windows, you used the cursor out of the window and over the representation of one of the windows "underneath." That window would immediately fill out, giving the illusion that it was "on top." (Levy 1994, 60; see Figure 6-3)

In Engelbart's system, the user somesthetically manipulated symbols in a virtual space that was not characterized by analogy to anything in the real world. Engelbart's model was conceptual only. He actually considered the virtual datascape as a "flying" space, which referred to a potential third dimension obviously elusive on paper. In the graphic interface developed by Alan Kay and his colleagues, on the other hand, the user transforms objects that analogically refer to real objects.

This distinction reflects Charles Sanders Peirce's famous discrimination of an "icon" from an "index": "the diagrammatic sign or *icon* . . . exhibits a similarity or analogy to the subject of discourse . . . the *index* . . . forces the attention to the particular object intended without describing it" (Peirce, 1996 [1931], 56). In Engelbart's NLS, the interface is indexical because NLS interface signs do not refer to any object in the world. Instead, they refer to the user's conceptual object, manipulated via the physical movement of the user's hand and arm. In the graphical user interface, signs do exhibit a "similarity" with the thing in the world that they represent: they are iconic previsualizations of objects that they participate in creating in the world: papers, documents, texts, pictures, and so on.[17] It is obvious from the start, therefore, that the graphical interface is iconic in essence, since with it, we move from an indexical manipulation to iconic visualization.

As Steven Levy realized, and as Alan Kay very often commented, this transition happened with the creation of an illusion. The virtual desktop was not a mere metaphor, since the user did not identify the false residual of the metaphor. Instead, it was an effect produced by the craft of the designer in making the user believe that there is a correspondence between the icons that he or she moves and transforms on the screen and the referential paper objects that they represent. For Alan Kay, the notion of the desktop as illusion should replace the idea of the desktop as metaphor in the designer's model of the interface not only because the responsibility of the analogy then migrates to the designer's side, but also, and more importantly, because it brings the "magic" back in the process of interface design and allows the designer to do more:

> One of the most compelling snares is the use of the word *metaphor* to describe a correspondence between what the users see on the screen and how they should think about what they are manipulating. My main complaint is that *metaphor* is a poor metaphor for what needs to be done. At PARC, we coined the word *user illusion* to describe what we were about when designing user interface. There are clear connotations to the stage, theatrics and magic—all of which give much stronger hints at the direction to be followed. For example, the screen as "paper to be marked on" is a metaphor that suggests pencils, brushes, and typewriting. Fine, as far as it goes. But it is the magic—understandable magic—that really counts. Should we transfer the paper metaphor so perfectly that the screen is as hard as paper to erase and change? Clearly not. If it is to be like magical paper, then it is the *magical* part that is all-important and that must be most strongly attended to in the user interface design. (Kay 1990, 199, emphasis in the original)

Of course, the user could be victimized by the illusion and lose control over the conditions of validity of the analogy on which the illusion, like the metaphor, stands. Kay understood this risk and pronounced himself for "understandable magic"—which would sound like an oxymoron to any practicing illusionist. He believed that the designer should be like a benevolent illusionist who would make his illusions transparent to his audience while performing them: the desktop illusion, this "magical paper" that the personal interface became, aimed at creating an iconic interaction transparent for the user and under the control of the designer. It is eventually in this sense that the notion of modelessness appeared as the conceptual invention of an illusion in the setting of PARC:

> An *intuitive* way to use the windows was to activate the window that the mouse was in and bring it to the "top." This interaction was *modeless* in a special sense of the word. The active window constituted a mode, to be sure—one window might hold a painting kit, another might hold text—but one could get to the next window to do something in it *without special termination*. This is what *modeless* came to mean for me—the user could always get to the next thing desired without any backing out. The contrast of the nice modeless interactions of windows with the clumsy command syntax of most previous systems directly suggested that everything should be made modeless. Thus began a campaign to "get rid of modes." (Ibid., 197, emphasis in the original)

The chord keyset was available on the Alto, but it was never used. Most of the CSL researchers and Rulifson, Tesler, Mott, and Kay agreed that the chord keyset was not useful in their new model of the interface. Some invoked the space it took on the desktop, but most referred to its "steep learning curve." Unlike the illusion produced by the modelessness of the graphical user interface, it was not "an *intuitive* way" to use a computer. Retrospectively, here is how Butler Lampson, for instance, summarized the fate of this device:

> The reason the chord keyset was so popular was that the NLS user interface was so terrible that it was almost impossible to use it without the chord keyset. There was so much requirements to flip back and forth between what you did with the mouse and what you did on the keyboard that it was vitally important to have the chord keyset. But as soon as people made a user interface that was even a little bit better, the chord keyset was no longer cost effective and people wouldn't use it. (Lampson, 1997)

Jeff Rulifson even told me that the NLS user interface was made over a weekend and never changed.

The definition of what made this new interface actually better relied on the social construction of the user among the PARC researchers. That construction treated the user as the subject of an illusion, characterized by a lowest common denominator in terms of computing skills, and prone to errors caused by being "trapped" in modes.

Part of the illusion was that the graphical user interface was modeless. As Kay himself said, "this interaction was *modeless* in a special sense of the word." In fact, it was not modeless at all. Actually, most computer scientists now agree on that point, and Donald Norman, for instance, has clearly shown not only the persistence of modes in later user interfaces, but also on the persistence of user errors associated with them:

> Why not just do away with modes? This was the opinion voiced strongly by Tesler (1981). But almost everything we do involves modes in one way or another, including working with so-called "modeless" computer systems such as the Apple Macintosh. Whenever dialogue boxes appear, or whenever the cursor changes from an arrow to an "I-beam" depending on its location on the screen, one is in a mode. Similarly, selecting an object in the Macintosh Finder can be viewed as changing modes. When no objects are selected, typing will usually have little effect. When an object is selected, however, typing may result in renaming the object—a common mode error in this interface. These examples serve to illustrate that what is actually meant by a "modeless" interface often refers to design in which contextual information is provided to minimize mode errors, and where modes can be easily entered and exited. (Sellen, Kurtenbach, and Buxton 1992)

Whatever the validity of this construction of the user, it did away with the heavy learning requirements imposed upon the user by Engelbart and finally sealed the fate of the chord keyset in the personal interface.

But the last step in the shaping of the personal interface did not happen at Xerox PARC. Xerox is famous for not being famous for the invention of the personal computer. As is widely known, literally every component of what eventually became the personal computer was present in Xerox PARC's Alto —the display with a graphical user interface, the mouse, and networking and e-mail capabilities. But a personal computer is a commercial product—"a $500 machine that anybody can buy"—and the product development of the personal computer failed at Xerox PARC. It did so for four main reasons.[18]

The first was corporate inertia. The Xerox Corporation saw itself as the leading company in the paper copier business in the 1970's. Its specialty was document reproduction via chemicals on paper. Xerox PARC was founded in order to make the Xerox Corporation "the architect of information" for the business office, in the words of C. Peter McColough, the Xerox company president in 1970. Xerox had just acquired a computer company, Scientific Data Systems, and saw the digital technologies of electronic computing as its future. But the development of personal-computer technologies at Xerox PARC occurred so rapidly that the Xerox Corporation was largely unprepared to receive them, to shift their corporate paradigm from paper to its virtualization, so to speak. The one PARC technology that was commercialized effectively by the Xerox Corporation, laser printing, was basically a copier technology. So the Xerox Corporation's image of itself as a copier company was an impediment to the transfer of personal-computer technologies from its R&D center in Palo Alto.

The second reason why Xerox PARC failed to develop the personal computer as a commercial product was itself personal. While the leader of the Computer Science Laboratory at Xerox PARC, Dr. Robert Taylor, was a psychologist with considerable experience in managing computer R&D, his boss, the director of PARC, Dr. George E. Pake, was a physicist. As Pake stated: "My scientific background was in experimental physics, and I knew very little about computers or computer science" (1985). The inevitable result was a certain degree of conflict between Pake and Taylor and a resistance to the flow of personal-computing technologies from Xerox PARC to the rest of the Xerox Corporation and thus to the marketplace.

Also, Xerox PARC was isolated (or insulated) from its parent company. No effective mechanisms were created for technology transfer from Xerox PARC to the manufacturing and marketing/sales divisions of the Xerox Corporation. When such a development unit was later created at Xerox PARC, the Systems Development Division (SDD), it was generally unable to form an effective bridge for technology transfer to the Xerox Corporation's operating units. PARC was located in the Stanford Industrial Park in Palo Alto, California, an ideal location for conducting R&D in personal computing, but at a great physical distance from the corporation's headquarters in Stamford, Connecticut, its manufacturing center in Rochester, New York, or its Office Systems Division in Dallas, Texas. Geographical distance diminishes the opportunities for frequent personal contact and thus makes technology transfer more difficult (Gibson and Rogers 1994). "PARC had weak ties to the rest of Xerox, and the rest of Xerox had no channel for marketing products based on the researchers' efforts" (Uttal 1983).

Finally, at the time, it was hard to see how the personal computer could become a commercially viable product selling at an affordable price. In 1975, the cost of computer memory had not yet begun to decrease to the point where a microcomputer realistically could be offered on the consumer market.

However, the Alto computer was built. As many as 1,500 Altos were available in 1978, either at Xerox PARC or in other institutions. The Star, too, was built. It was introduced as a commercial product in April 1981 with a base price tag close to eighteen thousand dollars. As a former Xerox executive summarized it, "it was a technological tour de force, but it was too expensive, no one understood it, and no one wanted it"(quoted in Smith and Alexander 1988, 238). In their retrospective on the Star project, its main designers gave it a more elaborate assessment:

> So, what have we learned from all this? We believe, the following:
>
> *Pay attention to industry trends.* . . . PARC researchers and Star's designers did not pay enough attention to the "other" personal computer revolution occurring outside Xerox. . . .
>
> *Pay attention to what customers want.* . . . The problem was not that Star lacked functionality, it was that it didn't have the functionality customers wanted. . . .
>
> *Know your competition.* Star initial per-workstation price was near that of time-shared minicomputers, dedicated word-processors and other shared computing facilities. Star was however, competing for desktop space with microcomputer-based PCs. . . .
>
> *Many aspects of Star were correct.* . . . Though the reorientation of the industry away from batch and time-shared computing toward personal computing had nothing to do with Xerox, PARC, or Star, it was an important part of the computing philosophy that led to Star. (Johnson et al. 1989, 25–26)

The "other" personal computer revolution that redefined the idea of the personal computer was indeed partly the result of the computing philosophy that had led to the Star and that had invented a personal user for the computer. The final stages of product development and marketing of the interface for the personal computer, however, occurred at Apple, not at Xerox.

Apple and The End of the Bootstrapping Process

The fairy-tale story of the founding of Apple Computer by Steve Jobs and Steve Wozniak, beginning with the Apple I and the meetings of computer hobbyists at the Home Brew Computer Club in a Palo Alto burger joint, is often told and need not be repeated here. It is necessary, however, to trace the path followed by Douglas Engelbart's innovations as they reached their terminus in the form in which they now are employed, a form very different from the one Engelbart had envisioned for them. And the incorporation of those innovations into the Apple computer via their further development at Xerox PARC forms the conclusion of that story. It also registers the ultimate translation of the conception of the user. At Apple, the user finally became "everybody," conceived this time as indeed everybody—as consumers of a commercial product, not candidates for coevolutionary change or as "Sally."

In November 1979, Steve Jobs visited Xerox PARC, and Larry Tesler demonstrated the latest implementation of Smalltalk on the Alto. In Tesler's words:

"I was about the only person there interested in personal computers, so they said, 'you can talk to these people from Apple'" (Rogers 1983, 89).

Tesler's own career trajectory led him to play the major part in the reshaping of Apple Computer in the early 1980's. In the late 1970's and early 1980's, Tesler was convinced that it was possible to implement on an eight-bit microprocessor the personal computing paradigm exemplified by Smalltalk:

> Of course we knew that eventually we would get to microprocessors . . . but we couldn't believe that you could do this stuff on an 8-bit. We felt that you needed at least a one-mip [millions of instructions per second], 16-bit processor to do any of this stuff. . . . So I wasn't even interested in the 8-bit ones. Larry Tesler was more interested than I was. So he actually put some effort into getting a version of Smalltalk running on some kind of 8-bit. (Kay 1993)

Tesler also was involved in the publishing business at two levels. The first of these was his involvement, prior to going to PARC, with Jim Warren and the Free University Newsletter. As Warren recalls:

> This was in the late 1960's, maybe the early 1970's. People's Computer Center was in one store front, around the corner was Whole Earth Catalog Order and Truck Farm . . . run by Stewart and Lois Brand. Another half block over was the Mid-Peninsula Free University Store. I was the general secretary of the Mid-Peninsula Free University. A guy named Larry Tesler . . . was the treasurer of the Free University. . . . We worked with each other in the Free U., on these newsletters, very frustrating, because it was a proportional-spacing typewriter, it wasn't programmable, you had very limited control. When he went to Xerox PARC, he started working on newspaper layout. Because of that experience in this radical antiwar hippie Free University, from that experience, it became obvious to him that if you want variable-size type and proportional spacing, you don't want a character-oriented machine, you want a bit-mapped machine. So he was successful in leading the fight to have the Macintosh come out as a bit-mapped machine. (Warren 1993)

Through his involvement in publishing activities in the context of both the counterculture and Xerox PARC, Tesler appeared as an effective bridge between the "serious" corporate environment of computing research and development and the hobbyist community epitomized by the Home Brew Computer Club.

Then, at PARC, Tesler was involved with the Ginn Publishing project, which led him to develop functions for computer editing such as cutting and pasting and the drag-and-drop capabilities of the graphical user interface:

> We worked with Ginn Publishing, which was a subsidiary of Xerox, and again we sent people off to study the editing activities that took place in that kind of environment, and it was very natural for them to cut out pieces of galley and paste

them all together. That's where the cut-and-paste model came from. And It turned out to be useful from a page layout or editing point of view, in text, almost universally. . . . And so, there was a school of thought within PARC, probably epitomized by Larry Tesler, that felt that the drag-and-drop, since Larry Tesler and Tim Mott were the two people who went off to study the Ginn people and ended up building a program for them, they really were enamored by the drag-and drop. . . . [The drag-and-drop model] came out of Apple's attempt, when Larry Tesler went to Apple, he did the user-interface design for [the] Lisa, and I think that the drag-and-drop sort of started emerging in the late Lisa early Macintosh days, because they were trying to address the complexity of the user interface, the clumsiness of the user interface based on cut-and-paste. (Irby 1992)

This involvement with publishing organized Tesler's contribution to personal computing and put him in the position of spanning boundaries between the community of hackers as early as the late 1960's and the more formal R&D environment of computer science at Xerox PARC.

Then, at Apple Computer, Tesler got the opportunity to set the agenda for the design of the Lisa and then the Macintosh in an institution that by then had become a perfect, if improbable hybrid of the two communities.

Jobs foresaw the potential of such a technology for a marketable product. Two major factors influenced the success of the technology transfer of the graphic user interface from Xerox PARC to Apple. Jobs and Wozniak were connected to the hobbyist movement of the early 1970's, and by 1979, Apple had successfully moved from this hobbyist market to the office market, thanks to Visicalc, the first spreadsheet program developed for the Apple II. "The two Steves—Jobs and Wozniak—they understood their market. The way they understood their market was twofold: 1) they were it, and that's the best way to understand a market, and 2) they just liked to go to the Homebrew Computer Club and having the neatest thing . . . The neatest thing available to that community" (Belleville 1992).

The first factor helped Jobs to realize a potential market existed for an individually owned personal computer. He wanted one. The second factor provided him with the interest and the connections to pursue the latest developments in office systems developed at PARC.

The failure of the Lisa system, in 1983, finally opened the way for a unified marketing strategy based on the Macintosh. First proposed in late 1978 by Steve Jobs, the Lisa computer was designed for general office use, "a high quality, easy-to-use computer for secretaries, managers, and professionals." In fact, a more specific representation of the user was "a business person whose day was constantly interrupted with spur of the moment requests to do one thing or another" (Ludolph, Perkins, and Smith 1989). Sharing some of the

Star's design principles, interface features, and marketing goals, the Lisa also shared its fate, and for some of the same reasons:

> All in all, Lisa was a spectacular achievement . . . still, by the time Lisa was ready for its public rollout, even the designers knew that, at the very least, Apple had a tough sell. Lisa simply cost too much . . . over $12,000.00. And Lisa ran painfully slow, not as slowly as the Xerox Star, perhaps, but still at a pace more glacial than frisky. . . . Apple had never really learned to sell computers to Lisa's target, Fortune 500 corporations. And it did not start with Lisa. (Levy 1994, 101–3)

From then on, however, Apple appeared as a leading force in the emerging market for microcomputers, moving away from the distributed office personal workstations of the 1970's such as the Alto, Star, and Lisa. At the center of the move to a market for personal computers that included "everybody" was the futher development of the mouse.

THE BUTTONS OF THE MOUSE

The issue seems innocuous enough: How many buttons should a mouse have? But there is hardly one major actor from the early days of personal computing who does not have a distinctive opinion on this subject, to the point that Bill Gates once said that "the number of buttons on a mouse is one of the most controversial issues in the industry. People get religious" (quoted in Levy 1984b, 76). But according to Stu Card, another major actor of this part of the story, "people who are mouse aficionados, like Engelbart and English, and me to a certain extent, are probably the least religious people about the mouse. Along with them, I see it as a provisional device that you might be able to do better with in some circumstances" (Card and Moran 1988, 526).

As we have seen, the invention of the mouse occurred very early at ARC, and its design was subject to a lot of discussions and user testing. The shape of the mouse slowly emerged, first in comparison with alternative pointing devices such as the light pen and tablet and then in competition with alternative designs based on the same principles and controlled by the knee, back, or hand. The mouse as a hand-controlled device in conjuction with the chord keyset was supposed to be part of the liberation of the hands of the user from the keyboard, and the three buttons of the mouse were related to different modes employed in the modal NLS interface.

At ARC, Bill English had been in charge of the mouse project. He wrote the original patent for the mouse and usually gets credits as the "co-inventor" of the mouse. English also was one of the first ARC members to leave the laboratory in 1970 to join the recently formed Xerox PARC, taking the idea of the mouse with him.

Like many devices and concepts transferred from ARC to PARC, the mouse underwent mutations at PARC. Compromises and consensuses made at ARC were requestioned, first at PARC and then at SDD, and then again at Apple. In particular, each institution had a different idea about what the number of buttons on the mouse ought to be, and these opinions resulted in different designs. For Bill English, "clearly, three was the right number . . . two is a good compromise. With one, you have to go through a lot of contortions to select things" (quoted in Levy 1984b, 76–77).

The first mutation of the mouse happened at PARC under Ron Rider's direction and transformed it from the ARC wheel mouse to the PARC ball mouse. According to Charles Irby (1992), the original wheel mouse "was not that different from the ball mouse. The ball mouse just has two little wheels inside that are picking up the motion from the rolling ball instead of the disks rolling on the table." This was not much of a design improvement, although some ergonomic issues served also as a justification at the time. There also were legal issues:

> The original device being an analogue device and being quite bulky in size, was not really amenable to large-scale use. It was too fragile and just didn't fit ergonomically. And I think that there was the issue that Engelbart and English had the patent on it and nobody wanted to pay royalty fees to them . . . there was a hole in the patent, and then at Xerox there was a guy called Ron Rider actually got a new patent on the ball mouse, which should have been covered . . . [but] because of the way the patent was worded they got it through the patent office. So Xerox actually has the patent on the mouse. (Ibid.)

This ball mouse, which still had three buttons, was part of the Alto design, and widespread use of it began inside PARC's community of researchers (Thacker 1988). Some researchers loved it. Some, like Larry Tesler and David Thornburg, hated it. They considered it "the least reliable component of the Alto and "totally inappropriate for drawing" (quoted in Perry and Wallich 1985, 69).[19] Some others, including Bill English, considered it as "an interim device, and wanted to see if it was possible to invent other devices that would improve on its speed" (Card and Moran 1988, 495).

Inside the company at large, the same phenomenon that occurred with the Alto, and pretty much sealed its fate, happened with the mouse. Xerox couldn't make commercial use of it. As Bill English (1992) recalls:

> Getting the mouse introduced, it's just amazing, thinking back . . . people had no concept unless they've been using it. Because Xerox came out with the 860 word processor, I think in 1979 or 1978, which was actually quite successful, it was one of the last self-contained word processors before people got PCs. It was a major Xerox product designed in Dallas. And we at PARC did our best to convince them to use a mouse for a pointing device. They absolutely refused, they wouldn't do

it, we could not sell them on the concept of the mouse, we showed them the re-port, we showed them the mouse, and what they did instead was to put a little finger-sensitive tablet on the keyboard . . . which was useless, it was so bad that finally they gave it up, but they wouldn't use the mouse . . . they said people don't want that extra thing on their desk . . . that was just really difficult to understand, in the same company . . . it was just crazy. . . . It wasn't until Apple picked it up. . . . I mean, it was the real change from there, Steve Jobs saw the technology at PARC and picked it up right away.

The mouse attracted Steve Jobs's attention during Larry Tesler's demon-stration of the Alto at PARC, and when Tesler moved to Apple a few months later, the mouse moved with him. This last move, at the end of the bootstrap-ping process, was the one that made a star out of the mouse, to the extent that many still believe that Apple invented the mouse. Although Apple never claimed such an invention, some of its employees still occasionally say that "we're the ones who perfected the mouse by getting rid of these extra buttons" (Bruce Tagliazini, quoted in Card and Moran 1988, 524). Indeed, the "but-tons controversy" got reopened at Apple and led to the disappearance of all the extra buttons: the Lisa and the Macintosh mice were to have one (visible) button. The rationale for such a decision was given by Larry Tesler:

> In any situation when there were arguments in both directions, unless one ap-proach was a big advantage for experienced users, we'd choose the one that made it easier for the beginner . . . in this case, we found that two buttons on the mouse were a slight advantage for experienced users, but not much. For beginners, when there were two buttons, they'd keep glancing down. With one button, they adapted right away. Since we had a very aggressive target—being able to learn the system in less than a half-hour—we couldn't have 20 minutes of getting over your fear of the mouse. (Quoted in Rogers 1983, 90)

Here again, the user was invoked as the decisive reason for a design choice.

Both comparative and design testing had been initiated at ARC. At Xerox PARC, both kinds of testing, under the supervision of Bill English, Stu Card, and later Charles Irby, were reinitiated. This usually means that prior testing is questioned, if not in its results, at least in its methodology, and that is what happened at PARC. The previous testing was questioned on its lack of a mea-sure of the effect of distance to target and on its methodology, which lacked an indication of the variability of the measures (Card, English, and Burr 1978). It was also questioned for its use of only one target size and its confusion be-tween large learning effects and device comparisons (Goodwin 1975). More generally, the ARC testing was faulted for being "more concerned with the evaluation of devices than with the development of models from which per-formance could be predicted" (Card, English, and Burr 1978, 601).

The leading actor in the PARC testing team was without contest Stuart (Stu) Card, a young psychologist who joined PARC in 1974. The shift from "an evaluation of devices" to the "development of models" signaled a major shift in the research strategy, best illustrated by Card's 1978 Ph.D. dissertation at Carnegie-Mellon and later expanded into the classic *Psychology of Human-Computer Interaction* (1983), which Card co-authored with Thomas Moran, another PARC psychologist, and Allen Newell, one of the leading Artificial Intelligence researchers of the ARPA contractors' community. As Card and Moran recall:

> The opportunity to tackle a new science of the user brought us to PARC in 1974 (collaborating with Allen Newell, as consultant). As other PARC researchers were beginning to pursue the vision of highly graphic, interactive, networked-based workstations, we were following a vision of our own. The idea was to draw concepts from cognitive psychology and artificial intelligence to create an applied cognitive science of the user. . . . In 1974, we were in the position of having to create a new field. Psychological theories and methodologies held the promise of being able to represent and manage complex cognitive tasks, but the only body of research pertaining to human-computer interaction was in the field of human factors, where studies were largely empirical and evaluative, concentrating mostly on sensory-motor questions like the best shape for a switch. (Card and Moran 1988, 493–94)

With this strategy, the testing phase was scientifically grounded in the testing and modeling of the user, as well as the device, the creation of a "science of the user rooted in cognitive theory."

From then on, the representations of the user would be rationalized: the user became an object of inquiry and the subject of scientific experiment. The first consequence of this, of course, was that, in order to be rationalized, the user first had to be at least minimally real. In the earlier phases of testing mouse devices, the user was a kind of a pretext, a resource to be mobilized temporally to justify the fate of the device. After the emergence of the "cognitive science of the user" proposed by Card, Moran, Newell, and others, the user-computer interaction became the focus of scientific study, and it finally was recognized that machines and their users share the same destiny.

Many measures and experiments carried out at PARC between 1974 and 1979 demonstrated the mutual implication of devices and their users, but none as well as the experiments on pointing devices. First, several pointing devices, including some built for the experiment, were tested in a comparative manner. Homing time, or the time to move the hand from the keyboard to the pointing device, and positioning time, or the time to move the cursor to the target for a standardized set of distances and target width, were measured for each device, along with error rates. The results confirmed earlier results: "none of the devices tested improved on the mouse either for speed or for error rates" (Card, English, and Burr 1978). But this first phase fell short of the expectations that Card and his colleagues had for the project: "this direct empirical comparison between devices was just the sort of methodology of human factors testing that we wanted to improve: we wanted to understand the reasons why the results came out the way they did" (Card and Moran 1988, 496). A second phase of the research was therefore initiated to do the conceptual modeling that would meet these expectations. This second phase involved the testing of "the performances on the continuous movement devices against the predictions of Fitts's law" (Card, English, and Burr 1978).

Fitts's law was the result of work spanning from 1954 to the late 1960's that established a relation between distance, size of the target, and hand movement time for pointing. In this second phase, each device was mathematically modeled, and these models were tested against the data until the model was in accord with what Fitts's law required. As Card and Moran recall (1988, 496), "the model for the mouse was particularly interesting. The mouse was best modeled by a version of Fitts's law." For Card and Moran (1988, 496), "the significance of this result is that this is the same law that describes movement time for the hand alone, with the same constant of proportionality. The limiting factor in moving the mouse, therefore, is not in the mouse, but in the eye-hand coordinate system itself." As Chuck Thacker, the leading engineer on the Alto, put it: "subsequent research has shown that the mouse is a Fitts's law device, in that it as efficient for target selection as manual pointing. The practical impact of this is that in the domain for which it was intended, the mouse . . . does as well as the limits of the human user allow" (Thacker 1988, 272).

These results had a profound effect on the way testing and research in general were conducted at PARC. Card and Moran (1988, 497) acknowledged that "these studies were heavily used in the debate within Xerox that led to the decision to depart from tradition by including the mouse with the new Star product." What is more, this change in the strategy of testing led to a new way to characterize the relation between the design and the user during the development process and directed the process of realizing the user.

The design-testing episode that dealt with the number of buttons reopened the question that the ARC people, under the direction of Bill English, had thought they had solved. In the framework proposed by Card and his colleagues, a number of alternative designs were studied, starting with as many buttons as the initial ARC mouse had: "We built mice that were ergonomically shaped and had a button under every finger, there were buttons on the side and there were buttons on the top. There were two problems with that. One is it was to easy in the course of moving the mouse to accidentally push a button.

And secondly, the user interface complexity that came about from having that many input devices was just overwhelming" (Irby 1992).

Two kinds of factors thus explained the problems that they encountered with a design presenting too many buttons: ergonomic factors and cognitive factors. The concern with ergonomic factors was in the established tradition of human-factors studies at that time. Inside the Xerox organization, this part of the work was carried out by a team at XDS, the old SDS, in Southern California, under the direction of Bill Bewley. According to Dave Smith, who made the weekly flight to Los Angeles:

> So then we said OK, one button . . . that was our first guess, that was the right number of buttons . . . we did some user testing . . . we had a group in El Segundo that did real user studies . . . they tested the mouse, and they found that one button was not enough. The problem comes when you try to make a multiple selection, or an extended selection, say of text. So you'd do it the way you do it on the Mac. You would place the cursor, hold the mouse button down and then drag it and you would drag out the selection until it goes just where you wanted it, and then let up. Well that's a hard operation for people. Dragging with the button down is simply a hard thing for people to do. You can learn it, but it's not a natural thing, and people make frequent errors with it. So we said, OK let's try a two-button mouse and see about that, still not as bad as a three-button. And so the second button on the Star was the extend button and to make a text selection you would click where you wanted to begin . . . and then you go to the way you wanted it to end and you click on the extend button . . . and if it was a discontinuous thing, like icons, you could use the extend button to click on multiple icons. (Smith 1993)

In Dave Smith's explanation, the decision to use a two-button mouse appears as the result of trial and error experiments: the second button helped to do things that were difficult with just one button. But this explanation was a reduction of a larger question that related the buttons of the mouse to the interface.

This question involved the cognitive processes of the users. With more than one button, the mouse was more than a pointing device. It was a specific part of the user interface, and several uses could be assigned to those buttons. The question of the number of the buttons on the mouse became related to the choices possible for displaying certain functions on the keyboard or on the mouse. In the language of PARC, these became known as "semantic" choices, what a user might choose to do to employ a certain function. Determining what semantics were most natural for users was done with the help of the methodology of user testing developed by Card, Moran, and Newell, and the results would finally determine the number of buttons on the mouse:

> That's in fact why we went to two buttons . . . we studied seven different mapping of semantics onto mouse buttons from one button to three buttons. . . . We video-

taped the users so we could see their face, their hands and what was going on the screen in a composite video image, so we gave them a whole bunch of exercises to do in all those different semantics, and each person was trained on just one set of semantics. And then we looked at the behaviors on how many errors they made, and how long it took to learn and all that stuff and it was fairly clear that two buttons was pretty optimum. One button put too much semantics on the mouse, and you ended up having to modify the semantics by pushing keyboard keys and various things like that, so it increased the complexity. And three buttons was just much harder to remember, even though it gave you more devices to spread the semantics, it also increased the complexity. (Smith 1993)

The user is socially constructed and socially situated in the processes by which technology is developed and diffused, and then the user is progressively realized in a particular social setting. The relations between designers and users are organized in the negotiations about the future uses of the technology, starting from abstract or virtual representations of the user in the mind of the designer and progressively approaching confrontations with real users. In this process, the kind of testing initiated at PARC by Card and his colleagues was a fundamental, but nevertheless limited move. This move, according to their claim, shifted the focus from a comparison between devices to a study of the human-device interaction. However, although this move demonstrated the interest of introducing the human aspect of the problem, it still fell short of fully realizing the user.

Instead, it reduced the user to a subject, in the scientific, not the philosophical sense—an object of study in which most of the qualities of the human being were deemed not to be of interest and bracketed out by the experimenters. The introduction of cognitive science as a way to introduce real users into the processes of technological development thus also limited conceptions of what real users might be and might do with the technology being developed.

Here, for example, is the characterization of the subjects provided by Card, English, and Burr (1978, 602) in the paper that reported the results of the experiment described previously: "Three men and two women, all undergraduates at Stanford University, served as subjects in the experiment. None had ever used any of the devices previously and all had little or no experience with computers. Subjects were paid $3.00 per hour with a $20.00 bonus for completing the experiments. One of the five subjects was very much slower than the others and was eliminated during the experiment." This choice of novice subjects was the obvious limit of this process, not because these subjects lacked experience with the devices, but because they were constructed as novices and as nothing else. Attention was paid to differences of sex, but their social identity was no concern of the experiment: college students were perfect subjects, because they were available, close by, and cheap. These subjects were only "half-real" or, in other words, they were model subjects, subjects who could be read as embodiments of the generic eye-hand system. The experiments were able to prove that using the mouse was as efficient as pointing, but people who point usually don't develop repetitive-stress injuries (RSIs). The limitations in the definition of the user imposed by the cognitive-science conception of the user as an experimental subject thus laid ample groundwork for subsequent unintended consequences of the technology.

To put it another way, the qualities of the "real" test subjects were selected in accord with and limited to the purpose of the testing, as the following statement by Larry Tesler shows:

> I really didn't believe in [the mouse]. . . . I thought cursor keys were much better. We literally took people off the streets who had never seen a computer. In three or four minutes they were happily editing away, using cursor keys. At that point I was going to show them the mouse and prove that they could select text faster with the cursor keys. Then I was going to show that they didn't like it. It backfired. I would have them spend an hour working with the cursor keys, which got them really used to the keys. Then I would teach them about the mouse. They would say, "that's interesting but I don't think I need it." Then they would play with it a bit, and after two minutes they never touched the cursor keys again. (Quoted in Perry and Wallich 1985, 69)

"Off-the street-people" were again a pretext to show something. They were "real," not mere embodiments of physiological and psychological models, but not seen as fully real. Their thwarting of the expected outcome of the experiment was viewed as merely within experimental parameters.

Thus, the emerging representation of the user at PARC, as we have seen, was a novice conceived and defined as the subject of an experiment in cognitive science. In comparison with the various versions of the user as conceived of as an intelligence worker, programmer, or computer person—in short, conceived of reflexively, as the experienced user—the PARC representation of the user once again implied a very different conception of the interface, reinforcing the shift from modal to what were supposed to be amodal or modeless interfaces.

The move from ARC's experienced users to the PARC novice user was further reinforced by the only feature of PARC's charter in relation to Xerox on which everyone agreed. Xerox was a "document company" and PARC's novice user was a document creator, most likely a secretary:

> First of all, it's important to understand that Xerox is a document-oriented company. . . . By far, the vast majority of the focus was on documents, and managing documents, and what goes into documents and how you print documents, store documents, and all that stuff. . . . Generally, we wanted to be able to address

> business presentations or business reports, but not with the emphasis on data
> analysis that goes into the numbers and so forth . . . but rather the formatting of
> the end product. That's the kind of market we were trying to serve. . . . It was de-
> signed from the very beginning to run on a LAN [local-area network], so we had
> planned this whole thing to be part of the rollout of LANs. We expected large cor-
> porations to be the early adopters of those, and have the population density of the
> right kind of users to make the cost justifiable. We had expected to be able to sell
> this at about $ 15,000 a site, per user. That's what we targeted. That price eroded
> rather quickly, of course. (Irby 1992)

This representation of the user in relation to a specific task, document management, was even carried out one step further when the principles of user-
interface design proposed by Charles Irby and his group were implemented.
As we have seen, the main principle was to go and study the "real users" in
real situations, as Larry Tesler and some of his colleagues did at the Ginn publishing subsidiary of the Xerox Corporation.

For Charles Irby, the real origin of the cut-and-paste model was the editing
practices of this specific kind of user, practices that were in use before the introduction of the computer. In other words, Larry Tesler and his colleagues
brought back from their study of the Ginn people a conceptual model of the
task, which they then implemented in the interface in terms of design principles derived from the Card, Moran, and Newell principles for the analysis
of human-computer interaction. But this specific representation of the task
was related to a specific activity, and problems occurred when it was time to
think of the interface as a unifying set of design principles for various different activities:

> And so, there was a school of thought within PARC, probably epitomized by
> Larry Tesler [that was] really enamored by the drag-and-drop, and I completely
> agreed with them in the text domain and in the page layout context, those are re-
> ally good paradigms. On the other hand, when we tried to apply it in a much
> broader set of domains, filing, editing graphics, doing database work, sending
> e-mail, all these other things, drag-and-drop was essentially necessary as an ad-
> junct to the cut-and-paste, because the notions of cutting and pasting just didn't
> apply anymore. So we ended up in Star and in Metaphor products going with the
> more general concepts of moving things and copying things. As a result certain
> things are a little bit more complicated but there's a tremendously larger set of uni-
> form behaviors across the entire product. (Ibid.)

Each developer had a different proposition for mapping the semantics on
the mouse on the basis of his study of a specific kind of user doing a specific
kind of task. By interiorizing the worldview or the conceptual model held by
specific users for whom he was designing, and by serving as an advocate in the

interface design process for practices based on that worldview, the designer yet again in effect became the user. In the first of Ezra Pound's *Cantos*, Odysseus digs an "ell-square pitkin" and in it slaughters animals for sacrifice and pours libations to obtain a prophecy (Pound 1970, 3–4). None of the hundred-odd cantos that follow escape that prophetic site. The same may be said for the designer of a new technology seeking a prophetic vision of the end user. Despite the arrival of the real user with the commercialization of the technology, and despite the best experimental evidence that cognitive science can offer about that user, the process of innovation finally cannot escape the necessity of taking the designer of the technology as also its preferred user. It cannot escape the reflexivity of the designer's vision.

CHAPTER SEVEN

"Of Mice and Man": ARPANET, E-mail, and est

I against my brother
I and my brother against our cousin
I, my brother and our cousin against the neighbors
All of us against the foreigner.

— BEDOUIN PROVERB, quoted by Bruce Chatwin, *The Songlines*

To this day, Engelbart is really pissed. . . . He is a bitter guy. . . . He shouldn't be because he is revered, but he is bitter, because he thinks that user-friendliness is a red herring and he is partly right.

— ALAN KAY (1993)

At Engelbart's ARC lab at SRI, as we have seen, the real user began to arrive when not just NLS system builders, but ARPANET users began to connect with the system, bringing with them the first outside criticisms of the system. The irony in this lies with the fact that ARC was involved in the building of the ARPANET in the first place, and served as the original Network Information Center (NIC) from the initial design of the network until the mid-1970's. Thus, one of the innovations in which Engelbart's lab participated helped to begin to undermine its central achievement, NLS.

TROUBLE AND DISSENSION: ARC AND ARPANET

The early history of the ARPANET has been well covered in the literature on the history of the Internet, and I do not intend to provide here a detailed synthesis of these studies.[1] But coverage of the Network Information Center inside Engelbart's laboratory more often than not is slight or nonexistent. Of the two first nodes on the ARPANET, the node at the University of California in Los Angeles (UCLA) is the one that gets all the press. The other, Engelbart's laboratory, never gets more than a couple of paragraphs, even in lengthy publications.[2] But Engelbart's lab played a significant role in the inception of what eventually became the Internet.

In 1965, when Robert Taylor, then assistant director of the IPTO, and J. C. R. Licklider proposed a network linking the IPTO contractor sites, the main purpose of the network was to be resource sharing, since Licklider and Taylor were concerned about the costs of the multiplication of the infrastructure investments funded by their office (Norberg and O'Neill 1996, 163). This contradicts the often-stated myth of its origin that claims the U.S. Department of Defense wanted a computer network reliable and robust enough to survive a nuclear attack. The effort to achieve the efficiencies of resource sharing drew on technology that made it possible to carry data on leased dedicated phone lines. That technology was packet switching.

Robert Taylor had enrolled Larry Roberts to take charge of the ARPANET project, and Roberts started at the IPTO in December 1966, as Taylor's assistant director. At the IPTO contractors' meeting at the University of Michigan in Ann Arbor in April 1967, Wes Clark had proposed to organize the network around small computers interfacing the main computer at each site to the communication network (Salus 1995, 20–21; Hafner and Lyon 1996, 72–74). After his return to Washington, Roberts wrote up Clark's suggestion as what he called a "Message Switching Network Proposal," which he circulated to the IPTO contractors. In this proposal, he named the small computers "Interface Message Processors" (IMPs) and described their functions and uses. Clark's suggestion of a subnetwork of identical and interconnected small computers was highly innovative and influential. It solved a number of problems: "putting IMPs into the network design made it easier for designers to specify most of the network: IMPs would communicate with other IMPs; there was no need to worry about the nature of various host computers"(ibid., 21). As Katie Hafner and Matthew Lyon realized, "not only did Clark's idea make good sense technically, it was an administrative solution as well. ARPA could have the entire network under its control" (1996, 73).

At first, most ARPA contractors "were not initially enamored with the idea . . . some of the people saw it initially as an opportunity for someone else to come in and use their [computational] cycles. They never had enough cycles" (Taylor 1989). But under the scheme that Clark and Roberts proposed, all that contractors had to do was work on what was needed at their site to connect their computer to the IMP and communicate with it, "without concern for the specifics of the network implementation" (Norberg and O'Neill 1996, 164). Hafner and Lyon report that "after word of Clark's idea spread, the initial hostility toward the network diminished a bit" (1996, 75).

In October 1967, Roberts presented his proposal in public for the first time at the Association for Computing Machinery (ACM) Operating Systems Symposium in Gatlinburg, Tennessee. For this presentation, Roberts still held to his original idea of a "message-switching network." In this organization, messages were discrete entities that would be routed in the network through switches that would store and forward them. But most available histories of the beginning of the ARPANET insist that at the time of this presentation, Roberts was not sure that message-switching provided the best means to carry the data, and that a discussion with another participant at the conference opened his mind to packet switching.[3] In this technique, messages are broken into discrete parts ("packets") that contain a header (source and destination information) and control information (for error checking) along with some of the text of the message. Every e-mail message displays these elements today.[4]

At the Gatlinburg conference, Roger Scantleburry, from the National Physical Laboratory (NPL) in England, gave a paper about their proposed Digital Communication Network. Roberts previously had met Donald W. Davies, a colleague of Scantleburry's at NPL, in a seminar on time-sharing at MIT in 1965 and had discussed with him and Licklider "networking and the inadequacy of data communication facilities for both time-sharing and networking" (Roberts 1988, 144). After Scantleburry's presentation, Roberts had a discussion with him and considered his suggestion that "packet switching offered a solution to his problem" (Norberg and O'Neill 1996, 166). After his return to Washington, Roberts read Baran's reports on packet switching and initiated contact with him.[5] In June 1968, Roberts described the ARPANET as a demonstration of the kind of distributed network recommended by Baran in his study.

During the winter and spring of 1968, Roberts contracted Elmer Shapiro at SRI, who was only distantly associated with the ARC laboratory, to study the "design and specifications of a computer network." This contract (ARPA order no. 1137) was the first explicitly paid-for ARPANET effort (Salus 1995, 25). After the initial stages of planning, most of the collaborative effort was taken on by the Network Working Group (NWG), a more formal reorganization of the informal committees of contractors decided by Larry Roberts (Norberg and O'Neill 1996, 167). In fact, Roberts organized the network implementation around three different teams with various contracts and links between them: the NWG itself;[6] Leonard Kleinrock and his team of graduate students (including Steve Crocker, Vint Cerf, and Jon Postel) at UCLA, which was to become the Network Measurement Center (NMC); and finally, Douglas Engelbart and his staff, which was to become the Network Information Center (NIC).

Early in the history of the NWG, Elmer Shapiro insisted that "the work of the group should be fully documented." Steve Crocker, one of the members of Kleinrock's team of graduate students, volunteered to write the first meeting note, which he labeled "Request For Comments" in order "to avoid sounding too declarative," according to Hafner and Lyon (1996, 144). The accumulated archive of Requests For Comments (RFCs) documents not just the NGW's work, but the role that Engelbart's crusade played in it—and in the development of what became the Internet and e-mail.[7]

The early development of the ARPANET occurred at the same time that Engelbart was starting to think about the diffusion of NLS, and, as we have seen, seemed to him to present the possibility of continuing the bootstrapping process outside the ARC lab, extending his crusade by building a community of users that would differ, to a certain extent,[8] from the reflexive users of the first phase:

> As we got our own NLS tools working, how were we going to learn more about it and involve other people? I was trying to tell them [his staff] that the only way I could picture it was by developing a community of users that was distributed around the world. I had started thinking about how that could be promoted and arranged. The people out there probably wouldn't be equipped with the kind of tools we had, but they could start getting value from their use somehow, or from our using them and handing them the products that we could gradually build up. More and more of them could potentially transport the actual tools into their environment and get it to evolve like that. I didn't think you could just merely say, "Here it is." It's too big a transitional step for someone just to adopt a really radical, whole different set of working tools. It would be a step-by-step way of doing it. It just interested me anyway, the collaboration among distributed people. (Engelbart 1996)

As early as 1966, Robert Taylor, a committed sponsor of the laboratory, discussed the opportunity provided by a network project with Engelbart. Engelbart's reactions, at first, were not too different from those of most IPTO contractors:

> Bob Taylor happened to mention networks to me some months before [at the spring 1967 IPTO contractors' meeting at the University of Michigan in Ann Arbor] I guess the summer before. I was thinking about all that and said, "Why would anyone want to do that?" I remember saying that. (laughs) About an hour later I was thinking, "Gosh, what a funny reaction on my part." Because with a little reflection and a talk with him, I realized what it could do and how it would fit into the community goals I'd been thinking of. (Ibid.)

During the Ann Arbor meeting, this realization became a fact when Engelbart volunteered to establish the Network Information Center in his laboratory:

> I sit there and think, "Damn, that's a marvelous opportunity. If I volunteered to form the library, there's a community. But if I go back home and tell my people that I have committed us to that, it would be a problem. We worked things out by consensus." But it just got more and more intriguing. Finally I volunteered, "Well, I'm interested in it. How about if I form an on-line library (I don't know if they called it the information center at the time) and run it for this community?" It ended up that my research was not that big a distraction. It interested me, anyway, and everybody was relieved I was doing it. Then it slowly got the ARPA office interested in this as something that was relevant to their own pursuit. It was three years before things were really operating, so in the interim, I did a lot of thinking and planning. (Ibid.)

This decision, however, was not exactly well accepted by his staff when he came back to SRI and told them that he had volunteered for the NIC:

> It wasn't [a consensus decision] at that time. That caused a lot of trouble and dissension. People felt outraged that they were researchers and that they were going to have to do a service business: to run a network information center. I tried to tell them, "Look, that's an immensely important exploratory act. It's a tremendous opportunity." That just didn't go over with them. Finally, some of the really good, supporting people in my group were going around saying, "It's better to give than to receive. It's better to give service." They wanted to support me. Some of them just got grumpy. There were a lot of problems through those periods. (Ibid.)

In spite of these early negative reactions, planning for the NIC inside ARC started with the first NWG meetings in 1967. Between 1967 and 1970, several staff members participated in those meetings and represented SRI and the laboratory. Elmer Shapiro at SRI provided an important link between the ARPANET NWG and the laboratory. In April 1969, Bill Duvall wrote RFC 0002 entitled "Host Software" and discussed "the various types of Links, including Control, Primary, and Auxiliary Links" (S. Crocker, in RFC 1000). It was the first of a long list of contributions from ARC/NIC.

In total, SRI-ARC-NIC authors contributed 84 of the first 727 RFCs (12 percent), and ARC's relative contribution then oscillated between 7 and 22 percent of the total RFCs per year, with two low points in 1970 and 1972.

But the contribution by ARC members to technical discussions tended to decline, with some renewed activity along the way, to be sure, while its merely administrative contributions increased until the NIC was moved out of the ARC lab. Clearly, the effort to bootstrap NLS out of the laboratory proved to be a relative failure. Instead of building a community of bootstrapping crusaders on NLS now made available to more user-programmers, the lab became a service provider for a community that was configuring itself in other ways and developing in other directions.

In 1969–70, all but one of the seven RFCs authored by ARC members were devoted to technical questions: Bill Duvall, Elmer Shapiro, Jeff Rulifson, John Melvin, and Bill English contributed on various issues related to the network implementation, in parallel with their contributions to the NWG. Of the twenty-six RFCs contributed in 1971 by the SRI-ARC authors, eleven were still devoted to technical contributions. The rest of the 1971 ARC RFCs were devoted to NIC business, and as the contributions to technical discussions declined, these purely administrative contributions grew.[9] In 1972, SRI-ARC authors contributed nine RFCs, all but one devoted to NIC business. The technical contributions of the ARC members seem to have stopped during that year.

Of course, some of the early key people at the technical level, such as Elmer Shapiro, Jeff Rulifson, and Bill English, had left the laboratory by then. Rulifson and English, for instance, along with some other ARC members, moved to PARC in 1971. The other ARC members had to pick up the slack, which limited their technical contributions to the ARPANET NWG for a while.

And technical contributions indeed resumed in 1973. SRI-ARC authors contributed eight RFCs that year, and this trend continued in 1974 and 1975, until the NIC moved out of ARC. From 1974 on, NWG contributions from ARC were limited to the work of two staff members who were not part of the early NLS development, and all their contributions appear to have been unrelated to NLS work at the laboratory.

E-mail and the Eclipse of NLS

The reasons that the effort to bootstrap NLS out of the laboratory failed involved more than just the ways in which, as we already have seen, opening the system to others precipitated the criticism of it as a fundamentally time-sharing design. For Engelbart, the communication features that had been built into NLS, which had been dubbed Mail and Journal, were crucial components in the second phase of his research program, moving from the augmentation of individuals to the augmentation of communities of people working collaboratively via ARPANET.

Mail and Journal were significant innovations, and work on ARPANET communications at ARC even extended to ideas similar to what is now called Java and finally beginning to be widely implemented. But there already were other electronic-mail technologies in use on the developing ARPANET, and the NLS version of e-mail and electronic communications was not able to displace them. This, too, helped thwart the spread of Engelbart's crusade by opening the NLS to use by others over the developing communications network.

Engelbart's ARPA assignment to establish the NIC was typically vague, and "contained no specific guidelines as to what form NIC services should take" (Engelbart et al. 1970, 126). On the other hand, when he took the initiative to ask his fellow contractors what services they expected from the NIC, he got another vague and "often contradictory" response: some thought that "there was little need for the NIC," whereas some others thought that the NIC should "supply initiative and leadership in the development of overall Network conventions and methodologies" (ibid., 126–27).

Confronted by such an uncertain situation, Engelbart decided that the NIC should provide two kinds of specific services: basic library services and on-line services. Basic library services covered the trivial aspects of the NIC management and were concerned with typical information-retrieval services such as accumulation, indexing, referencing, and storage of a "physical collection of information items in various sizes and media" (ibid., 129). On-line services, on the other hand, constituted a more interesting challenge for Engelbart and his staff, since providing such services meant harnessing the capabilities of the ARPANET:

> In designing the NIC, we were conscious of the fact that more was needed than just good library facilities. The technical sophistication of the tools we had available and of the users we would be serving demanded that we seek to make it possible for this community to derive significant advantages from the network in terms of increased communication of ideas, designs, criticisms, and comments on needs and possibilities . . . we were aware that it would not be sufficient merely to provide good technical features, but that the design must reflect the kind of coordinated user-system/service-system interface that we have felt is so important in the bootstrapping approach to the development of our own augmentation means. (Ibid., 126–27)

ARC developed Journal and Mail to provide these services. Engelbart planned to use the typewriter-oriented version (TODAS) of NLS to do so at first, and later to provide them with a display-terminal-based On-Line System. The vision of what could be done went well beyond e-mail to include functions that today are served by both the Internet and the World Wide Web:

> During the next year [1971] most remote on-line users will be served by TODAS, a typewriter-oriented version of our On-Line System . . . we are investigating ways of improving special aspects of the user's interface to the NIC—his query and browsing techniques, his means for doing bibliographic work, his means for publishing communiqués to the community, his means for staying in touch with current activities. . . . As soon as we have transferred our present systems onto the new PDP-10 computer and have achieved reasonable stability in system reliability and response, we intend to concentrate upon developing techniques to permit

general use of our NLS capabilities on a wide variety of remote display terminals, and we anticipate having a growing Network load of this type by next summer. (Ibid., 130–31)

From 1969 to 1971, during the planning stages of the NIC, Engelbart and his staff created several enhancements to NLS to provide these on-line services. In 1969, they worked on the design of a windowing capability for the system and implemented the Mail and the Journal features of NLS. In 1970 and 1971, these features were in regular use in the laboratory, and they implemented a version of NLS for the PDP-10 TENEX operating system (Engelbart 1988, 207–10). This latest enhancement made sense, not only because ARC was acquiring a PDP-10 to replace its SDS 940, but also because the PDP-10 was the time-sharing system used at most contractors' sites. In April 1971, 9 of the 25 computers connected to the first fifteen nodes of ARPANET were PDP-10s and 12 were PDPs.

The Journal and Mail features permitted use of NLS's linking capability to create an on-line index linking the information available in the NIC library. In the original design, besides cataloging and making use of links to point to something, Engelbart wanted what he called "back-links." The idea was to allow the user to track back all the documents pointing at a certain document, file, or statement that he or she was considering, thereby allowing queries in the form of "What among a certain corpus of documents is pointing at this document, file, or even statement?" (Engelbart 1996). The back links never got implemented. Instead, a more classic one-way indexing and transmitting system was developed around two subsystems resembling databases: the Identification System for the mail feature and the Number System for the Journal feature.

With the Mail NLS feature, an NLS user could submit a file or a part of a file to other users (individuals and/or groups) described in a distribution list specified as a list of unique identifiers ("idents"). At the time of submission, the user could contribute such information as: title, distribution list, comments, keywords, catalog of linked documents, and so on. The system could also automatically "expand" the group identification to generate a distribution list of its individual or collective members. This Identification System allowed queries to find a person's or a group's ident, as well as entry of initial identification information (Engelbart, Watson, and Norton 1973).

The Journal feature provided a permanent indexing and storage of mail submissions. At the time of its submission, the Number System automatically transferred a mail message to a read-only file identified by its unique catalog number. Catalog indexes based on message identification, name or ident of its author(s), and keywords were available. The user could consult such catalog indexes when editing a message in order to link it to previous messages. As Engelbart saw it at the time:

> The Journal system is part of the whole Augment, NLS integrated environment. Along with that, was the first really comprehensive mail system that I know about. The Journal feature is just one of the options. The concept is of making a permanent record, as though you'd published something, which then is always available. It's given a publication identifier that means you can always retrieve it. The operations of the system and some of the software that supports the operations and archiving and cataloging and all of that are built to support that. This was essentially in place by 1970. That's when the very first Journal item was started, probably in August 1970. As far as I know, it had a lot of the features that are only now emerging in modern electronic mail systems. (Engelbart 1996)

Other features allowed the use of "irregular Augment files" such as files (text or graphics) that other NLS users were working on, but that they had not submitted to the Journal yet, if those people made them accessible. The system also provided a way of analyzing a set of recorded exchanges, such as all the passages relevant to a given issue, identified by keywords or comments.

Massive use of the NLS mail and journal features in the NIC on-line services, required that most ARPANET users became NLS users—which was exactly what Engelbart had in mind when targeting the ARPANET community as the next bootstrapping circle. One way to make that possible was to make NLS compatible with the time-sharing operating systems that most users were using. The move from the SDS 940 to the PDP-10 TENEX took care of only approximately half of these users, however, and put a lot of pressure on the programmers at ARC. They realized that the NLS source code was too complex to be ported easily from the SDS to the PDP, and that NLS had to be reimplemented from scratch.[10]

Very early in the progress of the NWG, ARC staff member Jeff Rulifson proposed another way to take care of the other half of these users with his Decode Encode Language proposal. Basically, "the idea was to transport NLS-like interfaces over the net, just like Java today" (Rulifson, personal communication):

> The Decode-Encode Language (DEL) is a machine independent language tailored to two specific computer network tasks: accepting input codes from interactive consoles, giving immediate feedback, and packing the resulting information into message packets for network transmissin [sic] and accepting message packets from another computer, unpacking them, building trees of display information, and sending other information to the user at his interactive station. (Rulifson, RFC 0005: "DEL," June 2, 1969)

According to Jeff Rulifson, "it was generally agreed beforehand [before the initial NWG meeting] that the running of interactive programs across the network was the first problem that would be faced." During the initial ARPA NWG meeting at SRI in October 1968, the group, "already in agreement about the underlying notions of a DEL-like approach, set down some terminology, expectations for DEL programs, and lists of proposed semantic capability." A second round of meetings was later held in a piecemeal way: Crocker meet with Rulifson at SRI on November 18, 1968, and Stoughton meet with Rulifson at SRI on December 12, 1968 (Rulifson, RFC 0005, 1969). Steve Crocker gave an account of these meetings ("The Origins of RFCs") in RFC 1000 ("The Request for Comments Reference Guide" by Jon Postel, August 1987):

> The first few meetings were quite tenuous. We had no official charter. Most of us were graduate students and we expected that a professional crew would show up eventually to take over the problems we were dealing with. Without clear definition of what the host-IMP interface would look like, or even what functions the IMP would provide, we focused on exotic ideas. We envisioned the possibility of application specific protocols, with code downloaded to user sites, and we took a crack at designing a language to support this. The first version was known as DEL, for "Decode-Encode Language" and a later version was called NIL, for "Network Interchange Language." When the IMP contract was finally let and BBN [Bolt, Beranek, and Newman Corporation, to whom the IPTO had awarded the IMP contract in January 1969] provided some definite information on the host-IMP interface, all attention shifted to low-level matters and the ambitious ideas for automatic downloading of code evaporated. It was several years before ideas like remote procedure calls and typed objects reappeared.[11]

Their "evaporation" was one signal that Engelbart's dream to see NLS and his Mail and Journal features used by all ARPANET users would come to naught.

Indeed, the NLS Mail and Journal features themselves never attracted many users outside ARC. Instead, it was other, existing e-mail systems that caught everyone's attention. "It seems that the protocols that linked truly heterogeneous systems were the ones that got the most notice—for e-mail, IP, NFS . . . for everything on the ARPANET/Internet" (Rulifson, personal communication).

Since CTSS at Project MAC, most early time-sharing systems had provided a mailing application, but these applications were single-system based: users could communicate only with other users of the same system. The creation of the first electronic-mail capability over the ARPA network is usually credited to Ray Tomlinson at BBN in July 1970, with his SNDMSG application for the TENEX operating system.[12] Hardy (1996) reported, however, that "Tomlinson derived the network version of SNDMSG from two pre-existing software utilities. The first was an intra-machine email utility . . . the second was an early ARPANET file transfer program called CPYNET." Tomlinson worked at BBN when they traded their SDS 940 for the PDP-10, and he contributed afterward to the development of TENEX (Salus 1995, 95). His SNDMSG and READ-MAIL applications reflected previous developments at project MAC, to the point that Hardy quotes him saying that sending e-mail over the ARPANET was a "natural extension" of that system's capabilities.

For a while, ARPANET e-mail was indeed the most "natural extension" of TENEX: Tomlinson and BBN gave the program to the other sites on the network that were running TENEX, where it was inserted as the command MAIL and ran as an extension of the File Transfer Protocol (Salus 1995, 95). Soon it was adapted to the other computers on the network, such as the IBM 360 and the XDS Sigma 7. Other individuals, such as Steve Crocker and Larry Roberts himself, started to improve the application as soon as it was released. Larry Roberts's program was called RD, for "read." Vint Cerf recalled that

> Larry actually may have been the first one to write a reasonable program to parse e-mail. He wrote a TECO program that would . . . let's see, the way I remember it now is that we used to send e-mail on the Telnet channel of an FTP [File Transfer Protocol] connection. And the message would be appended to a file with a particular name, like mail.txt or something like that. It would be appended in a certain agreed way so that you could write a program, in this case a TECO macro, that would search down through the text file and pull up just the message itself. There was a header on the front of each message that said how many characters long the message was and you could skip from header to header and it would list the titles and the to and the from fields and the like. So that would have been . . . certainly demonstrable by the October 1972 time frame. I think the first real e-mail floated around somewhere as early as 1970. But it was not uniform everywhere. (Cerf 1990)

TECO stood for Text Editor and COrrector (and originally stood for [paper] Tape Editor and COrrector). It was actually quite a complicated programming language. It was sort of a programmer's text editor that could be used on-line or off-line with TENEX. Like NLS, it had one-character or two-character commands. According to Bob Kahn, "It was just the simplest, most straightforward editor you could imagine" (quoted in Cerf 1990).

Even inside ARC, NLS's supremacy over TECO was not unquestioned. Some members of the technical staff of the laboratory, such as Donald Wallace, would occasionally say that most of their work was done in TECO because they could do it much faster and with more flexibility than in NLS. Outside Engelbart's lab, the availability of a number of TENEX-compatible mail applications such as SNDMSG, READMAIL, RD, and others prevented the NLS mail feature from becoming predominant in the context of network mail between 1971 and 1977. ARC/NIC staff members still contributed to the Mail

Protocol discussions,[13] but they were in no position to impose NLS Mail as the application of choice. They still used it internally, however, in connection with the Journal.

But another of Engelbart's decrees proved to be controversial internally:

> We originally designed our Mail/Journal system to give the user a choice as whether to make an entry unrecorded (as in current mail systems), or to be recorded in the Journal. I knew that there would be lots of questions, and some quandary, associated with the question "to record or not to record." I assumed that many fewer items would be recorded than "should be"—as might be judged after we someday would learn the value and establish criteria for recording. So, I ordained that *all* entries would be recorded—no option. It put some people under considerable strain. (Engelbart 1988, 213)

Engelbart later reported that "a very valuable contributor, somehow felt violently opposed to the basic concept, and it possibly hastened his departure" (ibid.). Engelbart might have been referring to Rulifson, although Rulifson claims that he never felt "violently opposed to the basic ideas." Instead he thought that "Doug was way off base on some of his social ideas; just plain wrong," and that "the work on the off-line system was a waste of time." According to him, the basic reason why he left ARC was that he "wanted to have a job that allowed him to combine it with a thesis at Stanford" (Rulifson, personal communication). Whatever the reason for his departure might have been,[14] ARC indeed lost a valuable contributor when he left.

There were other sources of trouble at Engelbart's lab, as well, though, and they, too were related to Engelbart's crusade to produce not just new technologies, but new kinds of people to use them. Licklider's and Taylor's original idea conceived of the computer as a communication medium, as an interpersonal interface, a conception that other researchers in the IPTO community also shared. For example, David Clark, senior research scientist at MIT's laboratory for computer science, stated flatly that "it is not proper to think of networks as connecting computers. Rather, they connect people using computers to mediate. The great success of the internet is not technical, but in human impact. Electronic mail may not be a wonderful advance in Computer Science, but it is a whole new way for people to communicate" (RFC 1336, quoted in Hauben 1996). But for Engelbart, the implementation of such an interpersonal interface also was supposed to involve active research on the human side of the system, on the ways to improve group collaboration to take advantage of the newly acquired computer aids. That led him from the engineering challenges of the new technology to "social engineering" experiments. These experiments reveal the problems of the laboratory at the time of the beginning of the implementation of the ARPANET and the early developments at PARC.

OF MICE, AND MEN, AND WOMEN, AND EST

In the late 1960's, when Engelbart translated his early concept of the "intelligence worker" in the somewhat less elite-sounding notion of "knowledge worker" under the influence of Peter Drucker,[15] part of the cultural unacceptability of the notion of the "intelligence worker" was political. As one of my interviewees recalled, Engelbart "modeled the world not as a democratic environment where people would have computers of their own, and software would be tailored to a lower need, but software would be tailored to a higher need. And if you needed a year learning how to use a piece of software, hey, it takes time to learn a skill" (Belleville 1992).

Douglas Engelbart and his ARC group were not working in a cultural vacuum. The personal computer is in part the product of what in Europe was called "the generation of '68," and of its culture as it developed in the San Francisco Bay Area, from the Berkeley Free Speech Movement and antiwar agitation on through the San Francisco Summer of Love and the rise of the Human Potential movement.

> There was a whole 1960's thing . . . the Free University was in Palo Alto (laughs).
> There was a lot of stuff going on . . . psychodrama, est was going on, Esalen,
> down in Big Sur, the Whole Earth Catalog was right across the street at that time
> to SRI. . . . You know, I am from the East Coast and I found it too confining. California was wide open, particularly during this time: anything went. Of course a
> lot of people floundered. . . . I think that it helped a lot that there was sort of the
> perfect climate to put an engineering cast into, because they were just naturally
> looser. . . . It was a very nice setup generally . . . a little crazy. We had some riots
> at Stanford and stuff, that were unfortunate, and other things. But basically it was
> a very good setup I think. (Kay 1992)

Inside SRI, ARC was famous for its adoption of many countercultural trends and values. While the cultural strands of those heady days often are difficult to separate, for Engelbart and the ARC lab at SRI, the most important cultural influence was not the trend toward participatory democracy, but something quite different and more in line with the goals of Engelbart's crusade: the rise of interest in methods, both new and old, for unlocking powers supposed to be potentially present in those who sought to transcend their present state and conditions. This influence would have wide-ranging effects at ARC.

The POD People

One example is the PODAC episode, which occurred in the laboratory between January 25 and September 11, 1972. Engelbart had designed one integrated experimental plan in three distinct activities, PODAC, LINAC, and FRAMAC.[16] The line activity (LINAC) was designed "to carry out activities within the framework that move [the laboratory] toward the goals." The framework activity (FRAMAC) was designed to "discuss and set the framework goals." And the personal and organizational development activity (PODAC) was "the people's organization, representing all of the human beings that work in/for ARC" (JE#10225, April 25).

PODAC may be one reason why the ARC technical contribution to the Network Working Group slowed down in 1972, since it created a crisis inside ARC. Thanks to the Journal feature of NLS and Engelbart's order that everything should be recorded, the whole archive of PODAC-related Journal entries is still available for study.[17] Engelbart started the experiment with an internal ARC memo entitled "to launch PODAC" and distributed to the whole staff on January 25, 1972 (JE#8651). In this memo, he explained the purpose of the experiment and gave its main rules.

PODAC was to be "a separate organizational set-up from that for which we departmentalize our activities . . . in the business of setting and pursuing our goals":

> This whole activity is aimed at serving two needs that exist within ARC: We who tell the world that we are learning how to show other teams how to achieve greater goal-pursuit effectiveness must constantly examine ourselves . . . both as an organization and as individuals, while making a conscious effort to understand how we are doing, and how we can improve. I am quite convinced that unless there is a strong, constant, and pervasive attitude among us that we want to keep developing ourselves, and unless we consciously keep trying to do so, then we are fooling ourselves about seriously pioneering this augmentation SYSTEM stuff.

PODAC participation was mandatory for staff members in a weekly meeting of at least two hours, and the whole ARC staff was distributed in four groups, or PODs: Cedar, Fir, Oak, and Redwood, "aiming for balanced representation in age, sex, professional training, length of association with ARC, and work roles."[18] About this mandatory character, Engelbart was as clear as any leader could be in the early 1970's in the Bay Area: "I consider that attendance and participation will be part of the 'employment conditions' for working within ARC, and thus expect to press strongly for complete and consistent attendance."

Engelbart established the PODs as crossdisciplinary groups of approximately ten people with the express purpose that they would talk to each other. According to some staff members, the main motivation to start PODAC was the feeling that ARC was splitting into camps: the new ARPANET functions at ARC introduced a disciplinary divide between people working on the research activities ("programmers") and the service people hired for the NIC ("clerks"). Some members even claimed that PODAC was originally conceived as a kind of group therapy experiment.

This kind of a "social experiment" was not new to ARC or to Engelbart. As an individual, Engelbart had had some experience with encounter groups and had generally felt that his interaction with these groups had helped him "to understand himself better, to fully appreciate his attitudes and beliefs and integrate his thinking and opinions, and . . . to communicate better with the world outside himself" (reported in the minutes of the Fir POD meeting of April 18, JE#10125). After the 1968 demo, Engelbart hired several psychology consultants to work with ARC and experiment with various group-interaction methods in order to establish better communication in the laboratory.

In Engelbart's scheme, PODAC's purpose was to facilitate communication and interaction, but not to decide ARC's goals: it was "to be orthogonal to the management structure that commits resources, sets targets, hires, reviews, and is held accountable." However, he also insisted in the same "launching memo" that "better and more accurate statements of purposes, roles, modes of pursuing them, etc., are expected to be part of the product of the on-going PODAC," (JE#8651). This charter soon created tensions and problems within ARC. Facilitating people's understanding of themselves and their colleagues as part of the ARC community without giving them a way to have input into the goals and decisions of the organization was bound to cause problems. And it did.

Engelbart decided that he would not participate in any POD. He reported later that he felt that his presence was an "inhibiting factor," drawing too much attention away from the interaction among staff members during their meetings (minutes of the March 3 PODCOM meeting, JE#9561). In one case, it was reported that the dynamics of the group indeed were strongly influenced by his presence, even if the group had invited him ("Fir meeting of April 18," JE#10125). The report of the meeting emphasized this difference, stating that the dynamic tended "to become somewhat polarized into operating as a group vs. (or interacting with) Doug, rather than a group interacting within its own members." Since he had decreed himself apart from the groups and in ultimate control, this outcome seems inevitable. The issue of Engelbart's specific mode of leadership thus appeared crucial to the experiment from its start.

The minutes of the PODs meetings give us a good idea of their agenda, which was very much in tune with what appears retrospectively as the emergence of a culture of on-line computing. Topics addressed range from management problems at SRI stemming from the unusual working style of the programmers to more classic topics such as salary questions. In this respect, the PODAC archive represents a highly valuable witness to the emergence of this specific culture, one presented with the spontaneity and lack of formality that had been purposefully initiated with the RFCs and that we have come to expect from computer-mediated communication (see Star 1995):

The first three or four meetings . . . were pretty much the same experience that most of the PODs seem to be having from what I hear the members say. I enjoyed the experience, because my POD has some very outgoing, warm and interesting people in it. Even though all of them seemed to be on the defensive, their person-ality did come through and they began to be individuals to me instead of people I called to the phone. As a POD, we were having rather frustrating experiences in trying to find out what we were supposed to do . . . this frustration began to irri-tate us to the point where, without actually bringing it out and putting it into words . . . as a unit we suddenly stopped talking about PODs and wondering what PODs were going to do and started enjoying each other as people. We suddenly started TALKING to each other instead of making polite noises. ("POD Obser-vations," JE#9684, March 23)

As PODAC became more personal, the personal-development side of the activity at first took over the organizational side. Some members described these meetings as "bull sessions." Topics discussed covered "raising kids, philosophies of life, likes and dislikes, funny incidents in our lives, the dope rackets, 'hippies' as they are vs. as the general public thinks they are . . . you name it" ("Fir POD report of activities," JE#10188, April 11). In short, these discussions reflected the basis of the on-line computing culture at ARC in the general countercultural background of the Bay Area of the late 1960's.

But issues involving internal ARC organization arose that show there were causes of discontent among the staff members that revolved around what espe-cially in the context of the emphasis on participatory democracy in the 1960's and 1970's seemed to be the arbitrary and absolute nature of Engelbart's lead-ership. Participants strongly voiced serious concerns about the organizational aspect of the activity during some of the meetings: "There was widespread dis-satisfaction with the lack of well-defined roles, structure, and goals here at ARC . . . there were objections and dissatisfactions expressed about how Doug performs his role. There is an impression that Doug goes off in a corner and hatches ideas. People are uncomfortable with all the surprises. . . . Doug does not allow enough control, goal setting, participation for ARC in general" ("Communiqué from the Cedar 9," JE#8717, January 29).

Several people also felt that ARC was becoming more and more a service operation and less and less research-oriented, especially given its increasing ties with the government via ARPANET and with business via Xerox. Some tough questions were asked about the situation of ARC and NLS: "Can a com-munity like ARC support both research and service? If so, can guidelines be specified as to the extent of a service operation that can feasibly and peacefully coexist with research? Where and how far do we go with NLS—especially in light of Xerox?" ("Redwood POD notes," JE#9070, February 14).

The Cedar POD even indicated that they collectively felt that PODAC was a waste of time (February 16 communiqué, JE#9200). Walter Bass answered in a personal message "that he felt that it was time to begin an evaluation of PODAC," but also that "PODAC is undergoing birth pains at this time and that it is premature to throw out the baby until we've all given it a fair chance" ("Some thoughts about PODAC," JE#9220, February 17). The Redwood POD reported that "some people are obviously bored" and that they had held a discussion about the necessity to go on with the PODAC experiment (meeting notes for February 22, JE#9245).

The issue of the PODs' function in integrating new staff members into the ARC organizational and human culture, a process that, apparently without irony, actually was called "indoctrination," surfaced several times in POD meetings. Two of the most recently hired staff members, Paul Rech and Mike Kudlick, both managers, reported that they felt that "they had not been adequately warned about what to expect at ARC in the way of pressures to adapt to the atmosphere of social experimentation—e.g., PODs and our unorthodox management structure."

Engelbart had decided that there should be a super POD where representatives of the various PODs could discuss their respective experiences with PODAC. This entity was called PODCOM and it rapidly demonstrated that a crisis was developing over the nature of the organization and the role of the PODs in it. They could use the PODs to identify, elaborate, and express the concerns of the ARC community, but Engelbart did not have to pay any attention to them. Walter Bass reported that "the role and functioning of PODCOM has never been clear to all (if any) of us," but that many ARC staff members originally saw it as the way to give them a two-way channel for communication with the operational management of ARC and SRI. But Engelbart had rejected this idea from the start: "it's not true that PODCOM members will function as communication channels from Doug to the rest of ARC," Walter Bass reported. "Doug's experience with second parties communicating his ideas to third parties is that it doesn't work." Bass concluded that they needed "an entirely new organization to replace PODCOM" (minutes of the first PODCOM meeting, reported by Bass in JE#8735, dated January 31, 1972).

Kenneth Victor insisted "Doug has indicated that he is willing to use PODCOM as a vehicle for communication from the rest of ARC to him but not from him to the rest of ARC" and rightfully concluded that PODAC had "succeeded in formalizing a means for one-way communication (a very poor means of communication)" (personal message, JE#9244, dated February 22, 1972). The problem resurfaced again in a Redwood POD session when one member complained about the lack of feedback from PODCOM on issues raised in POD meetings. It was finally decided that PODCOM would change its organization and mode of operation. Walter Bass was chosen to be the chairman of PODCOM, Engelbart decided that he would not automatically attend PODCOM meetings, and more importantly, the function of PODCOM was somewhat revised, without, however, much changing the basic structure of decision making at ARC:

> PODCOM will be responsible for overseeing the POD activity and implementing established PODAC policy, fostering inter-POD communication, and seeing that the lines of communication between Doug and the PODs remain open. The question of how PODAC policy comes to be established remains open; basically, Doug will be held responsible for overall policy decisions, and PODCOM will attempt to guide Doug in making these decisions and will set policy itself (in a domain yet to be specified) with the advice and consent of Doug. (Report on PODCOM meeting 10 April 1972, JE#10086)

Engelbart therefore stopped attending PODCOM, but if he was willing to "not exert so much control over its activities," he nevertheless kept the prerogative to veto its decisions.

After an initial three months devoted to experimentation, according to Engelbart's design, PODAC underwent an internal evaluation. Each POD was asked to reflect on its own experience and discuss it with other PODs ("PODCOM Request for Comments on PODAC Evaluation," JE#10221, April 27). Some PODs considered the experiment very successful, while others disagreed and wanted to end it. For instance, the Oak POD reached no definite conclusions about the experiment, apart from some opinions relating to Engelbart's design philosophy and personality: "It takes three months to learn there's no way to wait out Doug" (Oak answers PODCOM questions, JE#10326, May 4).

The more successful PODs, on the other hand, proposed to continue with the experiment, albeit in a renewed form. The Fir POD put itself in an off-line status and proposed to give place to Special Interest Groups (SIG) focusing on "meeting effectiveness," "language and information," "effective group organization," "special skills," and—in a completely different register, hinting at even more problematic social experiments to come—"Scientology" ("A position paper on PODs and plans for further research from Fir POD (SIGCORE)," JE#10450, May 12). To mark this transition, Fir POD renamed itself SIGCORE, for the core group of people who decided to lead the experiment into its new form.

Some staff members from the other PODs, however, opposed this new development. Harvey Lehtman, for instance, commented that the Fir move was in contradiction with Engelbart's design for the experiment: "Such a move is tantamount to secession from the Union. . . . PODs should not deal with line activities. . . . It is too soon to go out of the small structure imposed by DCE" ("Reply to Fir memo (10450)," JE#10453, May 12). Diane Kaye insisted that the Fir proposal "really represents an attempt to get back into the comfortable familiar place of doing activities with only those people who share your particular point of view or special interest" ("Reply to Fir memo (10450)," JE#10454, May 12). Kenneth Victor went even further and questioned the validity of some of the Fir POD claims: "I personally question one of the underlying hypotheses of the SIGCORE paper, i.e., that Fir Pod has outlived its usefulness, and that all the members of Fir Pod are active and participating members" ("A personal response to Fir," JE#10468, May 16). The final word eventually came from the PODCOM chairman, Walter Bass:

> What evaluative processes have been attempted have reached no expressed conclusions, and we have no framework for PODAC evolution in which to discuss ANY specific proposals for changing (or not changing) the POD organization. Frankly we don't know what the hell is going on. In this context, the PODCOM reshuffling proposal is pure bullshit, and if that is the best PODCOM has to offer us, then perhaps PODCOM—and maybe the POD organization itself—has earned oblivion. ("Comments on PODCOM reshuffling proposal (11041)," JE#11059, July 14)

There was still an ultimate attempt to revive PODAC, though. In a PODAC Planning Committee meeting August 3, 1972, it was decided that the committee would change its name to PARSLEY (apparently not an acronym for anything) and attempt to "define purpose as its organization of POD activities and fostering PODAC participation among ARC members" (JE#11217). The committee announced that PODAC participation was then on a voluntary basis, even if it still stated that its goal was "ARC-universal involvement in PODAC." This new organization did not succeed in such an enterprise, and PODAC eventually died.

As part of the restructuring of PODCOM and of the whole POD experiment, Engelbart had once again opened the culture of the lab to outside influences, stating that "each POD should feel free to call on outside help from consultants . . . the POD members can do reading and searching for group interaction information on their own time outside office work; attend whatever lectures and/or classes or other means they might find to assist them in learning about encounter groups, T groups, and group dynamics, for the purpose of enhancing the POD work." He also made it possible for staff members to have up to 20 percent of the costs associated with these activities billed to SRI, with the proviso that it could not be higher than 10 percent of total salary time.

Some staff members took up Engelbart's proposition to call on external help. As early as April 21, the Oak POD arranged for the visit of Gus Matzorkis, a consultant in organizational development, which was followed on May 19 by that of another, Dr. Arthur Hastings. Jacques Vallée stated that "Dr. Hastings had been very interested in ARC, its problems, and its method of meeting them, but felt that there were some issues in ARC that are hidden, and have not been brought out into the open, and are not yet recognized" ("Minutes Fir POD/SIGCORE meeting," 24 May 1972, JE#10616, May 31). Gus Matzorkis eventually wrote a report based on his meetings with ARC members. The report, dated June 30, was submitted to the Journal on September 11, 1972 (JE#11732).

This opening to the outside marked the end of PODAC. The report concluded that:

> There is a largely unacknowledged clash of personal values systems in ARC. . . . There is considerably more formality in the ARC work culture than appears at first glance. . . . There is a tendency in ARC to sometimes be unduly tied down to the past, to be preoccupied with evaluating past decisions and events, to be carrying a load of yesterday's "unfinished business". . . . The relationships between Doug and ARC as a whole, and between Doug and various individuals and sub-groups in ARC, set much of the tone and pace of the work culture and provide the immediate setting or background for the major issues and problems in the culture. This dominance of the leader/others relationships is stronger here than in most work cultures.

No other PODAC-related Journal entries were submitted after this point. Both professional organizational consultants concluded that specific issues plagued the ARC work culture, issues that needed more than nice bull sessions to move toward a resolution. Most of these related to the specific kind of leadership that Engelbart exercised on ARC and appeared finally as built-in problems in an organization set up around one man's crusade. It is no wonder, then, that the last episode of this social experiment led toward "personal" rather than "organizational development," and to still more conflict between Engelbart and the participants in his crusade.

ARC *and est*

Along with the search for professional help from organizational development consultants, some ARC members turned to the personal-development movements that were so strong in the Bay Area at the end of the 1960's. In May 1972, the Oak POD started to "evaluate" an organization called Erhard Seminars Training: est—always lowercased. Paul Nathan Rosenberg, aka Werner Erhard, had launched est in October 1971 at the Jack Tar Hotel in San Francisco with nearly a thousand people in attendance (Pressman 1993). A former car salesman and autodidact who had been influenced by such self-help books as Napoleon Hill's *Think and Grow Rich*, Rosenberg created est as the kind of self-help program known to psychologists as "Large Group Self-Awareness Training." The seminar was built eclectically on the principles of Zen, Scientology, and other such philosophies and "philosophies."[19] Est lasted for almost fifteen years before Erhard repackaged it as the Landmark Forum.[20]

The Oak POD invited Stewart Emery from est to introduce the organization to ARC, and Walter Bass attended the seminars ("Oak Pod is evaluating Erhard Seminars Training," JE#10610, May 30). He came back very enthusiastic about est, saying that "the EST course is worth $150" and that "EST theory has a great deal in common with Augmentation Theory" ("Personal Evaluation of the est course," JE#10761, June 19). He managed to communicate his enthusiasm to Engelbart, who soon reiterated his proposal to pay for part of the cost of est to his staff members who were willing to enroll. Eventually Engelbart served on the board of est for a while in the 1970's.

The lack of PODAC Journal entries describing what happened next means that to document it, we have to turn from hard evidence to literature. Jacques F. Vallée,[21] who after his ARC career became a novelist and a student of unidentified flying objects (UFOs) and of putative alien contacts with earth dwellers, gave a "composite, imaginary, fictionalized" account of the est episode at ARC in his 1983 roman à clef *The Network Revolution: Confessions of a Computer Scientist*. Its portrait of the est episode at SRI, however, is very thinly disguised.[22] When I interviewed him, Jacques Vallée stood by his narrative, without the veil of fiction, this time (Vallée 1996). It is an account of how ARC and its crusade for the Augmentation of Human Intellect fell prey to the forces that rule such quasi-religious enterprises.

In Vallée's narrative, Pacific Research Laboratory (PRL) stands for SRI, "Stanley" for Engelbart, the Systematic Thought-Enhancement Machine (STEM) for NLS and/or ARC, and the Military Equipment and Gear Agency (MEGA) for ARPA. Aside from its semifictional and often ironic character, Vallée's account remains an insider's picture of what happened at ARC when the laboratory turned to est's version of the Human Potential movement's attempt to make people realize their full capabilities.

Eric Elzevier, Vallée's fictional surrogate, a marginalized outsider and observer in the classic manner of such narratives, tells the story of an experiment that ran amok because "the human factors came back and took revenge." Elzevier joins the STEM project in 1972, the same year Vallée joined ARC, "with some industrial experience with computers" (Vallée 1982, 100). At that time, at ARC/STEM, the situation was difficult: "the chief engineer [English] had resigned," the group was "riddled by conflict," and the strong countercultural bent of some of the young programmers was clashing with the idea of a MEGA funding of the project.[23]

According to Vallée's narrative, in the est episode, these young idealists actually were "expressing their identity, making it clear to the whole world that though they might be taking millions of dollars from the Defense Department to run their research, they were actually clever opportunists" using the government funding for higher, better ends—to realize "Stanley's" vision, now seemingly threatened with failure from without and from within:

> The STEM project was different, and they were going to prove it by enrolling in EST, a process about which they knew very little. The great mystery loomed above them, and it was their only opportunity to solve their personal and group conflicts. A dozen staff members caved in right away. They were ready for it. . . . They were professional people, for the most part, who accepted the blame for the current failure of the STEM. Since Stanley could not be wrong, they themselves must have been unworthy of his great plan, they must have failed in the great mission he had given them. . . . The first wave of believers dived into EST like a group of travelers lost in the desert, seeking salvation in the waters of some refreshing and mysterious river. When they came back to the office on Monday, it was hard to recognize them. They had not undergone a simple attitude change: it was transfiguration. . . . Nothing got done that day; they bathed for hours in the ebullience of their new spirit, and the others listened to their stories, which were couched in the new language that clearly eluded and excluded the rest of the group. . . . Other mysteries were implied by the First Wave proselytizers. They now knew how to be permanently happy. . . . They had achieved a superhuman state and had sneezed their last sneezes. The first wave put so much pressure on the group that a second splinter began to come loose from the STEM . . . EST had become like a wet blanket of conformity thrown over a nice bunch of individuals trying to live out Stanley's genial dream. The STEM idea had now been restructured to enclose even bigger and more inaccessible goals: universal happiness, permanently clear thought. Scientologists spend years and many thousands of dollars trying to get "clear:" EST covered the same ground in a few days for just 250 bucks. The Second Wave formed itself. (Ibid., 107–9).

Several aspects of this narrative echo Gus Matzorkis's insights on the problems of the laboratory: the focus on one man's "genial dream," the turn to the organization's past goals, the conformity. Moreover, it abounds with mystic, religious/cultish aspirations to turn doom and tragedy into "salvation" and "transfiguration." The crusade was failing on the shore of the promised land, its prophet entrenched in its vision, its soldier-priests lost in self-doubt. In the literature describing the anthropology of religions, this is the time of scapegoats and the murderous crowd.[24]

The ARC/STEM project as a whole had to prove that it was different, and at the center of a spreading crusade, but its contacts with the outside had amply demonstrated that it in fact was insufficiently differentiated from what was going on at other labs and, indeed, increasingly marginal with respect to unanticipated developments elsewhere. In addition, in Vallée's account, the staff at STEM is facing a paradoxical situation that undermines their sense of self-identity: its members can be mistaken for the "lackeys of the Master of War." STEM is funded by MEGA, and its prophet's crusade is paid for by the forces of destruction. At this crucial juncture, the prophet himself is speechless. He has lost his ability to convey the Word. Too busy fighting these evil forces on their own ground, he cannot find the energy to guide his converts spreading the Word. The Word has already been given to them, anyway: they should be convinced. All Stanley does at this time is repeat the gospel, over and over again. This is exactly what FRAMAC, the framework activity designed to "discuss and set the framework goals," did at ARC in endless meetings that turned toward the past, repeating for the new converts yesterday's Word, the prophet's epiphany.

In Vallée's account, the converts consequently start doubting the prophet, and this is what began to happen at ARC, as well. Stanley's followers know that they should not be mistaken for the "lackeys of the Masters of War," but STEM proves not to work. It does not solve the extremely urgent and complex problems it was designed to solve. The Word, Stanley's/Engelbart's promise of human augmentation, cannot be doubted, but the prophet who brought it can. As Engelbart did with PODAC and PODCOM, Stanley, the shepherd, casts himself apart and retreats: he does not belong anymore to the crowd of his disciples.

The crusade to develop and extend the potential of human beings to deal creatively with the challenges of the modern world thus finds itself in effect leaderless at the very time its goals and the self-descriptions of its adherents are being put in question by the marginalization of the entire enterprise. Then, another prophet, another master of the Word, offers a way out, allowing the crusaders finally to become one with the self-descriptions they have embraced, but failed to achieve. This is the ultimate goal of personal development. They can redifferentiate themselves, become again the "augmented individuals" they are supposed to be. This is where est comes in.

Werner Erhard was another prophet of augmented human potentials. Walter Bass said so in his report to ARC after his initiation, and Eric Elzevier, Vallée's outsider, says so, as well. Bass, the earliest convert, was the link: in spite of his contributions to PODAC, as the chairman of PODCOM, the one-way link to Engelbart, the original prophet, he also was a member of the POD that doubted him the most. He was the first to go to est and the first to see est as a way to redeem the ARC project. "Werner Erhard may well be the most capable 'Personal Development' man in the world today, and I imagine that he is very capable at 'Organization Development' as well, since his background is, in fact, in organization development," Bass wrote enthusiastically. The way to redeem an organization whose development seemed to have gone awry thus seemed to be yet another version of personal development.

In the est version, the obstacles to personal development lay within. MEGA is not the enemy, the est converts in Vallée's novel are able to conclude. The enemy is in us. And the techniques of est were well designed for the work of eradicating the enemy within: public disclosure of the individual's whole being, good and evil, sometimes under stress, sometimes with pleasure, in a manner that, even when satirized in the movie *Semi-Tough* (1977), has clear affinities with the techniques of brainwashing. Vallée says "they had gone through the humiliation, the stripping, the public flogging of their souls, the *animectomy*" (ibid., 110, emphasis in the original). Robert Todd Carroll describes the est method as "often abusive, profane, demeaning, and authoritarian." He quotes a former "adept" who describes the Landmark Forum experience that evolved out of est as follows:

> The Forum attempts to deconstruct personal attachments in a non-abusive manner by focusing your attention inward: The basis is being kept in a hotel ballroom for 10 hour days with little sleep, listening to the same thing over and over and over. Most of it consists of having people look at their childhood, and find the events that caused them to make decisions about other people, especially their parents. . . . You can't go to the bathroom when you want, you take meals in groups, there are strict rules about talking and conduct, and the leader won't hesitate to shame you into compliance. Much of it is psychology parlor tricks, like making a headache go away by imagining it as a physical void in your head, and imagining it being filled. This goes on for four full days.[25]

Insufficiently differentiated from others as crusaders for human augmentation, what Vallée calls the First Wave of converts, the lab members who first embrace est, are now bound together as one, differentiated from others by being wholly undifferentiated themselves, bonded together as individuals who have confronted the weaknesses that failed the crusade. The First Wave is a crowd that goes through an ordeal as a single person: in Vallée's narrative, its twelve members (!) are described in generic, undifferentiated terms: professionals, young and idealistic, be they programmers or clerks, men or women. They are saved, and they can go back to the Word and save it, as well. And they find a ready audience in what Vallée calls the Second Wave.

> The Second Wave was intense and sincere. PRL officials had gone into the ranks of many Silicon Gulch companies, to recruit a more serious cadre of managers

who would, they believed, restore their credibility in Washington. These managers had solid engineering degrees and production experience. Stanley gave them no authority and no means to use their experience, however, perhaps because he imagined the possibility that one of them would seize power. The result was a very confused bunch of middle-aged middle managers who had left their jobs in search of something more, because they thought there must be something more to life, indeed, than scheming down a career path at IBM or Varian. They had tried to recapture their creativity in the joy of research with this young, idealistic group, and they believed in what they had understood to be Stanley's goal. What's more, they knew they could turn it into a reality. Yet somehow they failed: the project had gone nowhere, they spent their time in agonizing meetings where no decisions were ever made. . . . Since the vision could not be wrong, there must be something really rotten about *them*, the old dinosaurs, the rejects of Computer Wonderland. . . . The suggestion of failure was there, under the surface, and the managers were emotionally vulnerable to it. . . . The Second Wave could not delay much longer their visit to EST. The younger group members dangled before them the rewards of acceptance and reconciliation, the open arms of a loving group, if they would accept the ordeal. They did. The following Monday, the gray-haired managers came to the office with the subdued glow of men who have found the inner truth, men who would never again be late for meetings, think less than clearly, or catch colds. (Ibid., 109–10)

The Second Wave turns to est for a different motive than the First Wave, but in the same fashion, as a crowd. Who could say if the Word has really touched them? "If they were so bright, after all, why didn't they stay at Varian drawing big fat salaries?" (ibid., 109). The redeemed converts of the first phase promise them the reward of acceptance at last. If they become "developed persons" they will eventually fit in.

If not, however, they will infect the whole enterprise, bring it low, perhaps even take it over. Notice the reiteration of the metaphor of the infectious cold betrayed by a "sneeze," in Vallée's account. It is the trope of the poison of doubt so common in persecutory texts (Girard 1982, 27).[26] But when the Second Wave has embraced est, the stage is set for catastrophe. STEM/ARC now is a mob of righteous converts who threaten to turn on anyone who differs from them. And they are in charge.

For those who had not yet taken EST . . . the pressure became unbelievable. For a while, it was a constant bombardment from group members who had gone through the Mysteries and now had a stake in the outcome. The whole world must go through EST to be saved, it was explained to Eric, or at least the whole STEM project. . . . In spite of their participation in the country's leading experiment in networking, the staff members at PRL were as vulnerable to this psychological pressure as any other group. . . . The First and Second Waves looked for other victims. They thought the task would be pretty easy because they had become the overwhelming majority. They formed a block around Stanley, who could hire and fire. They expected no organized resistance and they found none. Instead, they found individuals who could stand on their two feet and simply tell them to get lost. (Vallée 1982, 10–12)

These "individuals who could stand on their two feet," the few who are able to resist the pressure to realize themselves, are those who already have done so, those who are secure in their independent identities. First, there is Eric himself, whose "status in the team was peculiar." He could have belonged to the First or the Second Wave, since "he was from industry, like the managers of the Second Wave. But he was younger than the managers, and was known for his computer work among the peers of the hip programmers" (ibid., 110).

This technological ability appears in fact as a common feature of all but one of the resisting victims in Vallée's narrative. "Cliff," the second resister, "ran the network and was their only professional contact with the MEGA community." "Guru," the third, "was the only one in the group who knew the computer's operating system" (ibid.). "John," the fourth, "was the only remaining programmer from the team that had written the current version of STEM." That left "Wilma," who was different because she "was a strong, cheerful person" well versed in the esoteric traditions. She even "regarded that kid Erhard as of those Werner-come-latelies who had missed the whole point about initiation." "Wilma," though, epitomizes the personal level of development of all but one of the resisters: "Cliff . . . was intently studying the mystics," "Guru" had "already tried this particular style of domination and it didn't turn him on," and "John's real goal in life was to become a woodcrafter" (ibid., 111–12).

The resisting individuals are the real heroes of Vallée's account: "this was a revelation to Eric. He discovered the strength and the resilience of some team members whose real spirit he had never suspected." The resisting individuals are heroes because they already are fully developed people with some faith of their own and the technological or managerial abilities to be contributing members of the organization. They occupy strategic positions in the project and are essential to it. Of each of them, he says something like "it was impossible to get rid of him" (ibid.).

In the end, in Vallée's account, it is their resistance, not the pressure of the est converts, that prevails against the social and psychic tides ripping through the lab. "The Third Wave never materialized, and the apostles of EST realized they were wasting their time. The project conflicts deepened as time went on and as the glow of the EST experience gradually wore off. MEGA threatened to cut off its funding. People started coming to work late again" (ibid).

"And then one day, right in the middle of a staff meeting, Stanley sneezed" (ibid.) In the end, it is not the resisting individuals who suffer the catastrophe for which the est episode had prepared the lab. It is the prophet himself on whom the First Wave and the Second Wave turn. He becomes the victim, the scapegoat blamed for the failures of the crusade, failures that the others had attributed to themselves and had believed they had purged from themselves.

In Vallée's narrative, this sneeze closes the episode: the prophet himself is infected. In a conclusion to the chapter devoted to ARC, Vallée adds:

> The results were predictable. Armed with their new strength, those who had *not* taken EST began to look around. Eric remembers asking himself what he was doing there, and then he resigned, having spent less than a year in the project. Cliff, Guru, Wilma and John also resigned, what was left of STEM floated on for a little while, and then PRL managers succeeded in selling the project to a company that was looking for a document-preparation system. It had truly shrunk to that, to nothing more than a text-editor similar to those you will now find in the offices of any large newspaper. Once again, computer technology had devoured its own children. (Ibid., 113)

For Vallée, the infection was "the little terror of 'the Other Person,' which lurks in a dark corner somewhere in all of us," the sheer terror of unmediated communication (ibid.). In his narrative, the prophet carries the blame for this infection, for a terror that he could have dispelled, but did not.

In the ARC lab, the est episode affected staff members in a similar way: some resigned, gave up research, and moved to communes. Others became very sensitive to interactions (Lehtman 1992). Engelbart did not exactly solve his own "communication problems" with this experiment. Moreover, he entrenched himself even more in his gospel after this episode, continuing to face the same misunderstandings both inside and outside of his laboratory. Meanwhile, ARC floated on for a little while, too.

Chaos at the "Breakthrough Lab"

While the ARC lab internally was undergoing the throes of its agony over the apparent failure of its crusade, outside forces continued to put the crusade in jeopardy, as well. In the early days of 1972, ARC was facing a difficult situation: the relationship with ARPA-IPTO was getting very tense, as this excerpt from an internal ARC memo from Richard W. Watson reveals:

> On Jan 6, 1972 I had my first chance to check out my hypothesis about relations with ARPA when Doug invited me down to be around when Larry Roberts visited ARC with Steve Crocker. The visit frankly stunned me. The communication between ARC and ARPA about goals was nonexistent. Larry communicated clearly his displeasure with where he thought ARC was at, particularly with respect to the NIC which as I only realy [sic] understood later had had a bad his-

tory here. I got the strong feeling that if we did not get some kind of NIC on the air our funding might be cut; I got such feeling from Doug as well and that our June contract renewal was a key watershed coming up.

In my five years of selling research and development and interfacing with buyers of various kinds, I had never been in such a tense session; further my experience indicated that unless such a relationship could be reversed it was just a matter of time until funding was cut whether in a year or several years, but such relationship was not conducive to long term survival.

Shortly after I arrived Doug went to the IPT meeting in San Diego where he was given a rough time as he reported to all of us. This was more confirmation that we had to get a meaningful NIC on the air.

Later in the month I went to a NWG meeting at Ill. [The University of Illinois] and found that while things were more sympathetic there, ARC and NIC were somewhat of a joke. Throughout the following months as I met people I knew, I was constantly asked why I had gone to work for the AHI [Augmentation of Human Intellect] scandel [sic] as some put it. I was constantly defending the project and saying wait you'll see type of things. ("Some Background on Pressures Existing on ARC," JE#8634, January 24, 1972)

Internally, various contributions to the PODAC archives echoed this dissatisfaction from the ARPA sponsor. The minutes of the Fir POD meeting held on February 9, for instance, reported that "dissatisfaction was expressed with the apparent tendency of ARC to design processes and systems that are hurried, short-term, make-shift efforts for an immediate, urgent need to produce something and then allow that process to remain without redesigning for long-term and more efficient job handling" (MEJ 22-FEB-72, JE#9239). Some basic problems of the Journal system handling were especially mentioned. It was during that same meeting that Smokey Wallace stated that "most of his work was done in TECO [the Text Editor and COrrector] because he can do it much faster and with more flexibility than in NLS." Richard Watson discussed the philosophy of a real-world, money-making environment versus that of the "unpressured scientific research where a usable, practical product is not necessarily the goal." He insisted that since ARC was by then in a "mixed environment" (meaning NIC was a service facility and ARC was a research laboratory), it "behooves us to change our ways of thinking and working habits to fit that real-world environment for those products advertised to the real world." Some members of the group stressed the fact that NLS was a really good environment for programming, but that serious weaknesses appeared when practical business applications were concerned.

In several POD meetings, the question of the new users' needs was addressed over and over again. Bootstrapping to the next circle of users meant that the laboratory should be able to shift its mode of operation to serve a community of users with different needs and aspirations. The emphasis, however, was put on bootstrapping NLS, rather than on addressing the needs and aspirations of these new users. For the whole of 1972, the relationship with ARPA went through ups and downs, but the situation remained practically unchanged. In October 1973, in another internal memo, Richard Watson summarized this situation.

Watson insisted again on the fact that "there has been little or no feedback or guidance from ARPA in the intervening years as to what needs they would like met at what costs." More importantly, he insisted that this lack of guidance had become an impediment to the actual functioning of the NIC. For instance, Watson complained that ARPA had not set up any "explicit procedures associated with new sites coming on the NET to assure that the NIC receives timely notification (or any notification for that matter) and other information it needs for its data bases." The NIC's function was not only unclear, but also not exclusive enough, since there were by then "two or three other groups on the ARPANET providing related and occasionally redundant information services to the NET." But Watson insisted also on the fact that even if the NIC had made the effort to "try to make its management and guidance needs known . . . [it] probably need[s] to be even more forceful in the future." This could be read as an admission that the NIC had not done everything it could to make the situation better (JE#19870, October 26, 1973).

By late 1973, some inside ARC began to recognize that the very idea of bootstrapping NLS might be at the origin of some of the problems of the laboratory in its dealing with its ARPA sponsor: "ARC management, including myself, have seen the importance of the NIC to ARC in terms of what the NIC can contribute to ARC's broader goals," Watson wrote. He now realized that "the NIC has had to use NLS based technology to meet network needs and often has had to perceive these needs in NLS terms. This haw [sic] led to occassional [sic] distortions of actual needs and thus failures to perceive and meet actual network needs." Although he insisted that this kind of distortion could go both ways, Watson believed that the core of the problem was that "often NIC priorities have had to take second place to broader ARC objectives."

Also, Watson finally recognized the basic difficulty of carrying out research and service simultaneously on the same system: "the system on which the NIC has been based was not originally designed explicitly for many NIC functions, and while it is being adapted to meet NIC needs as part of its development evolution, it is incomplete and not finished through to the level of detail necessary for many NIC needs." In such a setup, two distinctive kinds of pressure apply: the system is under constant pressure to adapt to the needs of its clients and to the evolving representation of these needs, but it also suffers from the pressure that the changes brought about by the evolution of the research create. Watson insisted that "these factors make it hard to create a stable plan and to carry it out as new factors are constantly appearing on a daily and weekly basis to shift priorities or over come some new glitch."[27]

Elizabeth "Jake" Feinler, who was by then in charge of the NIC inside ARC, was prompt to respond to Watson. What appeared in Watson's memo as the result of a built-in conflict in ARC/NIC design became for her a source of complaints about the NIC. Issues ranged from "Lack of integration of the NIC into the framework of ARC," with the result that "we are frequently looked upon as a nuisance rather than as an integral part of the ARC R&D effort" and "Lack of committed programming support," forcing the NIC "to wait at the end of the line" with "little control over whether the final program suits NIC needs." They included "Lack of clerical help," "Lack of space on the current system," and "Lack of stated direction."

In 1973, there thus was still an internal division inside the laboratory over the decision to implement the NIC on the basis of the further development of NLS. While Engelbart conceived of the NIC as the vehicle to bootstrap NLS further, the NIC insisted that it was an activity in itself that could be considered as a worthwhile research and development activity. Feinler stated in her memo that the NIC could "create a whole new research area of resource sharing and information retrieval." But she also insisted that it would require that the NIC should stop being considered as a "foster child" and that it should receive "adequate recognition and support from within."

This final demand should be read in the context of the social experiments attempted by Engelbart with PODAC, LINAC, and FRAMAC. In late 1973, the problems that should have been dealt with in the PODAC experiment were still there. The est episode that marked the end of the experiment, as we have seen, concluded in a failure to settle the differences between the ARC members or to restore the link between the lab's staff and Engelbart. Watson diagnosed only the organizational problems stemming from the dual nature and the hierarchization of the goals of the laboratory, but Feinler was clear in her evaluation about the personal problems that these organizational problems created. According to her, individuals contributing to the NIC were still set apart as "a nuisance" or "system hogs" in late 1973. She finally insisted that the NIC members should be given "equal footing within the framework of ARC."

Donald "Smokey" Wallace, the model for Vallée's hero "Guru," summed up the situation of the laboratory in an internal ARC memo entitled "Of Mice and Man (a Revelation)." In the memo, Wallace lays out a program that parallels and parodies the situation at ARC. Wallace proposes an ironic variation on Engelbart's idea of developing a way to find a method for solving the modern world's complex and urgent problems:

> Historically our analytical techniques have not dealt well with problems of extreme complexity or that contained an inordinate number of independent variables. . . . Extremely Complex Problems generally have the following properties: 1) large number (approaching infinity) of independent variables, 2) lack of localization; and generally cause the following reactions in people attempting to deal with them: 1) Confusion, 2) Frustration 3) Chaos.
>
> If you accept the premise that the most pressing problem in modern society is that society's inability to solve extremely complex problems and that a major conceptual or methodological "breakthrough" is necessary to facilitate such solutions then it seems someone should set up a laboratory that would attempt to create (in a controlled way) the conditions of an environment necessary to maximize the probability of a breakthrough of the desired type.

Creating "the conditions of an environment necessary to maximize the probability of a breakthrough of the desired type" involves creating and sustaining confusion, frustration, and chaos in this laboratory's staff, but in a "controlled" and productive way. The attributes of the "breakthrough lab" thus differ from a "normal project." A lab based on confusion, chaos, and frustration would have different needs:

1. A director who is autonomous and really not a member of the project. This allows him to really be in control of the project. In essence he is the experimentator.

2. An inordinate number of intelligent people in order to maximize the chance of a breakthrough.

3. Unusually diverse professional and personal backgrounds in order to cover as much of society and technology as possible (cross fertilization).

4. The pseudo project should be in a high technology area.

5. Avoid success in traditional terms. This will cause a false sense of accomplishment and will make the project members complacent. (Remember the goal is a breakthrough, not a successful project.)

6. Maximize confusion, frustration and chaos. This is the general atmosphere for complex problems and a breakthrough is more likely under these conditions.

7. It is probably necessary (maybe not) that the members of the pseudo project not be aware of the labs real goals.

8. The members of the projects should be highly motivated to achieve the project goals (not the labs) even if ill or self defined.

9. All problems, even if simple, must be viewed in a higher context in order to make them complex (remember, these are the ones we are after).

However,

> care must be taken that the frustrations level of the participants must not become so high, or the incremental rewards so low, as to cause the subjects to leave the lab or the apparent normalcy of the project to become unstable. Such tools as apparent inept or indecisive management, fuzzy goals and unclear departmental or functional lines can, and should, be used as effective devices in creating an atmosphere of "creative frustration."

This, of course, was a description of the lab Engelbart had built.

> My breakthrough lab is really ARC. Quite frankly the frustration and chaos here has been driving me nuts. I just cannot accept the apparent madness of our situation. I have pieced together a conceptual model of what's going here at ARC that really explains the situation as I see it. . . . The experimentator in our BREAK-THROUGH LAB is DCE [Engelbart] and the mice are the members of the ARC staff. The confusion and seeming inability to get organized and the lack of goals are all calculated. The various groups and their diverse directions are all part of the plan to create the desired atmosphere in the hope that the much desired breakthrough will happen. I don't mean to imply that Doug is some demoniacal mad scientist, but it should be noted that he is tampering with our lives in a very significant way.

The end eventually justifies the means, even if these means "tamper with the lives of the staff in a very significant way." Ironically enough, the very word "breakthrough" was also at the core of the est gospel, which considered the experience of such a "breakthrough" as one of the most important goals of the seminars. And Wallace finally describes his attitude toward what he has realized about the lab in terms promoted by est. It is a "game":

> You may be surprised to learn, now that I understand the game here at ARC (or at least think I do) that I have not quit. After all, being a mouse running somebody's maze isn't a very nice way to think of one's self; however, I have played many games and most have been worse. The major frustration for me has been not understanding what has been going on. Now that I have put that behind me I can get to work and decide if I want to play and how I can get the most out of this new and certainly interesting game.

Internal disillusionment and external disregard sealed the fate of Engelbart's vision and led to his relative failure. Staff members continued to leave the laboratory, and the sponsors slowly pulled out. The IPTO ceased its funding in 1974, and SRI eventually sold the project to Tymshare in 1977. The system was sold again to McDonnell Douglas in the early 1980's, and Augment (the new name of NLS) slowly faded into oblivion.

Describing his career at a conference in 1986, Douglas Engelbart provided his own eulogy for ARC:

> I'm going to terminate at this point, since after 1976 we really had no chance to continue pursuing this "augmentation framework." It seemed no longer to fit in the pattern of the research at ARPA, or with what SRI wanted to do. When we landed out in the commercial world, we found that it wasn't what people there wanted to do, either. The AUGMENT system stayed alive in a sort of a funny, dumb way, often like taking a bulldozer in to help people work in their back yards. (Engelbart 1988, 229)

In one of his early insights into the possibilities of the personal computer, Engelbart had written: "The man-machine interface that most people talk about is the equivalent of the locomotive-cab controls (giving a man better means to contribute to the big system's mission), but I want to see more thought on the equivalent of the bulldozer's cab (giving the man maximum facility for directing all that power to his individual task)." But the individual tasks he once had in mind were considerably more important than helping people "work in their back yards."

When I met Engelbart in the early 1990's, he was desperately trying to continue his evangelism from the two offices that Logitech, a leading mouse manufacturer, was giving him to locate his "Bootstrap Institute." By all appearances, his crusade had come to nothing, its innovations appropriated to purposes foreign to its ends. As we have yet to see, however, appearances can change. As time sifts the ephemeral from what is more enduring, it is becoming clear that many of the basic issues about the nature of personal computing first raised by Douglas Engelbart continue to define its future, as well as its past.

Where Hand and Memory Can Meet Again

Notions of bootstrapping occur in many areas of technology because "designers often think of themselves as typical users" (Norman 1990, 155). But only a few manage to perpetuate their claim of representativeness. To do so, they need to demonstrate that the expertise they claim in designing a device will be translated adequately in the user's expertise in performing a task with that device. In Alan Kay's metaphor, the problem with bootstrapping in Douglas Engelbart's Augmentation Research Center was that while "Engelbart, for better or for worse, was trying to make a violin," "most people don't want to learn the violin." User-friendliness, not coevolutionary learning, became the norm in the design of human-computer interfaces.

We have seen how a particular network of incorporating practices, organizational forms, institutional self-definitions, and transfers of people and artifacts produced this norm, and with it the definition of the personal-computer user: the social construction of the personal interface happened as the social construction of user-friendliness, translated into the technical terms of "modelessness." From Douglas Engelbart's intellectual worker to "Sally" and eventually to Apple's consumer, the conceptualization and gradual realization of the user was a social process in which the designers' representations competed according to the relationships and strategies inside their communities and within their working environments. And what worked at one stage of the process did not necessarily promise success at another phase. For instance, the strength of Xerox PARC in the technological innovation of personal computing technologies did not guarantee its success in the later phases, such as commercialization.

But because the development of a technology in terms of the conceptualization and realization of the user is a process of social construction, not the inevitable and mechanized progress of mechanization itself, there is nothing inherent in what worked at any given stage or in what ultimately came to pass that necessarily discredits the viability of what did not. History tends to be written from the point of view of what prevailed, and that certainly has tended to be the case with the history of the origins of personal computing. But at the origin of personal computing there were conceptions of the person that went far beyond the conception of the user of the technology as a naive "everyone," simply a consumer. The future often is seen in terms of yesterday's questions, just as the past is seen in terms of what prevailed. But some of yesterday's questions remain unanswered about the future of the personal computer, and indeed, about the future of the person who used it. Clues to what those answers might be sometimes can be found by remembering and reevaluating what did not prevail.

ENGELBART'S KINESTHETIC SYSTEM: A HISTORICAL APPRAISAL

Engelbart's project to augment the human intellect focused on "increasing the effectiveness of the individual's use of his basic capabilities," and the decision to do so led him to investigate potential alternative means for learning and developing skills and artifacts related to input entry. But what *are* an individual's "basic capabilities"? In *Libraries of the Future* (1965), J. C. R. Licklider wrote:

> It is worth pausing to ponder how few well-developed skills there are that are both complex and widespread. Almost everyone can get about in three-dimensional space. Almost everyone can speak and understand one of the natural languages— perhaps not grammatically, but fluently. But relatively few people can do anything else that is even remotely comparable in informational complexity and degree of perfection. Of the remaining candidates for inclusion in the list of widespread complex skills, we may with some misgivings accept writing, and perhaps the playing of musical instruments. After this comes typing. And typing ends the list. It is possible that, in future decades, typing will move up past music and that it will become almost as widespread as writing and more highly developed. (98–99)

As we have seen, the hegemony of touch typing as an incorporating practice lay behind Licklider's conclusion that any other means of interfacing with the computer would be too difficult to learn and could not succeed for that reason. But as we also have seen, Engelbart had a much more generous conception of what a person's "basic skills" might be. As a result, Engelbart explored the possibility of using many different kinds of input/output devices as part of the human-machine interface, the mouse and the chord keyset being just two of them. Over the ensuing decades, however, the very fact that alternative input devices had been explored at Engelbart's lab was effaced. During the History of Workstations Conference held in 1986, Licklider himself remarked:

> There's the idea of instrumenting the body of the user. It hasn't gone anywhere so far really. . . . If we're talking about input, a thing that I want is instrumented fingers . . . and now I wonder why I'd have to have keys of any kind to type on, because if there are selectors on my fingers, then you don't need the keys. Incidentally, I've never heard anybody discuss this from an informational point of view, but it's obvious, if you just think of it, that typing is capable of transferring more information than is actually used because there's information in which finger touches the key as well as in the key that is touched. And if you could learn to type in such a way that you touched the same key with different fingers, that could be very useful. (Licklider 1988, 120)

Engelbart had envisioned instrumenting of the body of the user from the start, since he had proposed as early as 1962 "using physical-stimulus cues that are more effective for prompting desired physical responses than are audio or visual cues, which generally have to be given more higher-center processing in our brains before they result in the desired physical response than the direct physical-stimulus cues," and his research projects had included efforts to "see what skill can be developed for reading binary tactile signals corresponding to the transmission code applied directly to the fingers" via "a type of glove . . . individual finger caps."

Stu Card, during the participants' discussion after his paper at the History of Personal Workstations Conference, did not entirely efface the memory of Engelbart's innovative work, but he also did not display any understanding of the ideas that lay behind it:

> The reason that the mouse worked for Doug's system is that they had the other hand doing the functional keys, and so they could keep from overloading any one thing. You know, interfaces really take four hands to operate. It's unfortunate that people don't come with four hands, otherwise it would just be wonderful. It takes one hand for doing the functional thing, one hand for doing the mouse, and then two hands for typing in on the keyboard. You can look at various interfaces as ways of compromising and getting the number of hands down. (Quoted in Goldberg 1988, 525)

Card referred to the chord keyset when he talked about the "functional keys." What was important for Engelbart, however, was not the unavoidable design criterion that "humans have two hands," but the way the hands can function in relation to each other. What was *not* important was the putative inevitability of the standard QWERTY keyboard as the only way to provide for the manual input of texts.

Allen Newell, while a little more sympathetic toward Engelbart's achievement, likewise still found reasons to "explain" its failure:

> Doug has presented to us a notion that focused on what the human was doing. The key element for me in that is that the limiting channel is really the motor channel. As Doug does so effectively, and I can't do so, if we could just get it all going all at the same time, then we'd really allow the human to really communicate with the machine. There is a model of the human involved there. (Quoted in ibid., 489–90)

But improving the "model of the human" was what Engelbart's project was all about. Nothing proves a priori that "the motor channel," the collection of "low-level" motor skills, is a limiting factor constraining how humans work, on computers or anything else, and Engelbart assumed from the start that the agenda for "human factors" research should be to find to which extent learning *and* the development of the computer could improve both motor skills and how people use them to solve problems in the symbolic realm.

Today, however, the dynamic set in motion by Engelbart's technological innovations is making it increasingly difficult to continue to neglect or misunderstand them, or the cybernetic ideas behind them, or the vision of the future that informed them. Most of today's promises for a future of computing deal with the opening of another realm for social interaction—another realm for the expansion via the computer of what it means to be a "person." In this respect, claims about "cyberspace" or "virtual environments" now are widely used to represent the technological investment in our future.

The word *cyberspace* was coined by science fiction writer William Gibson in his 1984 book *Neuromancer*: "Case was twenty-four. At twenty-two, he'd been a cowboy, a rustler, one of the best in the Sprawl. . . . He'd operated on an almost permanent adrenaline high, a byproduct of youth and proficiency, jacked into a custom cyberspace deck that projected his disembodied consciousness into the consensual hallucination that was the matrix" (Gibson 1984, 5). In the same book, Gibson also introduced simstim, an interactive simulation system that allows the user to experience (to "flip in") somebody else's perception as if he were in his or her body: "Cowboys didn't get into simstim, he thought, because it was basically a meat toy. He knew that the trodes he used and the little plastic tiara dangling from a simstim deck were basically the same, and the cyberspace matrix was actually a drastic simplification of the human sensorium, at least in terms of presentation, but simstim itself struck him as a gratuitous multiplication of flesh input" (ibid., 55).

Cyberspace and simstim are the two polar opposite representations that currently inform our imagination about virtual reality: disembodied but highly

interactive ("a consensual hallucination") and/or vivid but passive ("the pas-
senger behind the eyes"). The coupling of both of these representations makes
possible what Brenda Laurel (1991, 188) considers the confluence of the three
enactment capabilities of virtual environments: sensory immersion, remote
presence, and tele-operation. Simstim is sensory immersion, cyberspace is the
remote presence of the consciousness, and tele-operation is the resulting action, action at a distance, action of a body that is not exactly the body of the
user any more, available only in cyberspace.

Although cyberspace, simstim, and their attributes were first given popular
currency by Gibson, they were anticipated—and in a limited way, achieved—
by Douglas Engelbart, whose hypermedia vision was of a multidimensional
and mutliformat dataspace in which users can "fly" (Engelbart 1992). For Engelbart, the "workstation is the portal into a person's 'augmented knowledge
workshop'—the [virtual] place in which he finds the data and tools with which
he does his knowledge work, and through which he collaborates with similarly
equipped workers" (Engelbart 1988, 187). From the beginning, he emphasized the sensorimotor aspects of this "portal," leading to the development of
the mouse and the principle that workstations need "three-dimensional color
display[s]" within which symbolic representations can be directly manipulated
(Engelbart 1962, 14).

The marginalization of Engelbart's projects with the development of the
computer as a commercial product for "everyone" has in the long run proved
to be only temporary. The massive success of the World Wide Web has put his
work in the forefront again. His NLS is now very often considered as the precursor of today's hypermedia, the original application in computerized systems
of the principle of hypertext envisioned by Vannevar Bush. (See, for example,
Berners-Lee 1997, 58). The World Wide Web is the 1990's implementation of
the 1980's science fiction representation of cyberspace, and NLS was its ancestor. The World Wide Web recapitulates thirty years of innovative work in
computer science and design, and packages computer-mediated communication in the form of a graphic hypermedium packet-switching network. (See
Figure C-1.)

Engelbart's conception of hypertext as implemented in NLS is essentially a
spatially distributed system for what has now come to be known as computer-
supported cooperative work or play. In the form either of a "cyberspace" network of stand-alone graphic computers or a "virtual reality" generated by a
simulation engine and accessed through elaborate input/output ("goggles and
gloves"), today's conceptualizations of the future of computing build on this
foundation. Like Engelbart's 1962 vision of the computer as prosthesis, they
extend the individual's capabilities beyond the capabilities of the unaugmented

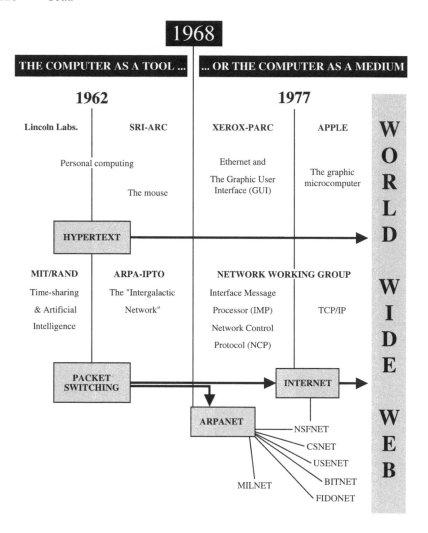

Figure C-1. The Genesis of the Personal Interface.

individual. As Ted Nelson, the conceptual inventor of hypertext, puts it, "The virtuality of a thing is what it *seems* to be, rather than its reality, the technical or physical underpinning on which it rests. Virtuality has two aspects: *conceptual structure*—the ideas of the thing—and *feel*—its qualitative and sensory particular" (Nelson 1990, 239, emphasis in the original). From the beginning, Engelbart always believed that these two aspects went together. Extending human cognitive capabilities would depend on extending human qualitative and sensory capabilities, as well.

"A LOT MORE CHANNELS": THINKING SOMESTHETICALLY

In 1965, at the same time that the mouse was created, André Leroi-Gourhan published an important book entitled *Gesture and Speech*. Leroi-Gourhan argued that human tools have exteriorized both cognitive and motor human abilities and have allowed a functional specialization outside the human body. However, he envisioned possible problems concerning the fate of the human hand in such an evolution. The physical and the mental are linked in such a way that the atrophy of one in the long run threatens to bring about the atrophy of the other:

> Originally it [the hand] was a claw or pincer for holding stones; the human triumph was to turn it into the ever-skillful servant of human technical intelligence. From the Upper Palaeolithic to the nineteenth century, the hand enjoyed what seemed like an interminable heyday. It still plays an essential role in industry, a few skilled toolmakers producing the operative parts of machines to be operated by crowds of workers requiring no more than a five-fingered claw to feed in the material or simply an index finger to push the buttons. But ours is still a transitional stage, and there can be no doubt that the nonmechanized phases of industrial processes are being gradually eliminated.
>
> The dwindling importance of the makeshift organ that is our hand would not matter a great deal if there were not overwhelming evidence to prove that its activity is closely related to the balance of the brain areas with which it is connected. "Being useless with one's fingers," "being ham-handed," is not a very alarming thing at the level of the species as a whole: A good number of millennia will pass before so old an organ as our neuromotor apparatus actually regresses. But at the individual level the situation is very different. Not having to "think with one's fingers" is equivalent to lacking a part of one's normally, phylogenetically human mind. Thus the problem of regression of the hand already exists today at the individual if not the species level. (Leroi-Gourhan, 1993 [1965], 255–56)

Leroi-Gourhan parallels this evolution of the hand with the dynamic of the liberation of human memory via books, punched index cards, and other "memory-collecting machines." For him, the evolution started with the opportunities provided by books, which he compares to "hand tools." Card indexes, on the other hand, are comparable to "hand-operated machines," while "punched index cards represent yet another stage, comparable to that of early automatic machines" (ibid., 264). About this later stage, he wrote:

> A punched card index is a memory-collecting machine. It works like a brain memory of unlimited capacity that is endowed with the ability not present in the human brain of correlating every recollection with all others.
>
> No progress beyond this stage has so far been made except in the matter of proportions. The electronic brain, although it employs different and more subtle

processes, operates on the same principles. . . . The artificial brain of course is still in its infancy, but we can already be sure that it will be more than just a nine days' wonder with limited applications. (Ibid., 264–65)

Engelbart understood that the future of the "electronic brain" would in the long run remain linked to the way humans have evolved to "think" somesthetically, using the whole collection of bodily sensations in the way they have learned to "think" with their fingers. In a meeting that Engelbart had with his staff at SRI during the autumn of 1972,[1] he declared:

I guess it can be assumed that our biological evolution hasn't been significant since before the time [we] had a very sophisticated or any kind of written language at least. . . . We could just wonder about how much there is to explore in a realm of mapping kinds [of] imagery and dynamics that are involved in the communicating processes in some kind of media and signal forms which are more akin to doing things spatially. Because your whole nervous system may well be much more adapted to the quick reception and quick effective coordinated reactions in a form like that. So you may well be someday sort of wired in kinesthetically to interact with it rather than just your hands the way there are now. . . . I am left with a strong feeling that there's a lot of future value to be gained in exploring portrayal forms and interaction forms that really bring in a lot more channels.

As Engelbart saw, these channels are not one-way inputs from the user to the machine, but feedback loops that also carry information from the machine to the user.

I began with . . . some sort of place in your head in which there is the formation of the message you wanted to communicate. In realizing that inside your head you need a process that transforms that into the signal forms for whatever channel you are using. Fingers on the keyboard or finger patterns on a keyset. . . . There are then some physical transducers that take those actions and convert them into the . . . signals, generally and then we have a computer process that can translate those into some standard form acceptable back into the computer. Now this is representative of what we do now. Do you realize that there usually are processes, feedback processes that come back to the person that . . . to go on a loop there's a process that takes interpretation and comes back into some kind of transducer that changes it to higher signals or some kind of stimuli that comes back and goes through a perception mechanism in your own body, back in here to be checked[?]

This is what the eye does, according to the highly influential article by Jerome Y. Lettvin, Humberto R. Maturana, Warren S. McCulloch, and Walter H. Pitt, "What the Frog's Eye Tells the Frog's Brain" (1988 [1959], 251), but it is not only the eye that does it. As James C. Bliss puts it, "the eye speaks to the brain in a language already highly organized and interpreted, instead of transmitting some more or less accurate copy of the distribution of light on receptors." But so do the kinesthetic senses when, for example, someone learns and employs the skill of touch typing, according to studies of that practice.

> Although it appears that visual guidance and feedback play a role in skilled as well as in unskilled typing, the primary source of sensory feedback in skilled typing is surely kinesthetic, including information about the position and movement of fingers as provided by muscles and joints. To a considerable extent, the development of skilled touch-typing can be viewed in terms of an increasing reliance on this type of feedback and a reduced reliance on visual feedback. This view conforms to the general principle proposed by Paul Fitts (1951), who stated that the transfer from vision to kinesthesis as the primary source of feedback characterizes the development of perceptual-motor skills. (Cooper 1983, 16–17)

Shifting from the merely visual to the somesthetic by incorporating the feedback loops of the kinesthetic senses thus is a quantitative change, not a qualitative change, a way to add "a lot more channels." But doing so also exemplifies the effects of one of Engelbart's basic principles: "after a certain degree of quantitative change, you almost invariably go into qualitative change" (Engelbart 1996). It is a difference that makes a difference.

Opening the visual dimension of the computer as a communication medium was one of the major contributions of Alan Kay and his research team at Xerox PARC in the 1970's. One of the major innovations of this group of computer scientists and designers was the "desktop metaphor" that many regard as today's "dominant paradigm of interaction with a personal computer" (e.g. Oren 1991). First on the Star computer, then on the Lisa and the Macintosh at Apple, and eventually on the IBM PC and its clones with Microsoft's Windows, the "desktop" became the first and most common "alternate reality," a successful illusion that allows computer users to visualize the computer environment in which they work.

This achievement is not without limitations, however, as its creators realized. The desktop metaphor was originally designed for systems like the Xerox Star, with a few hundred files on five to ten megabytes of storage, a machine quite different from present-day computers. As early as the beginning of the 1990's, it was clear that "the purely user-directed browsing style of the desktop is approaching its limits of utility, with the number of files on a single user's machine reaching 10,000 and with easy access to even more information across networks" (Oren 1991, 325). The problem, to paraphrase Ted Nelson (1993), is that we are now trapped by the success of the desktop metaphor in our thinking about personal computers.

The "desktop" is a visual feedback channel limited to two dimensions. As we have seen, the desktop metaphor developed out of the progressive realization of the user as the individual owner of a personal stand-alone computing system. In the process, the connectivity of the individual's system to similar systems and other users was pushed into the background, at least temporarily. But with the rise of the Internet and the increasing use of the personal computer as a means of making interpersonal connections, the limits of both the "desktop" and the visual channel itself are simultaneously becoming even more evident.

Jun Yoneyama reminds us that "in Heideggerian phenomenology, tools may be *ready at hand*, meaning that consciousness is focused at the object of work, and the tool is regarded as an extension of the body. If the tool somehow draws attention to itself, it is *present at hand*—the focus of the mind. This process of changing attention from work-object to tool is called a *breakdown*" (1997, 115, emphasis in the original). It is clear enough that trying to communicate with others via a "desktop" constantly invokes breakdowns by calling attention to the computer as a tool present at hand, rather than ready at hand. But so do alternative conceptions of the user interface derived from the tradition of artificial intelligence research, most notably the conception of the computer as itself an "intelligent agent" or robot.

The idea of the computer as an intelligent agent is nothing new. Alan Kay once attributed the idea of an "interface agent" to John McCarthy in the mid-1950's and the term itself to Oliver G. Selfridge a few years later, when they were both at the MIT (Kay 1984). In the AI tradition of regarding the computer as a "colleague," these conceptions treat the personal computer as a personified computer—a surrogate person. The result is a rampant anthropomorphizing of the machine via metaphors spanning the human-computer boundary, metaphors that mostly describe the computer in terms of human attributes: as a tool or factory, but also as an oracle (Janlert), brain (MacCormac), protagonist (Janlert), second self (Turkle, 1984), poison, sin, or idol (Mitcham).

Because it is evident from the nature of today's computer hardware and software that computer interfaces as intelligent agents are none of these things, however, today's personification of the computer still requires a "momentary suspension of disbelief" (Laurel 1991, 113). In the best tradition of the Artificial Intelligence program, they ask users to consider the agent in the narrative space of the interface to be a person enabling them to carry out a task in the "real, situated space" of their work practices. This creates a fundamental problem: it is the source of breakdowns.

The personification of the computer is supposed to render the computer "ready at hand," "naturalized" as a putative colleague or collaborator. But a colleague or collaborator requires a different kind of attention than a tool that is ready at hand does. The personified computer instead keeps presenting itself as "present at hand." Hence, the interface agent is necessarily a source of never-ending shifts of the attention for the user. Thus, the personification of the interface does not solve the problem of breakdowns: rather, it makes an essential source of breakdowns central to the interface. The necessity of the user's "suspension of disbelief" becomes a repeated necessity. The suspension of disbelief is no longer a one-time decision, but a decision reiterated with each breakdown. Ironically enough, this point seems to confirm Brenda Laurel's characterization of the interface agent as "an ill-formed presence or persona that belongs wholly to neither context, but attempts to mediate between them for the user" (1986, 75).

What have come to be called "direct manipulation interfaces" are supposed to have solved this problem. The idea of "direct manipulation" means that the interface is always "ready at hand." The term "direct manipulation" was coined by Benjamin Schneiderman to characterize the interfaces that offer a continuous representation of the object of interest, privilege the physical action of the user, rather than employing a complicated input-language syntax, and allow rapid, incremental, and reversible operations with immediate visual feedback (Schneiderman 1982, 251). Edwin L. Hutchins, James D. Hollan, and Donald A. Norman (1986, 91) consider that the "first major landmark" in direct manipulation interfaces was Ivan Sutherland's Sketchpad.[2]

As we have seen, the subsequent development of direct manipulation interfaces at Xerox PARC and Apple occurred via the search for user-friendliness and the various conceptions of the user that entailed. And giving users what they "want" still tends to be their justification today: "Users want comprehensible, predictable and controllable interfaces that offer end-user programming, control panels, style sheets, and effective dialog boxes. Overviews for visibility of the world of action, combined with rapid, incremental filtering and zooming offer appealing opportunities for designers" (Schneiderman 1997). But as we also have seen, both "users" and what they want, what is "user-friendly," are constructs of the designers of user interfaces within the constraints of existing incorporating practices.

If anything characterizes the difference between Engelbart's original conception of what the personal computer could be and what it has become it is the difference between ease of learning the human-computer interface, that is, "user-friendliness," and ease of use once the interface is learned. With Microsoft Windows and Apple's OS operating systems dominating the marketplace for user interfaces since the 1980's, the paradigm of the user-friendly interface has been the graphical user interface commonly called the WIMP, or window, icon, menu, and pointer interface. However, as we have seen, WIMP interfaces are still "marking interfaces" that in effect use "digital ink" to make marks on digital "paper" on a digital "desktop." The feedback loop is still limited to the visual channel, what appears on the screen, and the information bandwidth available therefore is limited to the display system. As a result, they cannot allow the kind of physical immersion that the design of a full-fledged system of virtual reality seems to require. Numerous people have realized this shortcoming since the end of the 1980's. For instance, Andries van Dam has noted that:

> I find it rather surprising that the third generation of WIMP user interface has been so dominant for more than two decades; they are apparently sufficiently good for conventional desktop tasks that the field is stuck comfortably in a rut. . . . [But] the status quo does not suffice . . . the newer forms of computing and computing devices available today necessitate new thinking about fourth generation UIs [user interfaces], what I call post-WIMP user interfaces. They don't use menus, forms, or toolbars, but rely on, for example, gesture and speech recognition for operand and operation specification. (1997, 63–64)

But even user-friendly interfaces have to be learned. In the end, the nature of the personal computer and its user interface comes back to the way in which the person involved, the user, is conceived. What can the user be expected to do, to want, to be? Reflecting on the lessons learned about interface usability over the past twenty years, Jeff Raskin, a crucial actor in the Apple implementation of the GUI, observed that:

> New input modes such as voice, . . . handwriting recognition, and direct mind to machine (MTM) links are less central to improving interface design than cognetic issues. While gloves and 3D input devices engender a lot of popular interest, the question of what are you going to have to do, say, write, or think in order to accomplish your goals generally goes unasked. I suspect most of us would prefer to use an MTM interface rather than type and shove a mouse around, but if the interface in which MTM is embedded is full of modal traps, complex navigational puzzles, and a multitude of details to be memorized, the improvement will be marginal and the interface will be as frustrating as anything now available. (Raskin 1997, 100)

One answer to what the user can be expected to do, to want, and to be has always been clear. It is summed up in van Dam's notion of an "ideal situation in which user-computer interaction is at least as natural and powerful as human interaction" (van Dam 1997, 67). But as we have seen, the breakdowns to which this leads are inherent in its conception. Yet the pursuit of direct manipulation via the ideal of user-friendliness and ease of use has confined the technology and the user alike in interfaces constricted by narrow input-output bandwidths and development paths boobytrapped with the limitations of modality and the marking interface.

We have seen throughout this book how ease of learning and ease of use very often have been considered to be in opposition, or even sometimes incommensurable. The future shape of the user interface may well lie in a reconciliation of these two opposite positions, in a third principle that would consider these two design objectives mutually constitutive. Ease-of-using requires ease-of-learning, and ease-of-learning does not mean anything if its does not lead to ease of use. Jeff Raskin has conceded this point:

> A central goal of interface design is to allow users to make their own task the exclusive locus of their attention, by designing the interface such that it can be reduced to habitual operation. Too much of the emphasis of current GUI design, due to the marketing needs of past years, is ease of learning at the expense of productivity. . . . As a result we have systems that are a combination of easy-to-learn menu-driven structures and relatively quick-to-use but hard to remember sets of keyboard commands. The user who desires efficiency eventually has to learn both. But the union of two strong systems does not make for a single, unified, correct one. It is a common myth that an interface is either easy to learn or easy to use but not both. (1997, 99–100)

It therefore is time to reflect once again on the benefits of interfaces that are easy to use, whatever it may take to learn them. As we have seen, the chord keyset and the mouse were parts of an interface designed with direct manipulation in mind, but quite emphatically with ease of learning not part of the enterprise. Engelbart's speculations about ways to instrument the body of the user for both input and feedback were direct-manipulation schemes in every sense of the term, but more so. What he expected the user of the personal computer to do, to want, and to be may well finally be what actual users find valuable and worth learning how to accomplish, using tools that finally make it possible to do so.

The user no longer can be considered merely as an imaginative projection of innovators in technology. The generic individual user of the early days of cognitive science, the asocial individual subject of psychological analyses, has turned into the situated member of a specific "market niche" engaged in specific tasks, in specific settings, with other members of (potentially) other market niches. Given that reality, tomorrow's user has to be considered as a biological and social entity fully involved in a never-ending interaction with the whole symbolic and material world of human experience. Like any other human interaction with the world, human-computer interaction is both a biological and a sociological process, as Douglas Engelbart knew.

As a result, the interface between the user and the personal computer cannot be considered solely as a symbolic space where materiality becomes a disembodied illusion. In fact, the past fifty years of computing advances have expanded the very idea of "reality," and current research programs cover the whole spectrum of these possible alternate realities, from the "classic reality" of ubiquitous computers in what has been ordinary daily life to the intermediate mix of "augmented realities" and eventually to the virtual realities of cyber-space and simstim.

In augmented realities, computer-generated information is superimposed onto the "real world" through a minimally intrusive head-mounted display or any other wearable output device. In this case, the human user is immersed at the same time in the "real world" and in an artificially generated, but also real world. In ubiquitous computing on the other hand, the world wears the com-puter, which computer is woven in the stuff of the world, the fabric of daily life. Mark Weiser, one of the foremost proponents of this research program even considers that

> The arcane aura that surrounds personal computers is not just a "user interface" problem. My colleagues and I at the Xerox Palo Alto Research Center think that the idea of a "personal" computer itself is misplaced and that the vision of laptop machines, dynabooks and "knowledge navigators" is only a transitional step to-ward achieving the real potential of information technology. Such machines can-not truly make computing an integral, invisible part of people's lives. We are therefore trying to conceive a new way of thinking about computers, one that takes into account the human world and allows the computer themselves to van-ish into the background. (Weiser 1995, 78)

If, or rather, when that happens, a personal computer and its interface with its user will not necessarily be individual objects that belong to a person, but ma-terial and symbolic devices that allow their users to act and interact as persons in whatever "reality" these actions and interactions might take place. If that is so, we will indeed need a new conception not just of the personal computer, but of the person as such.

KINESTHETIC MEDIA AND THE FUTURE OF THE PERSON

Like Jaron Lanier, I believe that

> what was once a research topic has become a controversy where practical deci-sions must reflect a fundamental ontological definition about what a person is and is not, and there is no middle ground.. . . . I have long believed that the most important question about information technology is "How does it affect our definition of what a person is?" . . . We cannot expect to have certain, universal agreement on any question of personhood, but we all are forced to hold an an-swer in our hearts and act upon our best guess. Our best guess runs our world. (Lanier 1995)

A good place to look for such a "best guess" is from within the cybernetic tra-dition itself—in Gregory Bateson's notion of an "ecology of mind," his frame-work for the exploration of the "natural history of the relationships between explicit, implicit and embodied ideas in the world of living things." Bateson's notion of "socialization" is a keystone in this conception of an approach the study of persons—to anthropology:

> First, "socialization" (by definition) requires *interaction*, usually of two or more organisms. From this it follows that, whatever goes on below the surface, inside the organism where we cannot see it, there must be a large part of that "iceberg" showing above the surface. We, biologists, are lucky in that evolution is always a co-evolution and learning is always co-learning. Moreover, this visible part of the process is no mere by-product. It is precisely that production, that set of appearances, to produce which is supposedly the "goal" of all that learning which we call "socialization." Moreover, this aggregate of externally observable phenomena, always involving two or more "persons," contains not only what has been learned but also all the imperfect attempts of both persons to fit together in an ongoing process of interchange. (Bateson 1991 [1975], 75, emphasis in the original)

For Bateson, this "set of appearances" that we call a "person," always involves what is beyond the individual, since a "person" is necessarily a socialized individual. And it also involves only the "large part of that 'iceberg' showing above the surface," since everything else "goes on below the surface, inside the organism where we cannot see it." Bateson makes this point clearer in a footnote: "the 'person' after all, is the *mask*. It is what is perceivable of a human organism. It is a unilateral view of the interface between one organism and another" (ibid.).

In this respect, Bateson's notion of the "person" actually dates back to the original Latin notion of *persona*, in the sense of the mask of tragic ritual, and most importantly in the sense of the mask of the ancestor. As the mask of tragedy, its meaning was reconstructed by the Latin etymologists as *per/ sonare*, the mask through (*per*) which the actor's voice sounds (*sonare*). But it is also the mask of wax cast on the face of the dead ancestor (*imago*), the *prosōpon* of the Greek tradition, which also meant the mask of the ancestor or his statue kept in the wings of the family house (Mauss 1950 [1938], 350, 352). Latin law founded the right of the *persona*, the true nature of the individual, on what was both a shift from and a continuity with its Greek Stoic origin:

> The word *prosōpon* had indeed the same meaning as *persona*, mask; but here it can also signify the character [*personnage*] that everyone is or wants to be, his character [*caractère*] (the two words are often linked), the true face. Very quickly, from the second century B.C., onward, it assumes the meaning of *persona*. Translating exactly as *persona*, person, right, it still keeps the meaning of a superimposed image: e.g., the figurehead of the boat (for the Celts, etc.). But it also signifies the human or even divine personality. It all depends on the context. The

word *prosōpon* is extended to the individual in its naked nature, mask torn off, and at the same time, the sense of artifice is kept: the sense of the intimacy of this person and the sense of character [*personnage*]. (Ibid., 355, my translation)

Here was the original double meaning of the persona, which both hides and reveals the true nature of the individual in respect to its origins, its genetic relatedness to its ancestors, and its individuality, its specificity as an actual entity. In this respect, the Latin *simulacra* and *imagines*, the masks and statues of the ancestors, were attributes of the person to whom they belonged: they were the evidences of his origin. The Roman senate always conceived itself as a finite number of *patres* representing the personae of their ancestors. The right of the person was founded in this origin: only the free man, of known origin, was a person. *Servus non habet personam*: in the Roman law, the slaves had no personalities, their bodies did not belong to them. They had no ancestors, no names. They existed only in the plural (ibid., 353).

Hence, personalization and socialization are the two sides of the same process of human becoming. Personalization puts the emphasis on the appearance of the unity of the subject, while socialization stresses the relatedness of members in their expression of a common form. The are both basically grounded in two dynamics: a continuous dynamic of genetic relatedness stemming from an origin and a dynamic of feeling that constitutes a common sense for this origin.

Bertrand Russell held that there were two ways to define a person: as derived from memory, since "each person's experience is private to himself, and when one experience consists of recollecting another, the two are said to belong to the same 'person,'" and as derived from the body, since "we can then define a 'person' as the series of mental occurrences connected with a given body" (Russell 1997 [1935], 140). "Consciousness" is an afterthought: it is the result of an articulation of the two previous elementary processes. Consciousness is the name human beings give to the realization of their dual nature as persons.

The computer will be "personal" when it allows its users to act as persons, understood in the sense just explained, to experience the world as both embodied mental occurrences and retrieved memories, united in actual socialized and enduring entities—when it becomes, like the person using it, personalized, a place where hand and memory can meet again in "an on-going process of interchange" with others. The computer will be truly "personal" when it enables its users to express the common form of their genetic relatedness. Obviously, human beings do not need the computer to do that, even if computers can contribute to the process. But the computer actually can contribute to that process, as a tool created by humans enabling humans to become themselves, to transform themselves and yet remain themselves, to become not post-human entities, but another kind of human.

A starting point, I think, would be the ability of the computer to allow humans to make full use of their bodies, to act inside the space that the interface presents *and* represents, to feel and experience tomorrow's worlds as bodies and minds through the symbolic and material space that the body's interface affords for exploration, play, and work. The social and cultural construction of the personal computer user, so far, has led to an overwhelming hegemony of the visual sense and symbolic coding, following in that a larger trend in modernity. The hegemony of sight (Robins 1996), and its correlated abstraction (Crary 1990), did not begin with computers.

Whether the computer could be interpreted as a person or as slave, whether it could be metaphorically considered as a conscious entity or not, is finally of little interest in regard to what the computer does. Nothing prevents a priori the computer from participating in the ongoing evolution of human beings in the way that tools have done for a long time. A coevolution of humans and their tools cannot be ignored or denied. At least, this coevolution can be observed and felt. At best, it may be influenced. If Leroi-Gourhan was right, the joint liberation of the hand and the memory are the two crucial characteristics of this coevolution. Conscious efforts to design personal computers should take this into account and strive for a harmonious human experience in its fullest expression, an experience that employs both hand and memory once more.

Douglas Engelbart's decision to "start with the basics" led him to put the emphasis first on sensorimotor processes, the lowest order of explicitly human processes in the system. The tactile is indeed first in the order of perception (Merleau-Ponty). Tactile (somesthetic) perception is the work of our skin. To see is to have at a distance, but to touch is to be. We need light to see, but we need nothing to touch. The skin is the medium of its own functioning. Gracefully, the blind watchmaker designed it in such a way that it did not become overwhelming. Our skin feels for a time only: past a certain threshold in the time of contact, we do not feel anything anymore. In our psychological development, if we believe Piaget, among others, the first "object" we recognize is our mother's breast. The mouth, a very special and sensitive part of our skin is the organ of our first contact with the world. It is our own interface with the world, the only part of us that is both inside and outside us, the place where as individuals we also become persons.

For the computer to ever be truly personal, it must be able to afford a real sense of presence for its users, stemming from the joint action of the full human senses. The personal computer, as a medium, should then allow the synesthetic and kinesthetic experiences of the unknown, of the place from whence, according to Whorf, metaphors arise. The only interesting virtuality is the virtuality of communication, of possible mutual understanding and collaboration. In 1941, just before his death, Benjamin Lee Whorf wrote the following lines:

> A noumenal world—a world of hyperspace, of higher dimensions—awaits discovery by all the sciences, which it will unite and unify, awaits discovery under its first aspect of a realm of PATTERNED RELATIONS, inconceivably manifold and yet bearing a recognizable affinity to the rich and systematic organization of LANGUAGE, including *au fond* mathematics and music, which are ultimately the same kindred language. The idea is older than Plato, and at the same time as new as our most revolutionary thinkers. . . . All that I have to say on the subject that may be new is of the PREMONITION IN LANGUAGE of the unknown, vaster world—that world of which the physical is but a surface or skin, and yet which we ARE IN, and BELONG TO. (1956 [1942], 247–48)

More than fifty years later, we are just beginning to experience the realization of such a premonition. But more than the widespread availability of easy-to-learn and easy-to-use computer interfaces, this vision still requires one more shift in our ways of thinking about the computer. From what I have shown here, it seems clear that this shift requires acknowledging the necessity of an open dialogue between the users and the designers of the technology based on a mutual human engagement. The computer will become a transparent medium, disappearing into the interaction it enables, only if we all realize that we engage in a communicative act each time we hit a keystroke, move a mouse, and tomorrow, maybe, touch the other side of the interface.

Personnel at Engelbart's SRI Lab

PROFESSIONAL (22)

Supervisory (1)

  Engelbart, Douglas *Director*

Software (13)

Andrews, Don	Leonard, Steve
Bass, Walter	Melvin, John
Church, Mary (Mimi)	Michael, Elizabeth
Duvall, Bill	Parsley, Bruce
Geoffrion, Ann	Paxton, Bill
Hopper, Dave	Victor, Ken
Irby, Charles	

Hardware (6)

Bates, Roger	Van De Reit, Ed
Baughman, Vernon	Yarborough, John
Ratliff, Jake	Hardy, Martin

Other (2)

English, Bill	*Assistant Director*
Norton, Jim	*Business Manager*

NON-PROFESSIONAL (10)

Ball, Geoffrey	*Research & Analysis*
Caldwell, Mary	*User Support*
Carillon, Roberta	*Administration*
Casseres, Dave	*Documentation*
Evans, David ("Dyvid")	*Research & Analysis*
Harris, Jared	
Meyer, N. Dean	*Software/User Support*
Row, Barbara	*Administration*

Trundy, Martha   *User Support*
Van Nouhuys, Dirk   *Documentation*

The following fifteen people affiliated with ARC prior to 1969 (that is, in or close to the laboratory) should also be included: Pat Connley, Elton Hay, Iris Hopper, Bonnie Huddart, Stevie Jenkins, Chuck Kirkley, Steve Levine, Don Lincicome, Jack Machanik, Steve Paavola, Jeff Rulifson, Judy Sass, Elmer Shapiro, Kaye Tomlin, and John Wensley. After 1970, ARC grew to a total staff of approximately forty-five people at its peak, and the Center was organized in two units, the second of which was the ARPANET Network Information Center (NIC).

The following 87 people worked for ARC at some point after 1970: Marilyn Auerbach Smith, Bill Barnes, Jeanne Beck Bear, Robert Belleville, Maxine Bolf, Beverly Boli, Rod Bondurant, Dave Brown, Mike Burke, Janet Chin, Jerry Coleman, Judy Cooke, Jan Cornish, Bart Cox, Bill Daul, Tom Davis, Chuck Dornbush, Linda Duckett, Joe Ehardt, Christina Engelbart, Jim Fadiman, Jake Feinler, Bill Ferguson, Pamela Garlick, Larry Garlick, Carol Guilbault, Ken Harrenstein, Marcelo Hoffmann, Kathy Holland, Tom Humphrey, Mil Jernigan, Dee J. Jones, Susan Kahn, Diane Kaye, Beverley Kelley, Gail Kintzler, Steve Kleiser, Mike Kudlick, Johanna Landsbergen, Jeanne Leavitt, Harvey Lehtman, Carolyn Len, Robert Lieberman, Dan Lynch, Karolyn Martin Switzer, Keith Maw, Dave Maynard, Adrian McGinnis, Susan Melvin, Laura Metzger, Marlene Meyer, Sandy Miranda, Beverly Morgan, Bonny Mosher, Jim Mulvaney, Jeanne North, Reddy Dively, Daphne O'Regan, Rene Ochoa, Cindy Page, Raylene Pak, Ray Panko, Jeff Peters, Andy Poggio, Jon Postel, Dave Potter, Allan Pratt, Helen Prince, Paul Rech, Raphi Rom, Caroline Rose, Marcia Keeney Rosenberry, John Rothermel, Mary Gayle, Glenn Sherwood, Dave Smith, Frank Snow, Israel Torres, Jacques Vallée, Nancy Vittum, Pam Vittum Andrews, Donald "Smokey" Wallace, Margaret Ann Watson, Richard Watson, Jim White, Priscilla Wold, and Nina Zolotov.

Preface

1. The two time lines of computer technology on pp. xviii and xix present such innovations and representative machines in a chronological fashion. I provide them to serve as references for the text.

2. Steve Woolgar convinced me long ago of the necessity of such means and purposes, but I decided here not to attack this directly.

3. Pickering (1995, 20), following Foucault (1972), considers "existing culture" as "the *surface of emergence* for the intentional structure of human agency." In this sense, "cultural production" is the process of this emergence with respect to machines, texts, music, or any other forms of arts and crafts. There might be something "scientific" in this approach, but that does not make it a necessary way to undertake the inquiry into this subject: it is just *one* way to do it and/or to talk about it.

Introduction

1. The sociotechnological shaping of the personal interface can be described as a set of negotiations between the actors involved in its temporal emergence. In the course of these negotiations, the actors mobilize resources not according to their possible categorizations in the social or technological realm, but according to a strategy that is both social and technological. The result of these negotiations is a sociotechnological system in which the uncertainty about the social identities of the major actors and the qualities of the technology is slowly diminished.

2. The word "compiler" was chosen by Grace Hopper from Remington Rand when she created the A-O compiler in 1951 for the UNIVAC. Martin Campbell-Kelly and William Aspray reported that she "chose the word *compiler* because the system would automatically put together the piece of code that made up the complete program" (Campbell-Kelly and Aspray 1996, 187).

3. For the description of the development of FORTRAN, see Campbell-Kelly and Aspray (1996), 188–92.

4. John Backus, the leader of the team of scientists who created FORTRAN reports that "just as freewheeling westerners developed a chauvinistic pride in their

frontiersmanship and a corresponding conservatism, so many programmers of the freewheeling 1950s began to regard themselves as members of a priesthood guarding skills and mysteries far too complex for ordinary mortals. . . . This attitude cooled the impetus for sophisticated programming aids. The priesthood wanted and got simple mechanical aids for the clerical drudgery which burdened them, but they regarded with hostility and derision more ambitious plans to make programming accessible to a larger population" (1980, 127–28).

5. This section on Douglas Engelbart's contribution to personal computing technologies relies on my interview with him (Engelbart 1992), as well as on four oral history interviews carried out by Henry Lowood, bibliographer for the History of Science and Technology Collections at Stanford University and Judith Adams in 1987–88 (Engelbart 1996).

6. See Augarten (1984) for a general overview of these various projects.

7. In August 1947, Henry Knutson of the ONR's Special Devices Center informed Jay Forrester, director of the MIT Whirlwind project, that "the tendency is to upgrade the classification [of military-funded research projects] and that all computer contracts are now being considered with the possible view of making them confidential." Quoted by Paul Edwards (1996), 104. See Edwards's chapter 4, "Why Build Computers," for more on the connection between the military and computing research after World War II.

8. Actually, the public awareness of computing suddenly increased with the part played by UNIVAC in the 1952 presidential election. It predicted Eisenhower's victory at 9:00 P.M. EST of the day of the election with only 7 percent of the votes in. Because most of the pollsters had predicted a close election, UNIVAC's prediction was not released until the computer was reprogrammed to give a result closer to what they anticipated. The final result proved to be very close to UNIVAC's first prediction, and CBS commentator Edward R. Murrow concluded that "the trouble with machines . . . is people" (quoted in Augarten 1984, 164).

9. However, since then, numerous controversies in historical accounts have neglected the "quasi-religious" aspect of these undertakings to make sense of the engagement of this generation. I do not intend here to take a position in those debates, but rather to try to locate them in the historical context of the post–World War II period, and not in the current semirevisionist discourses informed by later positions on this issue.

10. The Josiah Macy Jr. Foundation was named after a Quaker who had made his fortune at the beginning of the century in oil shipping. (See Heim 1993, 164–69 for more on the foundation).

11. The connection to Ashby's thinking is one of the very few influences that Engelbart acknowledged in the first expression of his Framework for the Augmentation of the Human Intellect: "It has been jokingly suggested several times during the course of this study that what we are seeking is an 'intelligence amplifier' (the term is attributed to W. Ross Ashby)" (Engelbart 1962, 19).

12. See Heims (1980), chapter 13, for an elaboration of this point.

13. Interestingly enough, this description of the "scout" comes from Stephen Toulmin's description of Gregory Bateson, one of the leading social scientists of the cybernetics circle (quoted in Heims 1991, 86).

14. This opposition may be one of the most profound legacies of the cybernetics program, as its resurgence in new literary science fictions of the 1980's dubbed

"cyberpunk" testifies. See for example Bruce Sterling's (1989) collection of stories on the Mechanist/Shaper narratives and Tom Maddox's (1991) analysis.

15. J. D. North, "The Rational Behavior of Mechanically Extended Man" (Boulton Paul Aircraft Ltd.: Wolverhampton, England, September 1954).

16. Here is Robert Taylor's recollection of this episode: "Licklider brought together this government committee of all the people who were supporting computer research in one form or another, and told us about this very modest program that he had just gotten under way, his 'modest' budget was greater than the sum of the other budgets represented in that committee. . . . ONR was represented. . . . the Air Force Office of Scientific Research was represented by Harold Wooster and Rowena Swanson. There was an Army Research office out at Durham, North Carolina, that was represented. I represented NASA. . . . The National Institute of Health was represented" (Taylor 1989).

17. This information was obtained during my own personal interview with Robert Taylor (1993) and confirmed in the Charles Babbage Institute oral history interview (1989).

18. For example, starting in 1965, Taylor annually called together the IPTO principal investigators for a two-day or three-day meeting. Taylor also visited each of his funded projects for several days each year, which provided him with an opportunity to observe various styles for managing research and development on computing. Later, after 1970, at Xerox PARC, Taylor was able to implement the management lessons that he had learned at ARPA from 1965 to 1969. This part of the history of personal computing is described in detail in Bardini and Horvath (1995).

19. This is Pamela McCorduck's characterization of IPTO management style (1979, 110).

20. In another interview, conducted by William Aspray (Sutherland 1989), Ivan Sutherland confirmed: "I would contrast the ARPA approach to sponsoring research with what I call the NIH and the NSF approaches, which are basically peer review approaches. . . . The ARPA approach has never had peer review mechanisms. It has been done basically on the individual initiatives of people in the office, with whatever advisors they had chosen to seek. But the director of ARPA and the director of IPT have had, in fact, a good deal of spending authority. . . . What the peer review mechanism is weaker at is activities, like in the computing area, where there is a big outburst of things happening, where an insight like that which Licklider had, that online computing is important . . . can make a big effect."

21. Alan Kay attended some of these meetings while he was a graduate student at the University of Utah in the late 1960's. He remembers them as very exciting, and especially emphasizes Taylor's social skill to get the contractors' brilliant egos and brains lined up (Kay 1992).

22. These responses were documented in the participants' discussion following Licklider's presentation at the Association for Computing Machinery Conference on the History of Personal Workstations in 1986. See Goldberg (1988, 126–30).

23. Bob Taylor confirmed during our interview that Licklider got to know more about Engelbart's research during a meeting of the committee that I discussed previously.

24. Historical note: this term derives from "bootstrap loader," a short program that was read in from cards or paper tape or toggled in from the front-panel switches. This program was always very short (great efforts were expended on making it short

in order to minimize the labor and chance of error involved in toggling it in), but was just smart enough to read in a slightly more complex program (usually from a card or paper tape reader) to which it handed control. This program, in turn, was smart enough to read the application or operating system from a magnetic tape drive or disk drive. Thus, in successive steps, the computer "pulled itself up by its bootstraps" to a useful operating state. Nowadays, the bootstrap is usually found in ROM or EPROM and reads the first stage in from a fixed location on the disk called the "boot block." When this program gains control, it is powerful enough to load the actual operating system and hand control over to it. See the *Hackers' Dictionary*, available on-line at the following ftp address: ftp://sailor.gutenberg.org/pub/gutenberg/etext92/jargn10.txt.

25. See MacCormac (1984), for an examination of the "brain as a computer" metaphor in the historical perspective of the eighteenth-century metaphor of "man as a machine." Also see Mitcham (1986) for a thorough survey of the classic studies concerning the human (social, cultural, ethical, and religious) dimensions of computers. Lars-Erik Janlert has focused on this representation of "the computer as a person," and concluded, at the opposite of the original eighteenth-century metaphor of "man as a machine," that "the person view, however, is the exact antithesis: *make man the measure of machines*!" (1987, emphasis in the original). From all this literature, I retain the idea that this metaphor goes both ways: It entails its user seeing humans as machines *and* machines as organisms.

26. Steve Woolgar (1987, 320) has analyzed the subsequent controversy between the "soft" and "strong" programs in AI (the "strong" version attempts to mimic cognitive behavior), and showed that it is "an argument about the relationship between science and technology."

27. In the context of the ARPA-IPTO contractors' community, Engelbart was in fact in a position of absolute minority, representing only his lab and himself, because this community, on the issues he worked on, was structured by the AI "clans": "So perhaps the most influential result of the Dartmouth Conference [the founding moment for AI research in the United States] itself was the social patterns it set . . . accusations of clannishness have persisted since 1956, and they aren't without foundation. . . . The major source of financial support in this country through the 1960s and early 1970s was ARPA . . . unlike many government funding agencies, ARPA does not use the peer-review system, but disburses funds based on its own judgment of the best people doing the best projects related to its mission. That judgment has been to concentrate resources, and has thereby enriched four main centers, which are again, Carnegie-Mellon University, where Newell and Simon work; MIT, where Minsky works; Stanford, where McCarthy works; and Stanford Research Institute, which is heavily populated with former students of these Dartmouth Conference participants" (McCorduck 1979, 109–10).

As we will see, the successive directors of the IPTO were fully aware of this, which does not mean that they necessarily believed the grandiose promises of AI research. J. C. R. Licklider, as we saw, seemed to believe in a future where "thinking" could be left to computers, as he stated later: "people like Minsky and McCarthy were primarily interested in artificial intelligence, and tended to view man-computer interaction as a neat and convenient thing to make it possible to write AI programs, whereas I thought there was going to be this interval between man's thinking about himself and machines taking over. I did not know how long the interval was, but it looked like a considerable interval, when working with the computer was of the essence. So, in short, I really believed it, and quite a few people in the area here thought that something really great was going to happen." Ivan Sutherland, his successor at IPTO, on the other hand, insisted that "the artificial intelligence people, I think, pioneered many of the advanced computing techniques: non-numeric programming; dealing with compiler languages; describing languages, and so on. I think that that whole effort has now reached a point where it is what is taught to undergraduates as computer science" (Sutherland 1989).

28. For a better sense of the historical context of the idea of time sharing, see Fredkin (1963) and "The Evolution of Time Sharing" in Wildes and Lindgren (1985).

29. Robert Taylor narrated this episode to me in our interview (1993) and in his Charles Babbage Institute oral history interview (1989). Licklider confirmed the whole episode from his point of view. In the same interview, Licklider remembers that the SDC contract represented more than half of IPTO's first-year budget (approximately seven million dollars), and that he "hated to see it [the AFSQ32] sit there being used as an old batch processor."

30. That is, since IBM supplied a "real-time package" to the 704 in the Computation Center. In its July 1961 Computation Center report, Dr. Corbató and his staff announced that the system was available for two users at a time (Wildes and Lindgren 1985).

31. It is not my purpose here to present a detailed sketch of the history of the artificial-intelligence community of researchers. Such a history has already been written in detail. See, for instance, McCorduck (1979). My point is rather to show the importance and the diversity of this community inside the IPTO contractors' community.

32. For example, during my interview Robert Taylor (1993) stated that Engelbart is "not exactly the best explainer of his own ideas," either orally or in his writings, as the style of the 1962 report clearly illustrates. The importance of this kind of "personality variable" is pervasive in the accounts of the actors and is related to the "frontier" quality of early computing.

33. Actually, in the ten oral history interviews of some of the major actors of the IPTO community that I downloaded from the Charles Babbage Institute project, only a couple still mention Engelbart's contribution for more than the mouse, and several do not mention him at all.

Chapter 1

1. In his chapter of the edited collection *The Boundaries of Humanity*, Allen Newell expresses dissatisfaction with metaphorical thinking in general: "it is clearly wrong to treat science as metaphor, for the more metaphorical, the less scientific." For him, AI is about a theory of mind, and not a metaphor for the mind: it should provide organized knowledge about the mind (Newell 1991, 161–63). In his general introduction to the same collection, Morton Sosna, however, echoes AI critics who "have questioned whether AI has remained, or can or ought to remain, unmetaphorical" (ibid., 7). Newell alludes to the relativist sociology of science—exemplified by Latour and Woolgar's *Laboratory Life* (1979)—and equates the "deconstruction of science" with "taking all science as metaphorical" (ibid., 160).

2. For Bush's work on the differential analyzers, see Owens (1991) and Wildes and Lindgren (1985), chapter 4.

3. As the arguments developed in this chapter will show, Weakland's intellectual pedigree is significant. John H. Weakland was a student of Gregory Bateson's who was trained in anthropology and quite familiar with Benjamin Lee Whorf's writings. Weakland also studied and collaborated with Margaret Mead, who herself, like Edward Sapir, Whorf's mentor and colleague, had studied with Franz Boas at Columbia University. In other words, Weakland was a younger member of an invisible college of anthropologists that included Benjamin Lee Whorf. Like him, Weakland was a chemical engineer whose fame would come from a different field of practice. He worked with Gregory Bateson at the Veterans Administration Hospital in Palo Alto and is credited with him for the invention of the double-bind hypothesis. In 1962, he joined the recently founded Mental Research Institute, where he worked for the rest of his career. Weakland was thus a founding member of the famous Palo Alto Group of psychologists.

4. For Nelson, hypertext was first conceived as a necessary tool for his work as an author. He calls it "the most fundamental tool of human thought," a tool that "allows you to see alternative versions on the same screen on parallel windows and mark side by side what the differences are" (Nelson 1993).

5. It seems to me that Nyce and Kahn commit a logical mistake when they summarize the results of their contributor Linda Smith in the following fashion: "Linda C. Smith . . . traces the various influences Bush's essay has had in the information retrieval research literature. She found that only a fraction of these citations focuses on Memex as a 'personal information system'" (1991a, 60). This is a case of a petitio principii. It begs the question.

Smith's citation analysis of "As We May Think" indeed identifies 375 citing documents, half of which were published in the period 1981–90, and she states that "the continuing high level of citation of the 1945 article in the 1980s can be attributed at least in part to the association of Bush with concepts similar to those underlying hypertext" (1991, 263–64). But this citation analysis was not performed on "the information retrieval research literature," but on a collection of documents indexed in the *Science Citation Index*, the *Arts and Humanities Citation Index*, and the *CompuMath Citation Index*. Smith even adds that "coverage of the citation indexes was supplemented by checking selected monographs and conference proceedings in such areas as information retrieval, library automation, and hypertext" (ibid., 263).

Nyce and Kahn's conclusion (but also their premise, if I am right) is a product of Smith's content-analysis scheme, which identifies "five categories that reflect citing authors' use of Bush's "As We May Think": "(1) historical perspective; (2) hardware; (3) information store; (4) association and selection; (5) personal information system" (ibid.). Smith's justification for the names that she gave to her categories is quite ambiguous: "Categories 2–4 reflect Bush's categorization of Memex . . . as 'a filing system, a repository of information, and a scheme of searching and speedily finding a desired piece of information'. . . . Category 5 applies to those citing documents which consider Memex as a whole" (ibid.). It is because she and Nyce and Kahn now consider the Memex as "a personal information system" that she can build such a category, after the fact. It is therefore quite predictable that "only a fraction of these citations focuses on Memex as a personal information system."

6. After he left MIT, he became president of the Carnegie Institution of Washington and directed the Office for Scientific Research and Development during World War II. For Bush's biography, see Zachary (1997).

7. Indeed, the consequences of Gödel's theorem could be understood as justifying a proposition such as "any boundary is arbitrary" and therefore observer-dependent. Because in this case, we, human beings, raise the question, it could be claimed that the answer is determined by the intellectual equipment required to express the question (i.e., language, in its metaphorical dimension). Unless, of course, you assume that there is such a thing as a "concept of boundary" independent of the word "boundary."

8. In this, the boundary metaphor is different in the case of the human-animal boundary, in which the topological implications are inclusive, rather than juxtaposive. As Bernard Williams (1991, 13) puts it, "we are a distinctive kind of animal but not any distinctive kind of machine."

9. See Hubert L. Dreyfus (1972 and 1979).

10. For the notion of "boundary object," see Star and Griesemer (1989).

11. The social context of Whorf's writings limited him to a weak formulation of his hypothesis. As George Lakoff points out, "one all-important thing should be remembered about Whorf. He did most of his work at a time when Nazism was on the rise in Europe and jingoism was prevalent in America. At the time, white people were assumed, even in much of the U.S., to be more intelligent than people with skins of other colors. . . . The very idea that 'uneducated' Indians, who were still considered savages by many, could reason as well as educated Americans and Europeans was extraordinary and radical. The notion that their conceptual system *better* fit scientific reality—that *we* could learn from *them*—bordered on the unthinkable" (1987, 330, emphasis in the original).

12. The excerpt of Engelbart's 1962 report surely conveys the impression that Engelbart directly quotes Whorf. It is obvious that it is not the case, but that Engelbart is giving here his own translation of the hypothesis.

13. During their training years as young mathematicians, from 1924 to 1926, both Norbert Wiener and John von Neumann spent some time in Göttingen, Germany, where their paths first crossed when they attended lectures by Heisenberg (Heims 1980, 51–52).

14. Korzybski summarized these three Aristotelian laws of thought as follows: "(1) The law of identity (Whatever is, is. {A thing is what it is}); (2) The law of contradiction. (Nothing can both be, and not be); and (3) The law of excluded third {middle} (Everything must either be, or not be)" (quoted in Paulson 1983, 47).

15. This point was made at the same time by the great Russian psychologist Lev Semenovich Vygotsky (1896–1934): "A word does not refer to a single object, but to a group of objects or to a class of objects. Each word is already a generalization" (1962, 5).

16. Margaret Mead, *Coming of Age in Samoa: A Psychological Study of Primitive Youth for Western Civilization*, 2d ed. (New York: Morrow, 1928) p. 145, quoted in Heims (1991), 269.

17. Numerous restatements of this point in the relativist literature in sociology of science and technology (e.g., Latour 1988)—not to mention the similar attacks on constructivists in the humanities—attest to the lasting effect of this misunderstanding.

18. Bateson (1979, 228) defines epistemology as "a branch of science combined with a branch of philosophy. As science, epistemology is the study of how particular organisms or aggregates of organisms *know*, *think*, and *decide*. As philosophy, epistemology is the study of the necessary limits and other characteristics of the processes of knowing, thinking and deciding." As an agronomist turned sociologist, I totally agree with this definition.

19. Petroski also claims that "understanding the development of the pencil, though it has spanned centuries, certainly helps us to understand also the development of even so sophisticated a product of modern high technology as the electronic computer" (1992, 334).

20. Douglas Engelbart certainly understood this point long before Petroski, as his own example of an "unnatural" tool, the "disaugmented pencil," shows: "One way of explaining to somebody why it could make a significant difference if you can do things faster, is to provide a counter example. So, I had them write with a brick taped to their pencil, because it's only a matter of happenstance that the scale of our body and our tools and such lets us write as fast as we can. What if it were slow and tedious to write? A person doesn't have to work that way very long before starting to realize that our academic work, our books—a great deal would change in our world if that's how hard it had been to write" (Engelbart 1988, 199–200).

21. Engelbart quotes Good's paper in one of the first papers he published (Engelbart 1961), and I found an annotated copy of the paper in Engelbart's personal archive. Engelbart especially noted a passage that states that "the tree of knowledge is a sort of banyan tree or rather a network. The network has nodes and roads. The roads are not equally good; good roads correspond to strong associations" (ibid., 284).

22. From the Greek *syn* (together) *aisthanesthai* (to perceive), synesthesia is one of these topics that has periodically reemerged on the scientific agenda since its first medical description in 1710, when Thomas Woolhouse, an English ophthalmologist, described the case of a blind man who perceived sound-induced colored visions (Cytowic 1993).

23. Since Whorf's writings, numerous results in cognitive science have shown that this connection deserves a central position in our understanding of the evolution of the human brain. Whorf (1956 [1941], 155) had certainly intuited some of these later results when he stated that "probably in the first instance metaphor arises from synesthesia and not the reverse." But to him, metaphor is nevertheless the key to reaching a higher level of consciousness: it is through the metaphorical capability of language that the introduction of natural language and of the whole body of the user are linked in the same project, augmenting the human intellect.

Somesthetic perceptions include tactile and kinesthetic perceptions. Tactile perceptions result from the sensitivity of the skin to various variable inputs, including pressure, vibration, temperature or electricity, and kinesthetic perceptions result from the sensation of movement (recognition of position, active and passive movement as well as resistance to movement) arising from the tendons, joints, skin, and muscle. For a general review of tactile communication before 1960 (and therefore before Engelbart's project), see Franck (1958) and for a more recent historical account see Krueger (1982).

24. In respect to the physical world, Bateson defined coevolution as "a stochastic system of evolutionary change in which two or more species interact in such a way that changes in species A set the stage for the natural selection of changes in

species B. Later changes in species B, in turn, set the stages for the selecting of more similar changes in species A" (Bateson 1979, 227).

Biologists define coevolution as "reciprocal evolutionary change in interacting species" (Thompson 1982, 3) and find the origin of this notion in the Darwinian notion of "coadaptation." Even if the word "coevolution" itself appeared prior to the mid-1960's in a few studies, according to Thompson (ibid., 4), "Ehrlich and Raven's (1964) study on coevolution in butterflies and plants was certainly the paper that established the coevolutionary perspective as a major framework within which to study the evolution of interaction." However, prior to Ehrlich and Raven's paper, some studies aimed at understanding the relationship between coevolution and population regulation without using the term "coevolution." Instead, they referred to "genetic feedback" (ibid., 5).

This link between evolutionary ecology and cybernetics through the notion of coevolution gained popular currency through the life and work of a former student of Paul R. Ehrlich's: Stewart Brand. According to his own account, Brand "was bit early by a series of biologists" including Ehrlich, who had supervised his undergraduate research at Stanford in 1959, and "last but deepest, Gregory Bateson" (Brand, in Kleiner and Brand 1986, 3). In 1968, Brand founded the *Whole Earth Catalog*, which he edited and published until 1972. In 1974, with the proceeds of the catalog, Brand founded *CoEvolution Quarterly* (CQ). Both the catalog and CQ were institutions of the counterculture in the late 1960's and early 1970's. In his introduction to a collection of ten years of CQ entitled *News that Stayed News*, Art Kleiner recalled that the catalog was "started by Stewart Brand in 1968 to cater (at first) to hippies living on commune" (Kleiner, in Kleiner and Brand 1986, xi). Like its predecessor, CQ went on "to spark the resourcefulness of a generation of people," the flower generation of the West Coast, who "reached for various things—some to stop the war in Vietnam, some to save various species, some to find a way to stay high" (Brand, in Kleiner and Brand, 1986, xi, 330).

Combining activism (be it political or ecological), practical and theoretical knowledge diffusion, and downright fun, Brand's publications helped like no other outlet to diffuse the particular mix of cybernetic thinking and evolutionary ecology that had its center in the notion of coevolution. For instance, CQ published a paper by Ehrlich on coevolution in its first issue (spring 1974), interviews and texts by Bateson in many issues (winter 1974, fall 1975, fall 1976, spring 1977, etc.), and a series of articles on James Lovelock's Gaia Hypothesis that the biosphere, the global system of life on earth, is one organism.

With such articles, the "scientific" intuition that there could be a coevolutionary process connecting the physical and the conceptual worlds started to pervade the entire counterculture and subsequently, the whole culture of the end of the century. Indeed the notion of coevolution continued to reappear during the 1990's, as much in scientific discourse as in popular discourse.

In *Co-Evolution: Genes, Culture, and Human Diversity*, William H. Durham, an anthropologist at Stanford University, proposed "an evolutionary theory of cultural change" and used it "to examine the range of relationships between genes and culture in human populations" (Durham 1991, vii), thus providing one of the leading accounts of coevolution from a sociobiological standpoint. In *The Fourth Discontinuity: The Co-Evolution of Humans and Machines*, Bruce Mazlich, a historian at MIT, extended this sociobiological account in a historical perspective and argued that "humans are on the threshold of decisively breaking past the discontinuity between themselves and machines . . . because they can now perceive their own evolution as inextricably interwoven with their use and development of tools, of which the modern machine is only the furthest extrapolation" (Mazlich 1993, 6). And in *The Symbolic Species: The Co-Evolution of Language and the Brain*, Terence W. Deacon, a biological anthropologist at Boston University, stated: "More than any other group of species, hominids' behavioral adaptations have determined the course of their physical evolution, rather than vice versa. Stone and symbolic tools, which were initially acquired with the aid of flexible ape-learning abilities, ultimately turned the table on their users and forced them to adapt to a new niche opened by these technologies. Rather than being just useful tricks, these behavioral prostheses for obtaining food and organizing social behaviors became indispensable elements in a new adaptive complex. The origin of 'humanness' can be defined as the point in our evolution where the tools became the principal source of selection on our bodies and brains" (Deacon 1998, 344–45).

Chapter 2

1. James C. Bliss was working in the laboratory adjacent to Engelbart's. They never collaborated formally, since that proposal was not funded, but they were both aware of each other's research (Bliss 1997). James Bliss worked for SRI until 1971 and later founded Telesensory Systems, Inc., a company that produced the Opticon, one of the most widely used commercial tactile stimulation devices.

2. The reference is to Paul Connerton, *How Societies Remember* (Cambridge: Cambridge University Press, 1989).

3. See Dunsheath (1969 [1962]), chapter 19, for an account of the history of the IEE.

4. The House American telegraph printer appears to be the contemporary of the British Bain and Wright machine, since it was invented in 1846. The *Encyclopaedia Britannica* at http://britannica.com, s. v. "Printing Telegraphs | Royal House and the Printing Telegraph," gives the following description of House's machine: "House's system employed a transmitting keyboard with 28 keys, each assigned a character. Behind the keyboard was a cylinder on the surface of which a series of pegs was set in a helix that took one turn around the cylinder. The cylinder was turned by a crank, and its motion was interrupted when a peg was blocked by a depressed key. Electric contacts that closed and opened the line, once for each letter, were positioned at the end of the cylinder. The resulting impulses through an electromagnet stepped a ratchet and printing wheel to corresponding positions at the receiver. When rotation stopped, a miniature press forced a blackened silk ribbon against an endless paper strip, backed by an embossed letter on the printing wheel, and the transmitted letter was printed."

5. I oppose Kittler's notion of "unlinking of eye and hand" mostly because of its supposed consequence on the changing "nature" of writing that Kittler described as a shift: "In the play between signs and intervals, writing was no longer the handwritten, continuous transition from nature to culture. It became selection from a countable, spatialized supply" (Kittler 1990 [1985], 194). More importantly, I oppose Kittler's idea that with the diffusion of typewriting was born a "play between type and its Other, completely removed from subjects," "inscription," the play that

actually replaced the "play between Man the sign-setter and the writing surface, the philosopher as stylus and the tablet of Nature" (ibid., 195).

To me, such an unlinking could have happened as one consequence of the development and diffusion of a *dispositif* that certainly included the typewriter or telegraph printer artifacts, but that, most importantly, also included the development and diffusion of the incorporating practice of touch typing. Such a learning process was in no case the most obvious part of the *dispositif*, but required the development of discourses, methods, and institutions devoted to its diffusion. Such a learning process, moreover, still required the human agency of gesture, the repetitive acquisition of practical routines, that in no instances could be "completely removed from subjects." According to Kittler (ibid., 195), "In typewriting, spatiality determines not only the relations among signs but also their relation to the empty ground." But what is an empty ground for the finger that hits the space key? What is spatiality for a kinesthetic system that bans the eye? Moreover, what part could the human gesture play in such a *dispositif*?

I do not think, as Kittler does, that "Whereas handwriting is subject to the eye, a sense that works across distance, the typewriter uses a blind, tactile power" (ibid.). What, except a comfortable tautology, says that the tactile sense is blind? If you know how to touch type (or play the piano), rather, your hands feel the empty ground (and hear the silence they produce). Touch typing and playing the piano are, in other words, two of the most interesting incorporating practices which are also synesthetic practices.

Kittler, and Seltzer after him, also might be wrong when they attribute the "front stroke principle" to Underwood. According to the Herkimer County Historical Society, this innovation appeared in a type-bar machine as early as 1883, with the Horton machine. The Underwood machine was, according to the same source "the first front-stroke machine to attain [commercial] prominence" (Herkimer County Historical Society 1923, 104).

6. This explanation did not settle the controversy among economists. S. J. Liebowitz and Stephen E. Margolis, in their "Fable of the Keys" reopened the debate in 1990 and challenged David's thesis. Their point was that the fact that the QWERTY keyboard remained the standard does not mean that the market mechanism was failing, since they held that nothing really proves that the QWERTY is less efficient than alternative arrangement of the keys. Liebowitz and Margolis also noted that "in the 1880s and 1890s typewriters were generally sold to offices not already staffed with typists or into markets where typists were not readily available." They also quote the Herkimer history about the existence of placement services operated by typewriter manufacturers. But contrary to David, they conclude that "since almost every sale required training of a typist, a typewriter manufacturer that offered a different keyboard was not particularly disadvantaged" (1990, 19). But when they claim that "the problem of implementing the conversion was not what kept the manufacturers from changing keyboards" and "the QWERTY keyboard cannot have been so well established at the time the rival keyboards were first offered that they were rejected because they were non-standard" (ibid.), they underestimate the network of commercial and educational institutions that was promulgating the QWERTY standard.

7. See the *Encyclopaedia Britannica*, at http://www.britannica.com, s. v. "Printing Telegraphs / Telecom Systems."

8. The important point here is that even if the QWERTY is clearly the dominant artifact for typesetting, its status remained challenged for nearly its whole history, and numerous special projects, applications, and artifacts were proposed using alternative designs for textual input. In her review of chord keyboards, Noyes (1983b) reported that these alternative designs were mostly experimented with for mail sorting (in England, Canada, and the United States) in the 1950's and 1960's, before any commercial application appeared in the 1970's.

After some pioneering, but not extensively reported work on a one-handed chord keyboard by August Dvorak in 1950, a few attempts to develop these devices were made in the 1950's and early 1960's. Dvorak is of course mostly famous for his multiple attempts to reform the QWERTY layout, leading to his 1936 Dvorak Simplified Keyboard (U.S. Patent # 2,040,248). The work cited here deals with his work on keyboard design for one-handed people. Noyes (1983b) cites these cases: Levy at the Toronto Post Office (1955), Klemmer at IBM (1958), Conrad at the British Post Office (1960), and Hillix and Coburn at the Navy Electronic Laboratory (1961). A variety of designs and key-mapping schemes were experimented with, but Levy's description appears to be the closest to Engelbart's system, since it was also composed of two five-key keyboards, each giving up to 31 alternative characters ($2^5 - 1$).

Several measures of the performance of typists using a chord keyboard were conducted during the same period. Ratz and Ritchie (1961) reported the results of their experiments in ranking the 31 possible chords on a five-key chording keyboard according to their difficulty as measured by the reaction times and a quantitative measure obtained for the distribution of the chords. They concluded that "the results show that motor system constraints are predominant over choice reaction time in determining speed on a chord keyboard" (Ratz and Ritchie 1961, 307). R. Seibel of IBM replicated the experiment the following year with a couple of minor changes and concluded that the training of the subjects was crucial for the improvement of their reaction times and information-transmission rates (Seibel 1962).

In 1965, R. Conrad and D. J. A. Longman published the most extensive experimental comparison of the standard typewriter versus chord keyboards available in the literature. They justified the attempt to reduce the number of keys to ten from the "generally accepted fact of the difficulty of making 'reach' movements quickly and accurately without visual guidance." Ratz and Ritchie reported "that little improvement took place after the second day [of practice]. Asymptotic behavior was reached rather quickly because the order of presentation was random" (1961, 304). Seibel argued with this result and concluded that "the lack of practice of the Ratz and Ritchie subjects appears to have produced a threefold (or more) overestimate of reaction times for the 31-chord keyboard" (Seibel 1962, 169). But Conrad and Longman failed to notice any significant difference of performance between groups of users of the two devices: "An experiment was carried out in which two groups of postmen were trained for seven weeks, one group at the chord keyboard, the other at the standard typewriter. The results showed that the chord group became operational about two weeks sooner than the typists. Beyond that point, improvement rates could be reasonably regarded as parallel, with the typist a little slower than the chord group with little difference in accuracy, other than that attributable to the special experimental conditions" (Conrad and Longman 1965, 77).

The subjects of the experiment were 46 postmen in their thirties who had never used a typewriter. The somewhat counterintuitive result of the faster operationality of the chord group is actually more complex than it appears and masks the fact that at the end of the training stage, the typewriter group had an average of about 10 keystrokes per operator per minute higher keying rate than the chord group. In other words, the typewriter group had a higher keying rate, but had taken longer to reach it (Conrad and Longman 1965, 84). Conrad's and Longman's results actually showed that the parallel increase of performance concerned a difference of performance in favor of the chord set of less than ten keystrokes per operator per minute, which may be too small to be considered significant according to the general accuracy permitted by the experimental conditions. But moreover, the design of the experiment was biased toward the chord keyset, since it assumed the subjects' same lack of the working knowledge of the device's mode of operation. Most people, however, had agreed since at least the 1920's that the already massive diffusion of touch typing favored the standard keyboard device for a "normal sample" of the population.

Chapter 3

1. Licklider started the study in November 1961, while he was still working at Bolt, Beranek, and Newman (BBN), assumed its direction while he took a leave in October 1962, to start up and direct ARPA-IPTO, and eventually finished the study with the writing of the report that became in 1965 the book *Libraries of the Future*.

2. Sutherland first reported his work on Sketchpad in January 1963 in MIT Lincoln Laboratory technical report # 296, before he presented it during the AFIPS Spring Joint Computer Conference in Detroit, Michigan, between May 21 and 23 under the same title: "Sketchpad: A Man-Machine Graphical Communication System." His dissertation work, under Claude Shannon, started in 1961 and benefited from the early advances of the East Coast researchers and especially Wes Clark's influence through his work on both LINC (Clark 1988) and the TX-2. Marvin Minsky and Steve Coons completed Sutherland's Ph.D. committee, and Douglas Ross "also provided many discussions" (Sutherland 1989).

3. For further description of the Sketchpad features, see Licklider (1966), 51–52.

4. The Whirlwind and SAGE programs are described by most recent historical accounts of computing, for example Augarten (1984), Lubar (1993), and Norberg and O'Neill (1996). Redmond and Smith (1980) give the most detailed description of the Whirlwind project, and Wildes and Lindgren (1985) give the most thorough description of the institutional setting at MIT.

5. William Ninke of Bell Labs, in his description of a subsequent graphic console describes the light button as follows: "a light button is a word or figure on the scope face which has a transfer vector associated with it. When the light button is touched by the light pen, the transfer vector is used to pass control to the appropriate routine. Placing control functions on the scope face has two advantages. First, only those controls which should be present at a particular stage of the problem are displayed. . . . Second, during most operations there is only one center of attention, the scope face, on which a user need concentrate. This allows smoother work on a problem" (1965, 845).

6. The information bandwidth of a given input device, w, is defined by the following equation: $w = \log_2(N^s)/t^s$, where N^s is the number of distinct states that the system can represent, $\log_2(N^s)$ is the number of bits necessary to represent all the states of the system, t^s is the time required to establish a state, and $1/t^s$ is the frequency at which random states are produced (Caswell 1988, 35–38). Note that in

the case of the light pen or any on-screen positioning device, the bandwidth is proportionate to the resolution and the dimensions of the screen of the display.

7. Haring also noted the discrepancy between the necessary display period of between 1 and 2 microseconds for a complicated flicker-free picture and the 8 microseconds limit of the then-available light detectors and photomultiplier tubes. He also mentioned the 40-microseconds decay time of the fastest phosphor layers.

8. Cliff Shaw reports that "the purpose of the JOSS experiment was not to make JOHNNIAC machine language available, but rather to provide a service through a new, machine independent language which had to be designed specifically for that purpose. It was to be an experiment with the goal of demonstrating the value of on-line access to a computer via an appropriate language, and was intended to contribute to a project with the long-range goal of a sophisticated information-processor. T. O. Ellis, I. Nehama, A. Newell, and K. W. Uncapher were the other participants in that project" (1964, 456).

9. GRAIL left many memories among some later key actors in the development of personal computing, such as Alan Kay: "Though everything was fastened with bubble gum and the system crashed often, I have never forgotten my first interactions with this system. It was direct manipulation, it was analogical, it was modeless, it was beautiful" (Kay 1993, 10).

10. The source that Norberg and O'Neill cite is T. O. Ellis, J. F. Heafner, and W. L. Sibley, "ARPA Semiannual Report No. 10," 22 June 1964, in the Keith Uncapher Papers, box 1, Folder: "Grail," Center for the History of Information Processing, University of Minnesota, Minneapolis: The Charles Babbage Institute.

11. Davis and Ellis described the device in a RAND memorandum (#RM-4122-ARPA) in August 1964 and presented it at the AFIPS Fall Joint Computer Conference with the same text, entitled "The RAND Tablet: A Man-Machine Graphical Communication Device."

12. Here is the original description of the tablet: "The basic building material for the tablet is 0.5-mil-thick Mylar sheet clad on both sides with ½-ounce copper (approximately 0.6 mils thick). Both sides of the copper-clad Mylar sheets are coated with photo resist, exposed to artwork patterns, and etched using standard fine-line etching techniques. The result is a printed circuit on each side of the Mylar. . . . The double-sided, printed screen is cemented to a smooth, rigid substrate and sprayed with a thin coat of epoxy to provide a good wear surface and to prevent electrical contact between the stylus and the printed circuit" (Davis and Ellis 1964, 327).

13. According to the *Encyclopaedia Britannica* at http://www.britannica.com, s. v. "Transducer," the term referred to a device that converted mechanical stimuli into electrical output, but it has been broadened to include devices that sense all forms of stimuli—such as heat, radiation, sound, strain, vibration, pressure, acceleration, and so on—and that can produce output signals other than electrical—such as pneumatic or hydraulic. Many measuring and sensing devices, as well as loudspeakers, thermocouples, microphones, and phonograph pickups, may be termed "transducers."

14. Later designs tried alternative signals. Larry Roberts (1966) described the Lincoln wand as an "ultrasonic position-sensing device," and Lewin from RCA labs (1965) proposed to make the pen the signal generator in the form of a magnetic field pulse, turning the device into an inductive transducer.

15. Engelbart's early proposal of the chord keyset considered the possibility of the total disappearance of the visual feedback loop in order to enter short textual commands. Here, the visual feedback loop could also disappear if the "electrostatic" sensitivity of the stylus was actually applied directly to the finger.

16. Owens also reports in a footnote that "Bush might not have known of the disc integrator when he devised the Profile Tracer," but adds: "However, variable friction gears much like the one he designed for the Profile Tracer were well-known to engineers." Indeed, Bromley reports that "the simplicity, ease of use, and low price of the Amsler planimeter . . . led to the manufacture of many thousands of the instruments in the nineteenth century—over twelve thousand by Amsler alone by 1884" (1990, 168).

17. Douglas Engelbart was, of course, aware of this connection, since he wrote in a later paper that "exactly the same phenomenon applied in the mechanical integrators of old-fashioned differential analyzers, was developed to a high degree of accuracy in resolving the translation components; we borrowed the idea, but we don't try to match the precision" (Engelbart 1973, 222).

Chapter 4

1. "The decisive step in the direction of a narrative conception of personal identity is taken when one passes from the action to the character. A character is one who performs the action in the narrative. The category of character is therefore a narrative category as well, and its role in the narrative involves the same narrative understanding as the plot itself. The question is then to determine what the narrative category of character contributes to the discussion of personal identity. The thesis supported here will be that the identity of the character is comprehensible through the transfer to the character of the operation of emplotment, first applied to the action recounted; characters, we will say, are themselves plots" (Ricoeur 1992, 143).

2. Madeleine Akrich (1992, 208) defined the "script" as follows: "A large part of the work of innovators is that of '*inscribing*' this vision of (prediction about) the world in the technical content of the new object. I will call the end product of this work a 'script' or a 'scenario.'"

3. "The word *black box* is used by cyberneticians whenever a piece of machinery or a series of commands is too complex. In its place, they draw a little box about which they need to know nothing but its input and output" (Latour 1987, 2–3). In fact, the "black box" metaphor has been central in the sociology of science and technology since the early 1970's to describe the processes it sought to demystify. Or better said, the "new" sociologists of science and technology have used this metaphor to characterize former sociology of science and technology that prevailed in "the early days . . . when scientific knowledge was treated like a 'black box' . . . and for the purpose of such studies, scientists might as well have produced meat pies" (Pinch and Bijker 1987, 21). The imperative to "open the black box of science and technology" came to be the catchword of the movement that sought to root its sociological analyses in the actual contents of the disciplines that it studies.

Progressively, though, the "black box" metaphor shifted from a way to characterize the sociology of science to a way to characterize science itself: scientists produce black boxes, not only "old" sociologists. In this extended meaning, a "black box" came to stand for any robust representation: "the assembly of disorderly and unreliable allies is thus slowly turned into something that closely resembles an organized whole. When such a cohesion is obtained we at least have a *black box*" (Latour 1987, 130–31, emphasis in the original). Enrolled as allies of the designer, everything and everybody, from the docile components of the system to gracious users, conspires in pursuing the success of his or her representation and leads to a massively diffused, properly used setup centered on a device, a matter of fact. A few years later, Madeleine Akrich, with Latour another member of the Parisian school of sociology known as the Actor/Network school, summarized these ideas beautifully in the case of the sociology of technology: "If we are to describe technical objects, we need mediators to create the links between technical contents and user. In the case of non-stabilized technologies these may be either the innovator or the user. The situation is quite different when we are confronted with stabilized technologies that have been 'black-boxed.' There the innovator is no longer present, and study of the ordinary user is not very useful because he or she has already taken on board the prescriptions implied in the interaction with the machine" (1992, 211).

In other words, the "study of the ordinary user" of stabilized technologies might not be very useful because he or she has been black boxed too: the prescriptions in the machine are also prescribed possibilities for the user.

4. From an interview with Douglas Engelbart available on-line at http://www.superkids.com/aweb/pages/features/mouse/mouse.html.

5. The interaction sequence was actually a little more complex than reported here, since the user first entered a "mode" (character, word, etc.) before entering the command. According to Alan Kay (1992), the "reason" for such a complex interaction sequence was a technological shortcoming of the analog design of the mouse: "The Engelbart mouse was an analog mouse and the pot[entiometer]s tended to drift. Part of the user interface was set up to compensate for that. So you had to tell the system as part of the command what kind of things you were trying to grab with the mouse, was it a character, was it a word. . . . If you were going after words, it was quite happy (laugh) because they were big compared to the pointer spot."

6. This cautious conclusion was not necessarily taken into account in later work based on these results, and numerous statements that the mouse was indeed the "best device for display selection" appeared in later accounts of the laboratory's achievements: for example, "the tests involved a number of devices, including the best light pen we could buy, a joystick. . . . To complete the range of devices, we implemented an older idea, which became known as our 'mouse,' that came through the experiments ahead of all its competitors and has been our standard device for eight years now" (Engelbart 1973, 221).

7. These subjects were members of the laboratory and the phrase "somewhat familiar" is explained by the fact that some of them just started working for Engelbart.

8. This move thus goes further than inscribing the user in the design of the device: at the time the device is tested, its takes the next logical step and assumes that this inscription leads to the incorporation of the appropriate practice. The apparent paradox thus dissipates, because previous inscriptions "naturally" lead to connected incorporations, because, as Katherine Hayles puts it, "As the body is to embodiment, so inscription is to incorporation. Just as embodiment is in constant interplay with the body, so incorporating practices are in constant interplay with inscriptions that abstract the practices into signs" (1999, 199). In the case of this particular stage of the technology development, testing, abstract inscriptions (formal representations of

the virtual user) are translated into incorporations, concrete materialized practices. The virtual user to be augmented thus becomes a reflexive user who has already acquired the correct incorporating practices.

9. In the interview with Douglas Engelbart available on-line at http://www .superkids.com/aweb/pages/features/mouse/mouse.html.

10. Some of these designs might not be as ludicrous as they may first seem. I was surprised to find recently a foot mouse offered in the in-flight mail-order catalog on the flight I was taking between Montreal and Los Angeles.

Chapter 5

1. Here is a summary of Engelbart's laboratory funding from 1965 to 1968.

1965 ARPA-IPTO support since February 1963, about $80,000 for that year. NASA support from midyear 1964 to midyear 1965 at a level of about $85,000.

1966 Joint ARPA/NASA support since February 8 (Contract NAS1-5904) for two years at a level of $250,000 per year. RADC support beginning 23 February 1966 (Contract AF 30(602)-4103) with a sum of $93,500, planned for one year (this sum was held in reserve and kept for the transition to the new computer system).

1967 Additional ARPA support (arriving May 12) of $565,500 to be used to acquire and support a time-sharing computer with multiple-CRT display stations until 8 February 1968 (channeled via RADC as an extension of the RADC contract mentioned above). Additional support ($24,000, running from 16 May 1967 to 15 November 1967) from the Special Operations Group of the U.S. Army. (Engelbart, *Quarterly Technical Letter Report 5*)

This *Quarterly Technical Letter Report* (Contract NAS1-5904 prepared for NASA, Langley Research Center), covers the Period May 9 through August 8, 1967. It is available on-line at: http://www-leland.stanford.edu/dept/HPS/TimLenoir/ Engelbart/Archive/ARNAS/ARNAS5.html.

2. This lack of belief in the commercial future of time-sharing is confirmed by Robert Taylor's account of his meeting with Max Palevsky, SDS chairman, in 1970, when Xerox bought SDS: "I started talking to Max about interactive computing, and time sharing. . . . Palevsky basically said that time sharing was not going to sell, and that he wasn't interested in it . . . the argument got heated. We couldn't even have a rationally based disagreement. So I all but threw him out of the office" (quoted in Smith and Alexander 1988, 62).

3. This second time-sharing system was developed on the famous PDP-1, the first machine created by Kenneth H. Olsen, his brother Stanley, and Harlan E. Anderson, the founders of the Digital Equipment Corporation (also known as DEC), in August 1957. DEC concentrated on minicomputers and shipped its first one in 1960, the PDP-1, for a price of about $100,000. PDP stands for Programmed Data Processor, and according to the legend, Ken Olsen, who had been "warned against mentioning computers when he went for a loan, passed off his intended company as dealing in Digital Equipment—even though he solely intended to manufacture computers." This and other background information can be found on the on-line version

of *The Hacker's Dictionary* at http//jargon /jargon_toc.html. An oral history interview with Kenneth Olsen is available on the site of the Smithsonian at http://www
.si.edu /resource /tours /comphist /olsen.html.

4. One understands better the excitement that Jeff Rulifson felt when one realizes
that he met Engelbart and the Project GENIE people at the conference where the 940
time-sharing system was first introduced.

5. Very few individuals though, had this opportunity, and a newer generation of
designers was soon to come. Here, for example, is how Chuck Thacker and Ed Mc-
Creight reacted to Wes Clark's question about the relationship between the Alto and
the TX-2: "So Chuck and I avidly read these things [the TX-2 papers published in
the Western Joint Computer Conference proceedings] and compared notes and, as I
said to Wes the next day . . . my only excuse was that I was in the eighth grade at the
time. We are all of a group of people of about the same age. People at the age we were
then have a feeling that it's all coming as a given, that somehow the world just arrived that way; and there was no need to explain it, and not much to really understand about what had happened before." Quoted in Goldberg (1988), 340. It might
have just "been that way," but some of them, maybe those a couple of years older,
had had the experience of the real thing.

6. In Great Britain, the Atlas computer at the University of Manchester became
operational in 1962. It was the first machine to use virtual memory and paging, although not for the purpose of doing time-sharing. Its instruction execution was
pipelined, and it contained separate fixed-point and floating-point arithmetic units
capable of approximately 200 Kflops [thousands of floating-point operations per sec-
onds] (Fotheringham 1961; Sumner 1962). The knowledge of the paging technique
had already well diffused in the U.S. computing community by the time Project GE-
NIE got started. The Project MAC effort in time-sharing announced its intentions
when it described MULTICS (for Multiplexed Information and Computing Service)
in a set of six papers presented at the 1965 Fall Joint Computer Conference. These
papers are currently available at http://www.best.com /thvv/papers.html.

In "System Design of a Computer for Time Sharing Applications," E. L. Glaser
from MIT and J. F. Couleur and G. A. Oliver from the Computer Division of General
Electric described and justified their use of the paging technique as follows: "The purpose of paging is to make the allocation of physical memory easier. One can think of
paging as the intermediate ground between a fully associative memory, having each
word addressed by means of some part of its contents, and a normal memory, having
each memory location addressed by a specific integer forever fixed to that physical location. In paging, blocks of memory are assigned differing base addresses. Addressing
within a block is relative to the beginning of the block. Thus if association and relative addressing are handled with a break occurring within a normal break of the word
(viz. in a binary machine block size is a power of 2), then a number of noncontiguous
blocks of memory can be made to look contiguous through proper association. The
association between a block and a specific base address can be dynamically changed
by program during the execution of appropriate parts of the executive routine."

However, by March 1966, the system was well behind schedule. MULTICS eventually got running in 1969, four years late, and General Electric and Bell withdrew
from the project. Norberg and O'Neill report that Bell Laboratories withdrew from
the MAC MULTICS project in early 1969 and went on developing UNIX, which was

named as a play on MULTICS (1996, 110). Licklider's original planning to fund Project GENIE as a counterpart to project MAC thus was justified by events. Moreover, the fact that GE withdrew its model 645 from the market a year after its announcement, stating that "what we had in our hands was a research project and not a product," gave him more reason retrospectively for having given project GENIE a mandate in tune with IPTO's second objective, industrial development. Quoted in Norberg and O'Neill (1996), 109.

7. See Dan Murphy's 1989 paper "The Origins and Development of Tops-20," available on-line at http://www.dbit.com/pub/pdp10/info/paper.t20 for more information on the history of paging.

8. As Donald Wallace said, the "copy-on-write feature" was available on both the SDS 940 and the PDP-10, but the way it got to be available on the PDP-10 is worth mentioning here. In 1964, DEC announced its PDP-6 model that was soon considered the machine of choice by most ARPA-IPTO contractors and was held in even higher regard by those involved in LISP programming. LISP was the language of choice for most researchers involved in AI research. It had been created by John McCarthy, one of the earliest proponents of time sharing.

Negotiations started between the Bolt, Beranek, and Newman Corporation and DEC to retrofit the paging techniques that they developed on their PDP-1 for time sharing. But in 1966, DEC announced that it was going out of the 36-bit computer business and terminated its PDP-6 line. BBN then turned to SDS and bought a 940. Later, DEC changed its mind and built the PDP-10, but in a design that was still not suitable for time sharing. BBN's experience with the 940 for two or three years led them to believe that they could do to the PDP-10 exactly what the Berkeley people had done to the 940, and they added paging. This was one of the origins of the famous TENEX operating system. According to Butler Lampson, "in that sense the fact that we did that [paging] was very influential to them, but the details of how exactly they did it were completely different. It was an influence at the highest level of conceptual influence" (Lampson 1997). I am giving a very basic historical sketch here. The reader interested in this issue should refer to Dan Murphy's paper previously cited.

9. John McCarthy, *Reminiscences on the History of Time Sharing* (1983), available on-line at the following URL: http://www-formal.stanford.edu/jmc/history/timesharing/timesharing.html.

10. Here is the original text of the announcement of the device in *Scientific American*, in March 1947: "The problem of giving automatically reproduced form letters that individually typed look has found a solution in a device called the Flexowriter Automatic Letter Writer. Operated by means of a perforated paper tape $7/8$-inch wide, it consists of an electric typewriter, an automatic perforator and an automatic writer. In preparing the form letter, the operator types manually the date and the name and address of the recipient. Then a switch is thrown, and the automatic writer takes over, controlled by the previously prepared tape."

11. Kenneth Olsen, in a Smithsonian oral history interview available on-line at the following URL: http://www.si.edu/resource/tours/comphist/olsen.html.

12. Robert M. Fano in a Siggraph 1989 special panel entitled "Retrospectives I: The Early Years in Computer Graphics at MIT, Lincoln Lab and Harvard," available on-line at http://www.siggraph.org/publications/panels/siggraph89/p02.html.

13. The flickering of the displayed picture is mostly an effect of the decay characteristics of the CRT phosphors used. The display of a spot results from the hit of an electron beam on the phosphor coat of the screen, and the persistence of the spot is determined mostly by the category of phosphor used. Phosphors are categorized by the length of time required for an image to decay to 10 percent of its initial value. However, Poole reported that "flicker has been found to be a function of the age of subject, wavelength of light, brightness variation, retinal location, light-to-dark ratio, and size of flickering object" (1966, 290).

14. Newman insists on the fact that "early display designers tended to view the display file with mixed feelings, for it was costly to provide the refresh memory" (1976, 1321).

15. The display generator is the circuitry that interprets the computer digital word and translates it into analog signals to generate the graphics on the screen. The display generator is essentially a digital-to-analog converter.

16. Machover reported prices ranging from approximately twenty thousand to two hundred and eighty thousand dollars for CRT display terminals consisting of a CRT and a display generator.

17. Lester Earnest to the list on the history of cyberspace (cyhist@sjuvm.stjohns .edu), dated Thursday, 15 August 1996, 11:14:31-0500, about their experience at the Stanford Artificial Intelligence Laboratory (SAIL). Information International Inc. (III) was the company that Edward Fredkin, one of the earliest proponents of time-sharing, and Benjamin Gurley, who had formerly worked at DEC, created in the early 1960's. See Norberg and O'Neill (1996, 93) for a description of how Licklider used III to fulfill what he referred to as a "hummingbird function" of transferring "Cambridge know-how" into the "California program."

18. See Machover (1967 and 1972) for an account of the availability and of the main characteristics of the commercial displays at the end of the 1960's.

19. Engelbart and his staff were fully aware of the advantages of the raster-scan display. For instance, Jeff Rulifson (1996) told me that he had come down and had seen a bit-map display in operation at RAND in the Uncapher and Ellis group as early as 1966.

20. Stan Augarten, "The Mouse That Roared," presently unavailable, but sometimes found on-line. Sutherland still reported in 1970 that "the task of sorting information from top to bottom and from left to right for presentation on raster displays has largely precluded their use for anything but presentation of text. In principle, however, a raster display has the potential of producing pictures with a range of light and dark tones, in color if desired, that provide a realism unequaled by the line drawings of a calligraphic display" (Sutherland 1970, 58).

21. A tape of the presentation can be ordered from the Association for Computing Machinery, 1515 Broadway, New York, New York 10036 and on-line at http:// www.acm.org.

22. Available on-line at http://www-sul.stanford.edu/depts/hasrg/histsci/ ssvoral/engelbart/start.html.

Chapter 6

1. The incorporating practice of chording should not be underestimated in its capacity for community building. To this day, some of the more convinced ARC

members still relate to this practice, as this message from a former ARC member shows: "I have never left ARC in spirit, but have applied many of the things I learned there to more conventional business problems elsewhere. My fingers fondly caress each one-button mouse I find, searching for the buds of the other two buttons. My left hand sporadically types 'Jump (to) Link' on the tabletop in binary chords [01010 01100] and nothing happens. My right hand clicks on now-ubiquitous URLs and I am again flying through information space as if nothing has happened . . . but of course it has" (Jim Norton, personal communication).

2. For a description of the early days of the ARPA network, see Roberts (1988).

3. Larry Roberts was then Robert Taylor's deputy director and succeeded him later as the fourth IPTO director.

4. Xerox hired Robert Taylor to help staff PARC on the basis of his experience and the network of contacts he gathered while he was working for ARPA-IPTO: "Taylor was known as the chief marble collector . . . the idea was to go to each of these places and get all the shooters, and get them into PARC. So in the '72–'73–'74 time-period, Taylor basically collected all the shooters. . . . he did really well. But all those people came . . . all that stuff was going on, and then, it just sort of got put together at PARC and everybody influenced each other and they managed to build, there was sort of a synergy of building stuff, but all the initial invention was back in the ARPA IPT community" (Rulifson 1996).

5. This claim might be misleading, since it could be read as implying that function keys are evolutions of the chord keyset. In fact, the necessity of chording in order to increase the number of key combinations appeared in many instances independently of Engelbart's proposed solution. For instance, Les Earnest reported recently in a message (dated August 17, 1996) to CYHIST, the on-line discussion list on the history of cyberspace (cyhist@sjuvm.stjohns.edu) the following story that happened in his laboratory at Stanford University: "Nicklaus Wirth had suggested a key idea (literally!) that was incorporated into THOR and ZEUS: adding a second "Control" key on the display terminal keyboards. . . . By using the second control key, prosaically called 'Control-2,' in conjunction with the Control-1 and Shift keys, each of the regular keys could have up to 8 distinct meanings. Combinations that used Control-1 or Control-2 were generally used to select editing modes or to move the cursor around the screen. This turned out to be a very powerful way to interact with the computer, though learning how to key the various combinations took some practice."

6. For this section on Douglas Engelbart's contribution, I again rely on my own interview as well on four interviews carried out by Henry Lowood, bibliographer for History of Science and Technology Collections at Stanford University, in 1987–88 (Engelbart 1996). I again thank Henry Lowood for giving me access to these materials.

7. The SDS 940 was already obsolete as a research machine when PARC started, mainly because its address space was much too small. The principal research machine in the ARPA community at that point was the DEC PDP-10, but PARC had a chance to purchase the SDS Sigma 7 at cost because Xerox in the meantime had bought the SDS company. According to Butler Lampson, however, "the problem with the SDS Sigma machine was that its software was totally unsuitable to do computer research, partly because it had a lot of problems, but mostly because everybody else who was doing computer research had decided to use TENEX. So there was an

enormous cost associated with cutting yourself off from the rest of the community" (Lampson 1997). Xerox was pushing the Sigma 7, though, and to have insisted on buying a DEC PDP-10 would have created a permanent ill will with SDS, since DEC was the main competitor of SDS, which now was rechristened XDS.

Thus, the first project started at PARC was building "their own PDP-10," the Multiple Access Xerox Computer (MAXC). Ed McCreight, who was working for Boeing at that time, was hired for this specific purpose. He joined most of the earliest PARC researchers in this project, which aimed at giving them a functional time-sharing system that could run TENEX, but also, for some of them, NLS.

8. The Data General Corporation was formed in 1968 by Ed de Castro, a former employee of DEC. Data General rolled out the Nova minicomputer with 32K of memory in February 1969 for an $8,000 introductory price tag, and the Nova 800 and 1200 in 1970.

9. Butler Lampson got his Ph.D. in electrical engineering from Berkeley in 1967, the same year that planning for Berkeley Computer Corporation started. The corporation was actually formed in 1968. The reason for forming BCC was that after finishing the 940, the group could not get more ARPA funding to go on scaling up their work, since it was not precompetitive research any more. SDS did not want to collaborate with the Project GENIE people to build the next machine, the Sigma 7. Actually SDS had been dragged kicking and screaming into doing the 940 by ARPA, by the Berkeley people, and by their customers (or at least some of them). So the Project GENIE people formed Berkeley Computer Corporation (BCC).

They wanted to and in 1968–69 finally did design and build a new machine totally from scratch: the BCC Model 1, a very ambitious machine. It had five different CPUs running two different instruction sets, microcoded on circuit boards. In theory, the machine was built to support several hundreds of low-demand users, 500 of them, as the new name of the machine, the BCC 500, said. But a temporary recession in the computing industry in 1970 marked the end of the BCC experience.

10. Charles Irby is getting lost in the jungle of TLAs, which, according to Steve Woolgar's joke, stands for Three-Letter Acronyms. UGH was the name of a subsequent implementation, written for the Alto in 1974 by Donald Wallace. Wallace told me that this implementation covered only the editing capabilities of NLS, and that he decided to name it UGH "as in revulsion" (Wallace 1996).

11. Illustrated by what Charles Irby calls their "new bible of user interface design," a Xerox document entitled "A Methodology for User Interface Design," written by Charles Irby, Linda Bergsteinsson, Thomas Moran, William Newman, and Larry Tesler in January 1977.

12. According to Smith and Alexander's version in *Fumbling the Future* (1988, 70), Gunning remained only briefly SSL manager because Robert Taylor "disliked Gunning's approach to organization. . . . Gunning had set up SSL as a collection of unrelated projects groups that lacked the coherence and the critical mass essential to significant advances in computer research." Whatever the validity of this claim, Gunning's dismissal proved to be crucial for the evolution of the representation of the user at PARC, since his new mission put him on the front line for the process of realizing the user.

13. Charles Simonyi was a former member of Project GENIE at Berkeley who had joined PARC in early 1972. While at PARC, he developed Bravo, which retro-

spectively can be seen as the ancestor of Microsoft Word. Simonyi joined Microsoft in 1980.

14. Mott declared in his interview with Smith and Alexander that he felt "totally at sea technically" at PARC: "there was so many new things that I had never seen before," even if he did hold a computer science degree from the University of Manchester in England (quoted in Smith and Alexander 1988, 106).

15. This echoed pretty well Rulifson's and Tesler's memo, which characterized the system as an "intuitive typewriter."

16. As Chuck Thacker says: "Back in the days when dinosaurs walked the earth (some of us still do). . . . I remember being overjoyed the day (I think it was in '70) that memory dropped below a penny a bit. This opened the world in wonderful ways." A full bit-map display (in which each screen pixel was represented by a bit of main storage) was now thinkable." This quote can be found at http://www2 .cs.washington.edu/people/faculty/lazowska/faculty.lecture/software/alto.memory .html.

17. In this perspective, Peter Bogh Andersen (1993, 15) used Peircean semiotics to argue that "computer-based signs have a larger 'iconic range' than other signs" and that "they can create some of their physical referents."

18. See Smith and Alexander (1988).

19. Thornburg justifies his position in the following way: "people stopped using drawing with rocks in Palaeolithic times, and there's a reason for that: rocks aren't appropriate drawing implements; people moved on to sticks."

Chapter 7

1. On the beginning of the ARPANET, see Norberg and O'Neill (1996, 153–96); Hafner and Lyon (1996), Hauben (1996), Salus (1995), and Abate (1999).

2. Peter H. Salus agreed with this evaluation in his review of *Where Wizards Stay Up Late: The Origins of the Internet*, by Katie Hafner and Matthew Lyon: "Hafner told me that their publisher had asked them to keep the cast of characters down. Credit where credit is due is more important than the putative thoughts of an executive at a media conglomerate. And on that basis it's tough to decide to devote a lot of space to Marill and describe a truly great man as 'Douglas Engelbart, a computer scientist who was at Stanford Research Institute (SRI).'" Salus, "The Vogue of History," *Matrix News* 6 (7), July 1996, available on-line at: http://www3.mids.org/ mn/607/hafner.html.

3. Salus (1995, 22–25), Hafner and Lyon (1996, 76–77), Norberg and O'Neill (1996, 165–66).

4. Paul Baran invented the technique for telephony at RAND, and the term "packet" was used for the first time in connection with computer networks by Davies in 1966. Baran et al. (1964), Roberts (1988,144).

5. Roberts reported that "some of the [RAND] reports were classified as not in the public domain. Therefore, neither Donald Davies nor I had seen anything of the work until we were deep into the design of our respective systems. The RAND work was very detailed. . . . Their hot-potato routing algorithm was a useful starting point for the ARPANET routing design" (1988, 147).

6. Norberg and O'Neill report that Roberts thought at first that "a committee cannot be expected to investigate and solve the more difficult, longer range problems,

particularly when the best solution may require considerable efforts for some of the members" (1996, 169). Roberts contracted a twelve-month study of host-to-host protocols to the Raytheon Corporation in September 1969. But Norberg and O'Neill also write that "Roberts changed his mind, however, and continued with the working group despite the difficulties."

7. Crocker detailed the use and style of these Requests For Comments (RFCs) in the third note, distributed two days later and entitled "Documentation Conventions": "The Network Working Group (NWG) is concerned with the HOST software, the strategies for using the network, and initial experiments with the network. Documentation of the NWG's effort is through notes such as this. Notes may be produced at any site by anybody and included in this series. The content of a NWG note may be any thought, suggestion, etc. related to the HOST software or other aspect of the network. Notes are encouraged to be timely rather than polished. Philosophical positions without examples or other specifics, specific suggestions or implementation techniques without introductory or background explication, and explicit questions without any attempted answers are all acceptable. The minimum length for a NWG note is one sentence. These standards (or lack of them) are stated explicitly for two reasons. First, there is a tendency to view a written statement as ipso facto authoritative, and we hope to promote the exchange and discussion of considerably less than authoritative ideas. Second, there is a natural hesitancy to publish something unpolished, and we hope to ease this inhibition" (S. Crocker, RFC 0003).

At the time of the writing of RFC 3, according to Crocker, the Network Working Group "seemed to consist" of Steve Carr (Utah), Jeff Rulifson and Bill Duvall (SRI), and Steve Crocker and Gerard Deloche (UCLA). The distribution list of the RFCs also included Bob Kahn (BBN), Larry Roberts (ARPA), and Ron Stoughton (UCSB). At the end of July 1969, the constitution of the NWG had changed slightly. It consisted then of Steve Carr (Utah), Elmer Shapiro and Bill English (SRI), Steve Crocker (UCLA), John Heafner (RAND), and Paul Rovner and Jim Curry (Lincoln Labs). The distribution list of the RFCs also included Ron Stoughton (UCSB), Bob Kahn (BBN), Larry Roberts (ARPA), and Jerry Cole (SDC). RFC 0010: "Documentation Conventions," by S. Crocker.

8. As we have seen, these users were still supposed to be computer programmers. That was the case of the earliest ARPANET users, since the network was envisioned by its promoters as a means to share computer resources.

9. Roberts gave ARC the original mandate to organize the NIC as a depository for information relevant to ARPANET users ("a library" in Engelbart's words), including network protocols and other information pertinent to ARPA resource sharing (Feinler [1977]). In 1970, the NIC published the first ARPANET directory, a list and description of every host computer on the network that highlighted the unique resources available on each machine and invited users to "visit them" and make use of them. As part of its mandate, the NIC also started in 1971 to publish regularly the network mailing lists (RFCs 0168, 0211), a list of the available RFCs (RFCs 0160, 0170, 0200), and a compilation of lists of relevant site reports (RFC 0182). Jeanne B. North was the author of most of these RFCs.

10. This reimplementation created an extra burden on the programmers and might have prevented them from contributing more to the design and implementation of the ARPANET protocols. However, if their contribution was limited by the huge effort needed to transfer NLS to the PDP, it was still a contribution, and some

ARC members played an important part in the earliest efforts to design the network that became the Internet.

11. DEL and NIL were perhaps "exotic ideas," but they were also quite innovative. Most accounts of the early history of the ARPANET protocols consider that "to say that this was optimistic is mild" (Salus 1995, 46), and that "these languages were more advanced than what was needed or possible at the time" (Hauben 1996). Using "a universal hardware representation" and a set of "Network Standard Translators" (NST) were indeed far-fetched ideas for the late 1960's, even if they could appear retrospectively as a great design basis for protocols over the network.

12. For the history of electronic mail, see Hardy (1996), Hafner and Lyon (1996), chapter 7, and Salus (1995), chapter 9.

13. Between 1971 and 1977, the NWG regularly discussed the mail protocol. ARC authors contributed abundantly to the discussions. Dick Watson initiated the debate (RFC 0196 and 0221, in July and August 1971) and participated in various other subsequent contributions (RFC 0278, in October 1971). Mike Kudlick called a meeting "to discuss a network mail system" (RFC 0453, February 1973) also attended by other ARC members, including Charles Irby, Dave Hopper, and Jim White. Jim White summarized the results of the meeting in a proposal to standardize mail handling over the network (RFC 0524, June 1973) and contributed from then on to the discussions (RFC 561). The NIC eventually issued a "Mail Protocol" document in RFC 0630 (April 1974). This protocol was slightly revised in the following years, leading to a "Standard for the Format of ARPA Network Text Messages" (RFC 0733, November 1977).

14. In a personal communication, Michael Friedewald told me that some other ARC members reported to him more pragmatic "reasons" to leave ARC: "they [Xerox] paid significantly higher salaries. It [Xerox PARC] was the 'Place to Be,' and many of the good people went there to carry forward their versions of Doug's vision." Some of the earliest ARC "renegades" had indeed moved to PARC to transfer NLS. Such was the purpose of the POLOS project, for instance.

15. The reference to Peter Drucker's work is acknowledged, for example, in a contribution to the Second Annual Computer Communications Conference (San Jose, January 24, 1972) entitled "Coordinated Information Services for a Discipline or Mission-Oriented Community," where Douglas Engelbart quotes Drucker (1966 and 1969).

16. Engelbart launched these three activities separately between the end of January and May 1972 in three internal memos in the NLS Journal: "To launch PODAC" (JE#8651, January 25), "To launch LINAC" (JE#10034, April 7), and "To launch FRAMAC" (JE#10331, May 4). The Personal and Organizational Development Activity (PODAC) dealt with "beliefs, interests, help[ing] people and the organization in dealing with the goals and line activities that result" ("Initial FRAMAC meeting Notes," JE#10457, May 23).

17. Inside this Journal archive, the messages devoted to PODAC were obviously of a special concern for Engelbart, since he asked that they'd be kept apart, in a "special binder."

18. The PODAC archive totals 59 Journal entries from eighteen authors. Four individual authors (BLP, WLB, MEJ, KEV) accounted for 33 entries (57.8 percent of all entries). In total, 35 individuals participated in PODAC. The following 17 individuals did not contribute to the Journal on PODAC: Lane, North, Peters, Rech, and

Van De Riet from the Cedar POD; Melvin, Page, Ratliff, and Wallace from the Fir POD; Hardeman, Limuti, Lister, Norton, and Paxton, from the Oak POD; Irby and Row from the Redwood POD. These 59 Journal entries were distributed in the various PODs as follows: 15 (four authors) for Fir, 17 (three authors) for Cedar, 12 (six authors) for Redwood, and 13 (four authors) for Oak.

19. In his memo describing his first experience with est, Walter Bass noted that "EST is NOT any of the following, although it has things in common with all of them: Autogenic Training, Encounter, Gestalt, Gurdjief, Positive Thinking, Prayer, Psychosynthesis, Psychotherapy, Self-Healing, Self-Hypnosis, Sensitivity Training, Sufism, Tao, Yoga, Zen" (JE#10761, June 19). Est appears indeed to have been a vast synthesis of much that was current in the Human Potential movements so in vogue in the late 1960's.

20. See Robert Todd Carroll's "Werner Erhard, est, and the Landmark Forum," in his *Skeptic's Dictionary*, available on-line at http://wheel.ucdavis.edu/btcarrol/skeptic/est.html.

21. Not to be confused with Jacques P. Vallée, a noted Canadian astrophysicist.

22. Other staff members confirmed the reading that follows through the recurrent use of a religious vocabulary (e.g., Donald Wallace) or the vividness of their memories some twenty years after the facts (e.g., Harvey Lehtman).

23. The conflict of values dividing hackers and hippies from straight managers, at a time when most of the funding in research in computing came from the military, is nothing special to ARC, either. During my interviews, I realized that these phenomena were actually going on long after the episode narrated here. Some of the key researchers at PARC had taken the est course, too, for instance (Belleville 1993).

24. This literature is most fully synthesized in the controversial work of René Girard, which in turn is most comprehensively laid out in his *Things Hidden since the Beginning of the World* (1987 [1978]).

25. Quoted in Andy Testa, "Landmark Education," available on-line at http://www.religio.de/therapie/landmark/landmark.html#2.

26. Michel Foucault reminded us in *Madness and Civilization* of the lasting presence of the trope of the infection in the religious discourse: "if the leper was removed from the world, and from the community of the Church visible, his existence was yet a constant manifestation of God, since it was a sign both of His anger and of His grace: 'My friend,' says the ritual of the Church of Vienne, 'it pleaseth Our Lord that thou shouldst be infected with this malady, and thou hast great grace at the hands of Our Lord that he desireth to punish thee for thy iniquities in this world'" (Foucault 1988 [1961], 6).

27. More precisely, Watson reported the following list of problems:

> Services have been advertised that had not yet been adequately debugged. Thus they were not workable for non-ARC users. At ARC non-workability could be easily reported, corrected or more readily forgiven.
> Commands at times were changed in NLS without adequate (or any) notice or documentation thus leading to upsets.
> Files were deleted or lost without notice.
> Links in files as part of NIC databases have occassionally [sic] been unreliable as data bases changed without adequate control over change procedures.
> Features needed by the NIC staff were not always developed on a timely basis or fully debugged.

NIC often has not known currently which were official network members or
how to reach them.

The answering service often has not kept up-to-date.

The NIC often could not provide users information about what features were
operational or when exactly they would be.

NIC never has had sufficient staff to collect, process and make available all the
information or background documentation needed.

Training and documentation were oriented toward general NLS use rather than
just specific NIC features.

NLS was highly oriented toward expert users rather than infrequent novices.

The catalog system has been difficult to run, debug and runs slowly on our
PDP-10. The catalog process of input, processing, and proofing was a
heterogeneous kludge of new and old methodology.

The Resource Notebook effort has not had adequate clerical support.

NIC staff were often not adequately trained to utilize NLS most effectively.

Coda

1. The transcript of the meeting belongs to the systematic record of the NLS journal entries after NLS went on-line (JE#1278, November 13, 1972, 13:17, transcription of FRAMAC).

2. Hutchins, Hollan, and Norman insist that: "There are two major metaphors for the nature of human-computer interaction, a conversation metaphor and a model world metaphor. In a system built on the conversation metaphor, the interface is a language medium in which the user and system have a conversation about an assumed, but not explicitly represented world. In this case, the interface is an implied intermediary between the user and the world about which things are said. In a system built on the model world metaphor, the interface is itself a world where the user can act, and that changes states in response to user actions. The world of interest is explicitly represented and there is no intermediary between user and world. Appropriate use of the model world metaphor can create the sensation in the user of acting upon the objects of the task domain themselves. We call this aspect '*direct engagement*'" (1986, 94).

The "direct manipulation interface" therefore appears as a general category of interface including the graphic interfaces, the WIMP interfaces, the post-WIMP interfaces such as gesture interfaces, and even the immersive interfaces of virtual reality applications. However, Susan Brennan argues that "the dichotomy between direct manipulation interface and conversation is a false one" (1990, 393). The fact that Hutchins, Hollan, and Norman consider that Sketchpad was the "first major landmark of direct manipulation interfaces," even if they acknowledge that its design goal was "to make it possible for a person and a computer to converse rapidly through the medium of line drawing" (Sutherland 1963), grants her this point: "First direct manipulation interfaces succeed *because* they share important features with real conversations. Second, when so-called 'conversational' interfaces fail, it is because they lack these pragmatic features—that is words alone do not a conversation make. Third, real conversations actually fulfill many of the criteria for direct manipulation" (Brennan 1990, 393).

Interviews

Andrews, D. 1996. Personal interview with the author, June 4, Mountain View, Calif.
Belleville, R. L. 1992. Personal interview with the author, December 16, Mountain View, Calif.
———. 1993. Personal interview with the author, March 19, Mountain View, Calif.
Cerf, V. 1990. Personal interview conducted by Judy O'Neill, April 24, Reston, Va. Center for the History of Information Processing, University of Minnesota, Minneapolis: The Charles Babbage Institute.
Clark, W. 1990. Personal interview conducted by Judy O'Neill, May 3, New York, N.Y. Center for the History of Information Processing, University of Minnesota, Minneapolis: The Charles Babbage Institute.
Deutsch, P. 1996. Personal interview with the author, May 29, Mountain View, Calif.
Engelbart, D. C. 1968. "Augmenting Your Intellect." *Research/Development*, August: 22–27.
———. 1992. Personal interview with the author, December 15, Fremont, Calif.
———. 1996. *Douglas Engelbart: An Oral History*. Four interviews conducted by H. Lowood and J. Adams, edited by T. Bardini. Stanford, Calif.: Stanford University Libraries. Available on-line at http://www-sul.stanford.edu/depts/hasrg/histsci/ssvoral/engelbart/start.html.
English, W. K. 1992. Personal interview with the author, December 15, Mountain View, Calif.
Irby, C. H. 1992. Personal interview with the author, December 11, Mountain View, Calif.
Kay, A. C. 1992. Personal interview with the author, December 17, Los Angeles, Calif.
Lampson, B. 1997. Personal interview with the author, July 17, Cambridge, Mass.
Lehtman, H. 1992. Personal interview with the author, December 14, Cupertino, Calif.
Nelson, T. H. 1993. Personal interview with the author, March 17, Sausalito, Calif.
Rulifson, J. 1996. Personal interview with the author, June 4, Palo Alto, Calif.

Smith, D. C. 1993. Personal interview with the author, March 17, Cupertino, Calif.
Sutherland, I. E. 1989. Personal interview conducted by William Aspray, May 1, Pittsburgh, Pa. Center for the History of Information Processing, University of Minnesota, Minneapolis: The Charles Babbage Institute.
Taylor, R. 1989. Personal interview conducted by William Aspray, February 28, Palo Alto, Calif. Center for the History of Information Processing, University of Minnesota, Minneapolis: The Charles Babbage Institute.
———. 1993. Personal interview with the author, Palo Alto, Calif., March 18.
Uncapher, K. 1993. Personal interview with the author, Los Angeles, Calif., February 16.
Vallée, J. 1996. Personal interview with the author, June 5, San Francisco, Calif.
Wallace, D. C. 1996. Personal interview with the author, June 3, Mountain View, Calif.
Warren, J. 1993. Personal interview with the author, March 17, Woodside, Calif.

Other Sources

Abate, Janet. 1999. *Inventing the Internet*. Cambridge, Mass.: MIT Press.
Akrich, M. 1992. "The De-Scription of Technical Objects." In *Shaping Technology/Building Society*, edited by W. E. Bijker and J. Law, pp. 205–24. Cambridge, Mass.: MIT Press.
Andersen, P. B. 1993. "Introduction." In *The Computer as a Medium*, edited by P. B. Andersen, B. Holqvist, and J. F. Jensen, pp. 9–15. Cambridge: Cambridge University Press.
Ashby, R. W. 1956. "Design for an Intelligence Amplifier." In *Automata Studies*, edited by C. E. Shannon and J. McCarthy, pp. 215–34. Princeton, N.J.: Princeton University Press.
Augarten, S. 1984. *Bit by Bit: An Illustrated History of Computers*. New York: Ticknor & Fields.
Backus, J. 1980. "Programming in America in the 1950s: Some Personal Impressions." In *A History of Computing in the Twentieth Century*, edited by N. Metropolis, J. Howlett, and G.-C. Rota, pp. 125–35. New York: Academic Press.
Baecker, R. M., J. Grudin, W. Buxton, and S. Greenberg. 1995. "Touch, Gesture and Marking." In *Readings in Human Computer Interaction: Toward the Year 2000*, edited by R. M. Baecker, J. Grudin, W. Buxton, and S. Greenberg, pp. 469–82. San Francisco: Morgan-Kaufmann. Available on-line at http://www.dgp.toronto.ed/OTP/papers/bill.buxton/haptic.html.
Baran, P. et al. 1964. "On Distributed Communications." *RAND Corporation Memos*, vols. 1–11. Santa Monica, Calif.: RAND.
Bardini, T., and A. T. Horvath. 1995."The Social Construction of the Personal Computer User: The Rise and Fall of the Reflexive User." *Journal of Communication* 45, no. 3: 40–65.
Bateson, G. 1977. "Afterword." In *About Bateson: Essays on Gregory Bateson*, edited by J. Brokman, pp. 235–47. New York: Dutton.
———. 1979. *Mind and Nature: A Necessary Unity*. New York: Dutton.
———. 1991 [1975]. "Some Components of Socialization for Trance." In *Sacred Unity: Further Steps to an Ecology of Mind*, edited by R. E. Donaldson, pp. 73–88. New York: HarperCollins.

———. 1991 [1980]. "Seek the Sacred: Darlington Seminar." In *Sacred Unity: Further Steps to an Ecology of Mind*, edited by R. E. Donaldson, pp. 299–305. New York: HarperCollins.

Bell, C. G. 1988. "Toward a History of (Personal) Workstations." In *A History of Personal Workstations*, edited by A. Goldberg, pp. 1–36. New York: ACM Press.

Berners-Lee, T. 1997. "World-Wide Computer." *Communications of the ACM* 40, no. 2: 57–58.

Bliss, J. C. 1997. Personal communication to the author, March 8.

Bohm, D. 1980. *Wholeness and the Implicate Order*. London: Routledge.

Bowker, G. 1993. "How to Be Universal: Some Cybernetic Strategies, 1943–1970." *Social Studies of Science* 23: 107–27.

Brennan, S. E. 1990. "Conversation as Direct Manipulation: An Iconoclastic View." In *The Art of Human Computer Interface Design*, edited by B. Laurel, pp. 393–404. Reading, Mass.: Addison-Wesley.

Bromley, A. G. 1990. "Analog Computing Devices." In *Computing Before Computers*, edited by W. Aspray, pp. 156–99. Ames: Iowa State University Press.

Bush, V. 1991 [1945]. "As We May Think." In *From Memex to Hypertext: Vannevar Bush and the Mind's Machine*, edited by J. M. Nyce and P. Kahn, pp. 83–107. San Diego, Calif.: Academic Press. Originally published in *Atlantic Monthly* 176, no. 1: 641–49.

Buxton, W. A. S. 1986. "Chunking and Phrasing and the Design of Human-Computer Dialogues." *Proceedings of the IFIP World Computer Congress*, pp. 475–80. Dublin, Ireland. Available on-line at http://www.dgp.toronto.ed/OTP/papers/bill.buxton/?chunking.html.

Campbell-Kelly, M., and W. Aspray. 1996. *Computer: A History of the Information Machine*. New York: Basic Books.

Card, S. K., W. K. English, and B. J. Burr. 1978. "Evaluation of Mouse, Rate-Controlled Isometric Joystick, Step Keys, and Text Keys for Text Selection on a CRT." *Ergonomics* 21, no. 8: 601–13.

———, T. P. Moran, and A. Newell. 1983. *The Psychology of Human-Computer Interaction*. Hillsdale, N.J.: Lawrence Erlbaum.

———, and T. P. Moran. 1988. "User Technology: From Pointing to Pondering." In *A History of Personal Workstations*, edited by A. Goldberg, pp. 493–526. New York: ACM Press.

Carroll, J. B. 1956. "Introduction." In *Language, Thought, and Reality: Selected Writings of Benjamin Lee Whorf*, edited by J. B. Carroll, pp. 1–34. Cambridge, Mass.: MIT Press.

Caswell, N. S. 1988. "Introduction to Input Devices." In *Input Devices*, edited by S. Sherr, pp. 1–70. Boston: Academic Press.

Clark, R. L., G. F. Groner, and R. A. Berman. 1971. *The BIOMOD User's Reference Manual*. Report to the National Institute of Health # R-746-NIH. Santa Monica, Calif.: RAND.

Clark, W. 1988. "The LINC was Early and Small." In *A History of Personal Workstations*, edited by A. Goldberg, pp. 347–94. New York: ACM Press.

Conrad, R., and D. J. A. Longman. 1965. "Standard Typewriter versus Chord Keyboard: An Experimental Comparison." *Ergonomics* 8, no. 1: 77–88.

Cooper, W. E. 1983. "Introduction." In *Cognitive Aspects of Skilled Typewriting*, edited by W. E. Cooper, pp. 1–38. New York: Springer-Verlag.

Crary, J. 1990. *Techniques of the Observer: On Vision and Modernity in the Nineteenth Century*. Cambridge, Mass.: MIT Press.

Crotch, Arthur. 1908. *The Hughes and Baudot Telegraphs*. London: Reutell.

Cytowic, R. E. 1993. *The Man who Tasted Shapes*. New York: G. P. Putnam's Sons.

David, P. A. 1985. "Clio and the Economics of QWERTY." *The American Economic Review* 75, no, 2: 332–37.

Davis, M. R., and T. O. Ellis. 1964. "The RAND Tablet: A Man-Machine Graphical Communication Device." Report #RM-4122-ARPA. Santa Monica, Calif.: RAND.

Deacon, T. W. 1998. *The Symbolic Species: The Co-Evolution of Language and the Brain*. New York: Norton.

Dertouzos, M. L. 1990. "Redefining Tomorrow's User Interface." In *CHI '90 Conference Proceedings: Empowering People*, p. 1. New York: ACM Press.

Dreyfus, H. L. 1972. *What Computers Can't Do*. New York: Harper Colophon.

———. 1979. *What Computers Still Can't Do*. New York: Harper Colophon.

Drucker, P. 1966. *The Effective Executive*. New York: Harper and Row.

———. 1969. *Ages of Discontinuity: Guidelines to Our Changing Society*. New York: Harper and Row.

Dunsheath, P. 1969 [1962]. *A History of Electrical Engineering*. London: Faber and Faber.

Durham, W. H. 1991. *Co-Evolution: Genes, Culture, and Human Diversity*. Stanford, Calif.: Stanford University Press.

Edwards, P. 1996. *The Closed World: Computers and the Politics of Discourse in Cold War America*. Cambridge, Mass.: MIT Press.

Ellis, T. O., and W. L. Sibley. 1968. "On the Problem of Directness in Computer Graphics." In *Emerging Concepts in Computer Graphics*, edited by D. Secrest and J. Nievergelt, pp. 123–30. New York: W. A. Benjamin.

———, J. F. Heafner, and W. L. Sibley. 1969. "The Grail Project: An Experiment in Man-Machine Communication." RM-5999-ARPA. Santa Monica, Calif.: RAND.

Engelbart, D. C. 1961. "Special Considerations of the Individual as a User, Generator, and Retriever of Information." *American Documentation* 12, no. 2: 121–25.

———. 1962. "Augmenting Human Intellect: A Conceptual Framework." Report to the Director of Information Sciences, Air Force Office of Scientific Research. Menlo Park, Calif.: Stanford Research Institute, October.

———. 1963. "A Conceptual Framework for the Augmentation of Man's Intellect." In *Vistas in Information Handling*, edited by P. W. Howerton and D. C. Weeks, 1: 1–29. Washington, D.C.: Spartan.

———. 1973. "Design Considerations for Knowledge Workshop Terminals." In *Proceedings of the AFIPS 1973 National Computer Conference*, pp. 221–27. Montvale, N.J.: AFIPS Press.

———. 1982. "Toward High-Performance Knowledge Workers." In *OAC '82 Digest*. Proceedings of the AFIPS Office Automation Conference. San Francisco, April 5–7: 279–90.

———. 1988. "The Augmented Knowledge Workshop." In *A History of Personal Workstations*, edited by A. Goldberg, pp. 187–232. New York: ACM Press.

———, et al. 1970. *Advanced Intellect-Augmentation Techniques*. Final report to NASA (Contract NAS1-7897). Menlo Park, Calif.: SRI.

————, and W. K. English. 1968. "A Research Center for Augmenting Human Intellect." In *Proceedings of the AFIPS 1968 Fall Joint Computer Conference* 33, pp. 395–410. Washington, D.C.: Spartan Books.

————, R. W. Watson, and J. C. Norton. 1973. "The Augmented Knowledge Workshop." *AFIPS Conference Proceedings*, vol. 42. National Computer Conference, June 4–8, pp. 9–21.

English, W. K., D. C. Engelbart, and M. L. Berman. 1967. "Display-Selection Techniques for Text Manipulation." In *IEEE Transactions on Human Factors in Electronics*, HFE-8, no. 1: 5–15.

Fitts, P. M. 1951. "Engineering Psychology and Equipment Design." In *Handbook of Experimental Psychology*, edited by S. S. Stevens. New York: Wiley.

Fotheringham, J. 1961. "Dynamic Storage Allocation in the Atlas Computer." *Communications of the ACM* 4, no. 10: 435–36.

Foucault, M. 1972 [1969]. *The Archaeology of Knowledge*. New York: Pantheon.

————. 1988 [1965]. *Madness and Civilization: A History of Insanity in Time of Reason*. New York: Vintage Books.

Franck, L. K. 1958. "Tactile Communication." *ETC.: A Review of General Semantics* 16, no. 1: 31–78.

Fredkin, E. 1963. "The Time Sharing of Computers." *Computers and Automation*, November: 12–20.

Garratt, G. R. M. 1958. "Telegraphy." In *A History of Technology*, edited by C. Singer, E. J. Holmyard, A. R. Hall, and T. I. Williams, 4: 644–62. Oxford: Clarendon Press.

Gibson, David V., and Everett M. Rogers. 1994. *R&D Collaboration on Trial*. Cambridge, Mass.: Harvard Business School Press.

Gibson, W. 1984. *Neuromancer*. New York: Berkley.

Gibson, W. B. 1980. *SRI: The Founding Years*. Palo Alto, Calif.: Publishing Service Center.

Girard, R. 1978. *Things Hidden since the Beginning of the World*. Trans. Stephen Bann and Michael Metteer. Stanford, Calif.: Stanford University Press, 1987.

Glaser, E. L., J. F. Couleur, and G. A. Oliver. 1965. "System Design of a Computer for Time-Sharing Applications." *AFIPS Conf. Proc.* 27: 197–202. Available on-line at http://www.best.com/~thvv/fjcc2.html.

Goldberg, A., ed. 1988. *A History of Personal Workstations*. New York: ACM Press.

Goldstine, H. H. 1972. *The Computer: From Pascal to von Neumann*. Princeton, N.J.: Princeton University Press.

Good, I. J. 1958. "How Much Science Can You Have at Your Fingertips?" *IBM Research and Development Journal* 2, no. 4: 282–88.

Goodwin, N. C. 1975. "Cursor Positioning on an Electronic Display Using Lightpen, Lightgun, or Keyboard for Three Basic Tasks." *Human Factors* 17, no. 3, 289–95.

Groner, G. 1966. "Real-Time Recognition of Hand-Printed Text." In *Proceedings of the AFIPS 1966 Fall Joint Computer Conference*, pp. 591–601. Washington, D.C.: Spartan Books.

Grudin, J. 1990. "The Computer Reaches Out: The Historical Continuity of Interface Design." In *CHI '90 Conference Proceedings: Empowering People*, pp. 261–68. New York: ACM Press.

————. 1993. "Interface: An Evolving Concept." *Communications of the ACM* 36, no. 4: 110–19.

———. 1994."Computer-Supported Cooperative Work: Its History and Participation." *IEEE Computer* 27, no. 5: 19–26.

Gurley, B. M., and C. E. Woodward. 1959. "Light-Pen Links Computer to Operator." *Electronics* 32, no. 47: 85–87.

Hafner, K., and M. Lyon. 1996. *Where Wizards Stay Up Late: The Origins of the Internet*. New York: Simon and Schuster.

Halasz, F. 1988. "Reflections on Notecards: Seven Issues for the Next Generation of Hypermedia Systems." *Communications of the ACM* (July): 836–52.

Hardy, I. R. 1996. "The Evolution of ARPANET email." Master's thesis, University of California at Berkeley. Available on-line at http://server.berkeley.edu/virtual-berkeley/email_history.

Haring, D. R. 1965. "The Beam Pen: A Novel, High-Speed Input/Output Device for Cathode-Ray-Tube Display Systems." In *Proceedings of the AFIPS 1965 Fall Joint Computer Conference*, pp. 847–55. Washington, D.C.: Spartan Books.

Hauben, M. 1996. "Behind the Net: The Untold History of the ARPANET." Available on-line at http://picasso.dei.isep.ipp.pt/docs/arpa.html.

Hayles, N. K. 1999. *How We Became Post-Human: Virtual Bodies in Cybernetics, Literature, and Informatics*. Chicago: University of Chicago Press.

Heim, M. 1993. *Metaphysics of Virtual Reality*. Oxford: Oxford University Press.

Heims, S. J. 1980. *John von Neumann and Norbert Wiener: From Mathematics to Technologies of Life and Death*. Cambridge, Mass.: MIT Press.

———. 1991. *The Cybernetics Group*. Cambridge, Mass.: MIT Press.

Herkimer County Historical Society. 1923. *The Story of the Typewriter, 1873–1923*. Herkimer, N.Y.

Hodges, A. 1992 [1983]. *Alan Turing: The Enigma*. London: Vintage.

Hofstadter, R. 1962. *Anti-Intellectualism in American Life*. New York: Vintage Books.

Hutchins, E. L., J. D. Hollan, and D. A. Norman. 1986. "Direct Manipulation Interfaces." In *User-Centered System Design: New Perspectives on Human-Computer Interaction*, edited by D. A. Norman and S. W. Draper, pp. 77–124. Hillsdale, N.J.: Lawrence Erlbaum.

Janlert, L.-E. 1987. "The Computer as a Person." *Journal for the Theory of Social Behavior* 17: 321–41.

Johnson, J. J., T. L. Roberts, W. Verplanck, D. C. Smith, C. H. Irby, M. Beard, and K. Mackey. 1989. "The Xerox Star: A Retrospective." *Computer* 22, no. 9: 11–29.

Kay, A. C. 1969. "The Reactive Engine." Ph.D. dissertation, Salt Lake City: University of Utah.

———. 1984. "Computer Software." *Scientific American* 251, no. 3: 52–59.

———. 1990. "User Interface: A Personal View." In *The Art of Human Computer Interface Design*, edited by B. Laurel, pp. 191–207. Reading, Mass.: Addison-Wesley.

———. 1993. "The Early History of Smalltalk." Los Angeles, Calif.: Apple.

———, and A. Goldberg. 1988 [1977]. "Personal Dynamic Media." In *A History of Personal Workstations*, edited by A. Goldberg, pp. 254–63. New York: ACM Press. Originally published in *Computer* 10 (March): 31–41.

Kittler, F. A. 1990 [1985]. *Discourse Networks 1800/1900*. Trans. Michael Metteer, with Chris Cullens. Stanford, Calif.: Stanford University Press.

Kleiner, A., and Brand, S., eds. 1986. *News That Stayed News, 1974–1984: Ten Years of* CoEvolution Quarterly. San Francisco: North Point Press.

Korzybski, A. 1926. *Time-Binding: The General Theory*. Washington, D.C.: Jas. C. Wood.

———. 1933. *Science and Sanity: An Introduction to Non-Aristotelian Systems and General Semantics*. Lancaster, Penn.: Science Press.

Krueger, L. E. 1982. "Tactual Perception in Historical Perspective: David Katz's World of Touch." In *Tactual Perception: A Sourcebook*, edited by W. Schiff and E. Foulke, pp. 1–54. Cambridge: Cambridge University Press.

Lakoff, G. 1987. *Women, Fire, and Dangerous Things: What Categories Reveal about the Mind*. Chicago: University of Chicago Press.

Lanier, J. 1995. "Agents of Alienation." *Journal of Consciousness Studies* 2: 76–81.

Latour, B. 1987. *Science in Action*. Cambridge, Mass.: Harvard University Press.

———. 1988. "The Politics of Explanation: An Alternative." In *Knowledge and Reflexivity: New Frontiers in the Sociology of Science*, edited by S. Woolgar, pp. 155–76. Beverly Hills, Calif.: Sage.

———, and Woolgar, S. 1979. *Laboratory Life*. Beverly Hills, Calif.: Sage.

Laurel, B. K. 1986. "Interface as Mimesis." In *User-Centered System Design: New Perspectives on Human-Computer Interaction*, edited by D. A. Norman and S. W. Draper, pp. 67–86. Hillsdale, N.J.: Lawrence Erlbaum.

———, ed. 1990. *The Art of Human-Computer Interface Design*. Reading, Mass.: Addison-Wesley.

———. 1991. *Computers as Theater*. Reading, Mass.: Addison-Wesley.

Leroi-Gourhan, A. 1993 [1965]. *Gesture and Speech*. Trans. Anna Bostock Berger. Cambridge, Mass.: MIT Press.

Lettvin, J. Y., H. R. Maturana, W. S. McCulloch, and W. H. Pitt. 1988 [1959]. "What the Frog's Eye Tells the Frog's Brain." In *Proceedings of the IRE* 47, no. 11: 1940–59. Reedited in W. S. McCulloch, *Embodiments of Mind*, pp. 230–55. Cambridge, Mass.: MIT Press.

Levy, S. 1984a. *Hackers: Heroes of the Computer Revolution*. New York: Bantam Doubleday Dell.

———. 1984b. "Of Mice and Men." *Popular Computing*, May: 70–78.

———. 1994. *Insanely Great: The Life and Times of Macintosh, the Computer that Changed Everything*. New York: Viking.

Lewin, M. H. 1965. "A Magnetic Device for Computer Graphic Input." In *Proceedings of the AFIPS 1965 Fall Joint Computer Conference*, pp. 831–38. Washington, D.C.: Spartan Books.

Lichtenberger, W. W., and M. W. Pirtle. 1965. "A Facility for Experimentation in Man-Machine Interaction." In *Proceedings of the AFIPS 1965 Fall Joint Computer Conference* 27, pp. 589–98, Washington, D.C.: Spartan Books.

Licklider, J. C. R. 1960. "Man-Computer Symbiosis." In *IRE Transactions on Human Factors in Electronics* (March): 4–11.

———. 1965. *Libraries of the Future*. Cambridge, Mass.: MIT Press.

———. 1966. "Graphic Input—A Survey of Techniques." In *Computer Graphics: Utility/Production/Art*, edited by F. Gruenberger, pp. 39–69. Berkeley, Calif.: Academic Press.

———. 1988. "Some Reflections on Early History." In *A History of Personal Workstations*, edited by A. Goldberg, pp. 117–25. New York: ACM Press.

———, and W. E. Clark. 1962. "On-Line Man-Computer Communication." In *Proceedings of the AFIPS Spring Joint Computer Conference, pp. 113–22. Washington, D.C.: Spartan Books.

Liebowitz, S. J., and S. E. Margolis. 1990. "Fable of the Keys." *Journal of Law and Economics* 33: 1–25.

Lubar, S. 1993. *Infoculture: The Smithsonian Book of Information Age Inventions.* Boston: Houghton Mifflin.

Ludolph, F., R. Perkins, and D. Smith. 1989. "Inventing the Lisa Interface." In a message sent by Rod Perkins to the multiple recipients of list cpsr-history@cpsr.org, Monday, June 17, 1996.

Lyotard, J.-F. 1994. "Can Thought Go on Without a Body?" In *Materialities of Communication,* edited by H. U. Gumbrecht and K. L. Pfeiffer, pp. 286–300. Stanford, Calif.: Stanford University Press.

McCorduck, P. 1979. *Machines Who Think.* San Francisco: W. H. Freeman.

MacCormac, E. 1984. "Men and Machines: The Computational Metaphor." *Technology in Society* 6: 207–16.

MacKenzie, I. S. 1991. "Fitts' Law as a Performance Model in Human-Computer Interaction." Ph.D. dissertation, University of Toronto.

Machover, C. 1967. "Graphic CRT Terminals—Characteristics of Commercially Available Equipment." In *Proceedings of the Fall Joint Computer Conference* 31, pp. 149–59. Washington, D.C.: Spartan Books.

———. 1972. "Computer Graphics Terminals—A Backward Look." In *Proceedings of the AFIPS Spring Joint Computer Conference* 40, pp. 439–46. Washington, D.C.: Spartan Books.

Maddox, T. 1991. "The Wars of the Coin's Two Halves: Bruce Sterling's Mechanist/Shaper Narratives." In *Storming the Reality Studio: A Casebook of Cyberpunk and Postmodern Fiction,* edited by L. McCaffery, pp. 324–30. Durham: Duke University Press.

Mauss, M. 1950 [1938]. "Une catégorie de l'esprit humain: La notion de personne celle de 'moi.'" In *Sociologie et anthropologie,* pp. 331–62. Paris: Presses Universitaires de France.

Maxwell, J. C. 1965 [1855]. "Description of a New Form of the Planometer, an Instrument for Measuring the Areas of Plane Figures Drawn on Paper." In *The Scientific Papers of James Clerk Maxwell.* New York: Dover. Originally published in *Transactions of the Royal Scottish Society of Arts 4.*

Mazlich, B. 1993. *The Fourth Discontinuity: The Co-Evolution of Humans and Machines.* New Haven: Yale University Press.

Mitcham, C. 1986. "Computers: From Ethos and Ethics to Mythos and Religion: Notes on the New Frontier Between Computers and Philosophy." *Technology in Society* 8: 171–201.

Moritz, M. 1984. *The Little Kingdom—The Private Story of Apple Computer.* New York: William Morrow and Company.

Murray, D. 1905. "Setting Type by Telegraph." *Journal of the Institution of Electrical Engineers* 34: 555–608.

———. 1911. "Practical Aspects of Printing Telegraphy." *Journal of the Institution of Electrical Engineers* 47: 450–529.

Nelson, T. H. 1990. "The Right Way to Think About Software Design." In *The Art of Human Computer Interface Design,* edited by B. Laurel, pp. 235–43. Reading, Mass.: Addison-Wesley.

Newell, A. 1991. "Metaphors for Mind, Theories of Mind: Should the Humanities Mind?" In *The Boundaries of Humanity: Humans, Animals, Machines*, edited by J. J. Sheehan and M. Sosna, pp. 158–97. Berkeley: University of California Press.

Newman, W. M. 1976. "Trends in Graphic Display Design." *IEEE Transactions on Computers* C–25, no. 12: 1321–25.

Ninke, W. H. 1965. "Graphic 1—A Remote Graphical Display Console System." In *Proceedings of the AFIPS 1965 Fall Joint Computer Conference*, pp. 839–46. Washington, D.C.: Spartan Books.

Norberg, A. L., and J. O'Neill. 1996. *Transforming Computer Technology: Information Processing for the Pentagon, 1962–1986*. Baltimore, Md.: Johns Hopkins University Press.

Norman, D. 1990. *The Design of Everyday Things*. New York: Doubleday.

Noyes, J. 1983a. "The QWERTY Keyboard: A Review." *International Journal of Man-Machine Studies* 18: 265–81.

———. 1983b. "Chord Keyboards." *Applied Ergonomics* 14, no. 1: 55–59.

Nyce, J. M., and P. Kahn, eds. 1991a. *From Memex to Hypertext: Vannevar Bush and the Mind's Machine*. San Diego: Academic Press.

———. 1991b. "A Machine for the Mind: Vannevar Bush's Memex." In *From Memex to Hypertext: Vannevar Bush and the Mind's Machine*, edited by J. M. Nyce and P. Kahn, pp. 39–66. San Diego, Calif.: Academic Press.

Oren, T. 1991. "Getting Back on the Trail." In *From Memex to Hypertext: Vannevar Bush and the Mind's Machine*, edited by J. M. Nyce and P. Kahn, pp. 319–38. San Diego, Calif.: Academic Press.

Owens, L. 1991. "Vannevar Bush and the Differential Analyzer: The Text and Context of an Early Computer." In *From Memex to Hypertext: Vannevar Bush and the Mind's Machine*, edited by J. M. Nyce and P. Kahn, pp. 3–38. San Diego, Calif.: Academic Press.

Pake, G. E. 1985. "Research at Xerox PARC: A Founder's Assessment." *IEEE Spectrum* (October), 54–61.

Paulson, R. E. 1983. *Language, Science, and Action: Korzybski's General Semantics—A Study in Comparative Intellectual History*. Westport, Conn.: Greenwood Press.

Peirce, C. S. 1996 [1931]. "A Guess at the Riddle." In the *Collected Papers of Charles Sanders Peirce*, edited by Paul Weiss and A. W. Burks. Cambridge, Mass.: Harvard University Press. Redited in Paul Cobley, ed., *The Communication Theory Reader*, pp. 48–60. London: Routledge.

Perry, T. S., and P. Wallich. 1985. "Inside the PARC: the 'Information Architects,'" *IEEE Spectrum* (October), 62–75.

Petroski, H. 1992. *The Pencil: A History of Design and Circumstances*. New York: Knopf.

Pickering, A. 1995. *The Mangle of Practice*. Chicago: University of Chicago Press.

Pinch, T. J. 1993. "'Testing—One, Two, Three, Testing!' Toward a Sociology of Testing." *Science, Technology and Human Values* 18, no. 1: 25–41.

———, and W. E. Bijker. 1987. "The Social Construction of Facts and Artifacts: Or How the Sociology of Science and the Sociology of Technology Might Benefit Each Other." In *The Social Construction of Technological Systems: New Directions in the Sociology and History of Technology*, edited by

W. E. Bijker, T. P. Hughes, and T. J. Pinch, pp. 17–50. Cambridge, Mass.: MIT Press.

Poole, H. H. 1966. *Fundamentals of Display Systems*. Washington, D.C.: Spartan Books.

Pound, Ezra. 1970. *The Cantos*. New York: New Directions.

Pressman, S. 1993. *Outrageous Betrayal: The Dark Journey of Werner Erhard from EST to Exile*. New York: St. Martin's Press.

Raskin, J. 1997. "Looking for a Humane Interface: Will Computers Ever Become Easy to Use?" *Communications of the ACM* 40, no. 2: 98–101.

Ratz, H. C., and D. K. Ritchie. 1961. "Operator Performance on a Chord Keyboard." *Journal of Applied Psychology* 45, no. 5: 303–8.

Redmond, K. C., and T. M. Smith. 1980. *Project Whirlwind: The History of a Pioneer Computer*. Bedford, Mass.: Digital Press.

Reiser, O. L. 1989. *Logic and General Semantics: Writings of Oliver L. Reiser and Others*. Edited by S. I. Berman. San Francisco: International Society for General Semantics.

Ricoeur, P. 1992. *Oneself as Another*. Chicago: University of Chicago Press.

Roberts, L. G. 1966. "The Lincoln Wand." *Proceedings of the AFIPS 1966 Fall Joint Computer Conference*, pp. 223–27. Washington, D.C.: Spartan Books.

———. 1988. "The ARPANET and Computer Networks." In *A History of Personal Workstations*, edited by A. Goldberg, pp. 141–71. New York: ACM Press.

Robins, K. 1996. *Into the Image: Culture and Poetics in the Field of Vision*. London: Routledge.

Rogers, E. M., T. Bardini, and A. Singhal. 1992. *Microcomputers in Development: Implications for Agricultural Extension, Education and Training*. Report to the FAO. Los Angeles: Annenberg School for Communication, 1992.

Rogers, M. 1983. "The Birth of Lisa." *Personal Computing*, February: 88–94.

Rosenblueth, A., Wiener, N., and Bigelow, J. 1943. "Behavior, Purpose and Teleology." *Philosophy of Science* 10: 18–24.

Ross, D. T. 1988. "A Personal View of the Personal Work Station: Some Firsts in the Fifties." In *A History of Personal Workstations*, edited by A. Goldberg, pp. 54–111. New York: ACM Press.

Russell, B. 1997 [1935]. *Religion and Science*. Oxford: Oxford University Press.

Salus, P. H. 1995. *Casting the Net: from ARPANET to INTERNET and Beyond . . . .* Reading, Mass.: Addison-Wesley.

Schneiderman, B. 1982. "The Future of Interactive Systems and the Emergence of Direct Manipulation." *Behavior and Information Technologies* 1: 237–56.

———. 1997. "Direct Manipulation for Comprehensible, Predictable and Controllable User Interfaces: Position Statement." In J. Moore, E. Edmonds, and A. Puerta, eds., *Proceedings of the 1997 International Conference on Intelligent User Interfaces*. Orlando Fl.: ACM.

Schultz, E. 1990. *Dialogue at the Margin: Whorf, Bakhtin, and Linguistic Relativity*. Madison: University of Wisconsin Press.

Seibel, R. 1962. "Performance on a Five-Finger Chord Keyboard." *Journal of Applied Psychology* 46, no. 3: 165–69.

Sellen, A. J., G. P. Kurtenbach, and W. A. S. Buxton. 1992. "The Prevention of Mode Errors Through Sensory Feedback." *Journal of Human Computer Interaction* 7, no. 2: 141–64.

Seltzer, M. 1992. *Bodies and Machines*. New York: Routledge.

Shanon, B. 1989. "A Simple Comment Regarding the Turing Test." *Journal for the Theory of Social Behavior* 19, no. 2: 249–56.

Shapin, S. 1984. "Pump and Circumstance: Robert Boyle's Literary Technology." *Social Studies of Science* 14: 481–520.

———. 1995. *A Social History of Truth: Civility and Science in Seventeenth-Century England*. Chicago: University of Chicago Press.

———, and S. Schaffer. 1985. *Leviathan and the Air-Pump: Hobbes, Boyle, and the Experimental Life*. Princeton, N.J.: Princeton University Press.

Shaw, J. C. 1964. "JOSS: A Designer's Point of View of an Experimental On-Line Computing System." In *Proceedings of the AFIPS 1964 Fall Joint Computer Conference*, pp. 455–64. Washington, D.C.: Spartan Books.

Smith, D. C. 1976. "Thoughts on the OIS Desktop," Xerox Information Technology Group, Systems Development Division, internal memorandum, November 12.

Smith, D. K., and R. C. Alexander. 1988. *Fumbling the Future: How Xerox Invented, and Then Ignored, the First Personal Computer*. New York: William Morrow and Company.

Star, S. L. 1991. "Power, Technology and the Phenomenology of Conventions: On Being Allergic to Onions." In *A Sociology of Monsters: Essays on Power, Technology and Domination*, edited by J. Law, pp. 26–56. London: Routledge.

———. 1995. *The Culture of Computing*. Oxford: Blackwell.

———, and J. R. Griesemer. 1989. "Institutional Ecology, 'Translations,' and Boundary Objects: Amateurs and Professionals in the Berkeley Museum of Vertebrate Zoology, 1907–39." *Social Studies of Science* 19: 387–420.

Sterling, B. 1989. *Crystal Express*. Sauk City, Wis.: Arkham House.

Stotz, R. 1963. "Man-Machine Console Facilities for Computer-Aided Design." In *Proceedings of the AFIPS 1963 Spring Joint Computer Conference*, pp. 323–28. Washington, D.C.: Spartan Books.

Sumner, F. H. 1962. "The Central Control Unit of the Atlas Computer." *Proc. IFIP Congress*: 291–96.

Sutherland, I. 1963. "Sketchpad: A Man-Machine Graphical Communication System." In *Proceedings of the AFIPS 1963 Spring Joint Computer Conference*, pp. 329–46. Washington, D.C.: Spartan Books.

———. 1970. "Computer Displays." *Scientific American* 222: 56–81.

Taylor, J. R., G. Gurd, and T. Bardini. 1997. "The Worldviews of Cooperative Work." In *Social Science, Technical Systems, and Cooperative Work*, edited by G. Bowker, L. Gasser, L. Star, and W. Turner, pp. 379–413. Hillsdale, N.J.: Lawrence Erlbaum.

Tesler, L. G. 1981. "The Smalltalk Environment." *Byte*, August: 90–147.

Thacker, C. P. 1988. "Personal Distributed Computing: The Alto and Ethernet Hardware." In *A History of Personal Workstations*, edited by A. Goldberg, pp. 267–89. New York: ACM Press.

Thompson, J. N. 1982. *Interaction and Coevolution*. New York: John Wiley.

Toulmin, S. 1980. In *The New York Review of Books*, April 3: 38.

Trigg, R. H. 1991. "From Trailblazing to Guided Tours: The Legacy of Vannevar Bush's Vision of Hypertext Use." In *From Memex to Hypertext: Vannevar*

Bush and the Mind's Machine, edited by J. M. Nyce and P. Kahn, pp. 353–67. San Diego, Calif.: Academic Press.

Turing, A. M. 1950. "Computing Machinery and Intelligence." *Mind* 59: 433–60.

Turkle, S. 1984. *The Second Self: Computers and the Human Spirit*. New York: Simon and Schuster.

Uttal, B. 1983. "The Lab that Ran Away from Xerox." *Fortune* (September 5), 97–102.

Vallée, J. 1982. *The Network Revolution: Confessions of a Computer Scientist*. Berkeley, Calif.: And/Or Press.

van Dam, A. 1997. "Post-WIMP User Interfaces." *Communications of the ACM* 40, no. 2: 63–67.

Vygotsky, L. S. 1962. *Thought and Language*. Cambridge, Mass.: MIT Press.

Weiser, M. 1995. "The Computer for the 21st Century." In *The Computer in the 21st Century*. *Scientific American* special issue, pp. 78–89.

Whorf, B. L. 1956. *Language, Thought, and Reality: Selected Writings of Benjamin Lee Whorf*, edited by J. B. Carroll. Cambridge, Mass.: MIT Press.

Wiener, N. 1961 [1948]. *Cybernetics or Control and Communication in the Animal and the Machine*. 2d ed. Cambridge, Mass.: MIT Press.

———. 1967 [1950]. *The Human Use of Human Beings: Cybernetics and Society*. New York: Avon.

Wildes, K. L., and N. A. Lindgren. 1985. *A Century of Electrical Engineering and Computer Science at MIT, 1882–1982*. Cambridge, Mass.: MIT Press.

Williams, B. 1991. "Prologue: Making Sense of Humanity." In *The Boundaries of Humanity*, edited by J. J. Sheehan and M. Sosna, pp. 13–23. Berkeley: University of California Press.

Winograd, T. 1990. "What Can We Teach About Human-Computer Interaction?" In *CHI '90 Conference Proceedings: Empowering People*, pp. 443–49. New York: ACM Press.

———. 1991. "Thinking Machines: Can There Be? Are We?" In *The Boundaries of Humanity: Humans, Animals, Machines*, edited by J. J. Sheehan and M. Sosna, pp. 198–223. Berkeley: University of California Press.

Woolgar, S. 1987. "Reconstructing Man and Machine: A Note on Sociological Critiques of Cognitivism." In *The Social Construction of Technological Systems*, edited by W. E. Bijker, T. P. Hughes, and T. J. Pinch, pp. 311–28. Cambridge, Mass.: MIT Press.

Yoneyama, J. 1997. "Computer Systems as Text and Space: Toward a Phenomenological Hermeneutics of Development and Use." In *Social Science, Technical Systems, and Cooperative Work*, edited by G. Bowker, L. Gasser, L. Star, and W. Turner, pp. 105–20. Hillsdale, N.J.: Lawrence Erlbaum.

Zachary, G. P. 1997. *Endless Frontier: Vannevar Bush, Engineer of the American Century*. New York: Free Press.

In this index an "f" after a number indicates a separate reference on the next page, and an "ff" indicates separate references on the next two pages. A continuous discussion over two or more pages is indicated by a span of page numbers, e.g., "57–59." *Passim* is used for a cluster of references in close but not consecutive sequence.

IMP (Interface Message Processor), 183–84, 191
Impact of computer technology, 16–18, 228
Incorporating practice, 67, 70, 78–79, 85, 93, 112, 114, 117, 215f, 223, 225, 244–45n5, 250–51n8, 254–55n1
Information, 12, 25, 37–40, 49, 52–53, 84, 217, 222; exchange, 34, 54; retrieval, 39–40, 188, 211, 240n5; processing, 44, 54, 132, 248n8; and somesthetic communication, 60–62, 223; graphic, 85, 134; bandwidth, 99, 114, 129, 225, 247–48n6; architecture of, 158, 167
—output, 85f, 101, 130–34, 190. *See also* Cathode-Ray Tube (CRT) screen; Display
Information International Incorporated (III), 131, 254n17
Information Processing Techniques Office (IPTO, ARPA), 21–23, 28ff, 86, 237nn16,18, 238n27. *See also under* Advanced Research Project Agency (ARPA)
Input-output devices, 4, 82, 158
Inscription, 71, 244–45n5, 250–51n8; practices of, 54
Institution of Electrical and Electronics Engineers (IEEE), 67, 138, 244n3
Intelligence amplifier, 11, 19, 236n11
Intelligence worker, 107–8, 112, 122, 154, 179, 194
Interactive computing, 19, 28–30, 251n2; character-based model, 125–26; statement-based model, 126
Interface, 1, 18–19, 53, 116; and natural language, 33–38, 42; and the body, 42–44, 53, 60, 102, 118, 216, 231; models of, 103–6; and narratives of interaction, 105, 224; marking, 114–15, 225; modal, 117–19, 172, 179, 226; modeless, 161–67, 179, 215; and intelligent agents, 224–25; and direct manipulation, 225–27, 248n9, 261n2; Windows Icons Menus Pointer (WIMP), 225–26
—graphical user (GUI), 117, 158–67,

170, 225–27. *See also* Cut-and-paste; Drag-and-drop
—and keyboards, 68–80, 111. *See also* QWERTY
—and learning, 54, 118, 155, 157, 163, 215, 225–27. *See also* User-friendliness
—of the NLS, 127–33, 166, 188. *See also* oN-Line System; Teletype
—and other input-output devices, 83, 86, 89, 93, 102, 111, 114, 177, 216. *See also* Cathode-Ray Tube (CRT) screen; Display; Light pen; Mouse; Tablet
Interface Message Processor (IMP), 183–84, 191
IPTO (Information Processing Techniques Office, ARPA), 21–23, 28ff, 86, 237nn16,18, 238n27. *See also under* Advanced Research Project Agency (ARPA)
Irby, Charles, 142, 144, 148, 156, 159–60, 173–74, 180, 256nn10–11, 259n13

Jobs, Steve, 169–71
JOHNNIAC, 6, 90, 248n8
JOHNNIAC Open Shop System (JOSS), 90, 248n8
Josiah Macy Jr. Foundation, 11, 25–26, 236n10
Joystick, 110, 250n6

Kahn, Robert, 192, 258n7
Kay, Alan, 149–52, 163–67; and "The Reactive Engine," 150; and the Dynabook, 151–52; and Smalltalk, 151, 169. *See also* Illusion; *and under* Interface: modeless
Kaye, Diane, 200
Kennedy, John Fitzgerald, 21
Kinesthesia, 54, 242n23. *See also under* Communication: somesthetic
Kirkley, Charles, 121
Kittler, Friedrich, 71, 93, 244–45n5
Kleinrock, Leonard, 184
Kludge system, 87
Knee-control, 112–13
Knowledge worker, 107, 109, 116–17,

WRITING SCIENCE